The Pennsylvania Nonprofit Handbook

Everything You Need to Know to Start

and Run Your Nonprofit Organization

9th Edition

Gary M. Grobman

 White Hat **Communications**

Much of the material in Chapter 4 and Chapter 16 of this publication is authored by Michael Sand and is reprinted with permission. The author gratefully acknowledges the contributions Mr. Sand has made to the material that comprises Chapter 15. The material in Chapter 7 is authored by Gerald Kaufman and Gary M. Grobman. Much of the material in Chapter 9 was rewritten by Melanie Herman of the Nonprofit Management Risk Center (NMRC). Some of the material in Chapter 20, 21, and 22 is based on the book Fundraising Online: Using the Internet to Raise Serious Money for Your Nonprofit Organization by Gary M. Grobman and Gary B. Grant and is reprinted with permission. Some of the material in Chapter 21 is based on the book The Nonprofit Organization's Guide to E-Commerce by Gary M. Grobman (White Hat Communications, 2001). Some of the material in Chapter 29 is co-authored by Gary M. Grobman, Gerald Gorelick, and Frederick Richmond, and it is used with permission from the authors.

Corrections to this publication, if any, will be posted at:
http://www.whitehatcommunications.com/nphome.htm

IMPORTANT DISCLAIMER: This publication is intended to provide general information and should not be construed as legal advice or opinions concerning any specific facts or circumstances. Consult an experienced attorney if advice is required concerning any specific situation or legal matter. Neither the author nor the publisher make any warranties, expressed, or implied, with respect to the information in this publication. The author and publisher shall not be liable for any incidental or consequential damages in connection with, or arising out of, the use of this book.

Contact the author in care of White Hat Communications, or by e-mail at:
gary.grobman@paonline.com

Printed in the United States of America.
ISBN: 978-1-929109-32-6

Library of Congress Cataloging-in-Publication Data

Grobman, Gary M.
  The Pennsylvania nonprofit handbook : everything you need to know to start and run your nonprofit organization / Gary M. Grobman. -- 9th ed.
    p. cm.
  ISBN 978-1-929109-32-6
  1. Nonprofit organizations--Pennsylvania--Management--Handbooks, manuals, etc. 2. Nonprofit organizations--Law and legislation--Pennsylvania--Handbooks, manuals, etc. I. Title.
  HD62.6.G763 2012
  658'.04809748--dc23
                        2011041843

Table of Contents

The Cost of Poor Quality
Quality in the Nonprofit Organizational Context

Chapter 29. Change Management

Total Quality Management
Business Process Reengineering
Benchmarking
Outcome-Based Management
Large Group Intervention

Chapter 30. Organization and Program Evaluation

Introduction
What is Program Evaluation?
Why Program Evaluation is Performed
Who Performs a Program Evaluation
Planning for Program Evaluation
Conclusion

Foreword

Joe Geiger, Executive Director
Pennsylvania Association of Nonprofit Organizations (PANO)

Congratulations! You have decided to be a part of the fastest-growing segment of business development in the United States. You are considering joining, or have already joined, over a million other nonprofits in the United States. They come in all sizes, shapes, and colors. The nonprofit sector's heritage includes helping in an emergency, encouraging the human spirit, educating and shaping values and goals, and being the first to offer a hand.

You have chosen to be a vital link in developing the fabric of the community. From the time our ancestors landed on Plymouth Rock (or staffed the Welcome Wagon that greeted those who did), people have worked together in formal organizations to better the human condition. The nonprofit sector has always been in the forefront of improving our society and the human condition.

Today, the nonprofit sector is in a very challenging period. Nonprofits are experiencing ever-growing scrutiny and demands for accountability. Service demand is increasing. There is more competition for charitable dollars. The public and government both are demanding that nonprofits improve their efficiency. This book will help you respond to these challenges.

As the Executive Director of PANO, I am pleased to be a part of the 9th edition of *The Pennsylvania Nonprofit Handbook*. Every week, callers to PANO ask questions: Should we start up? How do we get our tax exemptions? Where can we find grant funds? Should we merge? Should we contract with a for-profit to help us fundraise online? I am pleased to have a practical tool that can help answer these questions. This book will help to keep you on track. It is also an extraordinary resource for those who already manage or serve on the boards of nonprofit organizations. With practical advice on fundraising, communications, lobbying, personnel management, grantsmanship, and scores of other issues, it is a must for every nonprofit executive to have.

In summary, *The Pennsylvania Nonprofit Handbook* is at the top of the list of essential tools to have on your bookshelf. This book is must reading. While it will have value as a reference tool to be consulted when needed, I highly recommend that you read the book cover-to-cover to familiarize yourself with the panoply of issues facing the modern nonprofit in Pennsylvania.

J.M.G.
October 2011

Introduction

Americans of all ages, all stations in life, and all types of disposition are forever forming associations. There are not only commercial and industrial associations in which all take part, but others of a thousand different types—religious, moral, serious, futile, very general and very limited, immensely large and very minute. Americans combine to give fetes, found seminaries, build churches, distribute books, and send missionaries to the antipodes. Hospitals, prisons and schools take shape in that way. Finally, if they want to proclaim a truth or propagate some feeling by the encouragement of a great example, they form an association. In every case, at the head of any new undertaking, where in France you would find the government or in England some territorial magnate, in the United States you are sure to find an association.

—Alexis de Tocqueville
Democracy In America
1835

Little has changed about the American propensity to form benevolent associations in the 176 years since de Tocqueville wrote the above words. The modern charitable institution, however, may bear little resemblance to the typical charity of the 19th century. Burgeoning demands for services, increased government regulation, keen competition for funds, the advance of technology, demographic changes, and the public's changing perception of our institutions have all worked to increase the challenge to those in leadership positions with nonprofit organizations.

In our highly competitive, individualistic society, the nonprofit sector provides a way to express our humanitarian values, to preserve our cultural heritage, to promote various causes, to educate, and to enlighten. It is often through coming together in nonprofit organizations that our citizens exercise their constitutional rights to petition their government, engage in free speech, and exercise their freedoms of assembly and religion.

Nonprofits play a unique role as an intermediary between the citizens and their government. They maintain and transmit values to a degree that government has been unable to do.

Perhaps most important of all, nonprofits formulate much of the moral agenda for society. One only has to think of the response to the September 11, 2001 terrorist attacks, the environmental movement, rape crisis and domestic violence centers, public subsidies of arts and humanities, public awareness of AIDS and support of AIDS programs, and countless other issues that people coming together in voluntary organizations were able to put on the nation's agenda.

Virtually every single American is touched in some way by the services of this country's nonprofit organizations. Organizations such as institutions of religious worship, civic groups, hospitals, day care centers, libraries, colleges, symphonies, art museums, the Red Cross, Salvation Army, and the American Cancer Society work in partnership with government and the public to improve our lives and those of our neighbors. According to the Internal Revenue Service, there were 1,821,824 organizations that were exempt under Section 501(c) in FY 2010, 1,280,739 of which were 501(c)(3)s.

Historically, the primary distinguishing characteristic of the nonprofit sector is that it is mission- and value-driven. Nonprofit organizations exist to accomplish some social good, however that may be defined. A set of values and assumptions underlies this view of the voluntary sector, including altruism, benevolence, cooperation, community, and diversity. The privileges granted to the sector and public expectations are grounded in this belief.

Nonprofits in the United States sometimes take the form of soup kitchens, such as Our Daily Bread in Harrisburg, Pennsylvania, which operate on a shoestring budget and charge their clients virtually nothing for their services. They also take the form of enterprises such as hospitals, with budgets in the hundreds of millions of dollars, which often act in ways very much like their for-profit counterparts, seeking to maximize revenue and capture market share.

In January 2000, a Dauphin County (PA) Common Pleas Court county judge ruled against the tax exemption eligibility for Hershey Medical Center (HMC), affiliated with Penn State University. One of his objections was that the facility paid salaries to some individuals on staff in excess of a half-million dollars annually. Like almost all hospitals, HMC enters into sophisticated business arrangements. In 1997, the hospital merged with Geisinger, a for-profit health system. The merger shortly collapsed, chiefly as a result of conflicting organizational missions and cultures between the two parent organizations, in addition to financial and operational difficulties.

In contrast to the soup kitchen, the financial aspects of decision-making are of paramount importance to HMC's decision-making strategy. Yet, as one wag pointed out on the tangible benefits of a nonprofit being selected as a "Point of Light" by the White House, even a "point of light" has to pay its electric bill.

Neither Hershey Medical Center nor Our Daily Bread, about ten miles away from each other, is atypical of the nonprofit sector. While they may appear to be as different as night and day, they also share many things in common. Both depend on government grants, as well as donations from foundations, businesses, and individuals, to keep them operating in the black and to supplement fees for service. Both provide free services to those who are unable to pay for them. Both depend on volunteers. Both are governed by a board of directors, whose members do not share in any surplus revenues that may be generated, and that consists of unpaid volunteers from the community.

These are some of the aspects that differentiate nonprofit organizations from their government and private sector counterparts that also provide inpatient health care and food services. Nonprofit organizations, especially those qualified under section 501(c)(3) of the Internal Revenue Code, occupy a special and unique place in American society. Their uniqueness has many attributes.

All such organizations are supported by the nation's taxpayers. They are exempt from federal and state income tax. Contributors, for the most part, can deduct their contributions from their federal income tax (and from their state income taxes in most states). They are eligible to have their postage subsidized by the federal government. Many are exempt from state and local sales and property taxes.

Some people, including those who formulate tax and regulatory policies that apply to charities, have a vision of charitable organizations that resembles those of the 19th century. In that vision, staff consists of volunteers. Recipients of services are too poor to provide for themselves. Funding comes from wherever it can be found. An example of what this looked like is described on the Web site of Yale University's School of Medicine:

A 19th century hospital was predominantly a charity institution, although from the beginning, some patients paid for their stays. It was intended for the worthy poor, for sailors, and for other strangers in town. People of means, such as the donors who were members of the General Hospital Society of Connecticut, would receive medical care in their homes, and not in a hospital. The hospital as yet offered no advantages over home care. Physicians served in the hospital without salary on a rotating basis as attending physicians. They did so as a form of charity and civic duty, but hospital service also provided valuable experience, professional recognition, and the possibility of training students in the wards.

from *Connecticut and New Haven's First General Hospital: Hospitals in the Nineteenth Century;* Harvey Cushing/John May Whitney Medical Library; Yale University School of Medicine; *http://www.med.yale.edu/library/exhibits/hospitals/*

Benjamin Franklin convinced the Pennsylvania Legislature to participate in chartering the nation's first hospital, Pennsylvania Hospital. He received a commitment to match £2000 donated by private individuals with a like amount appropriated by the state government. Founded in 1751, the institution was created "to care for the sick poor of the Province and for the reception and care of lunaticks" (source: *In the Beginning: The Story of the Creation of the Nation's First Hospital; http://www.uphs.upenn.edu/paharc/features/creation.html;* University of Pennsylvania Health System, 2003).

The modern charitable institution, however, may bear little resemblance to the typical charity of the 19th century. Burgeoning demands for services, increased government regulation, keen competition for funds, the advance of technology, demographic changes, and the public's changing perception of our institutions have all worked to increase the complexity of decision-making to those in leadership positions with nonprofit organizations. Pennsylvania Hospital, started with perhaps a handful of employees, has evolved into the University of Pennsylvania Health System, with a workforce measured in the tens of thousands, making it one of the largest private employers in the entire state. Other nonprofits, such as educational institutions and other integrated health care systems, are on the roster of the state's largest employers. In fact, one such institution, the University of Pennsylvania, is the largest nongovernmental employer in Pennsylvania other than Wal-Mart (source: *http://www.paworkstats.state.pa.us/admin/gsipub/htmlarea/uploads/pasep_t50.pdf).*

The nonprofit sector's participation in the American economy is impressive. According to the Urban Institute's *The Nonprofit Almanac* (2008), the voluntary sector contributes at least 5% of our national economy and paid about 8.1% of all wages in 2006. The sector employed 12.9 million workers in 2005, or about 9.7% of non-farm employment. According to the U.S. Department of Commerce's Bureau of Economic Analysis, 2005 revenues of nonprofit organizations were $930 billion, with outlays during that year of just over $915 billion. In 2007, 383,000 nonprofit organizations reported to the IRS that they collectively controlled property, cash, and investments with a value of about $3.2 trillion (source: *http://www.irs.gov/taxstats/article/0,,id=102886,00.html).* This figure does not include wealth controlled by churches or small nonprofits that are not required to file Form 990 annual tax returns.

Most Americans recognize the value of nonprofit organizations in society. Of 142.35 million individual tax returns filed nationally for tax year 2008 by individuals and couples, 39.2 million claimed a tax deduction for charitable giving, totaling $161.87 billion in deductions, according to the IRS (source: *http://www.irs.gov/pub/irs-soi/10winbulindincretpre.pdf).* Many more billions of dollars were donated by persons who did not itemize, or who did not bother to declare the value of their charity on their tax returns.

The business community also donates billions of dollars each year to charitable institutions. More than half of individual taxpayers who take a deduction also make non-cash contributions, valued at $58.7 billion for tax year 2007 (source: *http://www.irs.gov/pub/irs-soi/10sprbulindcont07.pdf).*

According to the June 2011 annual report of *Giving USA*, published by the American Association of Fund-Raising Counsel Trust for Philanthropy, total charitable giving by individuals, corporations, and foundations ROSE over the previous year to an estimated 3.8% to $290.89 billion (source: *http://www.charitynavigator.org/index.cfm?bay=content.view&cpid=42*),

Billions of hours annually are volunteered to nonprofits. Independent Sector estimates that about 63.4 million Americans, or 26.8 percent of the adult population, gave eight billion hours of volunteer service worth $169 billion in 2009, based on an estimate that each hour is worth $20.25 (which increased to $21.36 for 2010) (Source: *http://www.independentsector.org/volunteer_time*). As those who volunteer can attest, the value to society, such as the relief of human suffering, far exceeds any dollar value.

It is difficult to foresee and anticipate all of the barriers that stand in the way of a nonprofit organization's creation and survival. One thing is certain—there will be barriers. Forming and running a nonprofit corporation, or any corporation, is a major challenge. Yet it is known that the accomplishments such organizations can achieve far exceed what any single person, operating without an organizational structure, can achieve alone.

Starting and running a nonprofit corporation in the 21st century requires political acumen, immense technical skill, vision, physical and mental stamina, and, perhaps most of all, luck and a sense of humor.

In the fall of 1984, the Internal Revenue Service, because of a computer glitch, lost $300 million in federal tax withholding payments of 10,000 companies. Even after the snafu was discovered, thousands of the companies received curt letters threatening that the government would seize their property and bank accounts if the tax payments were not made within 10 days. As a nonprofit executive who was on the receiving end of one of these letters, I can certify that "maintaining a sense of humor" was not easy at that time. Yet in the years after that IRS debacle, several more calamities beyond my control afflicted the nonprofit I ran.

There were times when running a nonprofit was no picnic. And then there were times when it was the most fun I ever had. I would like to think that if a publication such as the *Pennsylvania Nonprofit Handbook* had been around when I first started, my job would have been easier.

Purpose of the Handbook

As one might expect, a plethora of laws, regulations, court decisions, and other government policies apply to nonprofit corporations.

The purpose of this handbook is to provide answers to questions such as:

1. What does one have to do to form a nonprofit corporation in Pennsylvania?
2. What are the advantages and disadvantages of incorporating?
3. How does a nonprofit organization qualify and apply for 501(c)(3) status?
4. What kind of paperwork is involved in typical nonprofit operations?
5. What should be in a nonprofit corporation's bylaws?
6. How does a nonprofit organization qualify for discount bulk mailing privileges?
7. How does a nonprofit organization qualify for a state sales tax exemption?
8. Can a nonprofit organization engage in unrelated activities that generate income?
9. Will the tax exemption of a nonprofit organization be at risk if it engages in lobbying?
10. How do nonprofit organizations use the Internet to increase revenues?

This handbook cannot purport to answer every conceivable question, but it does attempt to provide sources for answers to many of the questions posed by nonprofit board members and staff. It also provides references to primary source material, much of it available on the Web, on important state and federal laws and regulations, sources for some of the most useful government forms, and sound advice about many nonprofit management issues.

What's New in the Ninth Edition

Among the new features that appear in this edition are—

- a set of sample bylaws that would be appropriate for many new startups,
- an expanded section on board member legal responsibilities,
- an expanded section on parliamentary procedure, and
- information about new technology applications, including social networking and mobile phone apps

Who Can Use This Book

This handbook will be a useful reference for—

- those who are considering forming a nonprofit corporation in Pennsylvania,

- those who need to keep current on laws, regulations, and court decisions that affect nonprofit organizations, including executive staff and board members of existing nonprofit organizations,

- those who will benefit from the advice included in this handbook on running a nonprofit organization, such as fundraisers, lobbyists, public affairs consultants, staff and leadership of funding organizations, and government officials, in addition to those who serve as the staff and board members of nonprofit organizations and their associations, and

- those who are students of nonprofit management at both the graduate and undergraduate levels.

This is the ninth edition of this publication. Every effort has been made to make this handbook as useful and free from errors as possible. It is the intent of the author to seek corrections as well as suggestions for improving this publication, and to incorporate these contributions in future editions. A survey/order form has been included in the Appendix to provide feedback to the author and publisher.

Acknowledgments

The author gratefully acknowledges the contributions of scores of individuals and organizations to this book. Among them are Kathleen Steigler and Linda Grobman, who edited the first edition of this book; Michael Sand, who wrote much of the chapter on boards, as well as the chapter on applying for grants; and Bob Mills, Esq., who was the initial author of the chapter on volunteer and staff liability, which has since been completely revised, updated, and expanded, thanks to the efforts of Melanie Herman of the Nonprofit Management Risk Center. Thanks are due also to those who reviewed and edited specific chapters of the previous editions, including Terry Roth, Esq.; W. Barney Carter; George Bell, Esq.; Bill Knoll, Classification Reform Instructor for the U.S.

Postal Service; Otto Hofmann, Esq.; Phil McKain; Jim Fritz, Esq.; Frederick Richmond; the late Steve Zneimer; Jim Redmond; Elizabeth Hrenda-Roberts; Ron Lench; Christine Finnegan; Joan Benso; Dick Shelly; John Briscoe; and Ken Wickham. Patricia Mogan, Standards for Excellence Officer of the Pennsylvania Association of Nonprofit Organizations (PANO), updated the section in Chapter 8 related to the Standards for Excellence program. I wish to thank John Hope, Linda Grobman, Barbara Blank, and Judy Grobman who reviewed and edited this edition and/or previous editions of this book.

I am also appreciative of the contributions to this publication made by Gerald Kaufman, executive director of the Awbury Arboretum Association, whose chapter on nonprofit ethics deserve to be shared with every board member and staff person who is affiliated with a charity. Joel Cavadel, an attorney from York, PA, made many contributions to the section on mergers and consolidations, for which I am most grateful. Esther Hyatt of Virginia Commonwealth University reviewed the chapter on evaluation. Nearly a score of members of the teaching section of the Association for Research on Nonprofit Organizations and Voluntary Action (ARNOVA) reviewed chapters of *An Introduction to the Nonprofit Sector,* a textbook based on a previous edition of this book. Some of their suggestions have been incorporated into this 9th edition. Some of the material in the chapter on change management was adapted from material on outcome-based management jointly written by Frederick Richmond and myself, and from material on large group intervention that Gerald Gorelick and I wrote together. Gary Grant and I wrote the material that comprises Chapter 22, Fundraising on the Internet.

Finally, a word of thanks to the Pennsylvania Association of Nonprofit Organizations, particularly to its executive director, Joe Geiger, for participating in this 9th edition. PANO is the authority Pennsylvania nonprofits turn to for information, products, services, and training to make them the best they can be.

G.M.G.
October 2011

Quick Start Guide
to Forming a Nonprofit Organization

The following provides an overview of 23 major steps involved in starting up a nonprofit corporation in Pennsylvania. The order in which these appear below is not necessarily the most efficient in every case (and many steps can be accomplished simultaneously), but it should be sufficient for most startups. Changes in laws and regulations will occur that may modify the contents of this list. Because this book does not provide legal advice relating to any specific fact situation, I recommend that you consider consulting a qualified attorney before starting up any corporation.

1. Choose the general purpose and mission of the organization, and write a description of it in a single sentence.
2. Conduct research to see—
   - whether there is a sufficient need for a new organization with that purpose
   - whether other organizations are already providing the service you propose to provide
   - who and how many will likely seek to be served by your organization
   - what federal, state, and local laws and regulations will apply to your organization
   - whether you will have enough startup income to finance initial expenses, and whether you can generate enough income (through sales of goods and services, grants, or donations) necessary to sustain your organization
   - whether there is sufficient interest in your community to build a board of directors for this organization.
3. Prepare a business and marketing plan if your startup is likely to require a substantial investment in startup funding.
4. Choose a unique business name, and check on its availability.
5. Choose an Internet domain name based on that name.
6. Choose a legal address for your organization.
7. Obtain an EIN number (your taxpayer identification number) from the Internal Revenue Service by filling out a Form SS-4. (This can be obtained online at: *http://www.irs.gov/pub/irs-pdf/fss4.pdf* by using the forms and publications finder using the term "SS-4" or by calling 1-800-829-FORM.)
8. Choose incorporators.
9. Prepare and file your incorporation papers with the Corporation Bureau of the Pennsylvania Department of State.
10. Place legally required advertisements about the incorporation of your organization in legal journals and general circulation newspapers (see page 31).
11. Obtain any required local business licenses.
12. Obtain business insurance, and consider obtaining directors' and officers' insurance.
13. Register with the Bureau of Charitable Organizations of the Pennsylvania Department of State if you will be raising $25,000 or more annually in charitable contributions.
14. Find out about legal requirements relating to employees if you plan on having them, such as federal income tax and Social Security tax withholding, state and local payroll tax procedures, unemployment insurance, and workers' compensation insurance; prepare job descriptions for staff, and develop personnel policies for employees.
15. Prepare draft organization bylaws.
16. Hold an organizational meeting of the board of directors and approve bylaws, approve organization bank accounts, elect organization officers, and schedule subsequent meetings.

17. Open a bank account for the organization.
18. Set up the organization's accounting/bookkeeping, financial reporting system, and other record-keeping systems.
19. Obtain office space if required, business cards, stationery, office equipment, and supplies.
20. Obtain an Internet host, publicize your e-mail address, and build your Web site.
21. Obtain any required state sales tax licenses if you will be required to collect sales tax on items you sell.
22. Apply for mailing permits.
23. If eligible, apply for a federal tax exemption using Form 1023 for 501(c)(3) status and Form 1024 for exemption under other sections of the Internal Revenue Code.

Chapter 1
The Decision to Incorporate

> Synopsis: Among the advantages of incorporating an organization are limits on liability, lower taxes, and increased organizational credibility. Among the disadvantages are loss of centralized control and increased paperwork, time, and expense of running a corporation.

Introduction to Incorporation

A corporation is a legal entity formed for business activities. Under state and federal laws, a corporation is treated as a separate "person" for purposes of making contracts, paying taxes, and being liable for the consequences of business activity. A nonprofit corporation, also called a "not-for-profit" corporation in some states, generally is not permitted to issue shares of stock, and does not provide shareholders with dividends from the profits that are received from operating the business. While nonprofit corporations can and do make profits, these profits may not inure to the benefit of the "owners" of the corporation— the board of directors or trustees. Rather, these profits must be used to operate and maintain the organization. Some states place limitations on the types of activities that are the primary purpose of the nonprofit corporation.

Pennsylvania law (15 Pa. C.S.A. §5301) lists the types of purposes for which incorporation as a nonprofit organization is permitted. These purposes include, but are not limited to—

> *athletic; any lawful business purpose to be conducted on a not-for-profit basis; beneficial; benevolent; cemetery; charitable; civic; control of fire; cultural; educational; encouragement of agriculture or horticulture; fraternal; health; literary; missionary; musical; mutual improvement; patriotic; political; prevention of cruelty to persons or animals; professional, commercial, industrial, trade, service or business associations; promotion of the arts; protection of natural resources; religious; research; scientific and social.*

Generally, there are three classes of nonprofit corporations:

1. Funding agencies (e.g., United Way, Jewish Federation, private foundations)

   The primary purpose of these organizations is to allocate funds, either those solicited as private donations or those already accumulated in an endowment or private fortune, for other agencies that provide actual services. Many of these organizations restrict their grants of funds to groups that provide a narrow range of services of interest to the funding organization. A Jewish federation is likely to make contributions solely to Jewish-affiliated organizations or others that principally serve the Jewish community. The United Way generally provides funding to social service agencies. Some foundations restrict their contributions to organizations promoting services for women, health-care related studies, or arts and humanities agencies.

2. Membership organizations (e.g., Common Cause, the Sierra Club, League of Women Voters)

   These organizations exist primarily to provide services (such as advocacy, information sharing, and networking) for their members, usually with a specialty of expertise.

3. Service agencies (e.g., hospitals, schools, day-care centers, family services)

> These organizations exist to provide specific services to the public. They often charge fees on a sliding scale for their services to fund the bulk of their budgets.

Each type of organization operates differently in many significant ways.

The decision to incorporate is a mere formality for most leaders who envision a large organization with employees, contracts, offices, property, and equipment. Corporate status in general, and nonprofit corporate status in particular, provides many advantages. Maintaining an unincorporated organization with annual revenue and expenditures comfortably in five figures is cumbersome at best, if not impossible. It is at the low end of the scale where the decision to incorporate is most important.

It would be ludicrous to consider incorporation for the Saturday morning running group get-together, which collects two dollars from each of its eight members to pay for the refreshments after the run. Yet, when the group expands to three hundred members, dues are collected to finance a race, the municipality demands that the club purchase insurance to indemnify against accidents, and the club wants a grant from an area foundation to purchase sophisticated race timing equipment with the intention of renting it to organizations that are hosting local 5K race fundraisers, then incorporation is clearly the option of choice.

Advantages and Disadvantages of Incorporation

The **advantages** of incorporation are the following:

1. Limited Liability. Of all the reasons to seek corporate status, this is perhaps the most compelling. Under all state laws, the officers, directors, employees, and members of a corporation, except under very limited and unusual circumstances, are not personally liable for lawsuit judgments and debts related to the organization. Thus, the personal assets of the organization's executive director or board members are not at risk in the event of a successful suit brought against the corporation, or in the event the organization goes out of business while owing money to its creditors. The assets of an organization may be minimal, while the individuals running it may have substantial assets. Corporate status protects those personal assets. Many people won't even consider participating in the leadership of an organization unless their personal assets are shielded by incorporation.

The Congress and the Pennsylvania General Assembly have enacted laws that are designed to expand the liability protection afforded to nonprofit boards of directors and volunteers (see Chapter 9).

2. Tax Advantages. In the absence of incorporation, income accruing to an individual running an organization is subject to federal, state, and local taxes at the individual rate, which is likely to be substantially more than the corporate rate. In the case of nonprofit incorporation, an organization can be exempt from many taxes, depending upon its type.

For organizations that are charitable, educational, religious, literary, or scientific, 501(c)(3) tax-exempt status is particularly attractive (see Chapter 8). Pennsylvania law exempts corporations that have federal tax-exempt status from state corporate income tax. Certain types of charities may be exempt from Pennsylvania sales and use tax and local property taxes, as well. Many types of charitable institutions, such as colleges and hospitals, which have substantial property holdings, would be taxed beyond their abilities to operate if they were denied tax exemptions. Many funding sources, such as government, foundations, and the public, will not make contributions to an organization that is not exempt under Section 501(c)(3), since this status provides a tax exemption to the contributor and assures that there is at least some minimal level of accountability on the part of the organization.

3. Structure, Accountability, Perpetuity, and Legally Recognized Authority. When people and organizations interact with a bona fide corporation, they have confidence that there is some order and authority behind the decision-making of that entity. A reasonable expectation exists that the corporation will continue to honor agreements even if the principal actor for the organization dies, resigns, or is otherwise disassociated from the organization. They know that there is a legal document governing decision-making (as detailed in the bylaws), succession of officers, clear purposes (as detailed in the Articles of Incorporation), a system for paying bills, accounting for income and expenses, and a forum for the sharing of ideas on policy and direction from the corporation's board members. So long as the necessary papers are filed, the organization will continue in perpetuity regardless of changes in leadership. This gives such organizations an aura of immortality, which is seen as an advantage in planning beyond the likely tenure of an individual board chairperson or executive director.

4. Ancillary Benefits. Nonprofit incorporation can provide lower postage rates (see chapter 24); access to media (through free public service announcements); volunteers, who would be more hesitant volunteering for a comparable for-profit entity; and the so-called "halo effect," in which the public is more willing to do business with a nonprofit because of a real or perceived view that such an organization is founded and operated in the public interest.

5. Strength of Collegial Decision-Making. Decision-making in an autocracy is clearly easier and more efficient than in an organization run as a democracy. Yet, there is a value in making decisions by building a consensus among a majority of members of a diverse, volunteer, community-based board. Members of a board often bring different experiences and talents and provide information that would otherwise not be available in making decisions. Issues are often raised that, if overlooked, could possibly result in disastrous consequences for the organization.

The **disadvantages** of nonprofit incorporation are the following:

1. Loss of Centralized Control. Many organizations are formed and run by a charismatic leader with a vision of how to accomplish a particular task or mission. Decision-making is enhanced without the distractions of the scores of issues that relate not to the actual mission of the organization but to the internal management of the organization. The very act of forming a nonprofit corporation can be draining—preparing and filing Articles of Incorporation, negotiating bylaws, finding quality colleagues to serve on a board of directors, hiring qualified staff if necessary, and dealing with the myriad of personnel issues that emanate from hiring staff, preparing budgets, raising money, and preparing minutes of board meetings. Even finding a convenient time and place where the board can meet to ensure that a quorum is present can pose a troublesome and potentially overwhelming problem at times.

Incorporation is a legal framework that trades off the advantages addressed earlier in this section with some serious disadvantages. Decisions can no longer be made in a vacuum by one person without oversight or accountability, but are legally under the purview of a board of directors. Decisions have to withstand scrutiny of all persons on the board, some of whom may be hostile or have personal axes to grind. By definition, boards of directors are committees, and committees often make decisions that are compromises to mollify members with divergent viewpoints and competing interests.

For those used to making quick decisions "on the fly" and who revel in not having their decisions subject to second-guessing, modification, or otherwise being meddled with, incorporation can be a personally shackling experience and can dilute one's control over the organization.

2. Paperwork, Paperwork, Paperwork. Even in the smallest nonprofit corporation, the paperwork load related to corporate status can at times be overwhelming. There are deadlines for virtually every filing. Keeping ahead of the paperwork wave requires discipline, commitment, and a sense of humor. Forms get misfiled, or otherwise lost in the bureaucracy or mail.

In some cases, failure to handle this paperwork can result in criminal penalties. There are penalties for missed filings (e.g., failure to file a timely 990 federal tax return results in a $20/day penalty, up to a maximum of $10,000, or 5% of the agency's gross revenues, whichever is smaller—and $100/day up to $50,000 for organizations with annual gross receipts exceeding $1 million). As soon as the first employee is hired, the paperwork wave accompanying that is substantial.

In the first year, the filings can be intimidating, time-consuming, and frustrating. A new corporation must develop a bookkeeping system that is understandable by the accountant who will perform the audit and prepare the financial reports, pass resolutions, file forms to open up corporate savings and checking accounts, order checks, file tax returns, and pay taxes. There are many federal, state, and local taxes, each of which requires its own filing at different times of the year. A new corporation must also reconcile savings and checking accounts, prepare board meeting announcements and minutes, devise a system to pay bills, and establish a process for the reimbursement of expenses. Other tasks it must accomplish are filing forms to protect its corporate name, preparing an annual report, adopting a personnel policy, purchasing office equipment, renting an office, preparing budgets, writing fundraising letters, and finding and retaining board members.

Few of these tasks have a direct impact on the actual work of the agency, but typically they will consume more time during the initial year after incorporation than does the work related to the actual mission of the organization. The only consolation is that after a few years, one becomes familiar with the required filings. Then they become routine and just a minor nuisance.

3. Expenses in Money and Time. Significant resources are required to establish a corporation and run it efficiently. No law prohibits running a corporation from one's home with a staff of volunteers. Legally, the only monetary requirement is to pay a fee to file Articles of Incorporation. Yet, doing so often sets off a chain of events that dramatically increases the organization's complexity. Opening up corporate bank accounts, doing expense reports, filing taxes, and doing the paperwork described above are difficult to accomplish solely with volunteer labor. Raising the funds necessary to hire a person to do all of this work—in addition to coordinating the actual work related to carrying out the actual mission of the organization—adds to this burden, and requires even more filing and paperwork.

Many of these tasks would be required even in the absence of a decision to incorporate. One can avoid much of the "wasted" time and energy by keeping "small," but this places a substantial limit to what one can accomplish. Experiencing the disadvantages of incorporation is the cost one incurs to receive the substantial benefits.

Nonprofit and Private Benefit

Nonprofit corporation status provides many advantages over comparable for-profits. Yet this status is not conferred without a cost. Generally, nonprofits must operate differently and with different motivations than their for-profit counterparts. There is a general legal doctrine that prohibits nonprofits from acting in a manner that results in "private inurement" to individuals, i.e., the transfer of earnings or profits from the corporation to its "owners." The basic principle at work here is that a for-profit is intended to benefit its owners, whereas a nonprofit is intended to further a purpose. Title 15 of the Pennsylvania Code includes the following:

§ 5545. Income from corporate activities.

A nonprofit corporation whose lawful activities involve among other things the charging of fees or prices for its services or products, shall have the right to receive such income and, in so doing, may make an incidental profit. All such incidental profits shall be applied to the maintenance and operation of the lawful activities of the corporation, and in no case shall be divided or distributed in any manner whatsoever among the members, directors, or officers of the corporation. As used in this section the terms fees or prices do not include rates of contribution, fees or dues levied under an insurance certificate issued by a fraternal benefit society, so long as the distribution of profits arising from said fees or prices is limited to the purposes set forth in this section and section 5551 (relating to dividends prohibited; compensation and certain payments authorized).

Section 5551 of Title 15 also includes the following section:

§5551. Dividends prohibited; compensation and certain payments authorized.

(a) *General rule.—A nonprofit corporation shall not pay dividends or distribute any part of its income or profits to its members, directors, or officers...*

(b) *Reasonable compensation for services.—A nonprofit corporation may pay compensation in a reasonable amount to members, directors, or officers for services rendered.*

(c) *Certain payments authorized.—A nonprofit corporation may confer benefits upon members or nonmembers in conformity with its purposes, may repay capital contributions...*

Section 5730 of Title 15 (Compensation of directors) authorizes a nonprofit corporation board of directors to "fix the compensation of directors for their services as such, and a director may be a salaried officer of the corporation." Pennsylvania law does not preclude the board of directors from serving as the nonprofit corporation's employees, provided they are not compensated unreasonably for their services. Yet there is a clear prohibition against the income received by the organization being distributed to these directors in a manner other than as "reasonable" compensation for services.

The term "reasonable" has been generally defined by the courts as compensation that is not excessive compared to individuals with similar expertise and responsibility in the same or similar community. Internal Revenue Service regulations (see Chapter 7) have been promulgated to place restrictions on compensation. However, there is no legal precedent for a doctrine that suggests individuals who work for charities or nonprofits should be paid any less than their for-profit counterparts.

In the 2001 book *Starting & Managing a Nonprofit Organization*, author-attorney Bruce R. Hopkins provides a useful chapter on the issue of private inurement in nonprofits.

There is nothing illegal or unethical about nonprofits selling goods and services and generating income. Nonprofits are becoming more sophisticated in finding new revenue sources to supplant the loss of government funds (see Chapters 20-22). Yet, nonprofits are distinguished from their for-profit counterparts by the destination of any profit. Chapter 25 includes a list of many of the important differences between nonprofits and for-profits.

Tips:

- Review Pennsylvania's nonprofit laws and decide whether your organization is willing to be subjected to the limitations and accountability required by these laws.

- Avoid incorporating if it is essential to maintain complete control of the organization, and if it is possible to keep the scale of operations small.

- Contact someone who runs a nonprofit corporation of similar size and type envisioned for your organization. Ask questions about paperwork requirements, office equipment, rental space, and the benefits and pitfalls of running such a corporation.

- If leaning toward incorporation, identify potential incorporators/board members who are—

  a. accessible, and not spread too thin among many other competing organizations,
  b. potential contributors to the organization,
  c. experienced fundraisers,
  d. knowledgeable about the issues of concern to the organization,
  e. respected and well-known in the community, and
  f. experienced in legal, accounting, and nonprofit management issues.

- If you find the requirements of incorporating your own organization too intimidating, consider seeking a fiscal sponsor (see Chapter 10).

Chapter 2
Steps to Incorporation

Synopsis: Organizational leadership must file the appropriate forms with the Pennsylvania Department of State's Corporation Bureau to incorporate an organization. Among important decisions to be made are choosing the corporate name, opting whether to have members, and choosing corporate purposes.

Introduction to Incorporation

While incorporation is a legal procedure, it does not require the services of a lawyer. However, lawyers with training and experience in Pennsylvania nonprofit law can be useful in reviewing, if not preparing, Articles of Incorporation and bylaws that are consistent with both statutory requirements and with the purposes of the organization. In 1988, the PA General Assembly enacted legislation (Act 1988-177) codifying its laws relating to associations and corporations. The provisions of more than 200 laws, enacted since 1838, were reorganized within a single document. Organizations should review the state laws applying to nonprofit corporations. There are several sources for the text of these laws.

The first is the 400-plus-page 1988 codification itself. It can be found in county law libraries, some public libraries, and many university libraries.

Of particular interest is Subpart C, Article B (Domestic Nonprofit Corporations Generally), sections 5301-5989 (pages 1652-1676). One should be aware, however, that some sections of current law that were not changed by the enactment of Act 1988-177 are excluded from this version.

Law libraries have copies of the Purdon's Pennsylvania Consolidated Statutes Annotated. Pennsylvania nonprofit law is codified in Chapter 15. Make sure in researching current law to refer to the most up-to-date supplement for use in the current year. This supplement will include all changes to laws made since the books were printed.

Role of Incorporators

Incorporators are those persons legally responsible for forming the corporation. It is common for one person to serve in this capacity, although several people may sign the Articles of Incorporation form as formal incorporators.

Incorporators frequently play a more active role than solely being a name on the Articles of Incorporation filing. If they act to promote the interests of the new corporation (e.g., raise funds, recruit personnel, negotiate leases, or purchase property for the organization), their legal status is augmented by the responsibility of serving in a fiduciary capacity. This legal status confers on them the duty to take actions in the best interest of the corporation rather than their own personal interest, and to disclose any conflicts of interest that may occur in their business dealings on behalf of the corporation.

By law, the incorporators make agreements on behalf of the corporation while it is in the process of legal formation. These agreements have no legal effect until they are approved by the corporation's board of directors, once the corporation legally exists. As a result, incorporators who make these agreements must make it clear to the other party that the agreement is not binding until the corporation exists as a legal entity and its board ratifies the agreement.

Once the Articles of Incorporation are filed and the state government agency with jurisdiction over incorporation (usually the Department of State) approves them, incorporators have no formal status, with one exception. They are invited to be present at the organizational meeting required by law, at which the board of directors is selected.

It is a common practice that the incorporators include members who will be serving on the first board of directors. Thus, care should be taken as to the qualifications of incorporators, since they may continue their association with the corporation as directors.

Choosing a Corporate Name

One of the most important and basic decisions in forming a corporation is choosing a corporate name. This name will be the organization's corporate identity, and the image created by it provides the first impression held by those outside of the corporation. "Short" and "descriptive" are two desirable characteristics in a corporate name. Many nonprofit organizations choose a name that gives the connotation of helping, or otherwise doing charitable activities in the public interest, rather than implying a for-profit motive.

If the organization plans to apply for 501(c)(3) status, it should avoid names that would be suitable for organizations whose activities are clearly not eligible for this status. The organization may wish to consider suitable acronyms comprising the first letter of each word of its name, but cute or frivolous acronyms often give an unprofessional impression. It is useful to check if any other organization is using the prospective name by using Internet search engines and the U.S. Patent and Trademark Office's database (see below).

The process of having to change a corporate name after incorporating and operating as a nonprofit often results in time-consuming and costly activities, such as changing the logo (see Chapter 24); reprinting stationery, business cards, checks, and brochures; and changing all of the legal forms relating to Articles of Incorporation, bank accounts, and contracts.

For obvious legal reasons, the name must be unique in Pennsylvania, although it is usually legal to adopt a name similar to another existing corporation after receiving permission from that corporation and filing the necessary forms to do so. The name must include a designator "incorporated," "corporation," "limited," "company"(or an abbreviation thereof), or "association," "fund," or "syndicate." Any corporation organized under the nonprofit corporation law may not express or imply a purpose to engage in activities as a governmental agency.

A name search should be performed with the Corporation Bureau to ensure that no other corporation, active or inactive, is using an identical or similar name. Bureau staff will check up to three proposed names during any single telephone call (717-787-1057). The Bureau permits the name to be reserved for $70 for a 120-day period prior to registration as a corporation.

Many corporations also choose to do a national name search and take steps to register their names with the United States Patent and Trademark Office as trademarks. This can be done only for those organizations that will be marketing goods and services interstate. The fee is $375 for paper filing and $325 for electronic filing using the Trademark Electronic Applications System (TEAS), which provides registration for ten years, assuming the owner certifies that the trademark has active status. See: *http://www.uspto.gov/main/faq/index_feefaq.html* for requirements to be eligible for a $50 discount by filing a TEAS Plus form. Obviously, if an organization has trademarked its name, it is not available for other organizations, even if that organization is headquartered in another state.

For more information or to obtain the correct forms, contact the Patent and Trademark Office:

U.S. Patent and Trademark Office (USPTO)
Commissioner for Trademarks
U.S. Department of Commerce
PO Box 1451
Alexandria, VA 22313
(571) 272-1000
(800) 786-9199
Web site: http://www.uspto.gov/trademarks/teas/index.jsp

Basic information about trademarks can be accessed at:
http://www.uspto.gov/

Choosing Corporate Purposes

It is generally advisable to state broad corporate purposes in a manner that permits the corporation to grow and change direction without requiring its Articles of Incorporation to be amended. However, the purposes should be specific enough to permit the corporation to be eligible for 501(c)(3) status, if this is expected.

The Internal Revenue Service (IRS) has provided guidance on drafting a purpose statement that will facilitate a successful 501(c)(3) eligibility determination. Two examples illustrate clauses that will satisfy the IRS:

1. charitable and educational purposes within the meaning of IRC 501(c)(3).
2. To grant scholarships for deserving junior college students residing in Gotham City.

"To operate a hospital" is an example of a purpose that is unacceptable to the IRS. The explanation provided by the IRS is that the purpose is ambiguous, since a hospital may be exempt or not exempt, depending upon how it is operated.

The IRS provides language that nonprofit organizations may use in their Articles of Incorporation if they choose a broad corporate purpose consistent with the first example:

This corporation is organized exclusively for one or more purposes as specified in Section 501(c)(3) of the Internal Revenue Code or the corresponding section of any future federal tax code, including, for such purposes, the making of distributions to organizations that qualify as exempt organizations under Section 501(c)(3) of the Internal Revenue Code, or the corresponding section of any future tax code. The corporation shall not carry on any other activities not permitted to be carried on by a corporation exempt from Federal income tax under 501(c)(3) of the Internal Revenue Code of 1954, as amended (or the corresponding provision of any future United States Internal Revenue law).

A second consideration when devising the purpose statement to facilitate exemption is to provide that the organization benefits an indefinite class of individuals, not specific persons. For example, if the purpose of the organization is intended to be establishing a scholarship fund for specific members of a family who were orphaned by the September 11th World Trade Center disaster, the purpose should be "to grant scholarships to deserving American students orphaned by terrorist attacks" rather than "to grant scholarships to the children of John A. Smith."

Research similar organizations and review their Articles of Incorporation to obtain ideas on framing your own organization's Articles of Incorporation.

Choosing to Have Members or No Members

"Membership" in the legal sense has a different meaning than those in an organization who pay dues. In the context of incorporation, having members refers to providing broad governance authority beyond an organization's board of directors. In general, it is desirable for most nonprofit corporations to have no members. This will ensure that all power and authority will be maintained by the board of directors, and it will prevent the difficult legal problems of expelling an individual member should that occasion arise. It is also expensive and time-consuming to conduct elections, change bylaws, and make major organizational decisions when all members have the legal right to participate. Outsiders, including those who would pay dues in exchange for participating in organizational programs and activities, can still participate in the activities of the nonprofit corporation without being legal members who are entitled to vote on the affairs of the corporation.

As with almost every issue, there are exceptions to this. Many organizations will find it desirable for each participant in the organization's programs and activities to have an equal voice in the internal governance of the organization. Many individuals bristle at the fact that a nonprofit organization's governance is often controlled by a self-selected group of individuals that sometimes are perceived by members to be elitist, paternalistic, or secretive about the organization's affairs. Some feel that having legal members is more egalitarian and democratic.

Additional Provisions

Many corporations that wish to qualify for 501(c)(3) status add a provision that will facilitate tax-exemption approval. One such provision is a statement forbidding the corporation from engaging in partisan political activity on behalf of, or in opposition to, a candidate or substantially engaging in lobbying. The language for this provision can be adopted from 501(c)(3) itself:

> *No substantial part of the activities of the corporation shall be the carrying on of propaganda, or otherwise attempting to influence legislation, and the corporation shall not participate in, or intervene in (including the publishing or distribution of statements) any political campaign on behalf of any candidate for public office except as authorized under the Internal Revenue Code of 1954, as amended.*

A second provision required for Section 501(c)(3) eligibility relates to corporate dissolution:

> *Upon the dissolution of the corporation, assets shall be distributed for one or more exempt purposes within the meaning of Section 501(c)(3) of the Internal Revenue Code, as amended or supplemented, or shall be distributed to the federal government or to a state or local government for a public purpose. Any such assets not so disposed of shall be disposed of by the District Court of the county in which the principal office of the corporation is then located, exclusively for such purposes or to such organization or organizations, as said Court shall determine, which are organized and operated exclusively for such purposes.*

A third provision required by the IRS for Section 501(c)(3) eligibility relates to private inurement.

> *No part of the net earnings of the corporation shall inure to the benefit of, or be distributable to, its members, trustees, officers, or other persons, except that the*

corporation shall be authorized and empowered to pay reasonable compensation for services rendered to the corporation and to make payments and distributions in furtherance of the purposes set forth herein.

Once the Articles of Incorporation are filed and approved, be sure that all actions taken on behalf of the Corporation will clearly indicate that they are actions for the corporation and not on behalf of individuals. Otherwise, such individuals may be personally liable for fulfilling the terms of contracts and other agreements, such as paying rent, staff salaries, telephone installation costs, and so on. One way to indicate that persons are acting on behalf of the corporation is to explicitly sign legal contracts and other documents as follows:

<u>(corporate name)</u>
By <u>(individual's signature)</u>
<u>(individual's corporate title)</u>

The Articles of Incorporation filing form (DSCB:15-5306) and other forms referred to in this section may be downloaded from the Corporation Bureau's web site at *http://www.dos.state.pa.us/ corps/site/default.asp.* One original should be mailed along with accompanying documents to:

Department of State
Corporation Bureau
P.O. Box 8722
Harrisburg, PA 17105-8722
Harrisburg, PA 17120

A $125 filing fee, made payable to the "Department of State," should be included with each application. Make sure you provide a check that has a name and full address on it, or it may not be accepted. Accompanying the application should be:

- a copy of the docketing statement (form DSCB:15-134A),
- a copy of form DSCB:17.2 (Consent to Appropriation of Name) or form DSCB:17.3 (Consent to Use of Similar Name), if necessary, and
- any required approval forms.

The department requires an actual street address or rural route box number. It will disapprove applications if a post office box is listed as the corporate address. It is acceptable to provide the address of a commercial registered office provider.

The incorporators are required by Pennsylvania law to advertise their intention to file, or that they have filed, Articles of Incorporation in two newspapers of general circulation, including one legal journal, if there is one for the applicable county. Most counties have a legal journal. In Dauphin County, for example, incorporators must publish an advertisement in the Dauphin County Reporter, a publication of the Dauphin County Bar Association. The names and addresses of legal journals from other counties are listed in Appendix D. You may wish to check with the department's Corporation Bureau to verify this address. Contact that office at (717) 787-1057. They are also posted online. From the Bureau's Web site *(http://www.dos.state.pa.us/corps/site/default. asp),* click on "additional resources." You do not have to send proof of the advertisement to the Corporation Bureau, but you should attach such proof to the minutes of the organization.

The department will send a confirmation of the filing of the application only if it receives a self-addressed, stamped postcard or envelope with the filing information.

Applications for Articles of Incorporation take about a week to process, not including mailing time. A copy of the application will be returned with the date noted and the Secretary of State's signature in the upper right hand corner of the Articles of Incorporation. This is the only confirmation organizations receive. The original will have been microfilmed by the department, and copies of it or any other Articles of Incorporation can be ordered from the department for a photocopy charge of $15 plus $3/page.

Other Required Reports to the Corporation Bureau

Pennsylvania nonprofit organizations are required to submit an annual report to the Corporation Bureau whenever there has been a change in corporate officers during the preceding calendar year. All nonprofit organizations that have not provided any recent filings with the Department, such as an annual report, are required to file a Decennial Report each decade, accompanied by a $70 fee. The next report is due during calendar year 2021. If an organization fails to file this report, the Bureau will release that organization's name for public availability.

Corporate Dissolution

Pennsylvania law (Title 15, §5971-5998) provides for procedures to voluntarily dissolve a nonprofit corporation, and the legal requirements affecting nonprofits that are involuntarily dissolved by government authorities.

In the event that a voluntary dissolution is desired even before a nonprofit corporation begins its operations, Articles of Dissolution may be filed with the Department of State, using form 15:5977. The filing fee is $70. The Articles of Dissolution must be ratified by a majority of the members (if the corporation has members) or incorporators, and include—

- the name and address of the corporation;
- the date of incorporation and the law under which the corporation was incorporated;
- a statement that the corporation has not received any property in trust, and has not commenced business;
- a statement that membership dues, other than the amount already expended for necessary expenses, have been returned;
- a statement that all liabilities of the corporation have been discharged, or that provision has been made to discharge corporate liabilities; and
- a statement that the majority of the members or incorporators have elected to dissolve the corporation.

In the case that business of the corporation has already commenced, the procedures become quite complicated.

Dissolution can be proposed by a majority of the Board of Directors "or other body," or through a petition recommending voluntary dissolution from members entitled to cast at least 10% of the votes that all members are entitled to cast. The question of whether the corporation should dissolve is then required to be voted on at a regular or special meeting of the members or Board of Directors. Written notice of the meeting must be sent to all members. The resolution shall be considered adopted upon approval of a majority of members who cast their votes or, in the absence of members, a majority of the Board of Directors. The action can be rescinded using the same procedure prior to the time that Articles of Dissolution are filed with the Department of State.

The Board of Directors has full authority to wind up the affairs of the corporation, which include mailing by certified or registered mail dissolution notices to all creditors, claimants, and municipalities in which the corporation has a registered office. State law (Section 5975 of Title 15) then requires the corporation to "as speedily as possible" collect sums owed to it, convert its assets into cash, and discharge its liabilities. Unless the bylaws provide otherwise, remaining assets shall be distributed to the members on a per capita basis. The only exception to this is that the assets of a dissolved 501(c)(3) corporation must, in most cases, be distributed to another 501(c)(3) organization.

The legal requirements for the involuntary dissolution of a corporation are much more complex. Nonprofits that face legal notices concerning involuntary dissolution need to seek immediate legal advice. Codified Pennsylvania law relating to involuntary dissolution may be found in Subchapter G of Title 15 (Sections 5981-5998) of the Pennsylvania Code.

Tips:

- **Review the legal requirements of Pennsylvania law for nonprofits (particularly Sections 5301-5999 of Title 15 of the Pennsylvania Code) to make sure the organization can and is willing to comply with them.**

- **Have a lawyer review, if not draft, the Articles of Incorporation.**

- **Include in the Articles of Incorporation additional provisions to enhance the prospects for achieving the appropriate federal tax status if such status is desirable. See Chapter 8 for additional details.**

- **Choose a short and descriptive corporate name.**

- **Check out your prospective name using popular Internet search engines, such as Google *(http://www.google.com)*, Bing *(http:/www.bing.com)*, and Yahoo! *(http://www.yahoo.com)*. Having a corporate name that is not unique in the world may not be illegal, but it could be confusing.**

- **Review publications published by the Small Business Administration (SBA) that will help you start up and run your organization. A good place to start is: *http://www.sba.gov/category/navigation-structure/starting-managing-business/starting-business***

- **Remember to provide a check to the Department of State that has a full name and address.**

- **Review publications published by Pennsylvania agencies to assist entrepreneurs who wish to start up a nonprofit organization in the Commonwealth. Among them are:**

  - *A Guide to Business Registration in Pennsylvania*, **provided by the Corporation Bureau (call 717-772-0677 to obtain a copy or point your browser to *http://www.scorecpa.org/businessguidetoregistrationPABusiness.pdf*)**

  - *Entrepreneur's Guide —Starting and Growing a Business in Pennsylvania*, **provided by the Department of Community and Economic Development (call 800-280-3801 to obtain a copy or point your browser to *http://www.fcadc.com/incentives/pdf/Entrepreneur_Guide.pdf*)**

Chapter 3
Bylaws

Synopsis: Bylaws provide general policy guidelines for nonprofit corporations. There are statutory provisions that go into effect automatically in the absence of comparable bylaw provisions.

Introduction to Preparing Bylaws

Pennsylvania nonprofit law requires each corporation to have a set of bylaws. Pennsylvania statute (15 P.S. §5309) provides that the incorporators must schedule a meeting of initial directors (or the incorporators, if the directors are not named in the Articles of Incorporation) for the purpose of adopting bylaws. State law requires that at least five days' notice be given for the organizational meeting.

The term "bylaws" is defined in law to be "the code or codes of rules adopted for the regulation or management of the business and affairs of the corporation irrespective of the name or names by which such rules are designated."

Certain provisions must by law be included in bylaws of Pennsylvania nonprofit corporations. Beyond legal requirements, corporate bylaws are a necessary and important document, and great thought and care should be exercised as to what will be included in them.

Typical bylaws include provisions governing the following 25 internal procedures and policies of the nonprofit corporation:

1. the purposes of the corporation, consistent with any federal tax law limitation or state laws governing lobbying or other activity;
2. limitations of liability of directors, consistent with PA law (see 15 P.S. §5552);
3. types of officers;
4. terms, powers, and succession of officers;
5. location of principal office;
6. whether the corporation will have members, or whether all powers will be vested in a board of directors;
7. how directors will be selected and how vacancies will be filled,
8. how many directors there will be;
9. length of terms of board of directors, limits on consecutive terms, and if and how such terms will overlap with other board members;
10. terms under which a member of the board of directors can be disqualified;
11. conditions under which the annual meeting and other regularly scheduled board meetings are held;
12. how unscheduled meetings of the board may be called;
13. terms under which notice of board meetings must occur;
14. what constitutes a quorum for the transaction of business;
15. how many directors are required to approve an action;
16. whether actions of the board may be ratified through the mail or by conference call, or require directors to be present at a meeting;
17. power of the chairperson (or president) to appoint committees, and to provide for rules, powers, and procedures of such committees;
18. whether alternates may be empowered to represent directors, and who selects them;
19. who is responsible for preparing board meeting minutes;

20. who is responsible for keeping and reviewing the corporate books, and dispersing corporate funds;
21. how amendments may be made to the bylaws;
22. terms and conditions regarding compensation, if any, paid to directors;
23. what committees are authorized, and what powers and duties they have;
24. the terms under which the corporation will be dissolved; and
25. which, if any, parliamentary procedure will be used at board meetings.

Legal Requirements of Bylaws in Pennsylvania

Pennsylvania law provides for some minimum standards with respect to bylaws of nonprofit corporations. For example, every Pennsylvania nonprofit corporation must—

- have a President, Treasurer, and Secretary (or officers who perform comparable duties). A single person may hold all three offices. The President and Secretary must be citizens of legal age. The Treasurer may be a corporation, or an individual citizen of legal age.
- not have meetings organized for the transaction of business unless a quorum is present.
- not expel a member of the corporation "without notice, trial and conviction, the form of which shall be prescribed by the bylaws."

Pennsylvania statute provides rules on many of the above bylaw options in the absence of explicit directions in the nonprofit corporation's bylaws. Thus, it is important to place provisions in the bylaws that will be intended to supersede these statutory legal guidelines, if the directors feel that the guidance provided in law is not acceptable to the corporation.

Among the provisions of bylaws that deserve the highest consideration and thought are the following, with some comments about the issues they raise:

Quorum Requirements

A quorum is the minimum number of members or directors required to be present for a meeting to be held for the legal transaction of business. The purpose of a quorum requirement is to assure that actions are taken by a representative number of duly authorized participants rather than by an elite few. Standard advice, in the absence of relying on any statutory requirement, is to set the quorum at the minimum number of people who will be expected to attend a meeting, taking into account emergencies, adverse weather conditions, or conflicts with competing meetings. If the bylaws permit it, board members may participate in meetings and be counted as part of a quorum if they are in communication by speaker phone or by conference call.

Since actions cannot be taken legally at board meetings without a quorum present, it is best to begin with a conservatively low quorum requirement. Then change the bylaws to increase that number as appropriate. Otherwise, it is possible that the corporation will never have a quorum for its meetings, even if the sole purpose of the meeting is to change the bylaws to decrease the number of directors constituting a quorum.

Voting Rights

Boards need to vote to formally demonstrate that they have taken actions. Many organizations can be effectively run by consensus rather than by formal voting, but even the most congenial and tolerant boards will eventually face issues that will divide them. In the absence of a provision in the bylaws, action may be taken at a board meeting with the approval of a majority of directors who are present at the meeting. Nothing prohibits a two-thirds vote from being required to ensure that actions are closer to representing a consensus. A two-thirds vote may be suggested for changing bylaws, or for changing membership dues requirements. Generally, a majority vote is sufficient for most routine board decisions, and avoids the inability to take positions and actions that can occur as a result of a two-thirds voting requirement.

Selection of Officers

Many organizations are attracted to the democratic notion of offices being opened to all. With such a policy, any director can run for an office, ballots are prepared, and the winner is selected by the majority (or plurality) of voters from the board of directors or the membership at large. Other organizations feel that democracy puts at risk an orderly succession and threatens the existing power structure. Orderly succession can be accomplished by providing for a nominating committee, appointed by the chairperson, which selects a slate of officers. This slate is then perfunctorily approved by the full board. Both systems have their advantages and disadvantages.

Some organizations utilize a third alternative that combines the two. The nominations committee recommends a slate of candidates, but the procedures permit other candidates to run, as well.

Executive Committees

Board meetings may occur at regular intervals, but issues arise in the interim that demand immediate attention. In such cases, it is valuable to have a mandated procedure for taking legally legitimate actions in the absence of board meetings. The mechanism to accomplish this is the executive committee, provided for in the corporate bylaws. While the executive committee typically is comprised of the corporation's officers, Pennsylvania law (Section 5731 of Title 15) authorizes nonprofit corporations to establish an executive committee comprised of one or more directors appointed by the board. The executive committee has all of the power and authority of the full board with the following exceptions:

1. The executive committee cannot fill vacancies on the board.
2. The executive committee cannot adopt, amend, or repeal bylaws.
3. The executive committee cannot have powers inconsistent with the resolution passed by the board establishing it.

Tips:

- **Review Pennsylvania law with respect to corporate bylaws. Identify which provisions are required, which provisions apply only in the absence of a different provision in the bylaws, and which act to pre-empt any statutory guideline.**

- **Give careful consideration to the more important bylaw provisions, such as—**

  a. quorum requirements;
  b. succession of officers;
  c. powers of the executive committee; and
  d. voting by the board of directors.

- **Have an attorney review the bylaws to ensure that they are in compliance with state law, and ensure that the organization's desires with respect to internal decision-making will be consistent with efficient operating procedures.**

- **Schedule an organizational meeting to approve the bylaws, and distribute a draft of proposed bylaws before this meeting.**

- **After a final version of the bylaws is approved, provide a final copy of the bylaws to all members of the board of directors.**

Chapter 4
Nonprofit Boards of Directors
by Michael A. Sand and Gary M. Grobman

Synopsis: It is a critically important function for nonprofit organizations to find and retain qualified, experienced board members and officers. Board meetings generally have a routine order of business and provide the forum for making organizational policy.

One important requirement of a nonprofit organization is the formation of a board of directors. The board has the responsibility to set policy for the organization in accordance with all applicable laws and to see to it that the policies are implemented.

Board Formation

The size of the board should depend on the needs of the organization. If the board's role is strictly policy-making and the policies are implemented by a qualified staff, a small board might be more appropriate. However, if extensive board time is required for fundraising or implementing programs, then a much larger board is in order.

The number of board members is set in the bylaws. One effective technique is to set a minimum and maximum number of board members and to allow the board to determine its own size within these parameters. Then the board can start small and add members as the need arises.

The term of board members must be included in the bylaws. Board members should have fixed terms of office. One common practice is for all board members to have three-year terms, with one-third of the members being elected each year. In this way, board continuity is assured. Some boards allow their members to serve an unlimited number of terms; other boards wish to limit the number to ensure new members with fresh ideas.

The election process should also be spelled out in the bylaws.

Most organizations have a nominating or governance committee that is responsible for recommending new board members to the full board. Additional candidates for board membership can be nominated either in advance or from the floor at the election.

The titles, duties, length of term, and process for the election of officers should be spelled out in the bylaws.

Organizational Officers

The elected officers of most organizations are similar:

Chairperson, Chair, or President
Leads the meetings of the organization. Appoints committee chairs. Either signs checks or delegates this duty to another individual.

Vice Chairperson, Vice-Chair, or Vice President
Assumes the duties of the president or chair in his or her absence, or upon his or her death or resignation. In many organizations, is given specific responsibilities,

either in the bylaws or by vote. In some organizations, automatically becomes the next president.

Secretary
Either takes minutes at the board meeting or approves the minutes if taken by another individual. Responsible for all official correspondence.

Treasurer
Responsible for finances of the organization. Usually makes financial reports to the board and signs checks.

Getting Good Board Members

Many organizations are finding it more difficult than ever to attract excellent board members. This is due to many factors, such as the large increase in the number of nonprofit boards, the increasing number of women in the work force, and the fact that upwardly mobile professionals often relocate.

To ensure excellence, many nominating committees meet several times during the year rather than just once to search for potential board members. One effective technique is to strive for a diverse board, and to list the types of characteristics desired. Some might be:

- *Expertise*: Some board members should have personnel management, fiscal, fundraising, or legal expertise.

- *Ages*: It is helpful to have older people represented, as well as youth and individuals in between.

- *Races and Religions:* All major races and religions in the community should be represented on a diverse board.

- *Backgrounds:* It would be helpful if some board members have corporate backgrounds, some are government leaders, and others have served on the boards of other nonprofit groups.

- *Users of the service:* Many boards include representatives of the client population being served.

The nominating committee or board development committee can search throughout the year for individuals with these characteristics, who are then asked if they want to be considered for board membership.

Each board should have a list of board member responsibilities. These might include attending board meetings on a regular basis, serving on at least one standing committee, and participating in fundraising. The list of duties should be provided to each prospective board member, and no board member should be elected who will not agree to meet these responsibilities.

Keeping Good Board Members

One technique for keeping good board members is to require all new board members to participate in an orientation program before they attend their first board meeting.

The first step in the process is to receive and review materials that all board members should have received previously. These include—

- articles of Incorporation;
- bylaws;
- funding applications;
- personnel, fiscal, and other board policies;
- annual reports;
- names, addresses, phone numbers, and biographical sketches of other board members and key staff members;
- list of committees and committee duties;
- minutes of the last several board meetings; and
- audits, budgets, and recent financial statements.

The second step is to hold a meeting with the board chair and the executive director. This provides an opportunity to ask questions about the materials received, visit the staff offices and programs, get an update of current issues, and review board member responsibilities.

Other steps to encourage productivity of board members include—

- giving board members specific projects. A board member who serves as the chair of a committee or who has specific fundraising responsibilities is more likely to stay active.
- keeping board meetings interesting,
- thanking board members for their work, and
- having social events periodically, in addition to formal board meetings.

One other technique is to remove unproductive board members quickly and replace them with new and productive ones.

Other ways to increase board productivity include—

- having a policy in the bylaws that missing a specified number of board meetings without a reason will result in automatic dismissal,
- re-electing only board members who have been meeting their responsibilities,
- calling board members who have not been active to ask them if there are any problems. In some cases, the chairperson should ask for their resignation if they do not agree to meet board responsibilities.

Board Responsibilities

Members of boards of directors have the following duties:

Personnel

The board hires the executive director. This is the board's most important responsibility. It then makes assignments to the executive director and monitors the executive director's performance. It is appropriate for the board or its Personnel Committee to do a formal performance appraisal of the executive director at least annually. The board approves salary scales and job descriptions for the other staff members, who are hired by the executive director. The board approves the personnel policies for the organization.

Finance

The board approves budgets for the organization. No funds are expended unless the funds are included in a budget approved by the board. The board approves spending reports, which are submitted on a regular basis.

Fundraising

All applications for funds are submitted to the board before being submitted to funding sources. The board also approves plans for special events fundraising, and board members are expected to participate in fundraising events.

Planning

Board members approve short- and long-range plans for the organization. They then monitor the effectiveness of the organization's programs to see if it has met the goals outlined in the plans.

Board Development

The board selects new board members and adopts procedures to see that excellent board members are selected and continue to serve.

Public Relations

Board members are aware of all of the organization's activities and encourage participation in appropriate activities by the community.

Advising

Board members advise the executive director on policy implementation as requested.

How Boards Function Effectively

Boards set policies only through a majority vote of their members at board meetings, unless the bylaws provide otherwise. For boards with staffs, one effective method of policy-making is to ask the staff to draft proposed policies. These policies are then sent to a board committee for review.

The chair of each committee should be a board member appointed by the board president. Members of committees are usually selected by the committee chair and may include non-board members.

All committees are advisory, except that the bylaws may permit the executive committee to act on behalf of the board between board meetings. Once a committee has approved a proposed policy, it is submitted to the board for approval. The board may delegate authority to committees to implement some decisions.

Board members who want a policy to be adopted begin the discussion by making a motion that it be approved. If another board member seconds the motion, discussion can begin; if not, the motion fails.

Once a motion is seconded, the chairperson opens the floor for discussion. Members are recognized by the chairperson before they may speak, and they can discuss only the motion on the floor. When the discussion has ended, the chairperson announces that a vote will be taken.

The easiest way to vote is by a show of hands. The secretary can then record the vote. If a majority approves a policy, it becomes the board's policy (unless the bylaws provide otherwise). It is the responsibility of the executive director to implement that policy.

The executive director receives instructions from the board at a board meeting. It is improper for individual board members to give assignments to any staff member without prior board authorization.

Holding High-Quality Board Meetings

One key factor in getting and keeping excellent board members is the quality of the board meetings. If board meetings are unproductive, board members tend to be unproductive.

An important technique for improving board meetings is to do as much planning *before the board meeting* as possible.

This might include:

- sending a notice of the date, time, and location of the meeting to the members several weeks before the meeting. Even if the board meets the same day of each month at the same place and time, a reminder notice is important.

- giving the board members the telephone number of the individual (usually the chairperson) to call if they cannot attend the meeting. This way, the chairperson can get input on important items from individuals who cannot attend the meeting. Also, if a quorum will not be present, the meeting can be canceled in advance.

- notifying members of important items to be discussed at the meeting. For major items, information or issue papers might be included in the meeting notice packet.

- including as many written items as possible with the meeting notice rather than distributing them at the meeting. This may include the minutes of the previous meeting and the treasurer's report, for example. Members then have an opportunity to read items before the meeting, and members who do not attend the meeting are kept up-to-date more effectively, and

- developing a preliminary agenda before the meeting. Committee chairs who will be asked to report at the meeting should be notified. Background reports should be developed for important issues.

The board meetings should start on time. Once the members know that every board meeting starts on time, it is much more likely that they will be prompt. Each board meeting should start with the distribution of a written agenda. The agenda should be as detailed as possible, listing each separate item to be voted on.

Once the secretary announces that a quorum is present, the chairperson asks all those present if there are any additional items for the agenda. Thus, there will be no surprises, and the chairperson can run the meeting more effectively. The chairperson has the option of referring new items to committees or postponing items until future meetings.

A typical order of business at a board meeting is as follows:

- *Approval of the Minutes of the Previous Meeting.* A formal vote is needed to approve the minutes. Minutes should be distributed to all members and should not be read aloud at the meeting.

- *Chairperson's Report.* The chairperson should state before each item whether it is informational only or requires board action. The chairperson should remind the members that only policy-making recommendations require board action.

- *Executive Director's Report.* This report should be in writing. If it is lengthy, it should be distributed before the meeting. The executive director should then highlight important aspects of the written report and take questions.

- *Committee Reports.* Committee reports should be in writing unless they are very brief. After giving the report, the committee chair should make specific motions when board action is required. Only policy items require board action; no board action is required when the committee chair is simply providing information.

- *Unfinished Business.* The only items belonging in this section are ones raised at previous board meetings. The chairperson should remind the members when the item was raised originally and why it was postponed.

- *New Business.* Major items of business are discussed as part of the chairperson's report, executive director's report, or committee reports. At the beginning of the meeting, members are asked if they have additional agenda items, and the chairperson has the option of placing some of these items under New Business.

- *Good and Welfare.* Many organizations provide an opportunity for members and guests to make short announcements, raise issues to be discussed at future meetings, or comment on items of interest.

- *Adjournment.* No formal action is needed. The chairperson announces the date, time, and place of the next meeting, reminds the members of steps to be taken before the meeting, such as committee meetings, and adjourns the board meeting.

After the board meeting, the minutes are sent to board members for their review. The minutes must include a list of attendees and the motions made and votes taken. Additional information may be included at the pleasure of the board. Many organizations include only the minimum required, and the minutes do not include individual comments made at the meeting. While the minutes need not be taken by the board secretary, they should be distributed under the signature of the board secretary.

Legal Responsibilities of Board Members

Being a board member of a nonprofit organization is not an honorary position. Pennsylvania law holds board members accountable for violating accepted standards of conduct and decision-making. Generally, boards may make bad decisions with impunity. But they are required to have made those decisions believing at the time that they were in the best interests of the organization rather than themselves, and consistent with the organization's mission.

Among the legal duties of board members are—

- *Duty of Care.* They must take reasonable care when making decisions for the organization.
- *Duty of Loyalty.* They must act in the best interest of the organization.
- *Duty of Obedience.* They must act in accordance with the organization's mission.
- *Avoid Conflicts of Interest.* They must not participate in decision-making in which they have a personal interest that may constitute a conflict of interest (Source: *Non-Profit Board Responsibilities* by Estela Kennen, *http://estela-kennen.suite101.com/nonprofit-board-responsibilities-a14806*).

Former Pennsylvania Attorney General Tom Corbett (the current Governor), in a booklet *Handbook for Charitable Organizations*, explains the "duty of care" standard he has enforced as—

> *When performing their duties, board members, senior management and members of committees must use the degree of care, skill, caution and diligence that a prudent person would use in handling corporate affairs. Decision-makers are required to make reasonable inquiries when analyzing contracts, investments, business dealings, and other matters. An individual who is acting in conformance with this standard will:*
>
> - *attend and participate in board meetings on a regular basis;*
> - *attend and participate in committee meetings when the individual is a member of the committee;*
> - *diligently read, review, and inquire about material that affects the corporation;*
> - *keep abreast of the affairs and finances of the corporation; and*
> - *use independent judgment when analyzing matters that affect the corporation....*
>
> *Board members, trustees and senior management have a fiduciary responsibility when handling finances and investments. That simply means, they must exercise the degree of care, caution and diligence that prudent persons would exercise in handling their own personal investments and finances. Individuals who have or claim to have special knowledge or skills in the area of investment will be held to a higher standard. Fiduciaries who carelessly or negligently invest funds may be personally liable for any losses sustained.*

He explains "duty of loyalty" to be—

> *Board members and senior management must always perform their duties in good faith with the best interests of the organization in mind. This means that they must not seek to derive private gain from business transactions that involve the nonprofit corporation or advance their own interests at the expense of the corporation. Acts of self-dealing constitute a breach of fiduciary duty which may result in personal liability to the nonprofit organization. Board members, trustees, and senior management should avoid conflicts of interest and even the appearance of impropriety. Individuals who take advantage of corporate opportunities to make profits for themselves at the expense of the corporation may be liable for the profits they received at the organization's expense.*

With respect to avoiding conflicts of interest, he writes that—

... It is particularly important for board members to disclose the following facts:

- *whether they have a potential conflict of interest with respect to any transaction, business decision or other matter in which the organization is involved;*
- *whether they have a financial, business or personal interest in an entity with which the nonprofit organization is or will be doing business;*
- *whether individuals related to them have a financial, business or personal interest in an entity with which the nonprofit organization is or will be doing business; or*
- *whether they serve as a director, member or employee of either a competitor of the corporation or a corporation with which the nonprofit organization is or will be doing business.*

The board should proceed with caution when any of the above facts are present because there may be a conflict of interest. An individual who has a potential conflict with respect to a particular transaction should disclose it to fellow managers and board members and abstain from participating in the negotiations and decisions surrounding that transaction. To avoid the appearance of impropriety, the individual who has the conflict of interest should not be present in the room during any discussions that relate to the transaction. (See: http://www.attorneygeneral.gov/uploadedFiles/Consumers/nonprofitbooklet.pdf)

In 2010, Mr. Corbett successfully prosecuted the Democratic Minority Whip of the Pennsylvania House of Representatives for, among other charges, conflict of interest with respect to a nonprofit. That official is now serving a 6- to 14-year prison sentence in a state correctional facility.

Relationship Between Board Members and Staff Members

The board of directors sets policy for the organization. Several examples of the types of policies set by the board are provided above. The only way policy can be set is by a majority vote of the board at a board meeting (unless the bylaws provide otherwise).

The executive director (or chief executive officer) attends all board meetings, and is responsible for implementing the policies set by the board. The executive director hires other staff members (whose salary levels and job descriptions have been approved by the board) to assist in implementing these policies.

When an item arises at a board meeting, the chairperson rules whether the item is a policy matter. If so, a vote of the board is required for action to be taken. If the item is not a policy matter, no board vote is taken. The purpose of the discussion is to provide guidance to the executive director on non-policy matters.

The executive director researches sources of funds and develops grant applications. Before a grant application can be submitted to a funding source, it should be approved by the board.

Certain types of communications between board members and staff members are not appropriate. For example, individual board members may not give assignments to staff members. Assignments are given to the executive director by vote of the board at a board meeting. The executive director is responsible for assigning tasks to other staff members.

Staff members should not complain to individual board members about programs, assignments, or policies. Complaints should be made according to specific procedures established by the board.

When a board member volunteers to help out in the office, that person must be treated as a staff person and no longer wears the "board hat." The executive director remains the person to make assignments to that person.

Parliamentary Procedure

Board meetings of nonprofit organizations may be formally or informally conducted, but its decisions made consistent with law and its bylaws are legally binding and may be enforced by a court. At times, decision-making can be a contentious exercise. Without an acceptance of basic rules for conducting meetings by those who attend, a meeting could become highly dysfunctional, with meaningful decision-making becoming impossible. Members may all decide to speak at once, may disagree on whether a decision has been really been made, may refuse to accept decisions made by the chair, or otherwise become frustrated when they don't feel that their participation has been treated respectfully and have been given a fair opportunity to voice their opinions and advocate for their positions.

Over the centuries, a set of standardized, basic rules for conducting meetings fairly has been developed. The standard used by many nonprofit organization boards is based on *Roberts Rules of Order,* first published in 1874. Henry M. Roberts, a West Point Graduate, based his manual on a 15-page set of parliamentary rules he developed to help him, his wife, and others who served on the boards of various nonprofit organizations (source: Darwin Patnode, *History of Parliamentary Procedure*). Roberts was influenced by the writings on the topic by Thomas Jefferson (*Jefferson's Manual,* which still serves as the rules of debate for the U.S. House of Representatives) and others that governed the debates of the Senate. And of course, these rules are based on rules of the English Parliament, from which the term "parliamentary procedure" derives its name.

Several other parliamentary procedure manuals are in use, among them the *Standard Code of Parliamentary Procedure* by Alice Sturgess (1950), George Demeter's *Demeter's Manual of Parliamentary Law and Procedure* (1969), and *Modern Parliamentary Procedure* by Ray E. Keesey (1974).

In nonprofit organizations, in which participants volunteer their time, it makes some sense to follow parliamentary procedure a bit more loosely compared to legislative bodies, keeping an eye on the objective of keeping meetings civil and assuring that decisions made by the board truly reflect either a consensus of members, or at least a majority. The more participants there are at a meeting, the more likely that increased formality will be productive.

There are clear advantages to conducting meetings using parliamentary procedure, including—

- There are procedures to ending debate, which in some cases could otherwise drag on interminably.
- Everyone with something to say has the opportunity to be heard.
- Debate on any issue remains on topic, and new topics are considered only after there is closure on the previous topic, or there is agreement to postpone closure.

- There is a procedure to reconsider decisions that may have been made in haste and without complete information.
- There are rules to deal with destructive, personal confrontations.

Typically, board meetings are conducted by the President (or Chair) of the board. It helps when that individual has a basic understanding of parliamentary procedure, although some organizations will hire a Certified Professional Parliamentarian with specific knowledge of parliamentary procedure to advise the chair. See: *http://www.jimslaughter.com/pdffiles/ASAEMatching99.pdf*

Many organizations will indicate in their bylaws that meetings shall use a particular form of parliamentary procedure, such as—

> *The rules contained in the current edition of Robert's Rules of Order Newly Revised shall govern the organization in all cases to which they are applicable and in which they are not inconsistent with these bylaws and any special rules of order the organization may adopt.*

For an explanation of Robert's Rules and details about how it works in practice, see the Robert's Rules Web site at: *http://www.robertsrules.com/*

Tips:

- **Develop a list of typical decision areas that are likely to arise in the course of routine corporate operations and reach a board consensus on whether the decisions should be made by—**

  a. **the executive director alone,**
  b. **the executive director, in consultation with the board,**
  c. **the executive director, in consultation with the board chairperson,**
  d. **the board alone,**
  e. **the chairperson alone, or**
  f. **a committee of the board.**

  Review, revise, and update this list annually.

- **Consider adopting a policy on the responsibilities and privileges of board members, and include a conflict-of-interest policy. A sample conflict of interest policy is provided in Form 1023 of the Internal Revenue Service, and more information may be found on the Web at: *http://www.idealist.org/ info/Nonprofits***

- **Become familiar with the basic procedures of Robert's Rules of Order.**

Chapter 5
Mission and Vision Statements

Synopsis: Mission and vision statements provide a foundation for your organization's future and help keep it focused on the purposes for which it was created. The mission statement includes the core organizational purpose. The vision statement describes the ideal future of the organization. Both are useful in maintaining the stability of organizations.

Every nonprofit organization should have a mission statement and a vision statement. Many nonprofit executives are confused about the difference between the two, and this is not surprising since organizational consultants disagree among themselves about what these should contain.

The Mission Statement

The mission statement should be a succinct description of the basic purpose of the organization, including the nature of the work to be carried out, the reason it exists, and the clients and constituencies it is designed to serve. It may also include some principles and values that are to guide the organization, although these can be enumerated in a separate values/principles statement.

The mission statement serves several purposes.

First, it is a core document guiding basic decision-making for the organization. The mission statement can effectively place constraints on decision-making that are inconsistent with the organization's core purpose, and thus provide a mechanism for organizational stability. Any decision made by an organization that would result in activities that contradict the mission statement should either not be implemented, or should require a major soul-searching by the organization's board of directors.

A second purpose is to provide the organization's board and staff with a useful short description of the organization. This permits all who work with the organization to be on the same page with respect to core purpose. The mission statement serves an important public relations function by explaining to important stakeholders, such as funders, government regulators, and clients, what the organization is about.

A third purpose is to serve as a way to focus all of your organization's staff and board on the primary reason for the organization's existence, so that internal activities and politics that might conflict with the true purposes of the organization can be reined in and resources are not diverted to purposes inconsistent with the core mission.

Many mission statements contain two parts, although the first part is sufficient. The first part is often referred to as the "umbrella," a short overview of the purpose of the organization. For example, the Pennsylvania Jewish Coalition's mission is "to monitor legislative and regulatory developments in Harrisburg that affect Pennsylvania's organized Jewish community." During the 13 years I served as the executive director of that organization, I must have recited that mantra a thousand times, and I can still do so in my sleep. This statement served an important purpose. It kept me focused on state matters at a time when there was a vortex of legislative and regulatory activity in Washington that threatened to divert me from doing the narrow task for which I was hired. Another purpose is that the funder, legislator, or member of the press who heard me recite it generally understood the role and essence of the organization.

A second part of the mission statement, which many, including myself, consider to be optional, provides further detail. One way to do this is to add the following after the umbrella: "In support of this mission, we…" followed by general, bullet-pointed objectives relating to, for example, increasing public awareness about the organization's goals and objectives; meeting the needs of clients; providing quality services; and maintaining relationships with officials from the government, the media, the advocacy community, and the public.

The Vision Statement

The vision statement is related to, but clearly different from, the mission statement. Its purpose is to convey the ideal future of the organization—what it hopes to become in the eyes of its board, staff, and stakeholders. One purpose of the vision statement is to inspire those in the organization to achieve goals. Another is to help frame decisions made by the organization in the context of achieving these goals.

Among the issues that might be appropriate in a vision statement include the organization's place in society, its intended growth, its use of new technology, quality improvement, its reputation in the community, and how the public perceives the organization's effectiveness and efficiency. Other topics could be how it will serve as a good organizational citizen in the community and a measurement of the degree to which it hopes to contribute to solving (or mitigating) particular social problems.

One of the best guides I have found on the preparation of mission statements and vision statements is a 1996 book, *A Guide to Strategic Thinking: Building Your Planning Foundation* by George Morrisey (Jossey-Bass).

Examples of Mission and Vision Statements

Mission Statement of the Pennsylvania Association of Nonprofit Agencies (reprinted with permission):

> *PANO leads Pennsylvania's Community Benefit Sector to achieve its fullest potential.*

Vision Statement of California State University, Monterey Bay (CSUMB)
http://about.csumb.edu/vision-statement

Vision Statement of Africare
http://www.africare.org/about-us/mission/mission.php

Vision Statement of the Young Adult Library Services Association (YALSA)
http://www.ala.org/ala/mgrps/divs/yalsa/aboutyalsab/yalsavisionstatement.cfm

Vision Statement of the Forestville (CA) Planning Association:
http://www.forestvillefpa.org/about/vision.html

Vision Statement of the Pennsylvania Society of Association Executives (PASAE):
http://www.pasae.org/pasae.php?mid=31

Online Resources to Explore

The Grantsmanship Center: How to Write a Mission Statement
http://www.tgci.com/magazine/How%20to%20Write%20a%20Mission%20Statement.pdf

Powerful Mission Statements - What? Why? How? - Part I
http://ezinearticles.com/?Powerful-Mission-Statements---What?-Why?-How?---Part-I&id=3592480

What's In a Mission Statement
http://familyfirstfoundation.org/faq/what_is_in_mission_statement.html

Tips:

- **Keep your mission statement focused on a narrow, specific purpose, to an extent that your organization won't be seen as potentially duplicative of other organizations in your area. In other words, carve out your own organizational niche, highlighting a unique service or serving a unique population of clients.**

- **Don't try to put too much into your mission statement; a single sentence is usually sufficient.**

- **Consider the mission and vision statements of similar organizations. You can find many examples on the Web.**

- **Periodically revisit your mission and vision statements to determine if they might be constraining your organization from adapting to new environmental conditions.**

Chapter 6
Strategic Planning

> **Synopsis:** Formal strategic planning is not for every organization. All stakeholders must be committed to successfully develop and implement a strategic plan. Although such plans require a major investment in money and time and have other institutional costs and risks, the benefits include enhancing the organization's ability to respond to internal and external threats.

Introduction

Strategic planning is a formalized process by which an organization makes a study of its vision for the future, typically for three years or more from the present. A strategic plan is an important management tool that can help organizational leaders consider the effects of advances in technology, changing markets for its services, the effects of government funding cutbacks, or the emergence of other organizations (both for-profits and nonprofits) that provide similar, competing services.

CEOs of organizations are often are so involved with putting out fires and responding to the challenges of day-to-day operations that it is a luxury to set aside time to think about the position of the organization even a year into the future. An organization's board is often ill equipped to consider changes in organizational structure and operations in the context of a regular board meeting.

Purpose of Strategic Planning

In his 1994 book, *The Rise and Fall of Strategic Planning*, Henry Mintzberg lists four reasons for organizations to do strategic planning: to coordinate their activities, to ensure that the future is taken into account, to be rational, and to control. Strategic planning is designed to suggest remedies for organizational problems before they blow up. Deep cuts in government grants, changes in markets, advances in technology, competition from for-profit businesses, and changes in demographics in an organization's service area all crystallize the need to change the basic way an organization does business.

Virtually all successful large for-profit businesses engage in a formal strategic planning process. The conventional wisdom is that businesses that do so, regardless of whether they are for-profit or nonprofit, are more successful over time than those that do not. However, Mintzberg cites scores of academic studies that show mixed results as to the benefits of strategic planning in business and industry, and concludes that the value of strategic planning is nebulous at best.

Putting that aside, a periodic strategic planning process provides the framework for a long-term assessment of emerging threats, and the opportunity to develop creative strategies to respond to them. The intent here is not to encourage or discourage nonprofits to engage in a formal strategic planning process; rather, it is to raise issues to consider in the event that this endeavor, for whatever reason, is under consideration.

Strategic planning requires the investment of both money and time. For most nonprofits, both are scarce. Thus, it is important that an organization's leaders systematically evaluate whether the benefits of preparing, updating, and implementing a periodic strategic plan outweigh the costs. Strategic plan preparation often involves the hiring of an outside consultant, plenty of meetings, and the involvement of board members, staff, and other organization stakeholders for an extended period of time.

The strategic planning process is fraught with danger. The contents of a final strategic plan often are totally at odds with the vision of the organizational leader who first suggested preparing one. The planning committee dynamics are often uncontrollable by the people who provide the organization with leadership. Organizational leaders may be uncomfortable sharing the organization's dreams and aspirations, its "dirty little secrets," and proprietary financial projections with a professional outside consultant, and may be even more reticent with community members of the planning committee. Yet, many agencies that successfully complete a strategic planning process improve their performance. Participating board members feel a renewed connection and bond to both the organization and their colleagues. Agencies that don't plan for the future, whether in a formalized process or informal board retreats, often suffer the consequences.

Strategic planning in the for-profit sector has been popular for several decades. In the for-profit world, strategic planning has the advantage of having each member of the committee, virtually by definition, already in agreement on the basic mission of the organization; that is, in short, to make as much profit as possible. There will be differences, of course, as to the methods used to accomplish this. In a nonprofit, there is not always agreement on the mission from the outset. In a hospital situation, for example, some planning committee members may view the mission as providing quality health care to the community. Some may feel it is to teach medical students, advance life-saving technology, increase "market share" by gobbling up other health care institutions, or serve populations not served by other institutions.

In a for-profit setting, the outcomes are easily measurable—net profit and market share are statistics easily compiled. In the nonprofit sector, consumer satisfaction, community benefit, and image in the community often are considered more important than bottom-line net revenue, and they are difficult to measure satisfactorily. In the nonprofit sector, board members may actually be concerned if the institution is making too much net revenue and not providing services to sectors of the market that would clearly result in revenue shortfalls. It is the nature of nonprofits that the institution is not motivated by private profit motive and, in theory, this can create conflicts. As a result of government cutbacks, tensions are mounting within nonprofit boards as they wrestle with difficult decisions concerning how to ease the financial crunch while maintaining traditional markets.

Making the Decision to Develop a Strategic Plan

The motivation for initiating a strategic plan comes from many sources:

Board Members. Board members who have participated in successful strategic planning as a result of their service on other nonprofit boards are often the source for initiating a strategic plan. Board members who run their own businesses or work for for-profit companies that routinely develop strategic plans also may raise this issue. Many who serve on nonprofit boards see strategic planning as a management and governance tool equal in importance to budgeting, and they cannot imagine an organization that doesn't initiate a formal process to look inward at least once every half-decade.

Funders. Some funders require the development of a strategic plan before they make grants to nonprofit charities. These funders want evidence that their contributions will be used prudently and cost-effectively and will influence the direction of the organization. A strategic plan developed as a result of such a requirement by a funder would obviously highlight changes in the organization's programs that are the direct result of the contribution.

Retirement of a Long-Term CEO. Many nonprofits were started by visionary leaders who ran the organizations by the seat of their pants. This "old school" of doing business may no longer be valid. New organizational leaders, many with MBAs, believe that nonprofit organizations are businesses, and the same management techniques they learned in business school are applicable to the philanthropic sector. The new school recognizes that the bottom line remains the principal concern of the organization whether or not the bottom line is interpreted as the net revenue at the end of the year or the number of satisfied clients served. The old school organizational executive is often skeptical, if not fearful, of strategic planning. Perhaps his or her vision of the organization has never been challenged, and a formal process to evaluate the organization from top to bottom, from the mission statement on down, is a threat to executive autonomy. In some cases, that skepticism is justified.

Once a new generation assumes the mantle of leadership, there is motivation to rebuild the organization from the ground up, starting with the mission statement and proceeding, in some extreme cases, to changing the model of the copying machine. A strategic plan is often the vehicle for the new leadership to assert its authority and provide a mechanism for a higher level of executive accountability.

Organizational Trauma. More often than not, it is an organizational crisis that triggers the decision for a strategic plan when an organization has no regular process to prepare one. The resignation or firing of a CEO is a traumatic event for any nonprofit. Sometimes, this event has occurred because of underlying unresolved issues and problems that may have developed and been inadequately addressed over many years. In the case of the involuntary separation, the organization's leadership has the opportunity to reshape the organization before a new executive takes over and molds the direction of the organization. Other traumatic events that may trigger the initiation of a strategic plan are the loss of a major funder; the establishment of competition from another nonprofit or for-profit; major damage to, or aging of, the organization's physical plant; liability suits; or quantum advances in technology that call into question the future demand for services by the organization.

Benefits of Strategic Planning

1. **It permits discussion of issues in a proactive rather than reactive mode.** Usually developed in an atmosphere that encourages creativity and brainstorming, the strategic plan may not only include concrete directions, but also provide an institutional set of core values. In a typical board meeting, there is simply no time to engage in a meaningful discussion about the long-term future of an organization. Many nonprofits are operating on the edge of financial chaos, often one failed grant application away from having to lay off staff or fold entirely.

2. **It requires an action plan to solve real problems faced by an organization.** The action plan is a template that the staff can use to implement the policies and desires of the board. Many CEOs complain that the board helps with solving problems, but fails to provide direction on the core values of the organization. A strategic plan explicitly includes those core values, and assists the CEO in creative strategies for solving current problems and anticipating future ones.

3. **It provides a formal mandate for the reallocation of resources to respond to changing conditions, and the means to obtain additional resources if required.** A successful strategic planning process that develops an aggressive plan to attack problems often energizes a moribund board.

4. **It builds inter-board relationships that might not otherwise exist, and creates a partnership among the board chairperson, board members, staff, funders, and other stakeholders.** Each has a role that is defined in the plan and, if bought into, the added responsibilities increase the available resources of the organization. The social contact that occurs at many board retreats, particularly those designed in bucolic settings away from the hustle and bustle of the organization, cement personal relationships among participants. This improves the bond between the organization and its leadership.

5. **It provides a mechanism for the board, staff, and organizational stakeholders to become more informed about the activities and problems faced by the organization.** It promotes, in many cases, a frank discussion by the organization's executive of problems that might not be shared within the context of a conventional board meeting. Many CEOs welcome the process in that it takes a burden off their shoulders and shares it with the organization's "owners" and constituents.

6. **It provides an opportunity to focus on the forest rather than the trees.** It is easy for a CEO to become lost in the mundane issues of personnel, budgeting, office management, board relations, and public relations, and virtually ignore issues relating to the actual purpose and mission of the nonprofit.

Costs of Strategic Planning

1. **Money.** Serious strategic planning costs money, a scarce resource for most nonprofits. Many nonprofits recognize that it is useful to have a trained, dispassionate consultant to assist in the planning process. There are costs to schedule planning meetings and travel to those meetings. Many organizations recognize the value of eliminating outside distractions to aid brainstorming, and thus schedule planning meetings at staff retreats held at attractive, isolated campgrounds, conference centers, business resorts, or hotels. There are costs of photocopying and printing all of the planning documents. There are opportunity costs, as well, because staff and board resources are diverted from other duties.

2. **Time.** Any realistic strategic planning process requires the allocation of precious staff and board resources. Meeting preparation, meeting attendance, minutes, preparation of draft and final strategic plans, and hiring a consultant all take time. It is not uncommon for a strategic planning process to take more than a year.

3. **Potential bad will.** As with any process, things can go wrong. Bad group dynamics can result in painful meetings and destructive outcomes. A group may spend an entire four-hour meeting arguing over trivial words in a mission statement. This can be frustrating for committee members who are more interested in developing an action plan to solve organizational problems. Strategic planning may bring board factions into collision, and meetings can degenerate into a test of wills. This may be healthy in the context of a committee rather than having a drag-out fight at a board meeting, but it means that to have a constructive planning process, personal baggage must be dealt with first. If the final strategic plan is not implemented, board members who participated may feel that the

organization wasted their time, and may not be as likely to participate in future efforts, or even may resign from the board. Current staff members may feel threatened that their jobs are at risk, and may look for other employment.

4. **Loss of Organizational Initiative.** A formal strategic plan may diminish an executive's initiative and quick response to changing conditions, because the preferred course of action is not in the strategic plan. The strategic plan may become outdated quickly and stifle a more appropriate response to changing conditions that were not anticipated in the plan. In addition, strategic planning often involves the board not just in setting objectives and outcomes, but also in determining the methods that should be used to achieve those objectives and outcomes. Many feel that this is the role of staff, not the board, and making it the role of the board takes away the flexibility necessary for executive staff to function effectively.

A Sample Strategic Planning Model

This chapter gives a cursory review of what a strategic plan is, its costs and benefits, some advantages and disadvantages, and some issues that often arise when nonprofits consider initiating a strategic plan. It is recommended that other specific resources be consulted when exploring the need for a strategic planning process, and several excellent sources are included in the *For Further Reading* section in the back of this book. The following is one model for developing a strategic plan and is a hybrid put together from several theoretical models.

Step 1. Decide whether to develop a strategic plan.

Consider the costs and benefits mentioned earlier in this chapter, and also the following questions:

- Is there enough time and money to allocate for this planning process now?
- Is the organization prepared to implement whatever plan eventually is approved, or will it sit on the shelf?
- Do we have a commitment from the organization's executive director, board chairperson, board members, and other stakeholders to develop a plan, or will we just be going through the motions?
- Are the organization's short-term problems so overwhelming that the organization is wasting time planning for the future when its continued existence is seriously threatened by current problems?

Step 2. Build the infrastructure necessary to develop a plan.

- **Appoint a planning committee of the board.** Include creative board members, funders, the CEO, chief financial officer, clients, and opinion makers from the community. Consider that any committee of more than 10 can become unmanageable. Some strategic planners recommend that the entire board serve on the committee.

- **Compile and distribute articles and related material on strategic planning to the entire board.** (For information on reprints or rights to photocopy this chapter or other copyrighted materials, contact the publisher of the material.)

- **Decide on whether the facilitator/consultant will be a board member or a private paid or volunteer consultant.** A board member already knows a lot about the organization, its strengths and weaknesses, its personnel, and all other members of the committee. On the other hand, that board member brings with him or her prejudices about colleagues and staff, and often has a point of view or hidden agenda that is not held at arm's length. A private strategic planning consultant has the experience to keep the discussion focused and follow the agenda. There are many consultants who have experience working with nonprofit agencies in designing the planning process itself, participating in orientation sessions for the planning committee, serving as a referee for dispute resolution, helping the committee reach consensus when that is desired, neutralizing oppositional or disruptive participants, and providing technical assistance.

A good consultant can organize the process and provide logistical support so that the board and staff will not be absorbed by the planning process mechanics. On the other hand, a bad consultant may influence the process beyond what is desirable, and constrain the participation of committee members. One must be careful to assure that the plan, if written by a consultant, is not a tepid re-write of the plan the consultant developed for a previous client, which may have only minimal relevance to the current client.

It is a good idea to informally survey comparable organizations to check out potential strategic planning consultants. Statewide associations may also be helpful in identifying consultants. Of course, it is vital that any contract between the organization and the consultant spell out exactly what services are required, the timetable, and the level of participation required by the consultant.

Step 3. Decide how many years the strategic plan will cover.

In general, small nonprofits choose a shorter time frame than larger nonprofits, perhaps two-four years for smaller agencies, compared to larger institutions, which prepare five-year plans.

Step 4. Put in writing the timetable and the process.

This includes the steps that are required and who is responsible for accomplishing each task. Among the tasks are—

- appointing the committee,
- hiring a consultant or facilitator,
- leading the orientation of the planning committee,
- choosing the meeting site,
- scheduling the meetings,
- writing the first draft of the plan,
- providing the procedures to review and revise the draft,
- writing the final plan,
- developing the process for the planning committee to approve the final plan, AND
- formulating the review and the process for the full board's approval of the final plan.

Step 5. Prepare a memo on what is expected of the strategic planning process.

This memo to the planning committee should highlight the major problems that are to be resolved by the strategic plan, such as how to review and update the mission statement, how to respond to potential cuts in government funding, how to respond to the new location of a for-profit competitor, how to deal with a change in the demographics of the people in the area served by the organization, and so on. The memo should note whether the planning report should be a consensus document (which does not mean that everyone must agree to its contents) or if majority rules after all points of view are heard.

Step 6. Have the board endorse the planning process, and allocate funds necessary for it to proceed.

Step 7. Appoint the committee, appoint or hire the facilitator/consultant, send out orientation materials, and schedule the first meeting.

The first meeting

The first meeting is usually an orientation session, which includes some of the following components:

1. A review of the purpose of the committee, the timetable, future meeting schedule, and meeting the facilitator.

2. A review of the current mission, history, short-term problems, long-term threats, staff resources, programs, activities, strengths and weaknesses, major successes and failures, core values of the organization, financial status, and future commitments. The CEO and CFO should be present to answer questions from the planning committee and to ask questions of the facilitator to establish ground rules for the planning process.

3. An analysis of the needs of the stakeholders, including those currently receiving service, and scenarios about how those needs may change. For example, is the population served by the organization changing demographically? Is government funding likely to drop? Is the community becoming poorer, limiting future fee-for-service revenue and requiring more non-fee revenue?

4. An analysis of institutional limits: population served by geography, age group, and income level.

5. An identification of what in the above can be changed by the organization as a result of strategic planning and what is the result of forces beyond the control of the organization.

The second meeting

The second meeting begins the brainstorming of the committee. This meeting examines the mission statement and reviews potential changes to that statement which—in some cases—might have been unrevised for decades. The facilitator may list various problems on the horizon of the organization, with the planning committee serving as a focus group—such as funding problems, changes in markets, competitors, outside threats from changing social, economic, political, or technological conditions, or demand for services. The planning committee is given a homework assignment to come to the third meeting with suggestions for solving these problems.

The third meeting

The third meeting consists of brainstorming on action strategies that will solve the problems identified at the first and second meetings. The facilitator lists each strategy and includes a table with the costs and benefits of each, the probability of success, and the pros and cons. Each strategy for each problem may be ranked based on the committee's assessment as to the value of the strategy.

The fourth meeting

The committee develops an action plan, with a timetable for implementation that includes coming up with the resources necessary to implement the action plan. The plan also includes a procedure to review the progress made in implementing the plan.

In the above model, a draft strategic plan can be accomplished with four three-hour meetings.

In *Managing a Nonprofit Organization,* Thomas Wolff outlines six levels in the linear model of strategic planning. In the linear model, the planning committee considers one level before proceeding to the next. This contrasts with the integrated planning model, which provides for many of these levels to be considered simultaneously, recognizing that the end result is interdependent upon each of the earlier levels.

Level 1. The planners consider the mission statement, which describes the purpose the organization is trying to achieve.

Level 2. Organizational goals are developed, providing the general direction in which the organization intends to go.

Level 3. Objectives and targets are set, indicating the outcomes the organization hopes to achieve.

Level 4. Strategies are formulated to meet the objectives and targets. These are the methods and ways the organization plans to achieve those outcomes.

Level 5. An action plan is developed to implement the strategies.

Level 6. An evaluation is performed after implementation, to review whether the outcomes were achieved and whether the strategies were successful.

For example, a hypothetical nursing home might have a planning document that, in an abridged form, is as follows:

Level 1. To provide quality long-term care services to the aging population of Anytown, for the purpose of improving the quality of life for those who need institutional care.

Level 2. To reduce the operating deficit and become the long-term care institution of choice in the community by improving quality of care.

Level 3. Increase non-fee revenue by 50%, and improve the cash-flow situation by taking advantage of accounting productivity. Improve government reimbursement by 25% within three years.

Increase the number of private pay residents from 30% to 50% within the next five years.

Level 4. Hire a development staff member.

Hire a lobbyist to assist the statewide association to increase federal and state funding.

Hire a marketing associate to place advertisements in publications read by active, upscale, middle-aged persons whose parents may be in need of long-term care services.

Level 5. Investigate the feasibility of marketing charitable gift annuities, and hire a consultant by July 15 to develop a program for residents and their families.

Aggressively go after accounts receivable, delay accounts payable for an additional 30 days, eliminate programs that are not profitable, increase fee-for-service revenues; increase fundraising; become entrepreneurial by selling clothing and health care equipment on the organization's Web site.

Place a classified advertisement in the newsletter of the state chapter of the Society of Association Executives for a registered lobbyist.

Hire a marketing associate by June 15, and use endowment funds for seed money, and assume the new staff member will generate at least enough income to finance his or her salary.

Level 6. One year after final approval of this report, require the executive director to prepare a progress report on whether the goals outlined in level 2 are being achieved, and what mid-course corrections to Level 5 are required to meet the targets of Level 3.

The process of planning each level can be discussed and refined for two hours or nine months. The parameters differ, obviously, for a hospital with a half-billion dollars in annual gross revenue, compared to a charity with $50,000 in annual gross revenue.

The actual plan may be written by the facilitator, the chairperson of the planning committee, or staff in consultation with the board and facilitator. In every case, the planning committee should review a draft of the plan before submitting its final version to the board. The board reserves the power to approve, disapprove, approve with changes, or send the plan back for revision.

Some of the changes that may be recommended by a nonprofit organization's strategic plan are—

- a mission change;
- a change in the character of services provided;
- a plan to expand or downsize staff;
- a plan to expand or sell capital equipment and/or physical plant;
- a plan to expand fundraising;
- a plan to retrain staff;
- a plan to move the organization's location;
- a plan to seek a merger with similar organizations;
- a communications plan to improve or modernize the organization's public image;
- a plan to hire a lobbyist, or form a statewide association representing agencies with similar problems or uncertainties;
- a plan to establish a for-profit subsidiary;
- a plan to seek, or refuse, government grants;
- a plan to liquidate the organization;
- a plan to professionalize the organization, or deprofessionalize it—e.g., a decision by a hospital to substitute nurse aides where registered nurses had previously been used;

- a plan to change the governance of the organization—increase or decrease board membership, change quorum requirements, change voting requirements, change committee structure, change the powers of officers;
- a plan to change the compensation structure to reward and improve productivity;
- a plan to change the organization's market niche;
- a plan to change into a for-profit;
- a plan to modernize the name of the organization; and
- a plan to introduce new technology

Some components of a strategic plan may be:

- a five-year projection of staffing patterns;
- a five-year projected budget;
- sources of revenue to implement changes stipulated by the plan;
- a marketing strategy;
- a schedule for periodically updating the strategic plan;
- a schedule for evaluating whether the plan is being implemented effectively and whether the strategies provided in the plan are successful;
- a physical plant/equipment plan; and
- yearly updates to the plan.

Tips:

- **Don't let a strategic plan sit on the shelf after investing time and money developing it.**

- **Know when to let a strategic plan sit on the shelf when conditions have become so turbulent or changed that it would not make sense to follow it blindly.**

Chapter 7
Nonprofit Organization Ethics

by Gerald Kaufman and Gary Grobman

> **Synopsis:** Nonprofit charities have a special obligation, both legal and moral, to uphold the highest standards of ethical practice, to be accountable to their boards and the public, to avoid conflicts of interest, and to treat their employees with dignity.

Introduction

Nonprofit organizations, especially those qualified under section 501(c)(3) of the Internal Revenue Code, occupy a special and unique place in American society. Their uniqueness has many attributes.

All such organizations are supported by the nation's taxpayers: they are exempt from federal and state income taxes; contributors, for the most part, can deduct their contributions from their federal income tax (and from their state income taxes in most states); they are eligible to have their postage subsidized by the federal government; and many are exempt from state and local sales and property taxes.

Ethics in the Nonprofit Environment

Among the general categories of ethical conflicts that are endemic to the nonprofit sector are accountability, conflict of interest, and disclosure. Specific issues of interest are relationships between board members and the staff; board members and the organization (such as business relationships); self-dealing; charitable solicitation disclosure; the degree to which donations finance fundraising costs rather than programs; the accumulation of surpluses; outside remuneration of staff; the appropriateness of salaries, benefits, and perquisites; and merit pay. For example, pay based on income received rather than mission accomplished is considered unethical. Staff members of charities are under more of an obligation not to exploit their position on staff for personal gain (such as charging a fee for outside speaking engagements on their own time) than their for-profit counterparts. Unlike their for-profit or government counterparts, charities generally are under an ethical, if not legal, obligation not to accumulate large surpluses. Salaries, benefits, and perquisites must be "reasonable," and prior to the promulgation by the IRS of regulations relating to this and other "excess benefit" transactions, the legal requirements applying to these issues were in a gray area.

The following sections include some issues relating to ethics that are appropriate for nonprofit boards and staff to consider.

Accountability

Accountability often is overlooked in discussions about ethics. Because of the unique status of 501(c)(3) organizations, they have a special obligation to the public to be accountable for the results of their activities that justify their tax exemptions and other privileges. Organizations should continually challenge themselves by asking if the outcomes produced are worth the public investment.

Nonprofit boards of directors have a special obligation to govern with integrity. Governing with integrity means that the organization recognizes that it is accountable to the public, to the people it serves, and to its funders. Accountability includes the concept that nonprofit organizations exist only to produce worthwhile results in furtherance of their missions.

In addition, accountability encompasses a core system of values and beliefs regarding the treatment of staff, clients, colleagues, and community. Yet, organizational survival needs too often undercut core values. Although everyone in the organization is responsible, it is the board's ultimate responsibility to assure that its values are not compromised, and that the activities are conducted within acceptable limits.

A more subtle issue of accountability is seldom discussed when staff will sometimes pursue grants and contracts, or engage in direct solicitation campaigns, for the primary purpose of growing. Boards sometimes ask whether the executive director "grew the organization" as the primary criterion for measuring success. Boards have an obligation to ensure that all activities support the organization's mission.

Conflict of Interest

A potential conflict of interest occurs any time organizational resources are directed to the private interests of a person or persons who have an influence over the decision. Examples might include the leasing of property owned by a relative of the executive director or a board member, the board awarding itself a salary, the organization hiring a board member to provide legal representation, or the executive director hiring a relative or a board member's relative.

A conflict also can occur when the person (or persons) making a decision expects something in exchange from the person in whose favor the decision is made. One example is the case in which an executive director retains a direct mail firm, and the executive director's spouse is hired by that direct mail firm shortly thereafter.

With regard to board members, the cleanest approach is to adopt a policy that does not allow any board member to profit from the organization. It is the duty of every board member to exercise independent judgment solely on behalf of the organization. For example, suppose a board member who owns a public relations business successfully argues that the nonprofit needs a public relations campaign and then is hired to conduct the campaign. The board member's self-interest in arguing for the campaign will always be subject to question.

Suppose in the above example the board member offers to do the campaign "at cost," and that is the lowest bid. It may be that even at cost, the board member's firm benefits because the campaign will pay part of the salary of some staff members or cover other overhead. It may be perfectly appropriate to accept the board member's offer, even though it is a conflict of interest. However, it is absolutely essential that the board have a procedure in place to deal with these types of issues.

Some organizations permit financial arrangements with board members, provided that the member did not vote on that decision. Given the good fellowship and personal relationships that often exist within nonprofit boards, such a rule can be more for show and without substance.

A similar problem can cause a conflict in the awarding of contracts to non-insiders. There may be personal reasons for one or more members of the board or the executive director to award contracts to particular persons, such as enhancing their personal or professional relationship with that person.

There are instances in which it is appropriate to have a contract with an insider, such as when a board member offers to sell equipment to the organization at cost, or agrees to sell other goods or services well below market value. Here, too, the organization should assure itself that these same goods or services are not available as donations.

It is essential for the board to confront and grapple with these issues and adopt a written policy to govern potential conflicts of interest, to avoid the trap of self-dealing or its appearances. Many potential abuses are not only unethical, but also illegal as a result of the Taxpayer Bill of Rights 2 (see page 68). A sample conflict of interest policy can be found at: *http://www.irs.gov/pub/ irs-pdf/i1023.pdf* (see page 25 of the form).

Disclosures

There is much disagreement within the nonprofit sector regarding how much disclosure is required to those who donate to charitable nonprofits. The first obligation of every organization is to obey the laws and regulations governing disclosure. Nonprofits have a legal and ethical obligation to report fundraising costs accurately on their IRS Form 990, to obey the requirement regarding what portion of the cost of attending a fundraising event is deductible, and to comply with state charitable registration laws and regulations.

Nonprofits face a more difficult ethical issue when deciding how much disclosure to make that is not required by law, particularly if the organization believes that some people may not contribute if those disclosures are made.

In the for-profit corporate world, the Securities and Exchange Commission demands full, written disclosure of pertinent information, no matter how negative, when companies are offering stock to the public. There is no comparable agency that regulates charitable solicitations by nonprofits. Nonprofits must be very careful to disclose voluntarily all relevant information and to avoid the kind of hyperbole that misrepresents the organization.

Another difficult issue is whether fundraising costs should be disclosed at the point of solicitation. The costs of telemarketing campaigns or of maintaining development offices are sometimes 80%, or even more, of every dollar collected. Some argue that people wouldn't give if these costs were disclosed. Others argue that if the soliciting organization cannot justify these costs to the public (and in many cases they are not justifiable), then the organization is not deserving of support.

Accumulation of Surplus

If the funds of a charitable nonprofit are to be used for charitable purposes, what is a reasonable amount of surplus to accumulate? One national charitable watchdog agency, the Better Business Bureau's Wise Giving Alliance, has suggested that a charity's unrestricted net assets available for use should be no more than three times the size of the past year's expenses or three times the size of the current year's budget, whichever is higher.

Organizations should consider the circumstances under which it is appropriate to disclose to prospective donors the amount expected to be used to accumulate a surplus. Clearly, if a major purpose of the solicitation is to build a surplus, that should be disclosed.

Outside Remuneration

Executive directors and other staff often are offered honoraria or consulting fees for speeches, teaching, providing technical assistance, or other work. The ethical issue is whether the staff person should turn the fees over to the nonprofit employer or be able to retain them. Potential conflicts can be avoided if the policy is based on the principle that all reasonably related outside income belongs to the organization. Thus, an executive director's honorarium for speaking to a national conference as a representative of the organization or as an expert in his or her field would revert to the employer, but a fee for playing in a rock band on weekends would be his or hers to keep.

An argument against this principle is that the employees' usage of their spare time should be of no concern to the employer. The argument on the other side is that the line between the employer's and personal time is not so easy to draw. Is it ethical for an employee to exploit the knowledge and experience gained on the job for personal gain? Are we buying only the employee's time from our employees, or do we expect that we are getting the undivided professional attention of that person?

If the board or executive director is silent on this issue, the assumption is that earning outside income is a private matter. It makes sense to have a clear policy on outside income before an employee is hired.

Salaries, Benefits, and Perquisites

Determining an appropriate salary structure is perhaps the most difficult ethical issue in the non-profit sector. Ethical considerations arise at both the high and low ends of the salary spectrum.

If an organization is funded by grants from foundations and corporations or by government contracts, the funders can and do provide some restraint on excessive salaries. However, if the nonprofit is funded primarily by individual donations or fees for service, such constraints (other than, perhaps, those relating to the intermediate sanctions regulations of the Internal Revenue Service—see below) are absent.

Boards fall into an ethical trap if they reward executive directors based on the amount of income received, rather than on how well the mission is accomplished. A board can consider many criteria when setting the salary of the executive director. These include the size and complexity of the organization, what others in similar agencies are earning, and whether the salary is defensible to the public. Some nonprofits include proportionality in their salary structures by limiting the highest paid to a factor of the lowest paid (e.g., the highest can be no more than three times the lowest).

As a result of enactment of the *Taxpayers Bill of Rights 2*, there are now *legal* as well as ethical restrictions about paying excessive compensation. Ethical management of employees requires that each person be treated with dignity and respect, paid a salary that can provide a decent standard of living, and given a basic level of benefits, including health coverage. A potential, critical conflict arises when a charitable organization working to spread its social values treats its staff in a way that conflicts with its organizational values.

Personal Relationships

Nonprofit organization executives and board members must be careful to avoid sexual harassment or behavior that makes an employee feel uncomfortable at best or threatened and intimidated, at worst. Employees should be treated fairly, which among other things, means that no favoritism should be permitted with respect to work assignments. Discrimination should not be permitted even if it doesn't meet the threshold required for legal violations.

Nepotism—the hiring of family members—should be prohibited. Nonprofit executives and board members should seek to keep personal friendships from influencing professional judgment. Managers shouldn't make it difficult for employees to maintain an appropriate work-family balance. Privacy and confidentiality of workers should be respected. A diverse workforce means that cultural differences among staff should be respected to the maximum extent possible.

Standards for Excellence

In 1998, the Maryland Association of Nonprofit Organizations initiated an ethics and accountability code for the nonprofit sector entitled *Standards for Excellence.* Along with the code, the program includes educational components and a voluntary certification process whereby charities can receive certification that they meet basic ethical and accountability standards. As a result of two major grants, the program has been expanded beyond Maryland to include nine other states (Florida, Georgia, Idaho, Louisiana, North Carolina, Ohio, Oklahoma, Pennsylvania, and West Virginia). Launched in July 2004, a national institute *(http://www.standardsforexcellenceinstitute. org)* now provides nonprofit organizations access to the educational tools to support implementing the Standards. The 55 performance standards required for an organization to be certified by the program are grouped in eight areas:

- mission and Program
- governing Board
- conflicts of Interest
- human Resources
- financial and legal accountability
- openness and disclosure
- fundraising
- public policy and public affairs

Participating charities may demonstrate that they adhere to the standards by participating in a peer review process. They submit an application, document their compliance with the standards, and pay a fee. If the peer-review panel affirms that the organization meets the standards, the organization receives a Seal of Excellence, with the expectation that having the Seal will provide the organization with increased credibility with donors and grantmakers. The full set of standards can be found at:

http://www.standardsforexcellenceinstitute.org

Among the standards are:

- On average, over a five-year period, a charity should assure that fundraising revenues as compared with expenses have a greater than a 3:1 ratio.

- Fundraisers, whether or not they are employees or independent consultants, should not be compensated based on a percentage of the amount raised or some other commission formula.

- Nonprofit organizations should have a conflict of interest policy and a procedure to provide board, staff, and volunteers with an annual opportunity to submit a conflict-of-interest statement, to disclose actual and potential conflicts of interest.

Taxpayer Bill of Rights 2—Intermediate Sanctions

The *Taxpayer Bill of Rights 2* was signed into law by President Clinton on July 30, 1996. The principal purpose of this law is to punish individuals affiliated with charities and social welfare organizations who are participating in financial abuses, and to provide the government with a sanction other than simply revoking the charity's exemption status. The law also includes expanded public disclosure requirements for annual federal tax returns.

Previous law required charities to make their 990 tax returns available for public inspection, but did not require that copies be provided. The law was changed to require that if a person requests a copy of the 990 in person, it must be immediately provided for a reasonable copying fee. If the request is made in writing, it must be provided for a reasonable copying and postage fee within 30 days. Organizations that make these documents "widely available," such as posting them on the Internet, are exempt, although they still must make the document available for public inspection. The law expands the disclosure that must be made on the 990, adding information about excess expenditures to influence legislation, any political expenditures, any disqualified lobbying expenditures, and amounts of "excess benefit" transactions.

This law increased the fine for failure to file a timely 990 from $10 per day to $20 per day, with a maximum of $10,000. Higher fines apply to organizations with gross receipts over $1 million.

Both state and federal law have prohibitions against "private inurement"— permitting a charity's income to benefit a private shareholder or individual. Legislation at the federal level to define what constitutes a prevalent form of private inurement and to refine the definition of a private shareholder was enacted. It aims to respond to alleged financial abuses by some organizations that were perceived as providing unreasonable compensation to organization "insiders."

To curb financial abuses, the law authorizes the IRS to impose an excise tax, 25% in most cases, on certain improper financial transactions by 501(c)(3) and 501(c)(4) organizations. The tax applies to transactions that benefit a "disqualified person," defined as people in positions who exercise substantial influence over the organization, their family members, or other organizations controlled by those persons.

Disqualified persons include voting members of the board, the president or chair, the CEO, the chief operating officer, the chief financial officer, and the treasurer, among potential other officers and staff. The benefit to the disqualified person must exceed the value that the organization receives to be subject to the tax. To avoid problems, tax experts are advising organizations to treat every benefit to a director or staff person as compensation, and reflect these benefits in W-2s, 1099s, and budget documents. Seemingly innocent benefits, such as paying for the travel and lodging expenses for a spouse attending a board retreat or a health club membership for an executive director, may trigger questions about excess benefit. Luxury travel could be considered an excess benefit.

Compensation is considered reasonable if it is in an amount that would ordinarily be paid for similar services by similar organizations in similar circumstances. The term "compensation" is defined broadly, and includes severance payments, insurance, and deferred compensation.

Most of the provisions relating to intermediate sanctions apply retroactively to September 14, 1995, the date the legislation was first introduced. Steep additional excise tax penalties, up to 200% of the excess benefit plus the initial 25% excise tax, apply for excess benefit transactions that are not corrected in a reasonable amount of time. An excise tax may also be applied to organization managers (a term that is meant to include an officer, director, trustee) who approve the excess benefit transaction in an amount of 10% of the excess benefit, up to $10,000 maximum per transaction.

Although these excise taxes apply to individuals and not to the organizations themselves, there is nothing in this law that prohibits organizations from paying the tax or purchasing insurance to cover an individual's liability for the tax penalty. However, if the organization does purchase this insurance, the premium must be considered compensation to the individual. This insurance could become the basis for an excess benefit if total compensation to the individual, including this insurance, exceeds the fair market value that the person provides to the organization in exchange for the total compensation that person receives from the organization. It makes sense to consult an attorney who is knowledgeable about the *Taxpayer Bill of Rights 2* if there are any unresolved issues that would make an organization's directors and staff vulnerable to an IRS audit.

The Internal Revenue Service published draft regulations on this section of the Revenue Code in the *Federal Register* on August 4, 1998. Final regulations were published in the *Federal Register* on January 10, 2001 that were temporary. Permanent final regulations were published in the January 23, 2002 issue of the *Federal Register*.

The final regulations provide more examples of situations that might be faced by charities. One change included in the final regulations is the safe harbor for organizations to rely not only on the advice of their attorneys (as was a feature of the draft regulations), but also on the advice of other outside consultants, such as their accountants.

Codes of Ethics

Ethics in organizations are enforced through the use of codes of ethics, codes of conduct, staff ethicists, ethics committees, policies and procedures relating to ethical dilemmas, and ethics training.

As explained by Dr. Jeremy Plant of Penn State University, a code of ethics is a systematic effort to define acceptable conduct. It may be general or specific, aspirational or legalistic. The code may be a simple list of ten golden rules, or a long, detailed, codified system of procedures and ideals. In the context of an ethics code, it may have the force of law (such as a statutory ethics code for public officials), be a collection of principles that are not law but are morally binding, or simply contain a system of symbolic principles for meaningful communication.

Unlike government (which has the taxing power) and for-profit business (which generates revenue through market transactions), charities generate much of their revenue through nonmarket mechanisms such as seeking donations (in the form of contributions from the public and grants from foundations and government). This form of revenue generation is a ripe area for fraudulent practices, and many of the ethics-related principles that differentiate nonprofit organizations from their government and private sector counterparts focus on this area.

In recent years, there has been a move toward turning nonprofit management into a recognized profession, with credentialing becoming available for fundraising executives, association managers, and nonprofit organization managers. Organizations such as the Association of Fundraising Professionals (AFP), the American Society of Association Executives (ASAE), and the National Council of Nonprofit Associations—and the state and local chapters of these organizations—have sought to professionalize their memberships.

Until 2003, there had been two major ethical codes focusing on fundraising standards for charitable organizations. The first, which was developed during the late 1980s and went into effect in 1992 (National Charities Information Bureau, 2000), is the National Charities Information Bureau's (NCIB) *Standards in Philanthropy*. Almost all of these ethical standards would have been meaningless in anything other than a nonprofit context. The standards were not enforceable by law, but served as a guide to both donors and those who run the charities. The standards were grouped into nine areas:

1. board Governance,
2. purpose,
3. programs,
4. information,
5. financial support and related activities,
6. use of funds,
7. annual reporting,
8. accountability, and
9. budget

The Council of Better Business Bureau's *Standards for Charitable Solicitations* were first published in 1974. Two revisions were made, the last being in 1981. A process was initiated in the fall of 1999 to help develop a third revision of the standards. The purpose of these standards was to "encourage fair and open solicitation practices, to promote ethical conduct by charitable organizations, and to help sustain public confidence and support of charities."

The fundamental goal of the revision effort was to create standards that were meaningful and relevant to donors, easily understood by users, and fair and not overly burdensome to charities; to instill public trust and support for philanthropy; and to be reasonable for the parent agency, the BBB, to administer.

In 2001, NCIB merged with the Foundation of the Better Business Bureau, and the new organization, the Better Business Bureau's Wise Giving Alliance, developed an updated code (BBB Wise Giving Alliance Standards for Charity Accountability), published in March 2003. The 20 standards that comprise this influential ethics code can be found at: *http://www.bbb.org/us/charity/*

Among the most controversial aspects of this code is the provision that calls for charities to allocate at least 65% of their donations for program expenses, spending no more than 35% of related contributions for fundraising. This is a higher standard than either the NCIB (60%) or the BBB's Philanthropic Advisory Service (50%) had enforced prior to the merger.

Other standards in this code provide for regular assessment of the CEO's performance, establishment of a conflict-of-interest policy, the completion of a written assessment of the charity's performance at least every two years, and standards protecting donor privacy. The new standard frowns upon accumulating unrestricted net assets available for use that exceed either three times the amount of the past year's expenses or three times the current budget, whichever is higher.

In December 2009, the Wise Giving Alliance announced that it was temporarily loosening its standards because of the severe recession. For the fiscal years ending in June 2008-2010, organizations still qualified for the Wise Giving Alliance stamp of approval if the organization spends at least 55% of donations on program expenses and no more than 45% on fundraising.

The national professional association of fundraisers also has an ethics code. The *Statement of Ethical Principles* of the Association of Fundraising Professionals (AFP) was adopted in 1991 when that organization was known as the National Society of Fund Raising Executives (NSFRE). AFP "exists to foster the development and growth of fund-raising professionals and the profession, to promote high ethical standards in the fund-raising profession and to preserve and enhance philanthropy and volunteerism" (NSFRE, 1991). This code was amended in 2007 and expanded to 25 principles.

AFP's ethics code consists of a set of general ethical principles, introduced by a preamble that recognizes the stewardship of fundraisers and the rights of donors to have their funds used for the intent they expect.

Many of these principles would be appropriate for any type of organization, such as to "foster cultural diversity and pluralistic values, and treat all people with dignity and respect" and "value the privacy, freedom of choice and interests of all those affected by their actions." Some of the principles are appropriate for public organizations, such as having an obligation to "safeguard the public trust" and others are parochial to the profession, such as to "put philanthropic mission above personal gain," and "affirm, through personal giving, a commitment to philanthropy and its role in society."

One year after the adoption of the AFP principles, the organization adopted its "Standards of Professional Practice" and incorporated them into its ethics code. Its 25 principles are mostly in the form of "members shall" and "members shall not."

A statement attached to the standards notes that violations "may subject the member to disciplinary sanctions, including expulsion, as provided by the (AFP's) Ethics Enforcement Procedures."

Some of these standards are perfunctory, such as "members shall comply with all applicable local, state, provincial, federal, civil and criminal laws." Others are general and broad, with implications that are not easily subject to interpretation, such as "Members shall not exploit any relationship with a donor, prospect, volunteer or employee to the benefit of the member or the member's organization." Among issues raised by the standards are conflicts of interest, truthfulness, privacy, and financial accountability.

Another issue raised in the principles that is of current interest in a number of professions is the standard that "Members shall not accept compensation that is based on the percentage of charitable contributions...." Some states have expressly prohibited lobbyists from signing contingency fee contracts in which they are paid only when they are successful in getting a bill or amendment passed by the legislature.

The theory is that such contracts encourage lobbyists to engage in efforts that go beyond the boundaries of acceptable behavior. On the other hand, contingency fees are routine for attorneys in civil cases. It is also not unusual for professional fundraisers to be paid a percentage of the amount they raise. Many in the field find that this practice promotes unethical solicitations (e.g., presentations that exaggerate facts, minimize disclosure, and other behaviors that intimidate and harass potential donors), and it is interesting that a major professional organization such as the AFP has taken an unequivocal position on this issue.

The standards are not enforceable by law, but serve as a guide to both donors and those who run the charities. For more information, contact:

Council of Better Business Bureaus
4200 Wilson Blvd.
Suite 800
Arlington, VA 22203
(703) 276-0100
http://www.bbb.org/us/Standards-Charity

A different set of ethical issues exists around disclosures to foundation and corporate funders. For instance, what is the obligation of disclosing changed circumstances after the proposal is submitted and before it is acted upon, such as when key staff members have announced plans to leave? If the organization knows that the changed circumstance might affect the decision, is it unethical not to disclose it?

In February 2004, Independent Sector adopted a *Statement of Values and Code of Ethics for Nonprofit and Philanthropic Organizations,* and recommended that it serve as a model. The statement identifies a set of values to which nonprofits may subscribe including commitment to the public good, accountability to the public, and commitment beyond the law. It also outlines broad ethical principles in the following areas: personal and professional integrity, mission, governance, legal compliance, responsible stewardship, openness and disclosure, program evaluation, inclusiveness and diversity, and fundraising. The full text can be accessed at: *http://www.independentsector. org/code_of_ethics*

There are many excellent publications on the subject of ethics. A few of them are:

1. **A series of articles by David E. Mason in *Nonprofit World,* published by the Society for Nonprofit Organizations.**

The Society For Nonprofit Organizations
P.O. Box 510354
Livona, MI 48151
(734) 451-3582
(734) 451-5935 (fax)
http://www.snpo.org

2. **Making Ethical Decisions** (33 pages, $12.95 plus shipping and handling).

Josephson Institute of Ethics
9841 Airport Boulevard
#300
Los Angeles, CA 90045
(310) 846-4800
(310) 846-4858 (fax)
http://josephsoninstitute.org/MED/index.html

3. **Ethics and the Nation's Voluntary and Philanthropic Community.**

Independent Sector
1602 L Street, STE 900

Washington, DC 20036
(202) 467-6100
(202) 467-6101 (fax)
http://www.independentsector.org

Conclusion

There are many other ethical issues that nonprofit organizations will confront on a regular basis, such as: personal use of office supplies and equipment; personal use of frequent flier mileage; the extent of staff and board diversity; and the use of private discriminatory clubs for fundraisers, board meetings, or other events. The list is endless.

What is important is that nonprofit organizations proactively engage in discussions about ethics and values on a regular basis, recognizing that the charitable nonprofit sector has a special obligation to uphold the very highest standards. Boards of directors of charitable nonprofits have an important role in this regard. Boards cannot play a more important role than assuring that nonprofits are accountable, and that they operate as mission- and value-driven organizations.

Many who choose to work in the nonprofit sector do so because the stated values of the sector and their personal values are in harmony. It is critical that such people be vigilant against the erosion of those very principles that attracted them to the work.

Only in this way can the public be assured that the charitable nonprofit sector remains worthy of its privileges and that the sector continues to occupy its special and unique place in our society.

Tips:

- **Challenge yourself and your organization to hold yourself up to the highest ethical standards, avoiding even gray areas of conflicts of interest and appearances of conflicts of interest.**

- **When in doubt, ask yourself, "How would I feel if my family and friends read about this on the front page of the daily newspaper?"**

- **Obtain salary surveys published by the Pennsylvania Society of Association Executives (PASAE), and determine whether anyone in the organization has an unreasonable salary.**

- **Demand that all business relationships with the organization be at "arm's-length," and obtain at least three bids on any work that costs at least $1,000, even if a board member claims that he/she will provide the product/service at cost.**

Chapter 8
Section 501(c)(3) Tax-Exempt Status

Synopsis: Federal 501(c)(3) tax-exempt status is valuable not only because of the tax advantages to the nonprofit corporation, but to the organization's contributors. Corporations with this status may not substantially engage in lobbying or engage in partisan political activities.

Introduction

After filing the Articles of Incorporation, achieving 501(c)(3) status should be the principal objective of virtually all nonprofits organized and operated for religious, charitable, scientific, literary, or educational purposes, testing for public safety, fostering national or international amateur sports competitions, and the prevention of cruelty to children or animals.

The federal regulation implementing Section 501(c)(3) tax-exempt status states (Reg. §1.501(c)(3)-1(d)):

> *(d) Exempt purposes. (1) In general.*
> *(i) An organization may be exempt as an organization described in section 501(c)(3) if it is organized and operated exclusively for one or more of the following purposes:*
> > *(a) Religious,*
> > *(b) Charitable,*
> > *(c) Scientific,*
> > *(d) Testing for Public Safety,*
> > *(e) Literary,*
> > *(f) Educational, or*
> > *(g) Prevention of cruelty to children or animals.*
> *(ii) An organization is not organized or operated exclusively for one or more of the purposes specified in subdivision (i) of this subparagraph unless it serves a public rather than a private interest. Thus, to meet the requirement of this subdivision, it is necessary for an organization to establish that it is not organized or operated for the benefit of private interests such as designated individuals, the creator or his family, shareholders of the organization, or persons controlled, directly or indirectly, by such private interests....*

For nonprofits whose activities are eligible, designation by the Internal Revenue Service for 501(c)(3) tax-exempt status is a major objective to be achieved as quickly as possible. This status confers several substantial benefits to the organization:

- The nonprofit will be exempt from federal income taxes other than unrelated business income taxes (UBIT). The current rate (as of 2011) of federal corporate income tax is 15% on the first $50,000 in taxable income, 25% on the next $25,000, 34% on the next $25,000, 39% on the next $235,000, and 34% on the rest up to $10 million. While many nonprofits will not generate large amounts of net revenue, particularly in their early years, it is a major advantage to have the option to capture this net revenue for future expansion, venture capital, and covering future operating deficits.

- Persons contributing to the nonprofit can take a deduction on their own income taxes for their contributions. Since the incremental tax rate for middle- and upper-income persons on adjusted gross income for the tax year 2011 was 10% (on income of 0-$8,500 for singles, $0-17,000 for married filing jointly), 15% (on income of $8,000-$34,500 for singles, $17,000-$69,000 for married filing jointly), 25% ($34,500-$83,600 for singles, $69,000-$139,350 for married filing jointly), 28% ($83,600-$174,400 for singles, $139,350-$212,300 for married filing jointly), 33% ($174,400-$379,150 for singles and $212,300-$379,150 for married filing jointly), and 35% ($379,150 and over for singles and married filing jointly), this represents an attractive incentive for persons to leverage their own contributions with the "tax expenditure" contributed by government.

• Many major donors (such as United Ways and certain foundations) will not make contributions to organizations that do not have 501(c)(3) status.

• The designation of 501(c)(3) status indicates a minimal level of accountability, policed by the Internal Revenue Service, which is a useful governmental stamp of approval of the charitable activities of the organization.

• In Pennsylvania, qualifying 501(c)(3) organizations may elect to self-insure for purposes of complying with unemployment compensation laws.

There are several disadvantages:

• A 501(c)(3) may not engage in partisan political activity on behalf of, or in opposition to, political candidates.

• Such organizations may not substantially engage in lobbying or propaganda.

• Such organizations have a higher level of accountability, and must, as all 501(c) exempt organizations, make copies of their 990 tax returns available in their offices upon request (see Chapter 1).

• There is a substantial application fee ($850 in most cases, $400 for smaller organizations, and $200 once the Cyber Assistant IRS online application becomes operational), and this fee is not refunded if tax-exempt status is denied.

Although not always the case, most incorporators of nonprofits have some altruistic motive for incorporating. The motives of the incorporators cannot be for personal gain. As one might expect, the motives are usually of an "eleemosynary" nature, i.e., related to charity.

Many nonprofit corporations are formed because a person or group of persons is frustrated with the lack of government action to solve a problem that, in that person's view, should be solved by government. Congress historically has recognized that government cannot do everything for everybody, even when the cause is just. Instead, Congress provides an opportunity for citizens to form organizations to do the activities themselves. They are rewarded by having certain privileges, such as the tax-exemption, provided that the activity falls within a statutorily enumerated list of activities.

Section 501(c) of the Internal Revenue Code lists more than 20 classes of activities that can qualify a nonprofit corporation for tax-exempt status. A list of these classes is provided in this chapter. Only one of these classes, 501(c)(3), permits a tax deduction for contributions made to organizations in that class, and requires that such organizations not engage in substantial lobbying or propaganda activities, or engage in political activities that advance the cause of candidates.

501(c)(3) status is not granted pro forma. There are stringent requirements for approval. Because of this, 501(c)(3) status is prized, and it is viewed by many in the public as a stamp of approval by the federal government. The fact is that 501(c)(3) status does not necessarily imply government's endorsement of the organization's activities. In FY 2010, the Internal Revenue Service granted 48,934 (c)(3) applications, denied 500, and took "other" action on 10,511, many of which were eventually approved after additional information was provided.

Successful application is facilitated by having certain provisions in the organization's governing documents. These provisions are discussed in Chapter 2.

How To Apply for 501(c)(3) Status

To apply, an organization needs the following forms and booklets from the Internal Revenue Service:

- Form SS-4—*Application for Employer Identification Number*
- Form 5768—*Election by an Eligible Organization to Make Expenditures to Influence Legislation*
- Package 1023—*Forms and instruction booklets for applying for 501(c)(3) tax-exempt status*
- Publication 557—*Tax-Exempt Status for Your Organization*

The above forms and booklets can be obtained at any local IRS office or online at the IRS Web site at: *http://www.irs.gov/app/picklist/list/formsInstructions.html.*

According to the IRS, it takes nine hours and 39 minutes to complete the basic form and several more hours to complete supplemental schedules. It also takes an additional 5.5 hours to learn about the law and how to complete the forms. It is advisable to be as careful as possible in completing the forms, since the wrong phrase can result in denial.

Some organizations are exempt from having to file the 1023. Among them are—

- those that will have gross receipts of less than $5,000 annually,

- bona fide religious institutions, and

- certain groups affiliated with a parent organization that already has tax-exempt status and will send a letter extending its exemption to them.

The Internal Revenue Service expects that an application for 501(c)(3) status will be filed within 15 months after the end of the month in which the Articles of Incorporation are filed. If the organization files on time and the application is approved, 501(c)(3) status will be retroactive to the date of the Articles of Incorporation. There is a form to file if the 15-month deadline is not met. For more information about this option, see IRS Publication 557.

Fees

There is an $850 application fee to file Form 1023. New organizations expecting gross receipts of not more than $10,000 for each of the first four years, or existing organizations that have not had gross receipts of that amount in each of the last four years, can qualify for a reduced fee of $400. The fee must be paid by check, but a corporate check is not required. The fee can be further reduced by utilizing the IRS's Cyber Assistant online filing program, although the likely launch date of this is expected to be in 2012.

Completing the Application

The best advice for filling out Form 1023 is to carefully read the instruction booklet and follow the directions. It sounds obvious, but many fail to do that and are surprised by delays in having their applications approved for organizations that are obviously qualified for 501(c)(3) status. Beyond that, however, here are four tips that experts offer to assist you.

1. Avoid an organizational name that would raise a red flag to an IRS examiner.

2. Have all governing documents (e.g., Articles of Incorporation and bylaws) include the language suggested in Chapter 2 with respect to corporate purposes, propaganda and lobbying, and distribution of assets upon dissolution.

3. Have an organizational conflict of interest policy that is consistent with what appears in the instruction booklet to IRS Form 1023 (or that can be found at: *http://www.irs.gov/ pub/irs-pdf/i1023.pdf)*

4. Provide a three-year budget that makes sense. First, it should be consistent with the fee schedule you are seeking, i.e., should average less than $10,000 per year if you want to pay the $400 application fee rather than $850. IRS examiners know you cannot possibly predict with any precision what your revenue and expenses will be for your completely new organization three years in advance. They just want something realistic. How does one do this? Experts suggest two approaches. The first, the expense approach, is you set the organization's goals, calculate what it would cost to accomplish those goals, and then develop a plan that raises that amount of money. The second, the revenue approach, involves estimating the amount of revenue you can reasonably expect to generate for the organization, through fundraising, membership dues, sales of goods and services, and grants. Then you decide how that amount of money could be responsibly spent. A third approach is to blend these two approaches. With either approach, make sure that the source of funds is broad enough to justify exemption as a public charity. If you receive funding from only a handful of sources, you may be eligible for tax-exemption, but as a private foundation rather than as a public charity. See below for an explanation of the differences.

Differences Between Private Foundations and Public Charities

Public charities and private foundations are both granted tax-exempt status under Section 501(c)(3) of the Internal Revenue Code. However, Section 509(a) differentiates organizations that receive their income from a broad range of public sources from those organizations that receive their income principally from one, or a limited number of sources plus investment income. Private foundations pay a federal tax on net investment income, must meet a minimum annual threshold for making distributions of their assets to charities, and are flatly prohibited from lobbying. To be considered a public charity rather than a private foundation, an organization must pass a public support test enforced by the IRS. There are two such tests, one of which must be passed for the organization to be considered a public charity. The test is based on financial data for a four-year period. If one test is passed, the organization will qualify as a public charity for the following two years. For information about these tests, see: *http://www.irs.gov/publications/p557/ch03. html#en_US_2010_publink1000200142*

Nonprofits that don't fit neatly into the public-serving or member-serving category are the 375,000 religious congregations, about 80% of which do not register with the IRS or file a 990 federal annual tax return because there is no requirement to do so. While these congregations exist primarily to serve their members, their tax treatment is as if they primarily serve the public. In fact, nonprofit organizations are not required by law to file for exempt status with the Internal Revenue Service provided they have a recognized creed or form of worship, are "sacerdotal" in character, carry on regular religious services, and operate for other than private gain.

There are several commercially available guides for filling out the Form 1023 in a manner that will maximize your chances for your application to be approved. Among them are:

> *How to Form your Own Non-Profit Corporation* (9th Edition) by Anthony Mancuso (Nolo Press, 950 Parker Street, Berkeley, CA 94710, 2009, $49.95).
> Sandy DeJa's e-book: *Prepare Your Own 501(c)(3) Application*, available at: *http://www.form1023help.com*
> (see also: *http://www.501c3book.org/* for free information about filling out this form).

Timetable

You can expect a form letter from the IRS within a few weeks of its receipt of your application acknowledging that it was received. Organizations that file an application requiring minimal decision-making by the IRS or that do not require a follow-up letter from them are processed in six-ten weeks. This applies to about half of applications. On the average, about 60% of all applications are quickly approved. Less than 1% of applications are denied. About a quarter of applications are neither approved nor disapproved, but include the granting of tax status different than the category applied for, those sent down from the IRS's Cincinnati Office (located in Covington, KY) to the IRS headquarters in Washington for more work, and those awaiting a response to inquiries for more information, among other reasons.

A Short History of Tax-Exempt Status

In ancient times, government, whether secular or non-secular, recognized that certain activities assisted the role of government and were deserving of tax exemptions. A passage in the Bible (Ezra 7:24) provides that "it shall not be lawful to impose toll, tribute, or customs" upon certain priests and their staff. Several thousand years ago, some of the best land in the Nile Valley was set aside tax-free by the Egyptian pharaoh for the priests of Osiris.

Modern tax-exemption law has its roots in England, with the passage of the Statute of Charitable Uses in 1601. According to *Unfair Competition? The Challenge to Charitable Tax Exemption*, by Harrison Wellford and Janne Gallagher, current U.S. tax-exemption law draws its roots from an 1891 court case in Britain *(Commissioners of Income Tax v. Pemsel)* that provided a judicial definition of charity strikingly similar to the American legal standard.

The modern federal tax-exemption can be traced to 1863, when the income of religious organizations was exempted from a corporate tax enacted to finance the Civil War. The first general U.S. corporate income tax, enacted in 1894, imposed a 2% flat tax and statutorily exempted charitable income. Section 32 of this Act extended this exemption to charitable, religious, educational, fraternal, and some savings and loan institutions. The 1894 Income Tax Act was eventually declared unconstitutional and subsequently repealed. Yet it served as the precedent for exempting organizations that were for "charitable, religious, or educational purposes."

A 1924 Supreme Court case, *Trinidad v. Sagrada*, decided that for purposes of tax-exempt status, the destination of the funds, rather than the source, was the key determinant. This case involved a religious order that sold food, wine, and other goods to support its school, mission, church, and other operations. Thus, tax-exempt organizations were permitted to run profit-making enterprises provided that the net profits were funneled to tax-exempt purposes. This policy was revised by Congressional enactment of an "unrelated business income tax" (UBIT) in 1950. The rationale for this was that charities were seen as competing unfairly with for-profit enterprises, the most celebrated case of which was New York University's ownership of a macaroni factory.

From 1909 to the present, many other categories of tax-exempt status were added by federal statute (see below), including labor, horticultural and agriculture organizations (1909), business leagues, chambers of commerce, scientific organizations, and mutual cemetery companies (1913), public utilities, social clubs, land banks, title holding companies, and farming associations (1916), societies for the prevention of cruelty to animals (1918), foundations and community chests (1921), and homeowner associations, fishing associations, and organizations that promote national and international sporting competitions (1976).

Following a 1917 tax increase to finance World War I, the Congress permitted a deduction for contributions made by individuals to exempt charities.

Tax-Exempt Status Other than 501(c)(3)

The Internal Revenue Code provides more than 20 other categories of tax-exempt status besides 501(c)(3). Those who wish to file for tax-exempt status under section 501(c) for other than 501(c)(3) need to request Package 1024 from the IRS.(Download at: *http://www.irs.gov/pub/irs-pdf/k1024.pdf)*

Among the other categories are:

> 501(c)(4)—civic leagues, social welfare organizations
> 501(c)(5)—labor, agricultural, or horticultural organizations
> 501(c)(6)—business leagues, chambers of commerce, trade associations
> 501(c)(7)—social clubs
> 501(c)(8)—fraternal beneficiary societies
> 501(c)(9)—voluntary employee beneficiary associations
> 501(c)(10)—domestic fraternal societies and orders that do not provide life, sick, or health benefits
> 501(c)(11)—teacher retirement fund associations
> 501(c)(12)—benevolent life insurance associations and other mutual businesses
> 501(c)(13)—cemeteries and crematoria
> 501(c)(14)—credit unions
> 501(c)(15)—mutual insurance companies
> 501(c)(16)—farmers' co-ops
> 501(c)(17)—unemployment compensation benefit trusts
> 501(c)(20)—prepaid group legal services organizations
> 501(c)(25)—title holding corporations or trusts.

With limited exceptions, these organizations have the same federal tax benefits as a 501(c)(3). One major difference is that with few exceptions, contributors cannot deduct the amount of their contribution from their personal income tax payments. For many of these organizations, there is no limitation against lobbying activities, and most are permitted to engage in partisan political activity (although there may be a substantial federal excise tax associated with political expenditures).

Tips:

- Before filing an application for exempt status, review Chapter 2 for provisions that should be in your organization's governing documents.

- Make sure you are not eligible for the discounted filing fees available to smaller organizations before sending a $850 check to the IRS ($400 if gross receipts for the first four years will average less than $10,000 annually).

- Consider developing a conflict of interest statement (see Chapter 7) and providing it to the IRS with other organization documents. There has been anecdotal evidence recently that some IRS application examiners, but not all, are requiring such a statement.

- Consider using the IRS Cyber Assistant online application process to apply for 501(c)(3) status, when it becomes available, to qualify for a further discount on the application fee.

Chapter 9
Liability, Risk Management, and Insurance

> **Synopsis:** Nonprofit organizations, like all others, are exposed to risk in a variety of areas. Staff members, volunteers, clients, and members of the general public may suffer injuries while participating in or attending an organization's activities. The nonprofit may be sued for a variety of alleged wrongful acts, from unemployment discrimination to negligent supervision to breach of fiduciary duty. Every nonprofit organization should consider how it will minimize its risks, even though state and federal laws provide some protection to nonprofit organizations.

General Liability Concerns of Nonprofit Corporations

Murphy's Law has many variations and corollaries. In its simplest form, it states, "If something can go wrong, it will." No one can foresee catastrophic events, and even if one could, it is virtually impossible to protect an organization against all possible eventualities.

A nonprofit corporation, like a business corporation, should take reasonable steps to prevent foreseeable, downside risks. A nonprofit should also examine ways to minimize the effect of losses that occur despite the organization's best efforts. A nonprofit, like any other business, could suffer personal injury or property damage claims caused by floods, fire, theft, earthquake, wind damage, building collapse, and slips and falls, just to name a few possibilities. Even when a claimant seeks a small amount, the effect on the nonprofit can be devastating in terms of resources that must be used to defend the case. These claims do not happen very often, but when they do, the results can be disastrous for the organization and its leadership.

Nonprofits are exposed to legal risks in many other areas. Many nonprofits engage in typical business transactions on a routine basis. They arrange for conventions, seminars, and other meetings. They publish newsletters. They are employers with the attendant risk that hiring, advancement, or firing decisions may be challenged based on contract rights, discrimination, or fraud.

A nonprofit corporation could be exposed to the antitrust laws if its membership has a competitive advantage. Nonprofit associations conduct a variety of programs that permit their members to self-regulate, such as by business or professional codes, product standards and certification, or professional or academic credentialing, to use but a few examples. These decisions are open to challenge by parties who feel aggrieved.

Liability of Officers, Directors, and Other Volunteers

Nonprofit volunteers are exposed to the same potential liability for actions in performance of their duties as individuals involved with business corporations. Volunteer officers and directors of nonprofit corporations are bound by the same basic principles governing their conduct as directors and officers of profit-making business corporations.

Nonprofit boards' legal duties include the duty of care, the duty of loyalty, and the duty of obedience. They owe a fiduciary duty of reasonable care and the duty to act in the corporation's and its members' best interest. This involves a duty of loyalty or good faith in managing the affairs of the corporation. These duties require individuals to use due care in the performance of their duties for the organization, to act in good faith in a manner that serves the mission of the nonprofit, and to put the interests of the nonprofit above their own personal interests when acting as a board member for the organization.

Although there are no statistical data available on whether lawsuits against nonprofits are increasing, the perception exists that this is true. Several factors may contribute to increasing liability exposure for nonprofit organizations. First, federal and state laws adopted during the past 20 years, such as the 1988 *Drug-Free Workplace Act* and the 1990 *Americans With Disabilities Act,* have fueled an increase in lawsuits against organizations. Second, the increased use of technology by nonprofits has resulted in new techniques for the collection and dissemination of personal and/or confidential information. Many feel that the techniques for preserving privacy and security in the nonprofit organization environment are not keeping pace with the technology for collecting and storing information, making organizations vulnerable. Third, nonprofits are engaging in business activities to an increasing degree to fund their programs. These activities, such as the sale of mailing lists, engaging in e-commerce, and publishing documents and selling them on the Web, may expose organizations to increased liability. And fourth, related to each of these three, nonprofit organizations are increasing partnering with for-profit organizations, making agreements by contract and delegating some of their authority to third parties that may not have the same interest in preserving the integrity of the nonprofit's "brand name" as that nonprofit.

Civil and Criminal Liability

Nonprofit organizations have two types of liability to consider. The first category is civil liability, which includes tort actions and contract actions. A tort is a civil cause of action, other than a breach of contract, for which the law provides damages. The damage may have been intentional or unintentional, but the action that caused the damage usually, but not always, does not fall to the level of being a crime. An example might be in subjecting a potential employee to employment discrimination. If the aggrieved person can prove in court that he or she was not hired because of unlawful discrimination, the trier of fact (a judge or jury) may find in the plaintiff's favor and award monetary damages.

A second type of liability is criminal liability. An organization's treasurer who embezzles funds may be charged with a crime and prosecuted in the criminal courts. In contrast to a civil trial that has a standard of "preponderance of the evidence," the criminal trial has a standard of "beyond a reasonable doubt." In contrast to a civil judgment, punishment for those found guilty of a crime may include a prison sentence and/or restitution.

Strategies to Minimize Exposure to Lawsuits

What can a nonprofit do to minimize its exposure to lawsuits? Among the strategies that can be considered are:

1. *Don't offer programs and activities that impose too high a risk on the organization.* This may be the strategy of choice if your organization does not have the funds to adequately train and supervise workers or if you typically hire low-salary, entry-level workers rather than those with experience who require higher salaries. Can you afford state-of-the-art safety equipment and are you willing to make this investment? When the nature of the service you want to deliver is simply "an accident waiting to happen," it may be best simply to avoid sticking your neck out. (I would be remiss if I didn't mention that many nonprofits make society better for all of us *because* they are willing to stick their necks out and

provide a needed service when neither government nor the private sector is willing to do so.)

2. *Change the activity or the procedures involved to reduce your organization's exposure.* This may take the form of doing background checks on potential employees. It may include periodically certifying that your workers are capable of performing their jobs and providing continuing education and training. Or it may simply be reducing the chances of criminal activity against one of the program participants by changing the time or venue of an event, or by providing additional security personnel.

3. *Finance the risk by transferring some portion of financial responsibility for loss to an insurance company.* It is important to keep in mind that not all exposures are insurable, and a nonprofit may not be able to purchase coverage for all of its risks.

4. *Share the risk with another organization that is better prepared or more appropriately positioned to deal with the exposure.* For example, an organization may choose to outsource client transportation to a provider that already has sufficient insurance to cover potential losses, and has experienced, licensed, and trained personnel (e.g., professional drivers, rather than your organization's volunteers).

Regardless of the strategy you choose, you should consider basic general liability insurance to cover personal injury and property damage claims. Consideration should also be given to purchasing directors' and officers' (D&O) insurance to protect volunteer leadership from personal legal claims. Finally, a similar but broader type of insurance policy dealing with general professional liability protects not only officers and directors, but all association volunteers and staff, as well. Fortunately, federal and state laws have been enacted to limit the liability exposure to those who volunteer for nonprofit organizations.

Volunteer Protection Act

The *Volunteer Protection Act* (VPA) was signed into law by President Clinton in July of 1997, with an effective date of September 16, 1997. The intent of the law is to provide limited legal immunity for the volunteers of charities under certain circumstances. The VPA provides some protection, but there are some limitations to its applicability. Among these limitations are the following:

- Protection applies only to volunteers—those who do not receive compensation for their services other than reasonable reimbursement of their expenses. Directors and officers are covered if their compensation is $500 annually or less.

- Protection applies only in cases in which the volunteer was acting within the scope of his or her volunteer responsibilities at the time of the incident.

- The liability limitation does not apply if the volunteer was required to be licensed or certified to perform an activity, and that volunteer lacked such certification or licensing.

- The liability limit does not apply if the person intentionally caused harm to others or showed flagrant indifference to the safety of those who were injured.

The immunity does not extend to harm caused by the operation of a motor vehicle, crimes of violence, activities not authorized by the organization, or to hate crimes, civil rights violations, damage resulting from the use of alcohol or drugs, or sexual offenses. It encourages states to grant liability immunity to nonprofit organization volunteers who are acting in good faith and within the scope of their official duties.

Nothing in the law provides immunity or protection for the nonprofit itself. Furthermore, the Act does not protect volunteers against large categories of claims to which volunteers are exposed, such as those alleging violations of civil rights laws (often involving employment cases), those alleging intentional harm, and suits involving the use of an automobile.

PA Statutory Nonprofit Organization Liability Limitations

1. Nonmedical Good Samaritan Civil Immunity

Governor Dick Thornburgh May 12, 1986 signed into law legislation adding a section to state law dealing with Good Samaritan immunity (42 Pa. C.S.A. §8332.1 et seq.). The first part of the law provides some limits to liability for civil damages caused by managers, coaches, umpires, and referees of nonprofit youth sports programs. The second part of this law provides broader protection to those who volunteer for charities. The statute provides some protection for a "person who, without compensation and as a volunteer, renders public services" to a Section 501(c)(3) organization. This act seeks to prevent successful lawsuits based on "simple negligence," and would permit a lawsuit only if "the conduct of such person (the volunteer) falls substantially below the standards generally practiced and accepted in like circumstances by similar persons performing the same or similar duties, and unless it is shown that such person did an act or omitted the doing of an act which the person was under a recognized duty to another to do, knowing or having reason to know that such act or omission created a substantial risk of actual harm to the person or property of another."

2. Directors' Liability Act

The Directors' Liability Act, enacted by the PA General Assembly in May 1986, provides a limit to liability for the directors of not only nonprofit corporations, but for-profit corporations as well. Act 1986-145 (15 Pa. C.S.A. §5713, et seq.) permits nonprofit corporations to eliminate, subject to certain exceptions, the liability of directors for monetary damages for acts that do not constitute self-dealing, willful misconduct, or recklessness. It applies to all nonprofits, not just 501(c)(3)s, but does not deal with the liability of officers. Furthermore, the liability provisions of this law do not take effect automatically, but require each corporation to amend its bylaws for this purpose. This bylaw amendment must be voted on by the members of the nonprofit corporation (or, in the case of a business corporation, by the shareholders). Directors alone may not adopt this bylaw amendment; it must be adopted by the organization's members, if it has members.

Act 145 permits directors to rely in good faith on information, reports, and opinions, including financial data, prepared or presented by officers, employees, counsel, accountants, and other professional experts and committees of the board. They are entitled to give consideration to the effects of corporate actions on corporate constituencies in addition to members of the nonprofit corporation.

If a bylaw adopted by the members of the corporation so provides, the personal liability of a director for monetary damages is restricted to a situation in which the director fails to perform the duties of office in a way that constitutes self-dealing, willful misconduct, or recklessness. An exception to this general rule applies in the case of liability under a criminal statute or for the payment of taxes. The Directors' Liability Act contains a statutory provision broadening the power of nonprofit corporations (and business corporations, as well) to indemnify and advance expenses to officers and directors who become involved in litigation or other proceedings. This change in the law permits corporations to indemnify officers and directors against whom lawsuits are brought, arising from their corporate conduct. The law provides that indemnification may be either by bylaw, agreement, or independent vote of members or directors even when direct indemnification was not previously thought possible. The corporation is permitted to create a fund to secure the payment of the indemnification.

The act simplifies and clarifies the authorization to advance reasonable and necessary expenses, with the proviso that repayment of the advanced amounts might ultimately occur if it is determined that the officer or director is not entitled to be indemnified. Of course, indemnification is no better protection than the total amount of money available to the nonprofit corporation. This may be one of the reasons insurance for directors' and officers' liability for nonprofit corporations costs more than for for-profit corporations.

3. Volunteer-in-Public-Service Negligence Standard Amendment

A third state law affecting the civil liability of nonprofit organization volunteers was enacted in October 2001. Act 2001-81 (42 Pa. C.S.A. §8332.4) applies only to volunteers of organizations that are exempt under Sections 501(c)(3) and (c)(4) of the Internal Revenue Code, as well as of the Commonwealth and local government agencies. This law parallels the same liability standard that the General Assembly enacted for purposes of the Nonmedical Good Samaritan Civil Immunity (see page 86).

While each of these laws has some benefit to limiting the exposure of civil liability for volunteers, these laws generally will not apply to acts or omissions relating to the transportation of participants in nonprofit organization activities and services.

Insurance for Nonprofits and Nonprofit Personnel

There are various forms of coverage that nonprofits may consider as they look for ways to finance insurable risks. The Nonprofit Risk Management Center has published a comprehensive guide on insurance for nonprofits and provides detailed information on a wide range of coverages available to and purchased by nonprofits. The $30 Guide, *Coverage, Claims and Consequences: An Insurance Handbook for Nonprofits*, is available at: *http://nonprofitissues.com/store/Coverage-Claims-and-Consequences-An-Insurance-Handbook-for-Nonprofits.html*

The most commonly purchased coverages are discussed below:

Commercial general liability insurance—Commercial general liability or CGL policies cover liability exposures that are common to all organizations. The policy actually includes a combination of three separate coverages, each with its own insuring agreement and exclusions: Coverage A (general liability), Coverage B (personal injury and advertising injury liability) and Coverage C (medical payments). The most common CGL claims against nonprofits are third party claims alleging bodily injury or property damage. While most CGL policies are based on standard wording available from the Insurance Services Office (ISO), there are dozens of different policies available to nonprofits and many more exclusions, endorsements, and other provisions that add or delete coverages. For example, one nonprofit may purchase a CGL policy that provides coverage for its special events, while another nonprofit may choose a policy that includes protection against suits alleging sexual abuse.

Commercial property insurance—Property insurance covers risk of loss to an organization's buildings or personal property. Coverage usually includes buildings, personal property of the insured, personal property of others on site and in the insured's possession.

Crime coverage—Many nonprofits purchase crime coverage, typically a package of policies that protect an organization against intentional theft by insiders, as well as theft of assets by third parties. Crime coverage generally includes a fidelity bond (also called employee dishonesty coverage) plus a basic menu of other coverages.

Directors' & officers' liability insurance—D&O insurance provides coverage against *wrongful acts* which might include actual or alleged errors, omissions, misleading statements, and neglect or breach of duty on the part of the board of directors and other insured persons and entities. Many D&O policies include employment practices liability coverage, protecting a nonprofit against claims alleging improper or illegal employment practices.

Professional liability insurance—Also known as *malpractice coverage* or *errors and omissions* (E&O) coverage, professional liability insurance protects against claims alleging negligence in the delivery of (or failure to deliver) professional services, such as medical services, counseling, legal services and more.

Workers' compensation and employers' liability insurance—Workers compensation coverage covers expenses an employer is mandated to pay by state statute to cover specific benefits for employee injuries. Employers' liability insurance protects employers from employee-related suits that are separate from WC claims.

Workers' Compensation Insurance

Every state, including Pennsylvania, has a workers' compensation law. Pennsylvania's workers' compensation law was enacted in 1915, and was one of the first examples of employer reform legislation enacted during a time when employers generally held all of the cards and thousands of workers were exploited and at the mercy of employers.

The purpose of workers' compensation is to provide income to workers injured on the job and to pay their medical bills. In exchange, the employee gives up the right to sue the employer. The income disabled workers receive is generally two-thirds of their base salary, with a maximum payment equal to the state's average weekly wage. For 2011, the maximum workers' comp benefit was determined to be $858 per week. This is a "no fault" system, designed to avoid costly and time-consuming litigation while streamlining the ability to provide benefits to eligible workers.

All Pennsylvania corporations, including almost all nonprofits, are required to participate in Pennsylvania's workers' compensation program. Corporate executive officers of nonprofit organizations who serve voluntarily, without pay, may apply to their insurance carrier (or to the Bureau of Workers' Compensation if they have no insurance carrier) for exemption from the law.

An exemption is also available to employees who are members of a recognized religious sect and adhere to its tenets and teachings that conscientiously oppose acceptance of insurance benefits. Corporations typically purchase worker's compensation insurance from a commercial insurance carrier. Because there is a standard rate for each class of employee set by the Pennsylvania Insurance Department, the insurance premiums are theoretically the same from company to company.

Several publications published by the Pennsylvania Department of Labor and Industry explain the state's worker's compensation program. All publications are available from the Pennsylvania Department of Labor and Industry's Web site.

Unemployment Compensation Insurance

The unemployment compensation program in Pennsylvania is a job insurance program. Its purpose is to provide some limited protection against loss of income for workers who lose their jobs through no fault of their own. Virtually all nonprofit corporations in Pennsylvania are required to participate in the program, which is financed principally by a payroll tax on employers (the state average is around 5%) of the first $8,000 in wages for each employee annually. The tax on new nonprofit organizations is 3.703% on the first $8,000 in taxable wages for each employee. The rate applies for the first couple of years. After that, the rate is set based on each corporation's history of employment. In the past, there also has been a requirement that workers contribute to the program by means of a payroll deduction. For calendar year 2011, the withholding rate was .08%. This rate is for nonprofits that select the "contributory" method of participating. Organizations that are 501(c)(3) tax-exempt may select to be "reimbursable" organizations under this program, and do not have to pay this tax—although they are liable for reimbursing the program for any benefits paid out to their employees.

The maximum weekly benefit under this program is two-thirds of the average weekly wage in the Commonwealth. For 2011, this maximum payment is $573 per week. There is an $8 weekly supplemental payment for those with two or more dependents.

Registration

All nonprofits that hire employees must register with the Pennsylvania Department of Labor and Industry. After registering (by filing a PA-100 form available from the Bureau of Employer Tax Operations Field Services offices), corporations automatically receive a quarterly UC-3 form (see Chapter 11).

Section 501(c)(3) Organization Reimbursement Election

State law permits, but does not require, 501(c)(3) tax-exempt organizations to elect the "Reimbursable Method" for complying with the unemployment compensation law. Under this method, the nonprofit 501(c)(3) is required to reimburse the Unemployment Compensation Fund for all regular unemployment compensation benefits that are expended. The federal government pays 50% of extended unemployment benefits to qualified workers. Congress often will extend the regular program during times of economic recession.

Organizations that select the reimbursable method will receive a Form UC-150, Notice of Amount Due for Compensation Paid, which is a bill. This bill must be paid within 30 days, even if a protest is filed within the 30-day period permitted.

The Bureau of Employer Tax Operations publishes a booklet titled *Employer's Reference Guide to Unemployment Compensation* (UCP-36) that provides the details of the program. This booklet may be obtained by writing to:

> Office of Unemployment Tax Services
> Bureau of Employer Tax Operations
> Labor and Industry Building
> Seventh and Forster Streets
> P.O. Box 60849
> Harrisburg, PA 17106-0849
> (717) 787-7530 or
> 1-866-403-6163

It is also available at:
http://www.portal.state.pa.us/portal/server.pt?open=514&objID=598469&mode=2

Another helpful booklet for nonprofits is:

Unemployment Compensation Information for Reimbursable Employers (UCP 16)—for Section 501(c) (3) organizations

This booklet can be accessed at: *http://www.dli.state.pa.us* (click on *Employers* under *UC pamphlets*).

Risk Management

The term "risk management" refers to management strategies your organization can utilize to protect its assets from erosion or loss. Every nonprofit has a wide range of assets, including personnel, property (real estate and personal property), income, and reputation. Risk management involves giving consideration to the risks an organization faces and deciding how the organization will respond to those exposures. Among the steps of a typical planning process are the following:

1. Identify potential exposure and risk to the organization's personnel, property, clients, funding, and reputation.

2. Evaluate and prioritize potential risks.

3. Develop strategies to address these risks.

4. Periodically evaluate and update your risk management plan.

The Nonprofit Risk Management Center offers a wide range of free and affordable services designed to help nonprofits cope with risk. These resources include free technical assistance, free online tutorials (including one on basic risk management), a large library of publications for sale, online and in-person conferences, and risk assessment software. Another online program helps nonprofits develop a customized risk management plan. Information on all of these resources can be found at: *http://www.nonprofitrisk.org*

Board Member Decision-Making

The Board of a nonprofit organization "owns" the organization in trust for the public. Ultimately, the board is responsible for assuring that the organization complies with all laws, and it is the board, not staff, that is responsible for protecting the assets of the organization. There are few cases in which board members have been found liable for making reasonable, good-faith, arm's length decisions even when hindsight has demonstrated such decisions to be "bad." More likely, board members have been liable for decisions made that involved self-dealing, obviously taken with criminal intent, or just plain "stupid." As Dr. Carter McNamara writes in Some Legal Considerations for Board Members (http://managementhelp.org/boards/liabilities.htm), "Directors must attend most board meetings, not just on occasion. Absence from a board meeting does not release the director from responsibility for decisions made. A pattern of absence may indeed be presumed to increase an individual's liability because she/he cannot demonstrate a serious dedication to the obligations of the position."

McNamara continues that board members are more liable for taking no action than for taking the wrong action for the right reasons. His advice is sage when he suggests that board members should be vigilant for something that smells "fishy" and shouldn't always assume that the information they receive is accurate.

In a booklet entitled *Handbook for Charitable Nonprofit Organizations*, available online (http://www.attorneygeneral.gov/uploadedFiles/Consumers/nonprofitbooklet.pdf), the Pennsylvania Attorney General, now the Governor, spelled out some of the specific responsibilities of nonprofit organization board members and senior management. See Chapter 4 for more about this booklet and the general topic of board member legal responsibilities.

Tips:

- **This chapter provides an introduction to some of the liability concerns facing nonprofits. Seek legal counsel before making any organizational decisions with respect to changing policy that could affect your exposure to liability, or about any liability suits and claims.**

- **Be certain you have an up-to-date personnel policy manual and that it includes a sexual harassment policy. Take steps to enforce these policies. While the policies should be customized to the needs of your organization, templates can be found in inexpensive computer files you can purchase from a general office supply store or find online.**

- **Provide detailed job descriptions even for volunteers. Some provisions of the federal immunity law apply only in cases in which volunteers are engaged in activities within the scope of their duties.**

- **Make sure that all volunteers are certified or licensed if they engage in activities that require certification or licensing for paid staff.**

- **If your organization transports clients, verify that volunteers have vehicle insurance and that all insurance policies for vehicles owned by the organization will cover damages caused by volunteers while driving those vehicles.**

- **If you serve on a board and disagree with a board decision being made at a board meeting that you feel may result in unreasonable increased liability exposure to you or your organization, ask that your objections be recorded in the minutes.**

- **Shop around for directors' and officers' insurance. Check to see if any policy you are considering will insure directors and officers for more than civil lawsuits.**

- **Make sure that those who hire employees are familiar with the questions they can and cannot legally ask (see Chapter 12).**

Chapter 10
Financial Management

Synopsis: All nonprofit corporations must keep certain financial records and create reports of their financial condition. There are three standards of financial verification used by accountants to verify financial data—audit, review, and compilation, with the audit being the highest level of scrutiny. *Line-item* and *program* budgets are the two major forms of budgeting utilized by nonprofit corporations. Nonprofit organizations must institute financial management systems to assure they will operate efficiently and effectively, and to minimize waste, fraud, and abuse.

The Importance of Financial Management to Nonprofits

Some of the most critically important duties of an organization's board and staff are to take steps to pay its obligations, invest its money, and plan for its financial future. Imagine the consequences that may occur if an otherwise "perfect," respected organization finds itself unable to meet its payroll because a large check anticipated from a funder failed to arrive in time. An organizational culture that condones stealing—whether in the form of allowing office supplies to be requisitioned for personal use, using credit cards to make personal purchases, or even not penalizing the use of long distance calling cards and photocopy machines for personal use—may experience a hemorrhage of organizational resources that could be fatal during tough economic times. Buyers who steer purchases to their relatives and friends rather than make dispassionate business decisions that are in the organization's best interest are subjecting the organization to a hidden "tax." Both board and staff leadership have a fiduciary duty to act in the best interests of the organization rather than in their own personal interest, and to manage the financial affairs of the organization prudently. To do otherwise is not only dangerous to the long-term health of the organization, but is both unethical and illegal, as well.

An organization's board and staff leadership are not the only sources of pressure to make its operations more "business-like," and to assure that each dollar expended is necessary and used effectively to further the organization's mission. Government and private funders are increasingly demanding efficiency, cost effectiveness, and outcomes that demonstrate real, measurable progress toward achieving program goals. The press has perhaps become more vigilant about monitoring the voluntary sector since high profile scandals involving respected institutions such as National Public Radio, American University, the United Way of New York City, the Association for Volunteer Administration, and the American Red Cross have made recent headlines.

Nonprofit organizations are increasingly operating in a competitive environment not dissimilar to their for-profit counterparts. They compete for grants and donations, for board members, contracts, volunteers, media coverage, and qualified staff. Failure to manage the financial affairs of an organization can be catastrophic, resulting in bankruptcy, cutbacks of services, layoffs, involuntary merger/takeovers, and dissolution.

Where the transfer of money is involved, there are always ethics and accountability issues of which to be aware. As a result of high profile financial scandals in the nonprofit sector, the elimination of waste, fraud, and abuse in nonprofit organizations is not simply a public relations problem. In 2004, the Finance Committee of the U. S. Senate launched an initiative focusing on devising changes to laws that affect how the sector will develop, whether its historical tax exemptions will be secure, and what disclosure will be required to assure the highest level of ethics and accountability of these organizations that are ostensibly formed for the public good rather than any individual pecuniary interest. Obviously, the financial management practices of the sector are among the prominent areas under scrutiny.

As this is being written, there is a climate of increased demand for human services and fewer resources to pay for them from all levels of government. Competent financial management is the glue that can hold a nonprofit organization together during tough times.

How Nonprofit Financial Management Differs From the Private Sector

The private sector's general goal is to make a profit for the organization with the highest return on investment (ROI), and it uses financial management as a tool for that purpose. In contrast, a nonprofit organization uses financial management to make the optimal use of resources to achieve its mission(s) and accomplish its goals. Rather than trying to maximize profit, a nonprofit organization seeks to maximize the production and delivery of goods and services, consistent with demand, to those who for one reason or another, cannot receive those goods and services from either government or the marketplace. It may be that this is because they cannot afford the market cost of the services. Or it could be that the organization provides collective goods that the government either chooses not to provide, or chooses to subsidize nonprofit organizations that will. Nonprofit organizations also advocate for various causes, knowing that they will never generate any direct income from providing advocacy services.

Generally, nonprofit organizations experience more of a political process in virtually every aspect of financial management compared to a private sector organization. And those involved in that political process are typically more diverse demographically and are not always on the same page with respect to the principal goal of the organization. In theory, the goal of for-profit organizations is to make as much profit as possible. A nonprofit organization may have many competing goals, some of which may be in conflict with each other. For example, a nursing home may want to increase its share of private-pay patients compared to those whose care is financed by Medicaid, but want to become the institution of choice for those who need care for Alzheimer's disease.

Because of the public benefits granted to nonprofit organizations, particularly those with 501(c)(3) tax-exempt status, the degree of accountability for funds is somewhat higher than for for-profit organizations. And because such organizations are entrusted with the care of people, many of whom are vulnerable and who have not voluntarily chosen that organization to receive services in the marketplace, there is an implicit acceptance by the public and government agencies that ethical standards are higher for such organizations than would apply to their for-profit counterparts (although many would argue that all organizations should have equally high ethical standards, regardless of their sector). Even with this being the case, there is no federal government regulatory authority over the financial management of nonprofit organizations comparable to that which the Security and Exchange Commission (SEC) has over stock-issuing corporations. If it did exist, such an agency might "impose uniform accounting standards on public charities, disseminate information on the financial conditions of organizations, and create channels through which donors, volunteers, clients, and community members could access and use this information," as Professor Peter Frumkin suggests in his book, *On Being Nonprofit.*

Components of Financial Management

As formulated by Jerome McKinney in his book, *Effective Financial Management in Public and Nonprofit Organizations,* the activities encompassed by financial management are a sequence of related activities, including planning, programming, budgeting, financing, controlling, and evaluating.

Planning involves assessing the organization's current and likely future situation, surveying its strengths and weaknesses, setting out its goals and objectives, and developing a roadmap to achieve them. See Chapter 6 for an in-depth discussion of strategic planning. There are financial implications to changes in market conditions, new competitors, new laws and regulations, additional paperwork requirements (such as might be required by a new government or foundation funder), and an increase in the demand for services—both an increase in the number of clients and an increase in the level of services required by each client—resulting from changing social, economic, or political conditions.

Programming is the scheduling of the activities the organization needs to engage in to make its goals become a reality. In this phase, the organization creates distinct programs. A program has been defined by Professor Carter McNamara as "a collection of organizational resources that is geared to accomplish a certain major goal or set of goals." Prudent financial management requires that financial data be segregated by program, so that the performance of each program can be independently evaluated. This is particularly important to nonprofit organizations, as funders—and to an increasing degree, donors as well—want their grants and donations used for a particular purpose that may be only one small part of the overall operations of the organization.

The "program" is intended to achieve a particular outcome. Resources are sought from government, foundations, and the public to finance any net loss that the organization would incur by conducting that program, whether or not fees are charged to those who benefit directly from program services.

Budgeting is the process for allocating expenditures to each program. A budget is defined as an itemized summary of estimated or intended expenditures for a given period, often for a given fiscal year. A "fiscal year" is a one-year period at the end of which all accounts are reconciled, and for which the one-year budget applies. It does not necessarily coincide with a calendar year. For example, the federal government's fiscal year begins on October 1. Many states, including Pennsylvania, begin their fiscal year on July 1.

Typically, an organization's budget is not only a document to control the activities of subordinates, but it is also a political document. A budget, either directly or indirectly, indicates the priorities of the organization. Annual budget documents in all three sectors usually indicate what was spent during the previous fiscal year, what is being spent during the current year, and what is proposed to be spent for the next fiscal year. Stakeholders reading the budget get a sense of the direction the organization is heading with respect to each of its programs, whether it is growing or declining, from where it is planning to get its funds, and its general financial health. One gets a sense from the budget about whether the organization is more comfortable outsourcing or performing tasks with its own personnel. Those who prepare an organization's budget should look at it in its entirety and think about what message it is sending. For more details about budgeting, see page 104.

Financing includes the activities necessary to obtain the resources needed in the budget. It may include borrowing from financial institutions to start new entrepreneurial ventures, or perhaps using endowment funds to serve as startup capital. It typically involves managing cash flow to assure that the organization has enough funds to pay its obligations, and policies relating to managing its cash and other assets. Fundraising, investment of surplus revenues, management of endowment funds, and use of funds generated by for-profit subsidiaries are among the activities that are included in the financing phase of the financial management cycle.

Controlling includes the development of a system that assures that the programs envisioned in the plans are being carried out appropriately. It also provides for feedback to warn when a program does not measure up to its expectations so that mid-course corrections can be implemented to get it back on track. Included in this phase of operations are policies to assure that the organization's assets—such as equipment and supplies, inventory of goods, and cash—are protected from inappropriate use or distribution. Most importantly, this includes systems that are designed to measure whether the implementation of programs is consistent with budget plans and projections, and to have procedures in place to expand, contract, or otherwise modify program operations when their performance differs from what was anticipated by the budget and planning documents. The basic accounting system; expense account policies; policies designed to minimize waste, fraud, and abuse; and the general Management Information System (MIS), if the organization has one, are among the systems that fall under this phase.

According to Thomas McLaughlin in his book, *Streetsmart Financial Basics for Nonprofit Managers*, there are six elements of an internal control system.

1. *Control Cues.* This involves management and leadership sending signals, both overt and covert, of proper ethical behavior, and training staff in appropriate control policies that promote accountability.
2. *Policy Communication.* This entails having written policies and procedures for issues relating to accountability and ethics when you can, but in the absence of that, being able to communicate to employees what is acceptable and what is not by e-mail, fax, interoffice memo, or voice mail.
3. *Segregation of Duties.* This involves breaking up work duties so that one person does not have total dominance over a portion of the financial system. For example, it might make sense for the person ordering the good or service, filling out the purchase order, writing the check, signing the check, mailing the check, and receiving the ordered goods to be different people within the organization. This becomes a challenge for organizations with only a few employees, but even for a one-person office, a system of checks and balances needs to be developed.
4. *Record-keeping.* This relates to documentation and recording of all financial transactions. Among ways nonprofits try to minimize their vulnerability to internal fraud and abuse is by using a reliable payroll service, contracting out accounts receivable, and taking advantage of those financial institutions willing to do cash management for organizations. Of course, doing so increases the organization's vulnerability to external fraud and abuse.
5. *Budgets.* The budget is perhaps the best strategy to control behavior, since if there are no funds in the budget, it is difficult for spending to occur that has not been preauthorized and planned for.
6. *Reporting.* McLaughlin's view is that "you only need five financial reports to control the average nonprofit corporation" (p. 207): the balance sheet, revenue and expenses, aged accounts receivables, cash flow projection, and utilization reporting (which generally refers to how many people are using the organization's services, and to what extent). By looking at these reports periodically, a manager ostensibly can see trouble spots.

Evaluation (see Chapter 30) provides data on whether the programs are accomplishing what they set out to do. It involves validating the efforts of what is working and providing enough information to eliminate components of programs, or entire programs, when it is determined that they are not working. Many funders require the independent evaluation of the specific programs they fund as a condition of the grant. Since the popularity of the "reinventing government" movement and outcome-based management, nonprofit organizations are under increasing pressure to evaluate programs based on outcomes rather than the more easily measured outputs (see Chapter 29 for more on this topic) . Regardless, systems to collect data that facilitate evaluation that are in place at the beginning before a program starts operating make evaluation easier than having to start from scratch after the program has been operating.

Generally, it is considered more efficient if all of the functions described in this financial management cycle are administered by one person. In smaller organizations, the executive director is responsible for all of the tasks involved that are described above. Larger organizations, however, will have one person (typically with the title of Chief Operating Officer or Chief Financial Officer) who will have these duties. In the case of the latter, as some high-profile criminal and civil cases have shown with respect to the for-profit sector, it is expected that there will be sufficient communication between the CEO and the CFO or equivalent. The CEO is ultimately responsible for the health of the organization, and simple ethics require that the CEO maintain a close watch over the financial affairs of the organization, even if a subordinate staff member maintains day-to-day control over the financial operation of the organization.

Controls for Waste, Fraud, and Abuse

There are two general classifications of systems that are used to control waste, fraud, and abuse in nonprofit organizations. The first is to discourage these before they occur. The second is to assist in discovering them after they have occurred.

The traditional method of thwarting waste, fraud, and abuse *before* they occur consists of—

1. *The independent auditor's annual audit and the annual management letter.* The management letter is an opportunity by the auditor(s) to point out any deficiencies seen in the operations of the organization that affect financial accountability and ethical concerns directly to the board. When you get a management letter that cites chapter and verse with respect to internal control problems, you need to deal with it (and quickly!). This requires a plan of corrective action that is approved by the board before implementation.
2. *Internal controls of the organization.* This consists of a system of checks and balances to assure that no one person (or perhaps even more than one) can control assets without appropriate accountability. This involves the requirement that expenditures be preauthorized by a responsible organization official in accordance with predetermined policies affecting disbursements. All expenditures are recorded by the accountant/bookkeeper, with appropriate documentation for the expenditure becoming part of the file. That financial officer has the responsibility to raise any questions about the expenditure. Oversight might include pre-audit checks of all purchase orders and vouchers, and review by someone other than the person requesting them before a payment is made, and separating those who order goods and services for the organization from those who receive the goods and services. It also might include spot checks of credit card transactions, long distance telephone bills, and cell phone accounts to assure that no personal expenses are charged to the organization.
3. *Policies requiring large orders of goods and services to be put out for bid.* This includes related policies that discourage purchasers from dividing up orders into small increments to undermine this policy. This does not necessarily mean that the organization must prepare a formal *Request for Proposal* (RFP) for every large purchase. But it should mean that quotes should be obtained from several qualified vendors and contractors for large purchases.
4. *Ethics policies that apply to organization resources are distributed to individuals.* These policies might apply to credit cards, telephones, Internet accounts, cell phones, and organization vehicles, for example. These ethics policies would also include what is acceptable with respect to receiving gifts. For example, those who authorize company purchases

would be prohibited from accepting gifts from suppliers other than *de minimus* gifts such as calendars. More substantial gifts, such as a box of cookies, would have to be shared with everyone in the organization. (The free vacation to Las Vegas as a thanks from the vendor to the organization's purchaser would have to be declined.) An ethics policy should also cover the issue of gifts made to staff members from those who receive services. All ethics policies should be reviewed at least once annually and updated as appropriate.

5. *Training all employees on how to deal with the elimination of waste, fraud, and abuse.* The philosophy inherent in this method is that it is difficult to deal with a "bad" behavior when an individual might not have a clear sense as to what that might be in every case. The training should include procedures for staff to report suspected cases of fraud.

6. *Severe penalties for violating the public trust.* This involves written policies that require those found to have stolen from the organization to be fired and referred to criminal authorities, or otherwise appropriately sanctioned by reprimand or suspension if the violation is in a gray area.

7. *Record keeping about all assets and taking a periodic inventory.* This is important so that when something is missing (such as a lap-top computer), an investigation can commence quickly.

8. *Electronic protection of records.* The purpose of maintaining backups is so have an electronic trail, if not a paper trail, in the event of a fire or flood that destroys paper records.

Methods used to find occurrences *after* they have occurred include—

- determining when an employee has suddenly adopted a high lifestyle beyond his/her known income;
- investigating when it becomes suspected that purchasers are funneling purchases to personal friends or relatives, or receiving expensive gifts from suppliers;
- taking swift action when there appears to be missing documentation, "lost" organization checks, or an increased backlog in recording transactions;
- randomly reviewing credit card transactions and organization telephone bills for personal expenses charged to the organization's account; and
- determining which expenses seem too high compared to what they have been historically, particularly when it is difficult to account for this with a reasonable explanation.

Basic Financial Statements

For a sample, actual document that summarizes the financial position of a nonprofit, the Association for Research on Nonprofit Organizations and Voluntary Action (ARNOVA), see Appendix I. There are four basic financial statements that are prepared by the organization's accountant:

1. *Balance sheet (Statement of Financial Position).* The purpose of the balance sheet is to demonstrate the financial position of the organization at a certain point, typically the end of a fiscal year, by comparing its assets (what the organization owns) to liabilities (what the organization owes). Current assets consist of the monetary value of what is owned by the organization other than long-term assets, including the cash in the checking account and cash equivalents, such as certificates of deposit; accounts receivable (minus the value of those receivables that are not likely to be collected, called "bad debts"); pledges receivable; grants receivable; the current value of investments (stocks, bonds, and other marketable financial assets); inventories of goods; and prepaid expenses and other deferred charges (such as, for example, a fully-paid life insurance policy that covers more than one fiscal year). Fixed assets (including the value of land, buildings, and equipment owned by the organization that has a life of more than a year) are those that are not likely to be con-

verted into cash at any time in the near future, such as stocks and bonds or real property owned by the organization.

Liabilities are debts that the organization owes to those outside of the organization. Current short-term liabilities include accounts payable, grants payable (for those nonprofits that make such grants), taxes owed but not yet paid (such as sales taxes collected and UBIT—unrelated business income taxes— that apply even to those organizations that are tax-exempt), and current loans. Long-term liabilities include long term loans, bonds, and mortgages. The report is called a balance sheet because assets and liabilities are brought into balance in the "bottom line" as a result of merging liabilities with the "net assets," also referred to as "fund balance"—the net value, the net worth, or the equity of the organization at that point in time.

2. *Income Statement.* Income statements consist of three parts, showing revenues, expenses, and the net difference between these two (positive if there is a profit, negative if there is a loss). That net difference can be distorted when an organization is on a cash basis of accounting, and there are either expenses or revenue paid out (or taken in, as the case may be), in a different accounting period. The accrual method of accounting overcomes this flaw (see page 102). Categories of income may include grants; donations; income from fees for services; income from for-profit subsidiaries; and sales of land, buildings, and equipment. Expense categories may include salaries, supplies, depreciation on buildings and equipment, administrative, general and fundraising expenses, and other expenses. The statement usually includes a line at the bottom comparing the net profit of the current year to the previous year, and the amount of this profit that has aggregated over time (called the "fund balance").

3. *Statement of Changes in Financial Position.* This statement typically includes the amount of cash from revenues; the amount of cash expenditures (and the difference between the two as net revenue or net loss); expenses from purchases of land, equipment, and income from the sale of these; and income from loans and bonds. The "bottom line" on this statement shows the net profit or loss and the cash balance, as well as how that cash balance compares to the previous year.

4. *Form 990—Return of Organization Exempt From Income Tax.* This annual information form has been required by the Internal Revenue Service since the 1940s, and was substantially revised in December 2007. It applies to most federally tax-exempt organizations with gross revenues of $25,000 or more. Organizations with gross receipts of less than $200,000 and total assets of less than $500,000 may elect to file the short version of the form, 990-EZ, or the 990-N e-postcard if gross receipts are normally less than $50,000. The filing deadline is four and a half months following the end of the organization's fiscal year. Organizations are required by law to provide a copy of their Form 990 to anyone who requests it, although organizations that make their returns "widely available," such as by posting their 990s online, are exempt from this requirement. The organization may charge a reasonable copying fee (none if the requester provides his or her own copying equipment on site) and actual postage costs. Form 990 requires detailed disclosure relating to Revenue, Expenses, Changes in Net Assets or Fund Balances (Part 1); Statement of Functional Expenses (Part 2); Statement of Program Service Accomplishments (Part 3); Balance Sheets (Part 4); a list of officers, directors, trustees and key employees that includes salary information (Part 5); and "Other" information that includes information about lobbying, fundraising, unrelated business income, in-kind donations, among other issues (Part 6). The fine for not filing this return is $20 per day, not to exceed the lesser of $10,000 or 5% of the gross receipts of the organization for the year. For large organiza-

tions (those with annual gross receipts exceeding $1 million), the penalty is $100 per day up to $50,000.

Fund Accounting

Separate accounting records are maintained for each fund of a nonprofit organization. The nonprofit establishes each of these funds to meet a specified purpose. A small-sized nonprofit may only have a single fund, called the general fund, operating fund, or unrestricted fund. Larger nonprofits may have several funds in addition to this general fund. Among the most common are—

Endowment Fund. A permanent endowment fund assumes that the financial principal remains unspent, but that the interest earned on this fund may be spent for either any purpose or a restricted, specified purpose.

Fixed Asset Fund. This fund includes the fixed assets of the organization and liabilities associated with the physical plant (both purchase and maintenance). Pledges to construct new facilities are included in this fund.

Restricted Funds. It is not unusual for donors to specify how their donations must be used. If the board does not have the power to use donations for any purpose it chooses, the donations are placed in a restricted fund and reported in a separate accounting statement of Income, Expenses, and Changes in Net Assets. Some nonprofits have funds established for each major donor.

Accounting rules tend to get somewhat complex and legalistic. Some donations have conditions attached before they can be counted on by the charity. Two examples of these are bequests and matching pledges. Rather than being included as assets in fund accounting, these donations are often disclosed as footnotes in the financial reports.

Cash-Flow Analysis

Nonprofit organizations, as with other organizations, benefit from performing a cash flow analysis. The analysis is designed to answer the questions of how much cash the organization needs to pay its obligations at each point in time, and when and from where is it coming at each such point in time. This analysis is necessary because revenue, such as that coming from grants, is not always received before expenses need to be paid. A year-long grant may be paid in monthly installments. But for organizations that write paychecks every two weeks, there are three payrolls rather than two every third month.

Utility bills (such as for heating in the winter and cooling in the summer), may be seasonal. The organization's annual fundraiser may create a spike in donations in May, a month or so before the end of the fiscal year. In short, a budget may balance appropriately based on a year of revenue and expenses. But if the expenses are incurred mostly before the income is received, the organization may find itself unable to pay its obligations. A cash-flow analysis will look at how revenues and expenses project each month, and determines whether there is a problem with having enough cash in the bank to write checks for obligations when they need to be written. When a problem is identified, there are often strategies for dealing with it. Some payments can be made in installments. Purchases can be put on a credit card until enough cash comes in. Accounts payable could be delayed a month or so to catch up, or the organization could seek a loan.

What is the FASB?

The Financial Accounting Standards Board is a private-sector organization founded in 1973 with the mission "to establish and improve standards of financial accounting and reporting for the guidance and education of the public, including issuers, auditors and users of financial information." Its accounting standards are promulgated with an open, participatory process, and are recognized by government agencies with statutory authority to enforce organizational accountability, including the Securities and Exchange Commission, and professional associations such as the *American Institute of Certified Public Accountants*. Indeed, while the board is independent of all government and professional associations, it consists of fifteen representatives from eight membership associations with an interest in financial reporting.

There are two important standards issued by the FASB that apply to nonprofit organizations.

FASB Statement 116 and Statement 117 were issued in June 1993, and apply to all charities with at least $5 million in assets and $1 million in annual expenses. They are generally required to be adopted for financial statements for fiscal years beginning after December 15, 1995. Statement 116 sets standards with respect to accounting for contributions made and received. Among changes in policy made by this statement is that donor pledges that are unconditional are counted as assets even though no actual payment on the pledges has been received. For a summary, see: *http://www.fasb.org/st/summary/stsum116.shtml*

FASB Statement 117 establishes standards for financial statements of nonprofit organizations. It requires, among other standards, that nonprofit organizations provide a statement of financial position, a statement of activities, and a cash-flow statement. Organizations must report total assets, liabilities, and net assets in a statement of financial position; report the change in an organization's net assets in a statement of activities; and report the change in cash and cash equivalents in a statement of cash flows. The main theme of FASB 117 is to take into account the presence or absence of donor restrictions and to group an organization's funds into three categories: permanently restricted, temporarily restricted, and unrestricted, applicable only to the organization's net assets. For a summary, see: *http://www.fasb.org/st/summary/stsum117.shtml*

Sarbanes-Oxley

The *American Competitiveness and Corporate Accountability Act*, commonly known as the Sarbanes-Oxley Act, was enacted by the Congress in 2002 as a response to corporate financial scandals, such as those at Enron, Arthur Anderson, and Global Crossing. Generally, this act does not apply to nonprofit corporations, although two provisions—those relating to protecting whistle-blowers and the destruction of litigation-related documents—do apply to both for-profit and nonprofit corporations.

Bookkeeping

Both state and federal law require corporations to record all expenses and income in an organized format. This can be done manually or by using one of many popular computer programs.

Several basic decisions must be made with respect to record-keeping. First, the corporation must decide on the period of its fiscal year. Because federal law requires the Form 990 nonprofit tax return to be filed within four-and-a-half months after the end of the fiscal year (technically, by the 15th day of the fifth month after the end of the fiscal year), that alone can determine when to begin the fiscal year. Other factors to consider are the fiscal years or the announcement dates of grants of major funding sources, using a calendar year for simplicity, or beginning the fiscal year as soon as the first corporate income has been received.

A second issue is to decide whether the bookkeeping system will be on a "cash" or "accrual" basis. Cash basis financial reporting recognizes a transaction the date income was actually received and deposited and when expenditures were made. The "accrual" method recognizes a transaction when it is made, i.e., when supplies are ordered, not when they are received. The "accrual" method factors in "accounts payable" (when the organization owes someone money, but has not actually sent them a payment) and "accounts receivable" (when there is a legal obligation to pay the organization something in the future, but the organization hasn't yet received payment). Most novices find the cash basis easier and simpler. The accrual method, on the other hand, gives a more realistic picture of the actual financial situation of the organization, and thus complies with generally accepted accounting principles.

The "cash" vs. "accrual" decision should be discussed with the organization's accountant, or whoever is likely to prepare the tax returns and annual financial report. The accrual method is the method of choice for all but the smallest of organizations. This is the time when the foresight of placing a certified public accountant or two on the board of directors can pay dividends.

Some funding agencies may have their own unique financial reporting requirements that must be complied with to qualify for grants.

Levels of Financial Verification

There are three levels of financial verification. In descending levels of scope and scrutiny, they are audits, reviews, and compilations. The level of financial verification required is often determined by the nature and source of funding for the organization. Many government grants explicitly require a minimum level of financial verification in their contracts. Such a contract may be a "pass-through" of funds from another source, and the original source may need to be tracked down to determine whether it has its own requirements. For example, a nonprofit organization may receive a grant from a United Way, but the funding is provided by a state government. As a result, the United Way may require financial reports from the nonprofit organization that will permit it to comply with its own reporting requirements to that state government grantor.

It is wise to request all financial reporting information, in writing, from any contracting organization that provides the organization with grant funds.

All of the three financial verification levels require that all organizational funds be kept segregated by the appropriate organizational accounts (and, of course, from the accounts of other organizations) and all transactions be accounted for. Thus, it is never good organizational policy to sign over an incoming check payment to a third party. Instead, deposit the check into the organization's account and then write a new check to the third party. While ignoring this advice may save the time of making a deposit and writing a check, it will result in a loss of "paper trail" necessary to determine who paid what to whom, when, and for what.

Many taxing authorities require an audit report when the funds in the contract are $100,000 or more in any single year. State and local governments generally require a review if funding is between $25,000 and $100,000 annually. If funding is less than $25,000, a compilation report is usually acceptable. Lately, the trend has been to increase these dollar thresholds. It is wise to research what thresholds apply to nonprofits in your locality, or which might be required by a particular funding organization.

Audit Report

The highest level of financial verification, an audit, is a complete arm's-length verification of the accuracy and reliability of account statements and financial reports. Records are systematically examined and checked to determine how they adhere to generally accepted accounting principles, management policies, and other stated policies. The purpose of independent audits is to eliminate bias, self-interest, fraud, and unintentional errors.

What does the auditor do? The auditor will request information from individuals and institutions to confirm bank balances, contribution amounts, conditions and restrictions, contractual obligations, and monies owed to and by your organization. The auditor will review physical assets, journals and ledgers, and board minutes to ensure that all activity with significant financial implications is adequately disclosed in the financial statements. In addition, the auditor will select a sample of financial transactions to determine whether there is proper documentation and whether the transaction was posted correctly into the books. In addition, the auditor will interview key personnel and read the procedures manual, if one exists, to determine whether or not the organization's internal accounting control system is adequate. The auditor usually spends several days at the organization's office looking over records and checking for completeness.

While an auditor can never obtain *absolute* proof of the representations made in a financial statement, the standard used is that of a "reasonable man" (or woman) who has "adequate technical training and proficiency as an auditor," according to the American Institute of Certified Public Accountants. Auditors have a professional code of ethics to ensure their independence from the management of the nonprofit organization they are auditing. Although they are paid a fee by the corporation, they are considered to be responsible to the public rather than to their corporate clients.

Many government agencies have audit requirements for recipients of their grants, as do many foundations and other umbrella fundraising organizations, such as United Ways and Jewish federations. Audits are often required by major umbrella fundraising organizations unless the revenues are relatively small.

The American Institute of Certified Public Accountants (AICPA) has prepared a comprehensive publication entitled *Audit and Accounting Guide: Not for Profit Organization*, published July 2007, specifically to assist nonprofit corporations in preparing for their annual audits. This *Guide* can be purchased for $86.25 in paper and $68 on CD-ROM (discounts available for AICPA members), plus $9.25 for postage and handling from:

American Institute of Certified Public Accountants
Service Center
220 Leigh Farm Road
Durham, NC 27707
(888) 777-7077 (option 1)
http://www.cpa2biz.com

Review

A second standard of financial verification, called a "review," is the application of analytical procedures by the accountant to the financial data supplied by the corporation. It is substantially narrower in scope than an audit. Much of the information supplied by the corporation is accepted at face value, although there may be a spot check to see if there are any glaring errors or inconsistencies between expenses recorded and the checks that are written. The examination of internal control and the proper allocation of income and expenses is similar to that of an audit report. Unlike an audit, the review will not include a formal auditor's "opinion" as to the compliance with generally accepted accounting principles.

Compilation

The third level of financial reporting/verification, a "compilation," calls only for the proper classification of assets, liabilities, fund balances, income, and expenses, from information supplied by management. Third-party verification of assets and liabilities is not required, although internal supporting documents may be used in their place. Spot checks are employed only when the accountant is aware of inconsistencies in other areas of the examination. As in a review, the accountant will not render an "opinion" on the accuracy of the report.

In the absence of legal requirements, it is good policy for nonprofits that expend more than a few thousand dollars to have at least a review. Many nonprofits have certified public accountants on their boards who may be willing to arrange for a review of the corporation on a *pro bono* basis.

Budgeting

Some nonprofits can exist for years using volunteer labor, donations of stamps, in-kind printing and other services, and have no need to raise money or make any expenditures. Others are more likely to have some staff and pay office rent or, if not, still have expenditures for workshops, postage, printing, telephone, and other typical corporate expenses.

The annual budget document is the blueprint for both spending and income. A poorly conceived budget can lead to the corporation's demise. On the other hand, a well-conceived, realistic budget can be the catalyst for program planning that provides a corporate life for many fruitful years.

Line-item and program budgets are the two major types of budgeting used by nonprofit corporations. Each has its advantages and disadvantages.

Line-Item Budget

The line-item budget is as it says—a list of various categories and the amount the corporation expects to spend for each category. Corporations, from the largest to the smallest, have some of the same categories in a line-item budget. Among the most common are these 26:

1. salaries,
2. consulting services,
3. professional services,
4. taxes,
5. fringe benefits,
6. telephone/wireless,
7. postage,
8. printing and photocopying,
9. travel,
10. workshops and conferences,
11. bank fees,
12. dues,
13. subscriptions and publications,

14. data processing,
15. equipment,
16. equipment maintenance and repair,
17. legal services,
18. insurance,
19. rent,
20. office supplies,
21. maintenance and repairs,
22. security services,
23. utilities,
24. bookkeeping and payroll services,
25. Web hosting services, and
26. miscellaneous

As an expense is incurred, its amount is entered in a journal prepared for this purpose, coded by its expense category. At the end of each month, the amounts of each category are aggregated on a ledger sheet called a "monthly summary." The monthly totals should be compared with the budget for each category to determine whether spending patterns are consistent with the budget. For example, an organization can have "annual conference" as a program, and include all expenses associated with it included, such as printing, postage, travel, consulting, and so on. Or as an alternative, the individual expenses of the conference for printing and postage could be included in the organization's regular printing and postage line-items.

The advantage of a line-item budget is the ease of assigning every expenditure. A dollar spent on paper clips is an expense for "supplies," and a dollar spent on Web hosting is an expense for "Web hosting." The disadvantage is that it is not always clear how much can be saved by eliminating any particular program of an organization, because the expenses of that program are subsumed within many different line-items, such as would be the case with the example of an annual conference.

Program Budget

The second type of budget is called a program budget. The program budget also contains various line-items, but the difference is that each program of a nonprofit, such as conferences, newsletter, membership, or publications, has its own budget within it.

For example, if the organization is having a conference, then the conference itself has a budget. Printing, postage, and telephone costs are attributed to the conference. Printing and postage costs may be associated with another program, as well, such as a newsletter.

The advantage of the program budget is that one can quickly determine the incremental savings that will accrue to the organization if a particular program is eliminated. The disadvantage is that it is not easy to allocate overhead costs—such as the CEO's salary and rent—to various programs.

It is not unusual for nonprofits to combine the two types of budgeting—to have a general line-item budget, but to allocate some spending in all categories to certain programs. For small nonprofits, line-item budgets are the easiest to prepare and follow, but program budgets provide better information.

The Budget Process

Each organization is likely to develop its own budgeting process, which evolves over time based on the personalities of its staff and board, the stability of its funding streams, the needs of outside stakeholders, and other factors. The following is one possible model.

Step 1. Begin the budgeting process at least three months before the start of the organization's fiscal year, allowing enough time for the board to approve the final budget after having the opportunity to provide feedback.

Step 2. Review all programs and management achievements. Compile a comparison of estimated costs to actual costs, which is called a "variance."

Step 3. Make estimates of expenses for commitments made for the upcoming year (in salaries, new programs, capital expenses) that did not require funding for the current year, such as new programs and the expansion of existing programs approved in the organization's strategic plan.

Step 4. Make estimates of expenditure increases resulting from predictable budget items, such as salary inflation adjustments and merit increases, rent, utilities, insurance, and other categories that grow as a result of inflation rather than expansion of services or programs.

Step 5. Make estimates of income—including estimated contributions, grants, fees, the sale of goods and services, and investment income.

Step 6. Adjust spending and income based on the organization's ability to build surpluses or incur deficits, but avoid making adjustments in income based on the need to balance a budget. The reason is that spending is more likely to be controllable compared to income.

Step 7. Submit the budget to the board for approval.

Step 8. Periodically adjust the organization's budget and resubmit changes to the board as new information is received.

Expense Reimbursement

Organizations incur expenses. Many of these can be paid conveniently by corporate check. Many others can be paid by corporate credit card, which is particularly useful for travel expenses. For reasons of good financial management, it is not atypical for newly formed organizations to require two signatures on checks. This is not unreasonable for recurring expenses that can be processed well in advance, such as paychecks, federal withholding, rent, major equipment purchases, and taxes.

However, requiring two signatures does present problems when making small, but reasonable, on-the-spot purchases. An expense reimbursement system should be designed to provide protection against one person making unilateral, capricious decisions on spending, but needs to be flexible enough to keep the organization from being hamstrung when trying to pay $25 for office supplies.

One suggestion is to set up an "imprest account" to pay routine office expenses, requiring only one signature. The authorized person (such as the executive director) has a reasonable sum to disburse from this checking account, which is entirely separate from the "master" checking account. The imprest account is replenished from the master checking account using a check that requires the usual two signatures, only upon a review by the chairperson or treasurer (or both) of what was expended—including supporting documentation, such as receipts. This account should provide an amount needed not only to pay reasonable expenses for the month, but enough to cover expenses for part of the following month, since several days or weeks may elapse during the processing of the expense report.

The organization's leadership should provide general guidelines as to what types of expenses are acceptable for reimbursement and what expenses should be absorbed by the staff. For example, hotel accommodations in any city can range from $50-$300. A dinner can be purchased for $5 or $75. Many organizations refuse to make decisions concerning what is appropriate, and instead provide a per diem allowance—a flat payment that is expected to pay reasonable travel expenses for each one-day period. The staff member then must absorb costs that go beyond this amount.

Many other expense issues arise that require board policies. How much should staff be reimbursed for mileage? What if a spouse attends a conference with a staff member and shares a room, resulting in an incremental cost increase? How will expenses be reimbursed that cannot be directly documented with a receipt, such as tips or parking meter expenses?

All of these issues can be resolved on an ad hoc basis, but it is useful to think about the nature of expense reimbursement before it creates problems. Many organizations have failed because their budgets were depleted by discretionary spending in the absence of an expense policy.

Fiscal Sponsorship

Social entrepreneurs often face a difficult dilemma once they decide to run with an idea to improve the quality of life for their communities. If they create a formal organization, they face spending countless hours building its infrastructure and complying with all of the legal requirements described in Chapters 2 and 3. Yet, if they choose to go it alone, they suffer the consequences of not being able to accomplish as much as they could by having a formal organization, and face the reluctance of donors to make donations to them. Grantors seldom are willing or able to fund individuals, and donors are often wary of making donations to organizations that do not qualify as 501(c)(3)s and permit those donations to be tax-deductible.

There is a third option beyond these two alternatives that is increasingly attractive, but relatively obscure—finding a fiscal sponsor. Perhaps this is not as obscure at first glance. Perhaps the majority of scientific research is carried out by individuals who are affiliated with universities. The grantor makes a tax-deductible check out to the university, and the university passes along most of the grant to the individual researcher and handles all of the administration.

This model can be, and has been, adapted for social entrepreneurship. A social entrepreneur, instead of creating his or her own 501(c)(3) tax-exempt organization, approaches an existing tax-exempt organization to serve as the fiscal sponsor. The entrepreneur becomes in effect an employee of that fiscal sponsor. The sponsor receives the grants and donations on behalf of the program being carried out by the entrepreneur, provides a salary and benefits, handles all financial transactions, and provides financial oversight over the program. The donors receive their tax benefits, and the entrepreneur is free to devote his or her energies to the program rather than administration.

One barrier to doing this is finding a willing fiscal sponsor. Among those that might be considered are those with an interest in supporting the mission of the program you plan to pursue. This might include foundations, United Ways or similar umbrella fundraising organizations, institutions of higher learning, professional societies, museums, health agencies, labor unions, religious institutions, and arts organizations.

Of course, if you choose this route, you must be willing to relinquish some control over the organization. Technically, you would be an employee of the fiscal sponsor, and the board of the fiscal sponsor is the de facto "ruler" of your organization rather than yourself. The agreement between your organization and the fiscal sponsor needs to be in writing and quite clear as to the responsibilities of each party. You will want everything spelled out about what control you will have, and whether you will have the ability to spin off your organization as a separate, independent organization in the future, should you desire to do so.

For a comprehensive online guide to considering whether to structure your organization via the fiscal sponsorship model, see the Foundation Center's tutorial at: *http://foundationcenter.org/getstarted/tutorials/fiscal/*

Online Resources to Explore

Business Owner's Toolkit: Small Business Guide
http://www.toolkit.com/

Guidestar—Nonprofit Resources
http://www2.guidestar.org/

Carter McNamara's Basic Guide to Non-Profit Financial Management
http://managementhelp.org/nonprofitfinances/index.htm

Nonprofit Good Practice Guide
http://www.npgoodpractice.org/

Idealist.org's Nonprofit FAQ—General Management
http://www.idealist.org/info/Nonprofits

Board Source/Independent Sector: The Sarbanes-Oxley Act and Implications for Nonprofit Organizations
http://www.boardsource.org/clientfiles/Sarbanes-Oxley.pdf

John Zietlow's Web site
http://www.johnzietlow.com/Nonprofit/Nonprofit.htm

Third Sector New England, Financial Management
http://www.tsne.org/site/c.ghLUK3PCLoF/b.1354161/k.F873/Articles_Nonprofit_Financial_Management.htm

Tips:

- **Before choosing either a cash or accrual basis of accounting, verify that your organization is not required to adopt the accrual method because of government or funder requirements.**

- If you are not the individual performing the accounting, yet are legally responsible for its accuracy, periodically examine the organization's books to see if there are any inconsistencies, or whether they are being kept sloppily.

- Have clear, written policies that inform staff of the need to avoid diverting organizational resources for personal use and the penalties for doing so.

- Keep duplicate paper and electronic copies of important financial records, and store them at an alternative physical site.

Chapter 11
Personnel

Synopsis: Nonprofit corporations with staff should have a written personnel policy. There are a number of state and federal laws that apply to nonprofits that have employees and many standard forms that must be filed to comply with these laws.

Introduction

Whether a nonprofit corporation has one salaried employee or hundreds, a written personnel policy can prevent disputes that, in some cases, can destroy an organization even before it gets off the ground. Obviously, a personnel policy for a small organization will be less complex than that of a large one. It is advisable to review personnel policies of several organizations of similar scope and choose among the provisions that are most sensitive to your organization's needs. It is not necessary to reinvent the wheel, but *having* a wheel is important.

Qualified and trained personnel are an organization's most prized assets. Staff members need to feel that the organization is flexible enough to respond to their individual needs. Conversely, the organization must have the ability to operate efficiently, effectively, and economically, and to treat all employees fairly and equally. A balance must be attained, and each organization can best determine for itself where the balance lies.

Before hiring the first employee, among the issues to consider and for which to develop policies are:

- Should staff be paid employees of the corporation, or should the corporation hire a consultant? (see page 120)
- What will be included in staff job descriptions?
- How much should each staff member be compensated? Should a staff person be paid on a salaried basis or by the hour?
- If an office is established, what should the office hours be, and where should the office be located?

It may be advisable for the organization to have a personnel committee. Its role is to study the issues raised in this section; develop a personnel policy for ratification by the board, if appropriate; and serve as the adjudicating body to resolve grievances by employees.

After a decision is made to hire employees, some of the issues to consider for inclusion in a personnel policy are the following:

- *Hiring policies*—How should job vacancies be advertised? Will there be affirmative action to recruit minorities? Should the search be national, statewide, regional, or local? Should current employees be given preference in hiring for vacant positions?

- *Firing policies*—What are the conditions that permit dismissal without appeal, such as "for cause"? Will there be severance pay? Will placement services be provided? Will notice be given of unsatisfactory job performance before dismissal?

- *Probationary periods of employment*—Should there be a period of probation during which an employee can be terminated without access to any grievance procedure or without receiving benefits, including leave?

- *Sick leave and vacation*—How many days will be allowed? Can they be accumulated, and if so, how? Will a doctor's note verifying a sickness be required?

- *Holidays*—Which holidays are paid holidays and which are optional? What is the policy with respect to the observance of religious holidays?

- *Personal days*—How many personal days will be permitted, and will they be accumulated? If not taken, will they carry over? Can they be "cashed in" upon retirement?

- *Overtime policies*—Which classes of employees are eligible for overtime pay? Is overtime mandatory if requested by the organization? Will overtime be compensated in salary or compensatory time?

- *Compensatory ("Comp") time*—Should comp time be granted in lieu of overtime pay? Should surplus comp time be required to be used for routine doctor and dentist appointments rather than sick leave?

- *Full-time vs. part-time status*—How many hours per week qualify the employee for benefits?

- *Health insurance*—Is there a group plan? Will gross salary be increased if an employee is covered by the health insurance policy of a spouse and agrees not to be covered by the organization?

- *Pension*—How long does it take for an employee to be vested? What is the employer and employee contribution required?

- *Life insurance, disability insurance, long term care insurance, and other insurance benefits*—Is there a menu from which to choose?

- *Employee evaluation*—Who performs the evaluation? How often will the evaluation be performed? Under what conditions may employees exercise their legal rights to examine their files? Who has access to personnel files?

- *Merit salary increases; cost-of-living increases*—What are the criteria used for salary increases, and how often and by whom are salaries reviewed?

- *Continuing education benefits*—Are they offered? Who has authority to approve requests? What are the time and cost limitations? When do employees become eligible?

- *Staff training/orientation*—Is a pre- or post-employment physical or other examination required? Is there a formal review for new employees concerning staff personnel policies? What type of training will be provided and who will provide it?

- *Maternity leave*—What documentation is required? What is the maximum leave the employee may take without losing her job?

- *Bereavement leave*—How long will such leave be, and which relatives will be included in the policy?

- *Family and medical leave*—For what purposes will this leave be granted, what documentation is required to accompany a leave request, will the leave be paid or unpaid, and what will the effect be on unused sick leave and vacation?

- *Pay for jury duty, military leave*—What is the organization's policy?

- *Sabbatical leave*—After how many years will employees qualify, for how long, and will this be paid or unpaid leave?

- *Expense reimbursement documentation*—How will expenses be filed and what expenses are eligible? Is there a flat per diem rate for out-of-town travel or reimbursement? What amount will be reimbursed for mileage?

- *Notice required for resignation*—What is the minimum notice required, and what are the sanctions for not complying?

- *System for resolution of employee grievances*—May employees appeal to the board of directors? Is there a committee for this purpose?

- *Disciplinary sanctions for rule-breaking*—Is there provision for suspension with or without pay?

- *Prohibition against secondary employment*—What types of outside earned income are prohibited or permitted?

- *Telephone policy*—What are the organization's policies with respect to personal calls at work (including reimbursement by the employee for toll calls), and personal use of cell phones provided by the organization?

- *Payroll*—Will salary be provided weekly, every other week, or monthly?

- *Use of the Internet*—What is the organization's policy for using the organization's Internet account for personal use, during working hours, and after working hours? What work-related information may not be shared on personal social networkng sites?

While the issues may seem overwhelming, a small organization may only need basic policies such as hours of operation, vacation and sick leave policy, benefits provided, and holidays. The rest can be determined on an ad hoc basis by the executive director, in consultation with the board's chairperson and/or the personnel committee, if there is one.

Major Federal Laws Affecting Employers

Taxpayer Bill of Rights 2 (P. L. 104-168)
This law was enacted on July 30, 1996, but its provisions relating to excessive income are retroactive to September 1995. It includes "intermediate sanctions" provisions that authorize the Internal Revenue Service to levy excise taxes on excessive compensation paid out by 501(c)(3) and (c)(4) organizations, and to penalize nonprofit managers who authorize such compensation. The law also provides for increased public disclosure of financial documents.

Fair Labor Standards Act of 1938 (52 Stat. 1060, 29 §201 et seq.)
Enacted in 1938, the law provides for a minimum wage, controls child labor, and requires premium pay for overtime.

Equal Pay Act of 1963 (P.L. 88-38, 29 § 206)
Requires that men and women performing equal work be paid equally.

Civil Rights Act of 1964 (P.L. 88-352, 28 §1447, 42 §1971, 1975a-1975-d, 2000 et seq.)
Prohibits discrimination, including employment discrimination, on the basis of race, color, religion, sex or national origin. Includes prohibition of certain questions being asked by prospective employers at job interviews.

Equal Employment Opportunity Act of 1972 (P.L. 92-2615 §5108, 5314-5316, 42 §2000e)
Amends the Civil Rights Act by expanding anti-discrimination protection.

Age Discrimination in Employment Act of 1967 (P.L. 90-202, 29 §621 et seq.)
Prohibits discrimination against persons age 40-70, as revised by the 1978 amendments.

Immigration Reform and Control Act of 1986 (P.L. 99-603, 7 §2025 and other references)
Requires employers to certify that their workers are not illegal aliens, and prevents discrimination on the basis of national origin.

Employee Retirement Income Security Act of 1974 (ERISA) (P.L. 93-406, 26 § 37 et seq., 29 §1001 et seq., and other references)
Requires accountability and reporting related to employer pension plans.

National Labor Relations Act of 1935 (49 Stat 449, 29 §151 et seq.)
Authorizes workers to form unions and other collective bargaining units.

Pregnancy Discrimination Act of 1978 (P.L. 95-555, 42 §2000e(k))
Amends the Civil Rights Act (which prohibits discrimination on the basis of sex) to change the definition of "sex" to include "because of or on the basis of pregnancy, childbirth, or related medical conditions."

Drug-Free Workplace Act of 1988 (P.L. 100-690, 41 §701 et seq.)
Requires organizations receiving federal contracts valued at $25,000 or more to certify that they will provide a drug-free workplace, notify their employees of actions taken against those who violate drug laws, and establish a drug-free awareness program.

Americans With Disabilities Act of 1990 (P.L. 101-336, 29 §706, 42 §12101 et seq., 47 §152, 221, 225, 611)
Prohibits employers with 15 or more workers from discriminating on the basis of disability.

Family and Medical Leave Act (P.L. 103-3, 29§2601 et seq.)
Requires businesses with 50 or more employees to provide certain workers with up to 12 weeks annually of family or medical leave to care for a sick spouse, child, or parent, or to care for a new child.

Uniformed Services Employment and Re-Employment Rights Act of 1994 (P.L. 103-353, 38§4301-4304).
Protects the job rights of individuals who voluntarily or involuntarily leave employment positions to undertake military service and prohibits employers from discriminating against past and present members of the uniformed services and applicants to the uniformed services.

The Patient Protection and Affordable Care Act (P.L.111-148, 29§1558). Among many other requirements, requires employers to report the value of health care benefits to employees on W-2s, requires nonprofit hospitals to meet certain criteria to maintain their federal tax exemptions, and provides small tax-exempt organizations with a refundable tax credit to subsidize the cost of providing health insurance to their employees, specifically targeted for those with low- and moderate-income. See: *http://www.irs.gov/newsroom/article/0,,id=220809,00.html?portlet=6*

Pennsylvania Laws Affecting Nonprofit Employers

Solicitation of Funds for Charitable Purposes Act (10 §161.1 et seq.)
Provides for regulation and disclosure of organizations that raise funds from the public for charitable purposes.

Child Labor Law (43 §41 et seq.)
Prohibits the employment of persons under 16 with limited exceptions, and provides labor standards for the employment of persons 16-18.

Corporation Not-for-Profit Code (Nonprofit Corporation Law of 1972 and Nonprofit Corporation Law of 1988—15 Pa. C.S.A. §7101 et seq.; §7301 et seq.; and 15 Pa. C.S.A. §5101 et seq.)
Contains codified statutes that apply to all nonprofit corporations in Pennsylvania.

Directors' Liability Act (42 §8361 et seq.)
Reduces the liability for directors of nonprofit corporations.

Equal Pay Law (43 §336.1 et seq.)
Requires employers to provide fair wages for women and persons 16-21, and to keep records of hours worked and wages paid to their employees.

Pennsylvania Labor Relations Act (43 §211.1 et seq.)
Protects the right of employees to organize and bargain collectively.

Human Relations Act (43 §951 et seq.)
Prohibits discrimination because of race, color, religious creed, ancestry, age, or national origin.

Employee Records Inspection Law (43 §1321)
Requires employers to make employee records with respect to qualifications for employment, promotion, additional compensation, termination, or disciplinary action available for inspection by the employee or his or her agent during business hours, and permits the employer to require that the inspection take place during the employee's or agent's free time, as the case may be.

Pennsylvania Lobbying Disclosure Law (Act 134 of 2006)
Requires persons receiving compensation to advocate the passage or defeat of legislation to register with the State, and to disclose certain expenditures and contacts.

Minimum Wage Act (43 §333.101 et seq.)
Sets the Pennsylvania minimum wage.

Pennsylvania Workmen's Compensation Act (77 §1 et seq.)
Provides for a worker's compensation program.

Unemployment Compensation Law (43 §751 et seq.)
Provides for unemployment compensation to workers who lose their jobs through no fault of their own.

Standard Paperwork for Corporations with Employees

Federal Forms

1. Form SS-4, Application for Employer Identification Number (revised 7/07)—This is the first federal form to be filed when starting an organization. Once this form is filed, the Internal

Revenue Service will establish an account for the organization and assign a federal tax number (EIN). This number will be the organization's account for paying taxes and is requested by other government authorities for tax purposes. It is requested by most foundations and grant makers, as well. This form should be filed at least a month before the number is needed. To obtain this form, call the IRS toll-free at 1-800-829-3676, or download it at: *http://www.irs.gov* (click on "Form SS-4" from the menu at the top, left).

2. Form W-4—Employee's Withholding Allowance Certificate—Each employee must file with the employer a copy of form W-4, which documents the number of exemptions and additional federal withholding requested. The information in the W-4 enables the employer to calculate how much should be withheld from gross salary (not including state and local withholding).

3. Circular E—Employer's Tax Guide—Employers need to obtain a copy of this publication (also known as Publication 15) for the current year (call toll-free 1-800-829-3676 to request this guide), to calculate the amount of federal income tax withholding, Social Security withholding (for calendar year 2011 set at 4.2% of gross wages up to $106,800 for employees and 6.2% for employers), and Medicare withholding (for calendar year 2011 set at 1.45% of gross wages each for employers and employees, without any ceiling). The amount of wages needed to earn a Social Security credit is $1,120 in 2011. So, workers will need to earn $4,480 in 2011 to earn the maximum four credits for the year. Most workers need 40 credits to be eligible for retirement benefits. These dollar thresholds are adjusted annually. For the latest information, see:

http://www.irs.gov/pub/irs-pdf/p15.pdf

4. Form 8109 Federal Tax Deposit—This is the form used to make payments to the IRS for business and withholding taxes. As of 2011, these payments are required to be made electronically using the EFTPS system, which debits the organization's bank account automatically. Form 8109 is also used for the payment of other taxes, including Unrelated Business Income Tax (UBIT) and Federal Unemployment Tax (FUTA). See: *https://www.eftps.gov/eftps/* for more information about electronic filing. Organizations that have payroll tax liability of $2,500 or less per quarter are exempt from electronic filing requirements, for the time being.

5. Form 941—Employer's Quarterly Federal Tax Return—Each quarter, the IRS will send a form for reconciling federal tax payments that were deposited for the previous quarter. The final line will indicate if the corporation owes any payments to the IRS.

6. Form 940—Employer's Annual Federal Unemployment (FUTA) Tax Return— Nonprofit organizations other than those with 501(c)(3) status are subject to FUTA taxes. This form must be filed if more than $1,500 was paid in wages during any calendar quarter or if the organization had one or more employees at any time in each of 20 calendar weeks during the previous two calendar years. The tax rate is 6.0% of wages on the first $7,000 of wages for each employee, reduced from 6.2% as of July 1, 2011. The net tax rate effective July 1, 2011 (which takes into account offsets employers receive for payments of state unemployment insurance taxes) is .6% of the first $7,000 paid to each employee. Quarterly tax deposits may be necessary, depending on the amount owed. These deposits are made in the same way as federal quarterly withholding deposits.

7. Form W-2—Wage and Tax Statement—This statement is given to all employees on or before January 31. It details their gross salary and amounts withheld in federal, state, and local taxes during the previous year. Employees file a copy with their Form 1040 personal income tax filing.

8. Form W-3—Transmittal of Income and Tax Statement—This return looks like a Master W-2, and aggregates information for all employees. It is filed with the Social Security Administration, accompanied by one copy of each employee's W-2. Employers may, but are not required to, file this form electronically.

9. Form 990—This is the tax-exempt nonprofit corporation's tax return, and was substantially changed beginning with the 2008 tax year (returns filed in 2009). Organizations with gross receipts of less than $200,000 and total assets of less than $500,000 may elect to file the short version of the form, 990-EZ, or the 990-N e-postcard if gross receipts are normally less than $50,000.

10. Form 990-T—This is a supplement to the tax-exempt nonprofit corporation's 990 tax return that reports gross income of $1,000 or more from unrelated business income during the fiscal year. See Publication 598 for more details. Note: A 2007 ruling by the IRS requires organizations to make their 990-T returns public beginning with the 2008 tax year, even if the organization is not required to make their 990 returns public. Thus, this requirement applies to organizations that have revenues less than the $25,000 income threshold that applies to 990 return public disclosure requirements, as well as places of religious worship.

11. Form I-9—This form is kept by the employer for each worker to certify that all workers are citizens, nationals, or aliens legally authorized to work in the United States.

12. Form 1099 MISC—This form must be filed if the organization pays more than $600 in the calendar year to those who are not direct employees, such as independent contractors. One copy is given to the individual on or before January 31. The other is sent with similar forms to the IRS on or before February 28, using **Form 1096** as a transmittal form.

State Forms

1. PA-100—Enterprise Registration Form and instructions. This is the form to request a state Enterprise Account Number, sales tax license, and sales tax exemption. Every organization in Pennsylvania that pays wages, offers products and services for sale, collects donations, collects taxes, is allocated tax dollars, or otherwise intends to engage in economic activity must register with the state using this form. First issued in 1995, this form combines several forms previously required, consolidating 36 pages into a single 14-page form with instructions, and most of these pages are specialized applications that can be ignored. It was last revised in March 2009. It can be accessed and filed electronically by visiting *http://www.pa100.state.pa.us/Registration.htm.* Organizations seeking a sales tax exemption, or a renewal of their exemption, must also file an REV-72. If this is the case, electronic filing of the PA-100 is not permitted. You are also required to file a paper version if you are applying for a Small Games of Chance license. The information provided is shared with the Pennsylvania Department of Labor and Industry, although it does not replace any forms required by that department. Thus, organizations that file the PA-100 and neglect to file Labor and Industry forms are likely to receive a notice to that effect. The department also publishes on its Web site a Retailers' Information Guide (REV-717), which explains the responsibilities of the sales and use tax laws in great detail, and provides a list of the addresses of local Revenue Department district offices. You can find it at: *http://www.revenue.state.pa.us/ portal/server.pt/document/630159/pa-100_pdf.* Many of the department's forms, including the PA-100, can be obtained online at its Web site: *http://www.revenue.state.pa.us*

2. PA-501/W3—Employer Deposit Statement and Return of Withholding Tax. Pennsylvania employers are required to file and remit employer withholding taxes using the e-TIDES system (*http://www. etides.state.pa.us*) or by telephone (1-800-748-8299). They must file quarterly if total withholding per quarter is less than $300, monthly if $300-$999 per quarter, semi-monthly if $1,000-$4,999 per quarter, or semi-weekly if more than $5,000 per quarter.

3. PA Form UC-2—Employer's Report for Unemployment Compensation. This is a quarterly return to report gross wages subject to unemployment compensation. The rate is printed on the forms provided, and applies only to the first $8,000 in gross wages for each employee for each calendar year. This form may not be filed electronically. 501(c)(3) tax-exempt organizations that select the "reimbursable" option file a different version of the form. For more information, click on "publications" on the Department of Labor and Industry Web site.

4. DSCB:15-5110—Annual Report, Nonprofit Corporation. A 1982 state law (Act 46) requires all corporations to file an annual report with the Department of State if there are any changes in the names of its officers. The form must be filed on or before April 30 each year. There is no fee for filing the form. The form can be filed in person or by mailing it to:

Department of State
Corporation Bureau
PO Box 8722
Harrisburg, PA 17105-8722

The form may also be obtained from the Bureau's Web site at: *http://www.dos.state.pa.us/portal/ server.pt/community/corporation_bureau/12457.* In addition, the Corporation Bureau requires every corporation to file a form every ten years if the organization has had no contact with the Bureau during that time. The charge for this decennial report is $70. Nonprofit organizations that file the annual report can avoid having to file the decennial report and paying the fee. The next decennial report is due during calendar year 2021.

5. PA-3—State Sales, Use, and Hotel Occupancy Tax. This is a return provided by the Department of Revenue to organizations that have sales tax licenses. A license is required for organizations that sell products and services, unless the sale is an isolated transaction. This form is filed by either telephone or the State's e-TIDES electronic filing system. New organizations file this quarterly, with due dates of April 20, July 20, October 20, and January 20.

6. REV-1752—Eligible Organization Games of Chance Application. This is the application for a small games of chance license, authorized by either the 1981 Bingo Law (P.L. 214, No. 67) or the 1988 *Local Option Small Games of Chance Act* (P.L. 1262, No. 156). The form was last revised in May 2011. The fee for initial applications and annual renewals is $100.

7. REV-915—PA Small Games of Chance Approval Form. This form is used to obtain approval for specific small games of chance, and requires information about the game's manufacturer, a description of the game and its rules, and the prize structure.

Tips:

- **Don't ever be "too busy" to comply with the law and fill out all of the paperwork.**

- **Make a copy of your organization's Form 990 Annual Tax Return available on your Web site to avoid having to make copies for members of the public who request their own personal copies.**

- **Download posters that explain Pennsylvania legal requirements that apply to employees at: http://www.portal.state.pa.us/portal/server. pt?open=514&objID=553565&mode=2**

Chapter 12
Hiring, Evaluation, and Firing

Synopsis: Nonprofits have options for staffing their agencies. A planning process is necessary when hiring and firing employees, and there are legal requirements for doing so. A regular evaluation process for staff and the executive director is recommended. There is a continuum for disciplining employees short of termination.

Introduction

Few can argue with the view that a nonprofit's human capital is its most important resource. The executive director influences the direction, morale, image, and financial stability of an organization. Yet, even the least senior employee can have a significant impact, negative or positive, on the organization. Employees can be creative, nurturing, versatile, ingenious, inspiring, and team building. And they can be disruptive, destructive, infecting morale, and creating scandal that can ruin the reputation of a charity that took decades to foster.

The scandal involving the United Way of America's CEO, William Aramony, convicted in 1995 on 25 counts of engaging in fraudulent practices and generally living lavishly at the organization's expense, is just one example of how a single individual can stain an entire sector. The shock waves from the New Era Philanthropy scandal are continuing to be felt. The forced resignation of the American Red Cross's chief executive in 2001, blamed in part on an alleged policy of deceptive fundraising, was front page news. And so was the forced resignation of the organization's 5th CEO in six years in November 2007 for alleged inappropriate behavior toward a staff member. More recently, damaging stories in the media about National Public Radio and the Central Asia Institute (run by the author of the best-selling book, *Three Cups of Tea),* the latter the subject of a *60 Minutes* investigation that aired in April 2011, have rocked the sector.

As our society becomes more litigious, poor performance by an employee can have disastrous consequences. Many human services nonprofits that work closely with aging populations, children, and people with disabilities have experience with defending the actions of their employees in court, and they are at risk for damage suits in the millions of dollars. In some cases, poor performance may be a matter of life and death for at-risk clients. The responsibility for choosing staff in a nonprofit should not be taken lightly.

Each hired employee is an investment by a nonprofit not only in the salary paid to him or her. The chemistry of an organization is changed by a new hire, and bad hiring decisions can haunt a nonprofit for many years or destroy it completely.

In recent years, nonprofits have lost the stereotype of having certain characteristics compared to their for-profit counterparts. That stereotype often viewed nonprofits as—

- less hierarchically structured,
- less willing or able to fire non-productive employees,
- more informally managed,
- paying less and providing fewer benefits for longer hours,
- more altruistically managed, with less emphasis on the bottom line, and
- more interested in their employees' personal satisfaction.

This stereotype may no longer be valid, or it is at least becoming frayed at the edges. Nonprofits today face many of the same competitive and financial pressures to succeed as their for-profit counterparts. Nonprofits are becoming more comfortable hiring MBAs and those with for-profit business experience to manage their enterprises, whereas once social work degrees were the educational pedigree of choice.

Many of the jobs available in the nonprofit sector are equally available in the for-profit sector. For example, both often require a CEO, accountants, legal staff, supervisors, receptionists, Web-masters, government relations personnel, public relations officers, administrative assistants, and secretaries. For many of these jobs, the actual tasks performed by nonprofit employees are indistinguishable from those performed by for-profit employees.

Regardless, it is important to recognize that those who apply for jobs offered by nonprofits may retain the stereotypical image. It is useful to consider whether a prospective employee may have an unreasonable expectation of working for a nonprofit. This can be assessed during the job interview.

Hiring requires a positive attitude, which is often missing on the part of the hirer. First, if the hiring is being done to replace a fired employee, or resigned employee, the hirer often is distracted by the disruption caused by the separation. The hirer often is in a position of having to perform a task that is not pleasant—putting aside current responsibilities to perform the job search and interview. Few, if any, managers enjoy this process.

Before embarking on hiring a new employee, it is useful to do some planning that considers:

- What are the tasks and duties the new employee will perform?
- Are these tasks absolutely necessary?
- Could someone already in the organization perform these tasks? Do these tasks require special education, professional credentials, and/or experience that are currently lacking?
- Can we obtain these services through means other than hiring an employee?
- How long will it take to hire a new employee, and will these duties still be required at that time?
- How will these tasks change over time?
- What can we expect in productivity of this new hire?
- What support services will this person require? For example, will we also have to hire a secretary or administrative assistant?

Options—Advantages, Disadvantages, Legal Considerations

Hired Staff—The Sunday paper classifieds are usually filled with hundreds of job openings from nonprofit organizations that have decided to hire full-time staff.

>**Advantages**: Employees have the most stake in the organization; they tend to be loyal, may work additional hours, and can be flexible in doing tasks not included in the job description when necessary.

>**Disadvantages**: Employees must be paid even when work is not required, require payroll taxes and expensive benefits, are paid for vacations and when sick, possibly disrupting work flow.

Paid Contractor—private for-profit companies and individuals market their services to nonprofits to perform tasks that are intended to obviate the need for hiring full-time workers. Among the most popular services that are outsourced by nonprofit organizations are payroll and accounting. Other services that are often outsourced to private companies are Web services, newsletter production and distribution, order fulfillment for goods and services, and fundraising.

Advantages: The nonprofit does not have to withhold income, Social Security, Medicare, state and local taxes, or pay unemployment and Social Security taxes. Contractors can be hired for short-term or long-term projects and can be terminated easily, do not require year-round benefits (although the equivalent is often built into the contract price), and do not obligate payment by the nonprofit unless the job is completed successfully. The contractor may have skills and resources that the nonprofit would not otherwise be able to afford, except on a temporary basis.

Disadvantages: Hiring independent contractors may be legal only under certain limited circumstances. The Internal Revenue Service Publication 15-A *(Employer's Supplemental Tax Guide)* provides details on the factors that indicate whether an individual is considered an employee or an independent contractor. This publication can be accessed at: *http://www.irs.gov/pub/irs-pdf/p15a.pdf*

Independent contractors sometimes charge steeply to cover overhead and marketing, as well as make a profit.

Volunteers—unsalaried workers, some of whom may be there not solely because they are altruistic and want to help, but because they may be fulfilling educational requirements, or disciplinary requirements ordered by a court (see Chapter 13).

Advantages: They do not require a salary, and they are there not for a paycheck but, with rare exceptions, because they want to be.

Disadvantages: They do not have the paycheck as motivation, generally work fewer hours than employees, and may leave the organization on short notice.

Temporary Hires—hiring people for short-term employment without a promise that the employment will continue beyond a certain date.

Advantages: They permit the organization to respond to seasonal fluctuations in workload.

Disadvantages: The recruitment and administrative burden of temp workers can be substantial.

Process in Hiring

Search Process. Many nonprofits, through their personnel committees, develop a procedure for hiring new employees. Search committees are often authorized by the board to develop job descriptions, prepare job notices, cull through résumés to identify several candidates to interview, and recommend a candidate to the board. Others entirely delegate the process to the executive director (unless, of course, it is a search for an executive director). In either case, the nine basic steps remain the same:

1. **Prepare a job description.** The job description is a useful planning document for the organization. It also allows prospective employees to decide if they are interested in, and capable of, performing the duties expected of them.

2. **Prepare a job notice.** The job notice provides standard information, such as job title, description of the job, education and/or work experience required, salary range, deadline for application, and the person to contact. Decide whether the notice will request applicants to send résumés or file applications provided by the organization.

3. **Advertise the job.** Jobs may be advertised in daily newspapers, trade journals and publications, the newsletter of a state association, through the State Job Service, with educational institutions, online through the Internet at general employment sites such as Monster *(http://www.monster.com)* and Career Builder *(http://www.careerbuilder.com)*, and, most importantly, internally. There are online job boards that target nonprofit sector employment, such as Idealist *(http://www.idealist.org)*, the *Chronicle of Philanthropy (http://philanthropy.org)*, the Foundation Center *(http://foundationcenter.org/pnd/jobs/)*, and Nonprofit Oyster *(http://www.nonprofitoyster.com)*. Many nonprofit organizations also include a current job opportunities listing on their own Web sites, as well.

4. **Review the applications.** Develop a process for reviewing and ranking for the purpose of deciding who will be invited for interviews. Remember to send a letter to those not interviewed, informing them that they were not successful.

5. **Interview candidates.** The interview should be a dialogue, not a monologue by the interviewer. Let the candidate talk, so the interviewer can make judgments about how articulate the candidate is. It is useful to be friendly, ask a few softball questions first, and perhaps make a comment about something interesting on the résumé, such as a hobby, professional association membership, or award. Ask about any years that appear to be missing from the résumé.

There are questions that should be asked by the interviewers, and questions that by law cannot be asked. Among the questions that may be asked are:

- What background and experience make you feel you would be suitable for this particular position?

- What is your educational background, and how has that prepared you for this position?

- What has attracted you to apply for a position with this organization?

- What experience, education, or background prepares you for this position that would separate you from other applicants?

- What former employers or teachers may be consulted concerning your abilities?

- What are your long-term professional goals?

- What are the two or three things that are most important to you in a new professional setting?

- What motivates you to perform? How do you motivate those who work with you or for you?

- What are some of your most important accomplishments in your previous position, and what did you do that was special to achieve them?

- Describe a situation in which you had a conflict with another individual, and explain what you did to resolve it.

- Are you more comfortable working with a team on a group assignment, or by yourself?

- What are your significant strengths and weaknesses?

- Why are you shifting direction in employment?

- Where do you see yourself professionally in five years?

- How do you feel about your current/previous employer(s)?

Among questions that you may *not* ask are:

- questions relating to an applicant's race, sex, sexual orientation, national origin, religion, or age

- questions relating to the applicant's physical and mental condition that are unrelated to performing the job

- questions that provide an indication of the above, such as the number of children, the applicant's maiden name, child care arrangements, height/weight, whether the applicant is pregnant or planning to have children, the date the applicant graduated from high school, and whether the applicant is a Sabbath observer

- whether the applicant has ever been arrested or convicted of a crime, without proof of business necessity for asking.

The Pennsylvania Human Relations Commission publishes a booklet on this issue, entitled *Pre-employment Inquiries: What May I Ask? What Must I Answer?* This 8-page booklet provides details on exceptions to the above prohibitions, the justification for these prohibitions and exceptions, and related issues raised by compliance with the *Pennsylvania Human Relations Act* and the *Americans With Disabilities Act.* It can be accessed online at: *http://www.phrc.state.pa.us/publications/literature/Pre-Employ%20QandA%208x11%20 READ.pdf*

For questions, contact the Commission at:

PA Human Relations Commission
Suite 300
301 Chestnut Street
Harrisburg, PA 17101
(717) 787-4410
http://www.phrc.state.pa.us/portal/server.pt/community/phrc_home/18970

6. **Select the best-qualified candidate.** This is different from selecting the best candidate. The best candidate within the pool of applicants may be identified easily, but if that person is not quite up to the task, it is a mistake to hire him or her. It is better to begin the search again, or try to find another way to have those duties performed without taking a chance that a bad hiring decision will harm the organization, perhaps irreparably.

7. **Verify information from the résumé and interviews; investigate references.** Under Pennsylvania law, you may not refuse to hire an employee based on a prior criminal conviction, unless that conviction specifically relates to the prospective employee's suitability for employment. The Pennsylvania Human Relations Commission recommends that if you do inquire about an applicant's arrests or conviction record, you should add, "A conviction will not necessarily disqualify you from the job for which you applied."

It is not unusual for job candidates desperate to make their résumés stand out to embellish their educational or professional qualifications. A few telephone calls can ferret out many of these. This is a wise investment; someone who is dishonest enough to falsify qualifications on a résumé is likely to be just as dishonest when it comes to other professional issues. Investigating references can often turn up reasons for not hiring someone. It is good practice to request permission from the applicant to check references and to contact previous employers. While a candidate may refuse for personal reasons to permit contact with a previous employer, it is sometimes, but not always, an indication of a flawed relationship. It is also advisable to perform a Google search on the candidate's name. This will likely give you some idea about the candidate's background and interests.

Among the questions that are appropriate when contacting prior employers are:

- How long did the applicant work for you?

- What was the quality of this applicant's work?

- What level of responsibility was the applicant given?

- How did the applicant get along with coworkers?

- Did the applicant show initiative and creativity? In what ways?

- Was the applicant a self-starter, or did he/she require constant supervision and direction?

- Was the applicant punctual?

- Is there anything you can tell me that would be relevant to my decision to hire or not hire the applicant?

8. **Make an offer to the candidate and negotiate salary, benefits, and other terms of the offer.**

9. **Put the offer in writing once the offer is accepted.** Use a contract, if necessary or desirable. Once the contract is signed or the offer is otherwise accepted, notify other candidates that they were not successful, and arrange an orientation session for the successful candidate.

Evaluation

Periodic staff evaluations are an important tool for executive directors and human resource managers to communicate important information to staff and obtain valuable feedback. One principal purpose of these evaluations is for the executive director to convey to the employee, in a measurable way, how well that employee is performing with respect to each of several areas of the position. This process is useful to both parties. Most employees want to do as well as they can, and the staff evaluation is an opportunity for the executive director to share potential shortcomings that might otherwise have been difficult to communicate.

The staff evaluation is an opportunity to focus on both strengths and weaknesses. Weaknesses are not necessarily the fault of the employee. In areas where improvement is needed, the executive director can suggest strategies, such as on-the-job training, mentoring, continuing education, and additional supervision, which can assist an employee in improving performance. Many nonprofit executives are reticent about approaching the subject of poor employee performance, and many employees are unaware that their managers feel that improvement is necessary. A regular staff evaluation can put in motion a series of positive steps that assist the employee in addressing shortcomings that might otherwise fail to be communicated. For problem employees, the staff evaluation is an opportunity to formally point out shortcomings in advance of disciplinary action or firing.

Staff evaluations are generally an annual affair, often scheduled a few weeks into a new calendar or fiscal year, or a month before or after the Annual Meeting.

In a typical staff evaluation process, certain questions are addressed, regardless of whether the evaluation is a simple 15-minute, informal meeting between the manager and employee or a formal process that involves filling out survey instruments that become a part of the employee's permanent personnel record and are the basis for merit salary increases.

There are many different formats, but many organizations have a formal personnel policy that requires all staff members to be evaluated (typically by the executive director, if the organization is small enough), with a written memo summarizing the results of an evaluation interview. The memo is shared with the employee, who signs it, acknowledging that it has been read, but not necessarily agreeing to the content. In many evaluation processes, the employee is provided an opportunity to respond in writing to any of the criticisms included in the evaluation, and this is included with any evaluation that is placed in that employee's personnel file.

Issues to be addressed should include:

- What goals were the employee expected to accomplish, and how successful was the employee in accomplishing these goals?
- What could have been done by the organization to help the employee accomplish more toward meeting these goals?
- What were the areas that the evaluator found to be the employee's strongest and weakest areas?
- What can the employee suggest to assist him/her to improve in those weak areas?
- What goals are expected to be accomplished before the next employee evaluation?
- How well has the employee gotten along personally with colleagues?
- How well has the employee worked with colleagues as a team to accomplish organizational goals?
- Has the employee shown loyalty to the organization by cheerfully taking on tasks when needed that may not have been in the job description?
- Has the employee favorably represented the organization outside of work?
- Has the employee demonstrated professional work habits by arriving on time, taking reasonable lunch and break time, and not being unnecessarily absent?

- What can the employee share about organization policies, procedures, and work processes that could be improved?

Evaluation of the Executive Director

The task of evaluating the Executive Director is relegated to the Board of Directors. A formal process to evaluate the executive director is appropriate annually. It can be performed by the Chair, the Personnel Committee, or a group designated by the Board that could consist of an ad hoc committee of board members. While an interview with the executive director is a major component, an evaluation of the executive director should also include feedback from staff members, grantors and other contributors, organization clients, and other stakeholders.

Some of the areas that may be evaluated include—

- success of the executive director in furthering the stated mission and vision of the organization and implementing the organization's strategic plan;
- financial management, including adherence to board-approved budgets, fundraising, and maintenance of financial viability of the organization;
- ability to maintain and improve staff morale and teamwork;
- ability to communicate with the board, staff, clients, donors, lawmakers and regulators, and the public;
- success in maintaining and improving public trust in the organization;
- success in collaborating with other organizations; and
- maintaining a highly ethical, credible, organization.

Firing

The loss of one's job is often the most stressful and traumatic event in a worker's life, with the exceptions of the death of a close family member or divorce. For most managers, having to fire someone is unpleasant at best, and it can be traumatic. In many cases, it represents a failure not just by the affected worker but also by the organization.

Managers must be careful about how the firing is done; employee lawsuits over firings are becoming more common. When a nonprofit is unionized, even firings for the most egregious offenses may be challenged. It is also important to make sure that there is the authority to fire. For example, the board chairperson may not fire the executive director without authority from the board, unless the bylaws provide for that. The executive director may not fire the communications director, for example, unless the organization's bylaws and/or job description of the executive director make it clear that he/she has this authority.

Planning Issues

Before firing an employee, it is important to do some advance planning. Among the issues to consider are how to deal with the workload performed by the fired employee, the effective date of the termination, what to tell coworkers about the action, how to ensure that the employee will not take away sensitive files and other materials, what to tell the employee about health and life insurance continuity and pension benefits, how to deal with separating personal property and organization property, how and when to terminate e-mail addresses and passwords, how much severance pay and other benefits to offer, and whether any letter of recommendation will be provided.

When to Fire

It is usually appropriate to summarily (without warning) fire an employee for gross misconduct that threatens the organization. Examples of this are drinking on the job, being convicted of a serious criminal offense, the willful destruction of organizational property, stealing from the organization, or causing harm to others (such as clients or other employees). Most unacceptable behaviors that eventually result in dismissal are not as abrupt, and it is only after the manager has attempted a series of mitigation efforts that have failed that the employee is told to leave. Among these behaviors are unexplained absences, chronic tardiness, insubordination, laziness, and general poor job performance. Many nonprofit managers are close to their employees and shy away from taking appropriate disciplinary action. They need to realize that the health of the organization requires discipline and that they are getting paid to ensure that the organization functions. Problem employees inhibit otherwise productive coworkers.

Discipline Short of Firing

Poor performance on the job may be the result of many factors. These might include personal problems of the employee, miscommunication by the manager, or skills required to perform the task that—for whatever reason—the employee does not have. Each of these has a remedy and, if the manager is flexible, dismissal can be avoided. For example, the birth of a child or serious illness of a spouse or other close family member can leave a valued employee temporarily unable to perform job duties. Some time off, flextime, counseling, or temporarily decreasing duties can all help. Continuing education can improve job skills. Improving communication from the manager, either "coaching" on how to do the job better, or at least providing some feedback on what is going wrong, can avoid the necessity of terminating an employee. Most employees want to do well, and many believe they are doing well but are never told that their professional work is actually considered poor by those who evaluate and manage them. For some employees, however, discipline is required.

Discipline Continuum

Discipline of employers can range from simply letting the employee know that something he or she did was not up to the organization's standards to more drastic actions, such as firing the employee. A discipline continuum consists of the following:

Verbal communication. Short of the gross misconduct referred to in the beginning of this section, this should always take the form of informal communication by the manager. It should be verbal, and one-on-one—definitely not in front of coworkers. The manager should explain the problem and seek an explanation from the employee of what the manager can do to help improve the worker's ability to perform. In many cases, this will be enough. Make a notation in your records when this communication was provided and what was said, and whether the employee acknowledged the problem and agreed to improve his or her performance.

Written warning. If there is no appropriate response to the verbal communication (e.g., the employee continues to show up to work late or misses reasonable deadlines), a written memo outlining the problem should be shared with the employee. It should not be accusatory, but should state that the employee is engaging in behavior that is unacceptable, needs to be changed, and that this memo follows up on a verbal communication.

Written formal warning. This involves a formal memo to the employee from his or her immediate supervisor, similar to the written warning, but notes that this new memo will become a part of the employee's permanent personnel file. The memo should make it clear that the person's job may be in jeopardy unless there is significant progress measured by a certain date, and that this progress will be evaluated on or shortly after that date.

Suspension without pay. Some employees just won't comprehend the seriousness of being late or being disruptive unless there is a real financial penalty attached. A one-day suspension, without pay, makes it clear that the manager has authority to take action and that permanent suspension (i.e., firing) is possible.

Firing. This is the last resort. In the larger nonprofit, this may actually have a beneficial effect on other employees if they feel that this troublemaker is hurting the organization. In the smaller organization, firing is rarely beneficial in the short term; a poor employee is often much more productive than no employee at all. In the nonprofit organization, firing should always be for cause. It is not appropriate to fire your administrative assistant who has been faithful, loyal, and productive for 10 years just because the daughter of your college professor moved to town and needs a job, even if the administrative assistant has a contract that provides for employment "at will." Even if there is no avenue for the fired employee to appeal, a nonprofit manager should be convinced that the firing is justified and could be defended in a court of law, if necessary. Some may have to defend the firing in court or before a grievance panel of some kind, such as a human relations commission. In recent years, courts have considered "wrongful discharge" suits and have awarded damages to fired employees who were dismissed unfairly. If in doubt that the firing is both legal and appropriate, consult an attorney.

How to Fire

It is common courtesy to make sure that the fired employee is the first to know, other than those up the chain of command who must know or be consulted first to obtain dismissal authority.

Fire the person in private, in a one-on-one situation, or with another supervisor present, as appropriate.

Explain to the person why he or she is being fired, and point out the previous attempts to reach accommodation. Don't turn the meeting into a debate or let the person plead for his or her job. By this time, it is counterproductive to rescind the decision. Explain that the purpose of the meeting, in addition to letting the person know about the firing, is to share productive information about procedures and benefits.

Explain applicable organization procedures, and benefits, such as severance pay, outplacement services, the effective date of the firing, when to turn over keys and files, and COBRA benefits. COBRA (the *Consolidated Omnibus Budget Reconciliation Act of 1985)* permits employees who retire, are laid off, who quit, or who are fired for reasons other than gross misconduct to continue to qualify for group health coverage for up to 18 months after termination, provided they pay the premiums. The manager may make suggestions about other jobs.

If appropriate, arrange for an exit interview, permitting the employee the opportunity to share information about the organization, job description, coworkers, job function, and so on. While this exit interview may not always be pleasant, the information provided may be invaluable.

Tips:

- **Make sure your policy is clear on what is permitted with respect to using the computer and Internet service provided by the organization, both on** organization time and personal time while in the office. For example, use of the computer to retrieve, store, or disseminate pornography should be expressly prohibited. Other policies should address other prohibited uses, such as visits to gambling sites, playing games, looking for other jobs, forwarding copyrighted material, hacking into the system, or using the organization hardware and/or software for other illegal purposes.

- Consult an attorney to resolve particularly sticky personnel matters.

- Keep good records of employee misconduct and what you did at every step to address the problem.

- Treat all employees as you would like to be treated if you were in the same position.

- Keep calm, even if the employee you are disciplining starts yelling, screaming, or crying.

- Consider the advance of technology on your personnel policies. Revisit your formal document at least annually.

Chapter 13
Volunteers

> **Synopsis:** Volunteers are a crucial strength for nonprofits. They can be highly motivated and can save organizational resources. There are significant disadvantages, as well. Managing volunteers requires many of the responsibilities of managing paid staff.

Introduction

Nonprofit organizations rely on volunteers to perform organizational functions from receptionist to board chairperson. Indeed, the term "voluntary sector" is a working synonym for "nonprofit charities."

Nonprofit organization budgets rarely permit salaries for all needed employees. During times of economic uncertainty, nonprofit organizations are particularly vulnerable to budget cutbacks, ironically at the very same time that the demand for their services increases. Using volunteers is an effective way to stretch limited organizational resources, build community support, improve communications, and tap hard-to-get skills.

The changing demographics in recent decades—more single-parent households, more two-parent working families, more women in the workforce, an increasing incentive to continue working to maintain income rather than retiring—demand that volunteer recruitment, training, support, and recognition change to meet new realities.

National statistics provided by Independent Sector validate the view that volunteering continues to be popular. According to statistics compiled by that organization, 61.8 million Americans, 26.4% of the adult population, volunteered eight billion hours in 2008, valued at $162 billion.

Volunteerism is alive and well in the United States. New public-private sector initiatives are strengthening the institutions that promote volunteerism. Partnerships are developing in schools, colleges, religious institutions, and the private sector. Successful volunteer programs tap "non-traditional" sources of volunteer strength. Increasingly, these partnerships are being directly encouraged by government.

President Bush spoke to the nation about changes to the federal budget he would propose in the wake of the September 11th terrorist attacks. In his January 29, 2002 State of the Union address, the President proposed establishing a new "U.S. Freedom Corps," which would also expand volunteer opportunities (see the Corporation for National and Community Service Web site at: *http://www.serve.gov/*). On April 27, 2006, President Bush issued an Executive Order requiring every federal agency to designate one staff member to serve as a liaison for volunteer community service.

In April 2009, President Obama signed into law the *Edward M. Kennedy Service America Act*. It authorizes a 5-year, $5.7 billion national and community service bill that triples the AmeriCorps program over an 8-year period. The law also authorizes transferable $1,000 education grants to those 55 years of age and older who perform community service activities. The President's budget request for community service activities for FY 2010-2011 was $1.416 billion, However, these programs were among the target of budget-cutting measures proposed by the Republican Congressional leadership in 2011, including a proposal by House Republicans to abolish the AmeriCorps program.

Interested organizations should monitor local newspapers and the *Federal Register* for RFP announcements, regulations, and briefings about the AmeriCorps program.

Pennsylvania has its own initiative called PennSERVE, headquartered in the Department of Labor and Industry. PennSERVE is the conduit for state and federal funds to promote volunteer programs in Pennsylvania, and currently is responsible for the AmeriCorps slots allotted to the Commonwealth. PennSERVE staff recommend that interested organizations call and get on the PennSERVE mailing list to receive notification about new funding availability. For more information, contact:

PennSERVE
Governor's Office of Citizen Service
1306 Labor and Industry Building
Harrisburg, PA 17120
(717) 787-1971
http://www.dli.state.pa.us/pennserve

Benefits and Considerations of Volunteers

Among the benefits of using volunteers are:

- They do not require salaries or fringe benefits. While this is the most obvious advantage, there may be other financial savings, as well.

- They are often highly motivated. Volunteers are there because they want to be, not because it is their livelihood. If it was "just a job," volunteers might be somewhere else.

- They can speak their minds without fear of loss of a livelihood. Volunteers can often be a useful sounding board. They are often less shy about speaking out than a paid employee might be.

- They may bring skills to the organization that it may not otherwise be able to find or afford.

- They may have a network of community contacts who may be a source of contributions, expertise, prospective staff, or additional volunteers.

Other considerations are:

- Just because volunteers are not on the payroll does not mean that the organization incurs no costs. Volunteers need telephones, work space, equipment, supplies, desks, and virtually everything else besides a paycheck. Training and orientation costs may be just as high as for salaried workers.

- Volunteer retention is often a problem. Paid employment elsewhere may replace volunteering. Family commitments or other duties may intervene. A volunteer can be easily captured by competing interests.

- Volunteers, just like paid staff, dislike dull, repetitive, uninteresting work. They are more likely to do something about it quickly than would paid staff.

- Volunteers are generally available for fewer hours per day and have a higher turnover than salaried employees. Many, such as students, volunteer for specific time periods and for short terms. They often require more hours of training and supervision per hour of productive work than employees.

Nonprofit Organization Volunteer Policy

To maximize the effectiveness of volunteer help, a carefully planned strategy is recommended.

Volunteer Job Description

Individuals are more likely to volunteer to assist an organization if they have specific information about the tasks they are being asked to perform. Before requesting volunteer assistance, develop a detailed job description that includes at least the following information—

- examples of duties to be performed;
- specific skills or training needed;
- the location where the duties will be performed;
- the hours per week required;
- the time period (e.g., weeks, months) the duties will be performed;
- the supervision or assistance that will be provided; and
- the training that will be provided.

Volunteer Recruitment

Active recruiting is required to maintain a dedicated volunteer pool. The following are some ideas for generating volunteers:

- Pass around a sign-up sheet at community speaking engagements where potential volunteers can indicate their interest. Be sure to provide space for addresses, telephone numbers, and e-mail addresses, as well as space to indicate specific skills or interests.

- Include information about volunteer opportunities in any public relations brochures, media stories, newsletters, and public service announcements. Many local newspapers have a regular column devoted to nonprofit organization volunteer opportunities.

- Ask users of the organization's services if they would like to volunteer, if this is appropriate.

- Target solicitation of potential volunteers to groups in the community that are likely to have time to share. Retired people, schoolchildren, and religious groups are excellent sources for volunteers.

- Post volunteer opportunities on your Web site and on general sites that permit the posting of volunteer opportunities, such as IdeaList (see page 135).

Interview potential volunteers as you would potential employees. Be sure their interests are compatible with the organization's. Find out what their motivation is for volunteering. Is it to perform a service or advance a cause? Is it to develop marketable job skills and make contacts? Is it to have a place to "hang out" and have access to a telephone? A volunteer can have the same organizational impact, negative or positive, as a paid staff member. The fact that a person is willing to work for free does not automatically make him or her the best candidate for the "job." The organization should not lower its standards in any way. Be sure that expectations are clear and performance is reviewed.

Tell potential volunteers about the organization and obtain basic information about them, such as their skills, training, and interests. Ask about their time availability. Once satisfied that the right volunteer is matched with the right job, review the volunteer job descriptions with them and ask them if they are ready to volunteer for specific assignments.

Orientation

Make certain that each volunteer receives a complete orientation before starting to work. In some instances, a group of volunteers may participate in a formal volunteer orientation program. In other situations, a one-on-one orientation at the work site is appropriate. It is important to include the following:

- an overview of the organization's mission,
- a description of the specific task to be performed,
- confirmation of the hours required,
- a statement of whom to contact if help is needed, and
- the individual to contact if an assignment will not be completed as scheduled.

Rewards

While volunteers don't receive a paycheck for their services, they should receive other types of payment. Remember to thank them for the work they perform. Both informal thanks and periodic formal award ceremonies to thank volunteers are appropriate. Encourage volunteers to attend training programs to update their skills. Include them in organizational social events. Remember that extra "payments" to volunteers will pay off in effective service to the organization.

Virtual Volunteering

A growing number of organizations are harnessing a new source of volunteers—those unable or unwilling to work on site, but who are eager to participate in volunteering for their favorite cause by working from their home or work computer. Virtual volunteering has obvious advantages for those who are elderly, disabled, caretakers, or who otherwise are restricted in their mobility or willingness to travel to a volunteer site. For many others who are too busy or otherwise unable to commit to a specific time and place for their volunteering, this non-traditional method opens up opportunities.

Virtual volunteers are being used to design and update Web sites, prepare newsletters, respond to requests for information, research reports, and prepare advocacy materials. Virtual volunteering has appeal to those who are too busy to make a commitment, but have the ability to fit in volunteer work from home on an ad hoc basis—provided they have a computer and Internet access. While there are some limitations involved in virtual volunteering (such as no hands-on supervision or the lack of face-to-face interaction), advances in technology are providing opportunities for people who otherwise would not make a commitment to volunteer. An eye-opening feature on virtual volunteering first appeared in the April 17, 1997, issue of *The Chronicle of Philanthropy*, with a second article on January 26, 2006 about this innovative strategy to exploit this resource.

Impact Online, an organization founded in 1994, administers a Virtual Volunteering Project. You can find information about how to begin, and you can even locate volunteers at this site, which can be found at: *http://www.volunteermatch.org/*.

Online Resources to Explore

IdeaList
http://www.idealist.org/

This site, sponsored by the New York-based Action Without Borders, is an excellent online resource for nonprofits. It boasts the participation of more than 61,300 organizations from virtually every country. Nonprofit organizations can join for free, although a donation is gratefully accepted. Member organizations may post information about their address, mission, contact person, telephone number, Web site URL, and e-mail address. The organizations are categorized by 46 types to facilitate searches by the public. Organizations post information about volunteer opportunities available, a job description, what skills are requested, and the dates that the volunteer is needed. There is an application form for posting organizations that is used to verify the information. At the time of this review in April 2011, 6,710 jobs and 12,288 volunteer opportunities were posted.

ServiceLeader
http://www.serviceleader.org

Service Leader is a project of the RGK Center for Philanthropy and Community Service of the LBJ School of Public Affairs (University of Texas at Austin).While there is some original material on this site, its primary value is having hundreds of links in one place devoted to volunteer management. These links are organized in categories such as *Volunteers in Schools* and *For Volunteer Managers.* Included on this site is the Virtual Volunteering Project, which includes a Frequently Asked Questions page, manuals, and other resources for use by agencies setting up a virtual volunteering program, and material useful to virtual volunteers. Click on *Documents* from the home page for *The Virtual Volunteering Guidebook* in PDF format, *The Future of Volunteering: Children Under the Age of 14 as Volunteers,* and other useful publications.

Carter McNamara's Managing Volunteer Programs
http://managementhelp.org/staffing/volunteers.htm

This area of Dr. McNamara's comprehensive site of nonprofit organization resources has excellent material on volunteer management, virtual volunteering, risk management relating to volunteers, and contributions to the *Nonprofit FAQ* that relate to volunteering. The material on volunteer job/task descriptions is particularly helpful.

Tips:

- **Interview all prospective volunteers.**

- **Make sure you clearly define duties and expectations, and review their performance.**

- **Have a policy for volunteer termination or reassignment, just as you would for paid employees.**

- **Consider having a formal awards ceremony for volunteers.**

- **Perform an "exit interview" with volunteers who leave or are terminated.**

Chapter 14
Charitable Solicitation Registration

> **Synopsis:** Pennsylvania requires almost all charities that raise at least $25,000 in contributions annually to register with the Bureau of Charitable Organizations before engaging in fundraising solicitations. Every printed solicitation and confirmation must contain a state-approved disclosure statement. A Unified Registration Statement is available, which is accepted by 36 states and the District of Columbia, to streamline submissions.

Introduction

Under Pennsylvania law (Act 1990-202), charities are required to register with the Department of State's Bureau of Charitable Organizations. The state registration obligation dates at least to 1919. Act 248, enacted June 20, 1919, required charities to file disclosure statements with the Board of Public Charities and pay a $2 fee. Subsequent revisions to the law were enacted in 1925 (Act 347), 1963 (Act 337), 1972 (Act 246), 1974 (Act 297), 1975 (Act 50), and 1982 (Act 90). Regulation of charities was expanded as a result of the enactment of the Charitable Organization Reform Act. Act 1990-202 was amended in July 1992 (Act 1992-92) to respond to many unintended negative consequences of the law, and to permit small charities to be exempt from burdensome paperwork requirements.

Disclosure by charities was augmented by enactment of the *Institutions of Purely Public Charity Act* (Act 55), signed into law in November of 1997. By September 2011, the Bureau reported that more than 10,500 charities were registered. In February 2002, Pennsylvania became the first state in the nation to permit charities to register electronically.

Institutions of Purely Public Charity Act Disclosure

Section 9 of the *Institutions of Purely Public Charity Act* requires all institutions of purely public charity to file an annual report with the Bureau of Charitable Organizations, even if they are not required to do so by Act 202. The report must be filed within 135 days of the close of the institution's fiscal year. It must include a copy of the annual return filed with the IRS, the date the institution was organized, information about any revocation of tax-exempt status by the IRS, and information about its affiliates. Religious institutions and institutions that receive contributions of less than $25,000 per year and have program service revenue of less than $5 million are exempt from filing this report. Payment of a $15 annual filing fee is required. Failure to file this report subjects the institution to an administrative penalty not to exceed $500.

General Charitable Solicitation Disclosure Law

In a manner not unlike Pennsylvania's lobbying law prior to 1998, charitable solicitation law was fraught with loopholes and provided the most minimal public disclosure. The public was unable to determine which charities were not allocating the funds they raised for charitable purposes. Public confidence in charitable giving was shaken by several egregious examples of certain charities being in full compliance with Pennsylvania law, yet reserving little or no revenues for the purpose for which they were soliciting. Scores of professional fundraisers would agree to raise funds for bona fide charities, only to provide token percentages of the money raised to the organizations. The rest they applied to fundraising costs—in effect lining their own pockets at the expense of the public.

Calls for reform came from both the general public and mainstream charities themselves. As the United Way of Pennsylvania explained in a January 1991 newsletter—

United Way of Pennsylvania testified in support of the legislation. United Ways and hundreds of other legitimate charities, which are 'squeaky clean,' are adversely affected and risk loss of public credibility and confidence as a result of a small but growing number of 'charitable' fundraising efforts which raise money solely or primarily for personal gain under the guise of charity.

Act 1990-202

The end result of this call for reform was the *Solicitation of Funds for Charitable Purposes Act,* Act 1990-202. Many in the philanthropic sector welcomed true reform in charitable solicitation disclosure. But there was concern among charitable organizations that the reporting and disclosure requirements of this law were, in some cases, burdensome and costly, and placed a real hardship on them. The General Assembly responded in 1992 by enacting amendments that had the objective of applying common sense to charitable solicitation regulation.

The major provisions of this act (Act 1990-202), as amended by the 1992 amendments (Act 1992-92) and 2001 amendments (Act 2001-45), are as follows:

1. Every "charitable organization" that solicits contributions from the public (including foundations and businesses) for charitable purposes must file a detailed charitable registration form with the Department of State. Charitable organizations that receive contributions of $25,000 or less annually are exempt from registration requirements, provided that they do not compensate persons to conduct solicitations.

   The term "charitable organization" is broadly defined as—

   Any person granted tax exempt status under section 501(c)(3) of the Internal Revenue Code of 1986 (Public Law 99-514, 26 U.S.C. §501(c)(3)) or any person who holds himself out to be established for any charitable purpose or any person who in any manner employs a charitable appeal as the basis of any solicitation or an appeal which has a tendency to suggest there is a charitable purpose to any solicitation...

   For certain organizations, there are exemptions and exclusions from requirements of the act, including some religious institutions, law enforcement and fire-fighting organizations, and certain veterans' organizations.

   The term "charitable purpose" is also defined broadly in Act 1990-202 to be—

   Any benevolent, educational, philanthropic, humane, scientific, patriotic, social welfare or advocacy, public health, environmental conservation, civic or other eleemosynary objective, ...

   The registration statement (Form BCO-10) must be refiled within 135 days of the close of the organization's fiscal year, and must include—

   • The organization's legal name, and names under which it solicits contributions.
   • Its principal address and telephone number.
   • Names and addresses of organizations that share in the revenue raised.

- The names and addresses of the organization's officers, directors, trustees, and the principal salaried executives.
- The type of organization.
- The date the organization first solicited contributions from Pennsylvania residents.
- The date the organization solicited and received gross national contributions totaling more than $25,000 during the fiscal year covered by the registration statement.
- Whether anyone is compensated for soliciting contributions in Pennsylvania, or whether there is an intention to compensate someone.
- A detailed financial report, including a balance sheet, statement of revenues, expenses, changes in fund balances, funds raised from solicitation, and a breakdown in expenses and, if the organization is not required to file a 990 with the IRS, a list of salaries and wages paid. If gross national contributions exceed $50,000, the report must be a compilation, review, or audit. If gross national contributions exceed $100,000, the report must be a review or audit. And if contributions exceed $300,000, the report must be an audit.
- Information about the organization's IRS tax-exempt status.
- Information about the purposes and programs for which contributions are solicited, and the manner in which the contributions are solicited.
- Whether the organization is registered to solicit contributions in other states or municipalities.
- Information about the organization's professional solicitors, commercial coventurers, and professional fundraising counsels.
- Information about parent and affiliate organizations.
- Contact information for all officers, directors, trustees, executive staff officers, those who are responsible for having custody of, or distribution of, contributions, for solicitation activities, and for keeping the financial records.
- Information about relationships (such as by blood or marriage) between a governing officer and fundraisers and/or vendors.
- Information about misconduct by officers, directors, trustees, or fundraisers.
- A copy of the organization's 501(c)(3) determination letter, if it has one.
- A copy of its latest IRS Form 990 federal tax return and Schedule A.

For the initial filing, the organization must provide a copy of its charter, Articles of Incorporation, bylaws, related documents, and tax-exemption status (along with its letter of exemption, if any).

Exemptions: Religious institutions exempt by the IRS, hospitals regulated by the Department of Health, registered educational institutions, and certain veterans' organizations, volunteer firefighters, ambulance rescue squads and their auxiliaries, are generally exempted from the registration requirements. Senior citizen centers, charitable nonprofit nursing homes, public nonprofit libraries, and parent-teacher organizations are generally exempt, as well. However, organizations that have a paid fundraiser are not exempt. Organizations not required to register may do so, but if they do, they must comply with all of the Act's requirements.

2. At the point of solicitation, the charity must disclose the name, address, and telephone number of a representative to whom inquiries can be addressed, a "full and fair" description of the charitable purposes, and, upon request, the source from which a copy of the organization's financial report can be obtained. Every printed fund solicitation or confirmation, or reminder of a contribution, including if the contribution was solicited and pledged orally, must include the following statement:

The official registration and financial information of (insert legal name of charity as registered) may be obtained from the Pennsylvania Department of State by calling toll free, within Pennsylvania, 1(800) 732-0999. Registration does not imply endorsement.

Exempt and excluded organizations are not required to print this disclaimer. Every oral solicitation by a professional solicitor must include a clear disclosure of the name of the professional solicitor, that the professional solicitor is being paid for his services, the name of the person acting on behalf of the professional solicitor, the name of the charitable organization, and a description of how the contribution will be used.

3. Professional fundraising solicitors (those who are paid to raise money for a charity) must file registration forms with the bureau and post $25,000 bonds.

4. Written contracts must be made between charitable organizations and their professional fundraising counsels (those who advise charities on fundraising plans for a fee) and between the charities and fundraising solicitors that disclose the fees and services that will be provided. These contracts must be filed with the Department of State.

5. The law requires filing fees of $15 for organizations with $25,000 or less in gross contributions, $100 for contributions of $25,001-$100,000, $150 for $100,00-$500,000, and $250 for more than $500,000. It requires a $250 filing fee for professional fundraising solicitors and fundraising counsels. A $15 fee also applies to persons or organizations that solicit contributions for the relief of a specific individual and that turn over all contributions collected to that individual; organizations that only use their own members to solicit other bona fide members of the organization; and certain veterans, volunteer fire, rescue squad, and ambulance organizations that did not receive contributions in excess of $100,000 and that did not use a professional solicitor.

6. There are stringent criminal penalties and civil penalties for violations.

Form Requirements

The Bureau of Charitable Organizations is aggressively enforcing this act. In 1992, the bureau was handing out token $100 fines to those it discovered were violating the law, with the message that its leniency was only temporary, until charities became familiar with the law. In recent years, the bureau has added investigation and audit staff, and has been working closely with the Attorney General's Office to crack down on violators. According to the bureau, more than 1,000 charities have been encouraged to "come into compliance" as a result of education, registration, and enforcement. The bureau has also mounted a public education effort to raise awareness about fraudulent fundraising practices. While willing to work with charities that are making good faith efforts to overcome compliance difficulties, the Commonwealth's enforcement efforts can be tough—the bureau's Web site as of September 2011 listed 301 names for which Cease and Desist orders against charities, solicitors, and fundraising counsels are outstanding.

A packet that includes the registration form, excerpts of the law, and instructions for filling out the forms may be ordered from:

Commonwealth of Pennsylvania
Department of State
Bureau of Charitable Organizations
207 North Office Building
Harrisburg, PA 17120
(717) 783-1720 or
(800)-732-0999

Regulation in Other States

All but 11 states (Delaware, Idaho, Indiana, Iowa, Montana, Nebraska, Nevada, South Dakota, Texas, Vermont and Wyoming) regulate charitable fundraising.

For charities that raise funds in more than one state (on the Internet or by direct mail, for example), complying with the requirements of each state can be problematic, expensive, and time-consuming. For several years, national and regional charities have legitimately complained about the impracticality of keeping up with the legal requirements for solicitation law compliance. An innovative project, the Unified Registration Statement, has addressed this concern.

The Unified Registration Statement

The National Association of Attorneys General and the National Association of State Charities Officials have developed the Unified Registration Statement (URS). This document can be downloaded from the Internet *(http://www.multistatefiling.org/)* in PDF file format. This format requires the use of Adobe Reader, which can be downloaded for free at: *http://www.adobe.com/products/reader.html*

Although each state regulating charitable solicitation maintains the practice of providing its own individual registration form, 36 states and the District of Columbia accept the URS for registration purposes—all but three of the states (Colorado, Florida, and Oklahoma) that require registration. Fourteen of the 37 jurisdictions that accept the URS (Arkansas, California, District of Columbia, Georgia, Maine, Minnesota, Mississippi, North Carolina, North Dakota, Tennessee, Utah, Washington, West Virginia, and Wisconsin) also require a supplemental filing. These supplemental forms are not extensive and are available on the Internet as an appendix to the URS forms (see: *http://www.multistatefiling.org/#no_states).*

Charities may print out the PDF file directly from the Internet (or save it to disk for printing out later), fill in the information, and file it with each participating state. Instructions are provided at the Web site for printing or saving the file. A version of the form in HTML can be found on the Web site to review, but this version is not acceptable for printing out and submitting to state regulatory offices.

The URS is continually being updated and improved in response to comments provided by participating charities and state regulators. As this book went to press, the latest version of the form was 4.01, which was made public in May 2010. The following Web site provides details about the latest version:

http://www.multistatefiling.org/#version

As of September 2011, the District of Columbia and the following states accept the URS for registration: Alabama, Alaska, Arizona, Arkansas, California, Connecticut, Georgia, Hawaii, Illinois, Kansas, Kentucky, Louisiana, Maine, Maryland, Massachusetts, Michigan, Minnesota, Mississippi, Missouri, New Hampshire, New Jersey, New Mexico, New York, North Carolina, North Dakota, Ohio, Oregon, Pennsylvania, Rhode Island, South Carolina, Tennessee, Utah, Virginia, Washington, West Virginia, and Wisconsin.

Each state has individual exemptions and exclusions from registration requirements (based on, for example, the type of organization or the amount of fundraising conducted annually). Also, each state requires different supporting documents to accompany the URS and charges an individual registration fee. Charities may still submit the state's individual registration form, but most charities soliciting in several states that accept the URS find it much more convenient to submit the standardized form.

The general Unified Registration Statement, version 4.01, consists of 22 questions on three pages. It requests—

- general information about the charity;
- whether there was a previous legal name used;
- information about misconduct by the organization's officers, directors, employees, or fundraisers;
- a list of states where the charity is registered and the dates and type of solicitation conducted;
- information about the organization's federal tax status;
- methods of solicitation;
- information about the purposes and programs of the organization for which funds are being solicited;
- the names, titles, addresses, and telephone numbers of officers, directors, trustees, and principal salaried executives;
- information that describes relationships (such as financial interest or relationship by blood, marriage, or adoption) between organizational leaders and professional fundraising organizations, suppliers, or vendors;
- information about felonies or misdemeanors committed by the organization's leaders;
- the names of those who are responsible for custody and/or distribution of funds, fundraising, financial records, and those authorized to sign checks;
- banks where funds are deposited, along with the account numbers and bank telephone numbers;
- the name and address of the accountant/auditor;
- the name and address of the person authorized to receive service of process;
- whether the organization receives financial support from other nonprofit organizations, shares revenue with other nonprofits, whether anyone owns an interest of 10% or greater in the organization, and whether the organization owns a 10% or greater interest in any other organization (and explanations for all of these);
- whether the organization uses volunteers or professionals to solicit directly to the public;
- a list of professional fundraisers, solicitors, fundraising counsels, or commercial co-venturers accompanied by information about their services, compensation arrangements, contract dates, dates of the campaign, and whether these persons/organizations have custody or control of donations; and
- the amount paid to these persons during the previous year.

It also requests financial information about the charity, including—

- contributions received in the previous year, fundraising costs from the previous year, management and general costs;
- fundraising costs as a percentage of funds raised;
- fundraising costs plus management and general costs as a percentage of funds raised; and
- program services as a percentage of total expenses.

Note that the URS can be used only for registration and registration renewal, not for the annual financial reporting required by almost all states that regulate charitable solicitation. A standardized reporting form for annual financial reporting is being developed.

Tips:

- If you know that your organization is not in compliance with charitable solicitation regulations, consider "turning yourself in" rather than being "caught red-handed." Most state regulators are more interested in bringing nonprofit organizations into compliance than punishing them. Your organization's penalty, if any, is more likely to be reduced if you make a good faith effort to correct past abuses or noncompliance.

- Take advantage of the Uniform Registration Statement if you are able to do so.

Chapter 15
Fundraising

Synopsis: The basic rule of fundraising is to ask—ask the right people at the right time in the right way. There are many conventional and creative ways to raise funds for a nonprofit organization.

ASK.

The rest of what is needed to know about fundraising—the amount to ask, whom to ask, when to ask—are technical details that will be expanded upon in this chapter. However, the simple task of asking for funds for an organization is the major point of this chapter, since it is rare, but not unheard of, that funds are sent to an organization unsolicited.

Most states, including Pennsylvania, require organizations to register *before* they raise funds for charitable purposes. Before launching a formal fundraising campaign, refer to Chapter 14 to ensure compliance with current state laws.

How Much to Fundraise

There are enormous differences in fundraising techniques if you're trying to raise $10 million for a new hospital wing or $1,000 to finance the costs of filing Articles of Incorporation, 501(c)(3) application, and a roll of stamps. There also are many similarities.

First, the organization must start with a reasonable budget plan. How much is needed to finance the organization's first-year activities? Will it have paid staff? Staff salaries, benefits, and payroll taxes generally are the largest line-items in any budget. The next decision that determines the magnitude of an organization's budget is whether it will have an office, which requires paying rent, telephone, furniture, equipment, and supplies.

A good practice is to prepare three budgets:

1. A "low-end" budget, which assumes a minimum level to get the organization off the ground. The organization would cease to function if revenue did not cover expenses in this budget.

2. A "middle-end" budget, which is as realistic as possible and considers the likely availability of funds for the year, and

3. A "high-end" budget, which is optimistic enough to assume the organization can pay for almost anything it seeks to do.

In asking for money, one should tailor the "pitch" to the demographics of the contributors. It helps to understand the motivation of the contributors, as well. People give money for a reason. It may be they share the organization's motivation for starting up. It may be they feel guilty because otherwise they would not be doing anything to address a problem. It may be they desire power in the organization that they can get only by being contributors. Givers may also be looking for ways to get a tax deduction, align themselves with a popular cause, or seek immortality (such as by contributing an endowed chair or building wing that would have their name on it). They may be contributing to an organization because they want a particular organizational leader to be their friend or to contribute to their own favorite cause.

The most successful fundraising is done by requesting contributions from people who have money to give away, who both know and respect the organization (or someone on its board or staff), and who are given reasons for contributing that are sensitive to their private motivations.

It is a good idea to select some board or advisory committee members based on their ability to tap funds from their friends and associates. Many of their well-heeled friends will write a check to virtually any cause solely because that influential board member picked up the telephone and asked them to do it.

The donations of board members are often an important source of revenue for new organizations. Many organizations will identify members of the community to serve on their boards because of their willingness and ability to make substantial financial contributions rather than having governance expertise.

Board members are usually—but not always—delighted to donate when asked, recognizing that the organization, to be successful, does need some start-up funding, and it would make them look foolish if the organization is stillborn as a result of lack of seed money.

It is not unusual for external funding sources to consider the extent to which board members make contributions. Therefore, the participation percentage of board member contributions may be as important, or more so, as the dollar amount raised from them.

Always suggest an amount when asking for a donation. Of course, the solicitor should consider the ability of the person to give that amount. The solicitor also should give examples of how that specific amount will be used to benefit the organization (e.g., "Your $2,000 donation will purchase the computer system the office needs...").

IRS Substantiation Rules

The federal *Omnibus Budget Reconciliation Act* (OBRA), enacted in 1993, imposed new restrictions on charities and donors with respect to the substantiation of donations made beginning with the 1994 tax year. The law requires charities to provide a contemporaneously written acknowledgment of contributions of $250 or more when requested by a donor; the donor may not take a charitable tax deduction without having such a written acknowledgment.

The practical effect is that charities are sending these statements routinely to their donors as a part of a "thank you" letter. The written acknowledgment must include the amount of cash paid or a description of property transferred by the donor, a statement of whether the donor received goods or services in exchange for the donation, and a good-faith estimate of the value of such goods and services, if any.

Additional requirements of this law apply in cases when charities provide goods or services in exchange for the donation. If the donation is in excess of $75, the charity must provide a written a statement to the donor that the deductibility of the donation is limited to the excess of the amount donated over and above the value of the goods and services provided, and an estimate of the value of these goods and services provided by the charity. For example, if a 501(c)(3) organization holds a fundraising dinner and estimates that the costs for catering and entertainment are $45 per person and the charge is $100 per ticket, federal law requires disclosure to ticket holders that they can deduct a contribution of $55 per ticket purchased. IRS Publication 1771 provides examples of fact situations that require this disclosure.

Final regulations issued in December 1996 by the IRS provide some guidance to charities on several issues. First, charities may ignore benefits provided to members that can be used "frequently," such as gift shop discounts, free or discounted parking, or free or discounted admission to the organization's facilities or events. Second, there are safe harbors (examples that an organization can follow and avoid violating the law) for benefits of minimal value. One safe harbor permits a donor to deduct the entire value of the contribution if the benefit received has a value less than 2% of the contribution or $97, whichever is less. For example, a $1,000 contributor may receive a T-shirt and mug as a thank you gift without tax penalty to the donor, provided these gifts have a value of under $20.

A second safe harbor applies in the case of small contributions when the benefit received is relatively small. This applies to contributions of at least $48.50 when the value of the benefit provided to the contributor is less than $9.70.

The dollar thresholds mentioned above were for calendar year 2011. Each year, the IRS adjusts these numbers (referred to as the "de minimis threshold amounts") for inflation. Current thresholds can be obtained by downloading Publication 1771 from the IRS Web site (http://www.irs.gov/pub/irs-pdf/p1771.pdf) or by calling 877-829-5500.

Charities must provide written substantiation of a donation to volunteers who wish to claim as a deduction the cost of unreimbursed expenses of $250 or more. The regulations also require that institutions such as colleges that raise money by offering their alumni the right to purchase hard-to-get athletic tickets must consider 20% of the payment for the tickets as the fair market value for the right to purchase them. This amount may not be deducted.

There are many gray areas with respect to substantiation issues. It makes sense to consult an attorney familiar with this issue if there is any question about whether your organization is in compliance with IRS requirements.

Sources of Funding

Among potential sources for funding are:

1. **Umbrella Fundraising Groups** (e.g., United Ways, Jewish Federations, Catholic Charities, Junior Leagues, and similar service organizations)

   In addition to providing an important source of funding, membership in a federated fundraising organization provides added visibility and community endorsement. This is especially important for agencies that lack name recognition. Membership in a federated fundraising organization carries no iron-clad guarantee that funding levels will be sustained or increased (especially in a recessionary and highly competitive fundraising environment). However, member organizations fulfilling priority needs of umbrella groups can count on relatively stable funding.

   Although members sometimes chafe at accountability, program, and fundraising requirements imposed by umbrella organizations, few would trade their federated funding for total independence. While it sometimes appears that existing member agencies have a total lock on funding, the trend in recent years has been toward funding "cutting-edge" programs that are highly responsive to critical community needs.

2. Foundations

Major foundations usually require written proposals, many of which can be time-consuming to prepare. There is also a time lag between when the application is submitted—and, perhaps, a response to questions from the foundation on issues that were not adequately covered by the application—and when the "check is in the mail."

Many smaller foundations are managed by the philanthropists themselves who establish the foundations for tax purposes. The benefactor may write a check as soon as the request for funds is received.

Most foundation proposals can be prepared by someone without special training or education. The trick is to research the kinds of organizations and activities of interest to the foundation and tailor the grant application to that information. It is also vitally important to tailor it to the application guidelines of the foundation, since many proposals are rejected on technical grounds even before they are judged on their substance.

Many local libraries have sections devoted to foundation fundraising, including research materials with the names, addresses, and type of funding provided by each foundation.

According to Giving USA's 2011 annual report on philanthropy, foundations are responsible for just 14% of philanthropy, $41 billion of the $290.89 billion donated in 2010. However, the individual gift may be quite substantial, and the awarding of a major gift by a name foundation can have benefits beyond the financial reward. It can serve as a catalyst for other grants and give the beneficiary organization increased credibility.

3. Direct Mail

The key to direct mail fundraising is a mailing list of people who are likely to consider making a contribution. Professional services sell mailing lists categorized by various interests and demographics. Organizations may wish to send a few newsletters to such a list, and then follow up with a direct mail appeal. If an organization is a membership organization, its members are among the first who should receive an appeal for voluntary contributions. After all, they have already indicated their interest in the organization's activities and are most likely to know what the organization is doing and how its funds are being spent.

Others to include on solicitation lists are—

- persons who benefit from the service provided by the organization and families of such persons, if this is appropriate,
- individuals who are in attendance at your speaking engagements, and
- persons who make contributions to similar organizations.

A fundraising letter should appeal to some basic instinct that will make the reader have an irresistible urge to run to his or her checkbook and write a check to the organization. Appeals that honestly portray the needs of the organization and the importance of the services it provides are a basic component of direct mail letters. Among the most popular appeals are those that generate:

- *Guilt.* Make people feel guilty that they are not participating in solving some urgent problem.

- *Affiliation.* Appeal to the need to belong to an organization that is doing something worthwhile.

- *Self-interest.* Find some way to show that by helping the organization, donors' own lives will be improved in some way.

- *Ego.* Make prospective donors feel they are wonderful people only if they make a contribution.

- *Idealism.* Appeal to the idea that the world or community will be a better place for everyone and that only a chosen few selfless people will help this cause.

- *Religious obligation to give to charity.* Religious organizations have relied on this for years, but many secular organizations find this line of appeal equally effective for certain target audiences.

4. Businesses

Many organizations receive operating funds and in-kind contributions of services, equipment, and supplies from businesses in their communities. These businesses may include—

- employers of board members;

- suppliers of goods and services to the organization;

- businesses that make contributions to other nonprofit organizations in the community;

- businesses that sell goods and services to board members, members, or clients; and

- major employers in the community.

Rather than visiting a business "cold," it is effective to involve representatives of businesses in the organization's program before asking them for funds. Among ways to do this are:

- Have business representation on the board.

- Establish a "business advisory committee" consisting of local businesspeople.

- Invite business representatives to an "open house" to see the organization in action.

- Place business representatives on the organization's mailing list. Send them the newsletter and newspaper clippings about the organization's accomplishments.

- Invite business representatives to speak to the organization's board or membership about their products and services.

Many business corporations have established foundations that are specifically staffed to consider funding requests from charities.

5. Telephone Solicitation

Similar to direct mail, telephone solicitation is effective if done with the right list of names and correct telephone numbers. A college making calls to its alumni using student volunteers will certainly have a much better response than if it makes calls at random. Similarly, an organization is well served if it can tailor calls to those with a likely interest in its purpose. Note that charities are exempt from the federal "do not call" law.

6. Government Grants

Millions of dollars in federal and state grants to nonprofits that still go begging for takers. The trick is to identify the source of funds and determine eligibility. The *Catalog of Federal Domestic Assistance* is available in many libraries. It can also be found on the Internet, in searchable format, at *https://www.cfda.gov/*. This document provides a summary of available federal grants and the qualifications and conditions for applying. Using the site at *http://www.grants.gov*, you can identify and apply for federal government grants entirely online (see page 206).

Government grants usually are accompanied by lots of paperwork and operational requirements, some of which may be inconsistent with the manner in which an organization intends to operate. The Istook Amendment, actually a series of amendments placing curbs on public advocacy and lobbying by organizations that receive federal grants, was successfully added by Rep. Ernest Istook (R-OK) in 1995 to appropriations legislation. An amendment by Rep. Istook to the conference report of H.R. 2673, the $373 billion Consolidated Appropriations Act, considered December 2003, prohibited transit agencies receiving federal funds from displaying advertising from groups that want to decriminalize marijuana and other Schedule I substances for medical or other purposes. It would not be unexpected for the Congress to approve additional curbs on advocacy by nonprofit organizations that receive federal funds. In 2006, language was attached to H.R. 1461, the *Federal Housing Finance Reform Act,* that would have placed similar restrictions on nonprofit organization advocacy. As passed by the House, the bill would have disqualified nonprofit organizations from receiving grants under a new Affordable Housing Fund if they engage in partisan or nonpartisan voter engagement activities, certain grassroots advocacy, or lobbying at any point from one year before applying through the grant period. It did not become law, however.

If you are applying for government grants, learn about any additional requirements to be in compliance with the law.

7. Revenue-Generation Other Than Voluntary Contributions

The following are strategies used by nonprofits to increase income:

- newsletter subscriptions;
- newsletter advertising;
- annual fundraising dinner;
- reception or testimonial dinner for a famous person or someone well known in the field of expertise of the organization;
- sale of publications;

- fees for services to clients;
- sale or rental of mailing lists (make sure the buyer will use the list in a manner consistent with the organization's goals and it will not resell the list to others);
- small games of chance (provided they comply with state regulatory laws);
- wills, bequests, charitable gift annuities, and other planned giving strategies;
- social events (e.g., bus trips to sporting events);
- newspaper and Internet advertising to request contributions;
- in-kind donations;
- card calling (using board and organizational members to do peer one-on-one solicitation);
- fees from workshops and conferences;
- sale of exhibit space at workshops and conferences;
- special fundraising events such as bake sales, flea markets, house tours, walk-a-thons, and running races; and
- auctions of donated items (including those from celebrities) at a special event or one conducted over the Internet or at a live event.

Searching for Funding Sources Online

Government agencies at all levels, foundations, and corporations have billions of dollars to give away each year to support the missions of worthy charitable organizations. Some of these grants come with substantial strings attached, and others can be used for almost any reasonable purpose. What they have in common is that information about these funding sources is usually posted on the Web sites of the funders, in addition to being available in databases that are often searchable by categories that will help you target your search.

It wasn't too long ago that nonprofit organizations were comfortable with budgeting thousands of dollars for thick directories of these funding opportunities. Now, many of these directories are available for a reasonable fee on CD-ROM, by subscription on the Internet, or for free at scores of Web sites. If you are looking for funding from such grantors, you need to know about these sites, which will save you countless hours of search for the funds you need.

Of the almost three hundred billion dollars raised annually by charities, perhaps only 17% or so comes from sources other than individual donors, such as foundations run by individuals, families and corporations, community foundations, and corporate giving programs. Yet, there remains a certain caché to having a grant come from a prestigious foundation, providing your organization with instant credibility. The Internet has made it much easier to identify potential funders, using online directories and databases that are searchable by the funder's program priorities, geography, and type of support. Today, every major foundation has a Web site, as do many of the smaller ones. Among typical documents posted are mission and values statements, annual reports, newsletters, grant opportunities, biographies of staff and leadership, funding priorities, guidelines and deadlines, information about previous grants made (including amounts of funding awarded), and, to an increasing degree, application forms that can be submitted electronically.

Identify most likely funding sources

The first objective in a search for funding sources is identifying potential grantmakers that have a history of awarding grants in your charity's area of interest in your geographical area. Among the obvious targets are—

- private foundations—non-governmental organizations with an endowment derived principally from a single source (individual, family, or corporation) that makes grants for charitable purposes;
- corporate giving programs—grant-making programs within a for-profit business;
- public foundations—charities that make grants to unrelated organizations and individuals;
- community foundations—charities that make grants to organizations within a specific locality or region; and
- government—federal, state, regional, and local governments.

Identify foundation funding

Many nonprofit organizations depend on foundation support to maintain their programs. But with all the progress offered by the Internet, foundations will not come to your site to give. Despite that, grant writers were among the first to benefit from the access the Internet provided them to look for and approach foundations whose objectives match their missions and to manage the process of applying for grants.

Through the Foundation Center's Web site *(http://foundationcenter.org)*, grantseekers can find a particular foundation or research those most likely to be attracted to their programs by areas of interest, type of funding, or the geographical region they support. The Foundation Directory, long a vital resource for fundraisers, is available online here.

Fundraisers can read a foundation's guidelines on its Web site and learn how to apply. Many allow proposals to be sent online or by e-mail. The Internet provides a convenient way to ensure that you are sending the best possible proposal, and it helps foundation staff, as they have to answer fewer questions. Fundraisers should always consult a foundation's Web site before contacting a program officer with questions. It is wise to become intimately familiar with a foundation by reading through its site before and during the process of applying.

Foundation staff frequently complain when charities call with questions that were clearly answered on their Web site. Demonstrate to them the courtesy of looking there first. At the same time, while it has become increasingly possible to find a grant and apply for it entirely online, this is not recommended. Make "personal" contact with the grantmaker before applying. Tell the staff if you found useful information at the site. This should be done by telephone or letter. However, follow-up e-mail requests for information or responses to questions are perfectly acceptable.

Some of the information you can find at a foundation's Web site includes announcements about grants the funder has already made, contact information, strategic plans, annual reports, and other documents you will find useful in crafting your proposal. You can often find useful information from the grantmaker's federal tax return (usually a 990 or 990PF) at such sites as Guidestar *(http://www2.guidestar.org)* or Charity Navigator *(http://www.charitynavigator.org)*. The searchable GrantSmart database *(http://www.grantsmart.com)* has more than 675,000 federal tax returns from more than 107,000 private foundations and charitable trusts. You can also use popular search engines such as Google *(http://www.google.com)* to find general information about the grantmaker, those that have received funding from it, and the grantmaker staff.

Thank and acknowledge support

Cultivate a strong relationship by publicly acknowledging foundation support on your organization's Web site. Do this in much the same way as you might your individual donors, through donor listings, or even a dedicated page or online press release announcing the gift and describing the foundation's history and matching objectives. If you have done this, be sure to let the foundation know how you have acknowledged its support.

Access free and low-cost databases

Want to search community foundations by state? Point your browser to: *http://www.tgci.com/ funding.shtml* to tap into the Grantsmanship Center's database. You can find grant sources organized by topic (e.g., children and youth, recreation, arts & cultural activities, and the aged) at: *http://staff.lib.msu.edu/harris23/grants/index.htm*

Visit the Foundation Center *(http://foundationcenter.org*—see "finding funders") for searchable databases that help identify potential funding sources. Here you can find basic information about thousands of private and community foundations, including their assets, amount of grants, contact information, and Web site address.

The Chronicle of Philanthropy has a subscription-based database that includes information about all foundation and corporate grants published in that publication since 1995. If you are a subscriber to the print version (a must read for all who need to, or want to, follow what is happening in the nonprofit sector), you can use the search engine free for searches involving the last two issues.

Government Grants

The Catalog of Federal Domestic Assistance *(https://www.cfda.gov/)* has been available free online in a searchable format since the mid-1990s. The latest version of this Web site has much more useful information for grantseekers than was available a decade ago, including a database on more than 2,100 federal grant assistance programs. Here you can find access to the print editions, and find federal government grants offered in your organization's niche using a keyword search.

Consider government grant sites

Grants.gov, launched in October 2003, takes the online search for federal government funding to a higher level. The objective of this site is to level the playing field so all eligible organizations, regardless of their size or grantsmanship sophistication, can have a fair opportunity to receive federal grants. The site directs grant seekers to funding programs offered by 26 grant-making federal agencies that aggregately award over $400 billion annually to state and local governments, academia, nonprofits, and other organizations. It not only makes it easier for organizations to find grants of interest, but also streamlines the paperwork needed to apply for them and permits the entire process to be conducted online. All application forms, financial report data in support of organizational audit and performance measurement activities, grant management procedures, and information about grant programs have been standardized across these participating organizations.

The site hosts everything an organization needs to find, apply, and manage a federal grant. Even grant notifications are made electronically. Site visitors download forms, work on them offline, and then submit completed applications electronically, saving hours of time and money. The site is divided into sections that help you engage in a six-step process, consisting of finding grant opportunities of interest, downloading the grant application package, registering with a Central Contract Registry, registering with a credentials provider, registering with grants.gov to submit grant applications, and logging on. There is even a toll-free number to use to request assistance. This site is the first place to go if you have any interest in federal grant funds.

Other places to look for information about federal government grants include—

http://www.fundsnetservices.com/searchresult/8/Government-Funding.html
http://www.usa.gov/Business/Nonprofit.shtml

Don't forget that many states, counties, and individual municipalities also make grants to non-profit organizations. They often have searchable Web sites that can help in identifying funding opportunities.

Finding Corporate Support

Corporate funding sources that are not foundations do not file a 990. However, there are databases, some free and some subscription, which permit you to check them out as well. Among them are EDGAR *(http://www.sec.gov/edgar/searchedgar/webusers.htm)* and Hoover's *(http://www.hoovers.com)*. Edgar includes all filings of publicly-traded companies with the SEC since 1994. The annual filing, form 10-K, includes a lot of basic financial information, some of which may be of use to fundraisers. Hoover's includes information on both public and private companies. Some of the basic information can be viewed for free, but more detailed documents and databases require a subscription. There are other, less well known, sources for information about corporations of use to grantseekers, such as David Lamb's Prospect Research Page *(http://www.lambresearch.com/CorpsExecs.htm)*, which has plenty of links to corporate information. You can also find corporation information at Yahoo! (see *http://biz.yahoo.com/ne.html)*.

Of course, you will want to visit the corporation's Web site and learn more about its products and services, financial information, annual reports, newsletters that may provide details about how the organization is involved in its community, and biographies of key leadership.

Find in-kind donations

One thing that distinguishes corporate giving from its non-business counterparts is the willingness to make in-kind donations of company-produced products. Corporations give a staggering amount of products to charity. According to a survey of 150 of the largest corporations conducted by the *Chronicle of Philanthropy,* as much as 30% of total giving by these organizations consisted of in-kind gifts, more than $1 billion in 1999. The same survey conducted five years later found that two individual pharmaceutical companies, Pfizer and Merck, each reached or exceeded this amount in in-kind donations. And, in 2009, this survey found that Oracle (software), Comcast (cable, telephone, Internet), and Abbotts Laboratories (pharmaceuticals), Eli-Lilly (pharmaceuticals), Bristol-Myers Squibb (pharmaceuticals), Microsoft (software), IBM (software), and Johnson and Johnson (consumer products, medical devices, pharmaceuticals) joined those two companies in donating at least $100 million in in-kind products and services with such in-kind donations comprising at least 60% of their total charitable donations.

Several intermediary Web sites have sprung up to find matches between corporations willing to provide such in-kind donations and charities that can put the products to good use. In 2007, Goods360 *(http://good360.org,* formerly known as Gifts-in-Kind *http://www.giftsinkind.org)* alone distributed an estimated $900 million worth of goods, partnering with firms such as Office Depot, Gillette, IBM, Avon, and General Motors (each of which was honored with a "Light of Hope" Award for its efforts). According to the organization, more than 12,000 charities currently benefit from these donations, which come from 2,800 donors. The Web site provides an easy way for 501(c)(3) organizations to register, and there is an annual registration fee, as well as shipping and handling costs to receive goods. For example, the site was offering 5,000 diapers to member charities for an administrative fee of $569.99 at the end of April 2011.

Many organizations depend on corporate support. Corporate investment in nonprofits is based on entirely different motivations from individual philanthropy. Corporations are looking for mutual benefits. Some corporations support programs in their communities hoping that community building activity will strengthen and support their workforce. Others seek marketing benefits and value associations with organizations whose cause and good name will encourage consumers to purchase their products or services. Corporate fundraisers need to be skilled and knowledgeable in both building good relationships with corporations and helping their organizations think creatively about how they can benefit commercial enterprises.

Design your Web site to facilitate corporate support

Perhaps the Internet's primary value for corporate philanthropy is in visitor traffic. The fundraiser's Internet strategy must touch on both the organization's Web site and the corporation's. Banner ad space or recognition of corporate sponsors on an organization's Web site is important. Conversely, allowing companies to use your logo and name on their site will have a similar beneficial value, spreading the name of your organization and information about its mission to the company's stakeholders.

Some organizations develop a corporate sponsors page, typically linking logos to the corporation's Web site. These can link specifically to pages at the company's site that talk about your work, creating a "two-way street" for Web surfers. The company page might focus on the link between the particular product or service and the organization's mission. For example, a company selling baby care products might wish to be identified with an organization providing services related to infant health or child welfare.

These relationships tend to be active partnerships. Therefore, a Web strategy should be particularly dynamic—relating perhaps the regular progress toward the organization's goals with the success of the fundraising relationship.

Employee giving programs

Another form of corporate giving is the employee giving program. Companies with large numbers of employees may encourage them to support a particular organization with which they have a relationship. Employees may give individually or participate in fundraising events. Large nonprofits may also seek support from their own employees.

Because workplace giving operates as a special campaign, it may be worth creating a separate Web page for this, including integrating the option to give online and reporting progress to date toward a particular goal.

Hiring a Consultant

There are hundreds of honest, hard-working, professional fundraising consultants who will, for a fee, provide an organization with fundraising advice or even handle all of its fundraising. There also are hundreds who are not reputable. Most states, including Pennsylvania, regulate this industry, and there are opportunities to obtain information about them before making a hiring commitment. The Pennsylvania Association of Nonprofit Organizations may be able to help you identify candidates for this duty. Since most states require these consultants to register, you can look at these records (some states post reports online) or contact organizations that have hired them to see if they are pleased with the services being provided.

Tips:

- Review other organizations' solicitation materials and use effective presentations as a model for solicitation.

- Keep a file of newspaper clippings about benefactors in the community and others who would have a potential interest in the work of your organization. A few well-placed and well-timed telephone calls can be effective in reaching these influential people.

- Involve everyone in the organization in the fundraising effort. It is not prudent to isolate fundraising from the programs the organization funds.

- Always thank each donor, regardless of the amount received. A $2 check from an individual may have required as much personal sacrifice as a $1,000 check from a wealthier contributor.

- Take advantage of a member benefit of PANO—a free electronic subscription to a weekly electronic newsletter from GrantStation *(http://www.grantstation. com/)* with scores of current grant opportunities. PANO membership also provides a discount to GrantStation services, including its Find-a-Funder database.

Chapter 16
Writing Effective Grant Proposals

by Michael A. Sand

Synopsis: Grant applicants should research the grantor before applying. They should not deviate from the format of the grant application except with express permission. There is a formula to follow for effective grant applications that, among other components, emphasizes the needs of the community, not those of the applicant.

Introduction

Competition for government, corporate, and foundation grants is increasing. At the same time, funding from government sources for human services is shrinking, and the demand for human services is skyrocketing.

In response, charities are becoming more sophisticated in the ways they seek alternative sources of funding. Many are hiring development staff with specialized training and experience in obtaining grants. Others without the resources to make such a major investment are forced to do what they can. The purpose of this chapter is to provide a framework for the preparation of proposals for those without substantial grantsmanship experience.

It is often useful for grant seekers to develop the attitude that the relationship between them and the grantors is collaborative. True, all of the wonderful plans you have in mind will never come to fruition without the funds. However, the grantor needs the creativity, dedication, staff resources, and vision provided by the grant recipient. A grant proposal that is seen as simple begging is not as likely to be as successful as one that encourages the grantor to become a partner in an effort that will have substantial benefits to the community.

Before embarking on a costly and time-consuming search for grants, verify that the purpose of the grant is consistent with the organization's mission. Some organizations apply for grants simply because the money is available and obtainable, and they have a plan to win it. However, a successful grant application may result in the organization losing its focus if the grant is inconsistent with its direction.

Even if the grant's purpose is consistent with the mission, consider whether the project is viewed as constructive by the organization's stakeholders, such as members of the board, clients, and staff. It may be useful to convene a focus group to gauge whether the grant would truly be beneficial to the organization and its clients.

In addition, organizations should consider cash-flow issues, grant eligibility, the politics of the grant, and the source of the grant. The check from the funder may arrive months after the organization has committed itself to hiring staff and paying other project costs. Is a source of funds available until the grant funds are received? Are there laws or other grant requirements that must be adhered to that, for any reason, you are unable or unwilling to honor? Have the grants for which you are applying been promised informally in advance to other organizations? Does the grantor have a reputation for making unreasonable demands on the organizations it funds?

Researching the Grantor

Once you believe a funding source may have funds available, do not begin to write the grant application until you have tried to find the answer to several questions. Try to obtain an interview with a representative of the funder before beginning to fill in the funding application. In any case, you should have the following information before beginning the proposal-writing stage:

1. The application format

Why write a 30-page application when a three-page application would have been funded? Why write a three-page application and not get funded when a 10-page proposal would have been accepted? Many government agencies will send you a *Request for Proposal* (RFP) that will outline exactly what should be included in the application. Many larger foundations will provide specific instructions.

If you are given written instructions by a funding source, do not deviate from these instructions without permission. One major reason grants do not get funded is that the writer does not follow the instructions to the letter. Even minor deviations can make the proposal ineligible. If you believe a particular instruction does not apply to your situation, request written permission from the funder to make changes.

2. Motivation of the funding source

Many funding sources specialize in awarding grants for specific purposes. An organization will not receive a grant from such a funder unless the proposal clearly is responsive to the vision and mission of the funding organization. When applying for a government grant, for example, obtain and study the legislative history that led to a funding appropriation. When applying for foundation funds, be sure to obtain the donor's funding instructions. Many corporate and family foundations have a priority listing of the types of programs they fund and will be glad to share this information.

3. The amount of funds awarded by the grantor per award, and the amount of total funds awarded

This will be extremely helpful information if you can obtain it. In many instances, a government agency has a specific allocation of funds for a particular program. Large foundations set specific priority areas and make general allocations in the priority area. Foundation directories provide information about the priority areas of grantors and are available in most public libraries. It just makes no sense to develop a grant application if the funds awarded by the source are too small for the organization's program needs.

4. Successful applications that were funded in previous funding cycles

Perhaps the best indicator of the types of funding applications that will be successful is a review of actual applications that have been funded. A strong argument can be made that government agencies have an obligation to provide you (as a taxpayer) with copies of funded applications. While you may have to review the applications at the agency's headquarters or pay for duplication, you should be able to review past grants.

Many foundations will provide a list of the previous year's grants and the total of each. You can contact a funded organization and ask for a copy of its application. While lists of past grants are often difficult to obtain from businesses, many annual reports and business newsletters include a list of grants that have been awarded and their sources.

5. The names of individuals making the funding decisions and their backgrounds

When writing a grant application, it is important to know who will be reviewing it. If the reviewers have extensive expertise in your field, you will not have to define every term. In many instances, however, a foundation trustee or a business official on the allocations committee will not have any knowledge of your particular field. You will then have to carefully explain your services in layman's terms, spell out every abbreviation, and define each technical term you use.

6. The criteria used in making the grant selection

Knowing the selection criteria can be crucial in determining how to write a grant. Many grantor agencies have limited amounts of funds and will give preference to smaller grants. Others will make the selection based on non-cost factors and then negotiate the cost of the proposal. Knowing whether it will be helpful or harmful to have political officials contact the grantor agency is important information.

Sections of a Grant Application

1. Cover Letter

Many grant applications specifically request a cover letter and define what information should be included. If this is not expressly prohibited by the grant application format, write a short cover letter on the organization's stationery that—

- is addressed to the appropriate individual at the grantor agency, making sure the name, title, agency name, and address are absolutely correct;

- contains a one-sentence description of the proposal;

- provides the number of participants, jobs obtained, or other units to be funded by the grant;

- lists the total amount of funds requested; and

- provides the name, address, and telephone number of the individual at the requesting organization the grantor can contact to request additional information.

2. Executive Summary

Include in this section a succinct summary of the entire proposal.

3. Introduction

Provide important information that may not appear elsewhere in the grant application. Items you might include are—

- your organization's mission;
- how long you have been providing the type of service included in this program;

- a brief history of your organization;
- major indicators that you are capable of operating programs efficiently and effectively
- If there are eligibility requirements in the proposal, a statement that you are eligible to receive the funds;
- IRS Section 501(c) tax-exempt status determination letter;
- outline of letters of support from past clients, representatives of cooperating agencies, and legislative officials (The letters themselves should be included as appendices to the application.); and
- a statement of how you will obtain funding for the program at the end of the grant period.

4. Need

For a grant to be funded, the organization must demonstrate the need of individuals in the community for the service to be provided. What is the extent of the need and how is the need documented? The need described should be the need of the individuals in the community for the services, not the need of the organization. Rather than stating, "We need a counselor because our organization doesn't have one," or "The funds for the one we had were cut back by the government," estimate the number of individuals who need counseling services. The need should be the need in your coverage area. While national or statewide figures might be given, if you serve a particular county, the estimate of need for that county should be provided.

The need should be the need for the particular service you are providing. If you provide services for victims of domestic violence, for example, the estimated number of victims of domestic violence should be provided, rather than unemployment figures or other available statistics. The need should be quantified. How many individuals do you believe are eligible for the particular service you provide in your coverage area?

Common sources of data are—

- **Census Data**—Make certain you are using data from the most recent census. In most cases, earlier data are outdated.

- **County Planning Departments**—Call the office of your county government to find the telephone number for your county's planning department.

- **State Agencies**—The Departments of Education, Health, Labor and Industry, and Public Welfare are all excellent sources of data.

- **Local Governments**—Local police departments are excellent sources of crime data, and local school districts can provide educational information.

- **Self-generated data**—In many cases, you can provide the data from sources within your organization. Sources might include—

  a. waiting lists,
  b. letters from potential clients requesting a service (with identifying information deleted),
  c. letters complaining that a particular service is not in existence,
  d. testimony at public hearings,

e. Information obtained from questionnaires administered to present clients asking them to list other services they might like, and

f. community surveys.

5. Objectives

Objectives are the proposed results of the project. Objectives should have the following characteristics:

- They are measurable. How many individuals do you estimate will participate in your program?

- They are time-based. How many individuals do you estimate will participate in your program in the next three months? In the next year?

- They are realistic.

The information needed to measure objectives can be obtained as part of the program funded by the grant. Do not list objectives in your proposal that are impossible to measure.

6. Project Description

Here is where you will outline your program. An easy way to remember what to include are the 6 W's of program writing:

- **Who?** Who are the clients? How are they selected? What are the restrictions (e.g., age, income, geographic)? Who are the staff members?

  If you are asking the funding source to pay for new staff members, include a job description and a qualifications statement that lists the education, experience, and other job requirements. If you are applying for funds to continue existing staff, include a résumé and a biographical statement for each staff member.

- **What?** What services will be provided? What will be the benefits of this program? What are the expected outcomes? For educational programs, include a course outline. You may include relevant sections of an operations manual. For other programs, a narrative outlining the services would be appropriate. Still others might provide a "day in the life of a client." What outreach efforts will be made?

- **Where?** Where will the services be provided? Give the addresses of all main and field offices. If you will be obtaining new space with the program funds, what type of space are you seeking?

- **When?** What are the hours that services will be provided? On which days during the year will services be provided? It is also useful to provide a timetable for project implementation.

- **With whom?** What other agencies are participating with you in the provision of services? For example, include agencies referring clients to you. Outline the agencies to which you refer clients. It is important to obtain letters from the other agencies confirming any relationships you describe.

- **Why?** Why are you providing these services rather than alternatives? Are you utilizing any unique approaches to the provision of services?

7. Budget

If it is not clear from the grant application forms, ask the funding source how much financial detail is required. Many businesses, for example, may only require the total amount you are going to spend. On the other hand, most government agencies require a line-item budget that includes a detailed estimate of all funds to be spent. Such a budget might be set up to include the following:

- **Personnel costs** (salaries, fringe benefits, consultant and contract services)

- **Non-personnel costs** (travel, office space, equipment, consumable supplies, and other costs such as telephone, postage, and indirect costs)

Some grantors may require your organization to contribute a matching share. If you are permitted to include in-kind or non-cash expenditures, use the same budget categories as above. In the personnel category, for example, you would list the worth of the time volunteers are contributing to your program. In the non-personnel category, you would include the market value of the equipment donated to your program.

8. Evaluation (see Chapter 30)

Inform the funding source that you will be conducting an evaluation of the services you are providing.

- **Detail who will participate in the evaluation process.** Outline the participation of board members, staff members, clients, experts in the substantive field, and representatives of the community in the evaluation process. Some grantors require an independent evaluator.

- **Explain what will be evaluated.** List some of the issues the evaluation team will consider. For example, the evaluators will review whether the need was reduced as a result of providing the services. Were the objectives met? Were the services provided as outlined in the Project Description section? Will the budget be audited by an outside firm and, if not, who will review the receipts and expenditures?

- **Specify what type of evaluation will be provided.** Provide in as much detail as you can how the program will be evaluated. If formal classes are provided, include the pre- and post-test you will use to evaluate them.

If a client questionnaire will be used, attach a copy to the application. Describe how the program data will be reviewed in the evaluation process. Include a description of the audit or the process you will use to review the budget items.

9. Conclusion

In no more than two or three paragraphs, summarize the proposal's main points and the reasons the community will be improved as a result of successful completion of the project.

When you have finished writing your grant application, ask yourself the following questions before you send it to the funding source:

- Is the application free of the jargon of your field?
- Are all abbreviations spelled out the first time you use them?
- Have you followed all of the instructions in the Request for Proposal (RFP)?
- Are all words spelled correctly? Remember that your computer's spell-checker only tells you that the words you use are spelled correctly and in English, not that they are the correct words for the context.
- Is your application interesting to read?
- If you were the grantor agency, would you fund it?

Finally, get the application in the hands of the grantor well before the deadline. The fundraising field is replete with horror stories about multi-million dollar proposals that were not even considered because someone put the application in the mail and it didn't arrive until well after the deadline. Make sure there is enough postage if the application is mailed. It is highly recommended that applications be either hand-delivered or sent by a trackable, overnight courier, such as UPS or Federal Express. Make several office copies before submitting the original, and be sure that you provide the number of copies requested by the grantor.

Tips:

- **Double check your proposal for spelling and grammar, that all pages are included in the proposal (i.e., the last page was not left in the copy machine as a result of making a copy of the submission for your files), that the correct number of copies is provided, and that all attachments are included.**

- **Hand deliver your grant proposal, or use a trackable, reliable delivery service. Track the package to see if it has arrived prior to the deadline. This is not the time to save a few dollars by putting your proposal in the mail.**

- **Even if your proposal is rejected, send a short thank-you letter to the funder for the opportunity to submit the proposal, and expressing a willingness to maintain a relationship with respect to future funding opportunities.**

- **Be careful what you wish for; you might get it. Begin thinking about how to administer a grant even before you apply for it. You may decide that the stress of winning a particular grant might be too much on your organization.**

Chapter 17
Lobbying

Synopsis: Lobbying by nonprofit corporations is not only legal, but should be encouraged. There are effective strategies for communicating with legislators in person, by letter, or by telephone. Pennsylvania requires lobbyists to be registered and report expenditures.

Lobbying is the time-honored tradition of communicating with elected or appointed officials for the purpose of influencing legislation and other public policy. The word itself derives from the outer room of the legislative chambers where paid professionals congregated, seeking to button-hole legislators before they cast their votes. In recent years, the term has developed a pejorative character as the public, justified or not, perceives special interest lobbyists as using their influence to work against the public interest. This general mistrust of lobbyists has been exacerbated by a corruption scandal that rocked the nation's Capital in 2006 involving the lobbying efforts of Jack Abramoff, an independent lobbyist, with close ties to Congressional leaders and the White House.

Organized lobbying is an effective way to communicate an organization's views on a pending issue, to promote a favorable climate for those served, and to directly influence the outcome of decision-making. Lobbyists are employed by organizations who view themselves as working in the public interest—speaking for the poor and disenfranchised, improving the environment, establishing programs to serve the disabled, or expanding government support for vital human service and community needs.

Whether referred to as "advocacy," "government relations," or "lobbying," it is a right afforded by the First Amendment to the U.S. Constitution relating to freedom of speech, as well as the right to petition to redress grievances. Many of the public policy decisions made in Washington, state capitals, and cities and towns have a direct effect on nonprofit organizations and the client interests they serve.

Many nonprofits are expressly created to advance one cause or another whose fate is considered by a government body.

Pennsylvania Legal Requirements for Lobbying

A completely revised lobbying law took effect in Pennsylvania on January 1, 2007, replacing the 1998 lobbying disclosure law. A Commonwealth Court decision in 2000 had declared that law to be unconstitutional, and a 3-3 vote by the Pennsylvania Supreme Court in 2002 failed to overturn that decision. As a result, Pennsylvania was the only state in the country that did not regulate lobbying for several years, although at one point, the State Senate adopted rules regulating lobbying of that body.

The *Lobbying Disclosure Law* was enacted on November 1, 2006. It is much broader in application compared to the laws it replaces, and covers lobbying of the House, Senate, and executive branch. Over the objections of the Pennsylvania Association of Nonprofit Organizations, the law applies to lobbying by charitable organizations, and considers advocacy activities tantamount to lobbying.

The Act defines a lobbyist as—

> *Any individual, association, corporation, partnership, business trust or other entity that engages in lobbying on behalf of a principal for economic consideration. The term includes an attorney at law while engaged in lobbying.*

The term "lobbying" is defined as—

> *An effort to influence state legislative or administrative action. The term includes (1) direct or indirect communication; (2) office expenses; and (3) providing any gift, hospitality, transportation or lodging to State official or employee for the purposes of advancing the interest of the lobbyist or principal.*

Lobbyists must register with the Pennsylvania Department of State within 10 days of acting as a lobbyist. There is a $100 biennial registration fee. Exemptions from registration requirements are provided to the media, volunteers who don't receive any compensation for their lobbying, those who receive less than the $2,500/quarter spending threshold, employees who lobby less than 20 hours per quarter on behalf of their employer or all of their principals, and representatives of bona fide churches protecting their free exercise religious rights. There are fines assessed against those who fail to register, fail to file reports, or who file false or misleading information. A lobbying ban for up to five years is an additional potential sanction available to enforcement authorities.

Pennsylvania Reporting Requirements

Under the new law (Act 134), expense reports must be filed quarterly, due within 30 days after the quarter that is covered by the report. Reports are required when total expenses for lobbying activity exceeds $2,500 for a registered principal in any calendar quarter. Those who are registered as lobbyists must file a statement when their expenses don't reach that threshold.

Reporting includes—

- contact information;
- total lobbying costs;
- costs for gifts and hospitality. All gifts valued at more than $250 to a legislator, regulator, or staff member must be disclosed. Hospitality includes meals, beverages, recreation, and entertainment, but does not include the costs of receptions; and
- costs of direct communication. The term is defined as—

> *an effort, whether written, oral or by any other medium, made by a lobbyist or principal, directed to a state official or employee, the purpose or foreseeable effect of which is to influence legislative action or administrative action. The term may include personnel expenses and office expenses.*

- costs of indirect communication. The term is defined as—

> *an effort, whether written, oral, or by any other medium, to encourage others, including the general public, to take action, the purpose or foreseeable effect of which is to directly influence legislative action or administrative action. The term includes letter-writing campaigns, mailings, telephone banks, print and electronic media advertising, billboards, publications and educational campaigns on public issues.*

The term does not include regularly published newsletters distributed primarily to an organization's members.

A copy of the law, regulations, registration and reporting forms, and additional details may be found at: *http://www.dos.state.pa.us/campaignfinance/site/default.asp*

For more information, contact:

Pennsylvania Department of State
Division of Campaign Finance and Lobbying Disclosure
210 North Office Building
Harrisburg, PA 17120
(717)787-5280

Federal Legal Requirements for Lobbying

Lobbying is regulated at both the state and federal levels. Although there may be similarities between state and federal requirements, lobbyists must register separately with federal and state regulatory offices.

Federal Requirements

The *Lobbying Disclosure Act*, PL 104-65, was enacted on December 19, 1995, and provides major changes in registration and reporting requirements for lobbying the Congress and the Executive Branch. The bill also includes a provision (Section 18) that places restrictions on the lobbying by nonprofit civic leagues and social welfare organizations, among others, which receive federal funds. The effective date of the act was January 1, 1996. Minor changes were made by the *Lobbying Disclosure Technical Amendments Act of 1998*. On September 14, 2007, President George Bush signed into law the *Honest Leadership and Open Government Act*, which made substantive reforms affecting lobbying, a response to a major scandal. This law made major changes in lobbying reporting requirements, gift disclosure, and travel financed by lobbyists. Of particular importance are the following:

* Lobbying disclosure forms are required to be filed quarterly rather than semi-annually.
* Thresholds for reporting lobbying expenses were reduced.
* Information requirements for reporting and disclosure were expanded.
* New reports are required relating to political contributions made by, or transferred to politicians by, lobbyists.
* With some exceptions, gifts to members of Congress and their staff from lobbyists are prohibited.
* With some exceptions, lobbyists, or organizations that employ them, may not pay for the private travel of members of Congress or their staff.
* Lobbyists may not participate in privately funded Congressional travel.

The *Lobbying Disclosure Act* defines "lobbying contact" as—

> *any oral or written communication (including an electronic communication) to a covered executive branch official or a covered legislative branch official that is made on behalf of a client with regard to—*
>
> *(i) the formulation, modification, or adoption of Federal legislation (including legislative proposals);*

> *(ii) the formulation, modification, or adoption of a Federal rule, regulation, Executive order, or any other program, policy, or position of the United States Government;*
> *(iii) the administration or execution of a Federal program or policy (including the negotiation, award, or administration of a Federal contract, grant, loan, permit, or license); or*
> *(iv) the nomination or confirmation of a person for a position subject to confirmation by the Senate.*

It defines "lobbyist" as—

> *any individual who is employed or retained by a client for financial or other compensation for services that include more than one lobbying contact, other than an individual whose lobbying activities constitute less than 20 percent of the time engaged in the services provided by such individual to that client over a six month period.*

A packet of materials, including a copy of the *Lobbying Disclosure Act*, registration and expense reporting forms, instruction booklets for filling out the forms, and answers to frequently asked questions, can be obtained by contacting—

Secretary of the Senate
Office of Public Records
232 Hart Senate Office Building
Washington, D.C. 20510
(202) 224-0758

Unless they are self-employed, individual lobbyists do not register with the House and Senate. The law requires registration by lobbying firms, defined as entities with one or more employees who act as lobbyists for outside clients. A separate registration is required for each client. A typical nonprofit that has one or more employees who engage in lobbying activities is required to register, provided that its expenses attributable to lobbying exceed $10,000 in a semi-annual period (either January 1-June 30 or July 1-December 31). Registration is required no later than 45 days after a lobbyist first makes a lobbying contact or is employed to do so, whichever comes earlier. To register, the organization must electronically file a Form LD-1 in duplicate with the Secretary of the Senate and the Clerk of the House:

Secretary of the Senate
Office of Public Records
232 Hart Senate Office Building
Washington, D.C. 20510
(202) 224-0758

Clerk of the House
Legislative Resource Center
B106 Cannon House Office Building
Washington, D.C. 20515
(202) 226-5200

Registration discloses general information, a description of the registrant's business or activities (e.g., social welfare organization), and a list of employees who act or are expected to act as lobbyists (an employee is not considered to be a lobbyist if he/she spends less than 20% of his or her time lobbying). Also disclosed are an indication of the issues to be lobbied (selected from a list of 74 general categories, such as "welfare"), and the specific issues to be addressed, including specific bill numbers or executive branch activities.

Online forms and instructions can be found at: *http://lobbyingdisclosure.house.gov/*

Expense Reporting Requirements

Registered organizations are required to file four quarterly reports each year. The reports are due 20 days after each quarter. One copy each must be filed with the Secretary of the Senate and the Clerk of the House. Organizations employing lobbyists must report whether their lobbying expenses were less than $5,000, or more. If lobbying expenses were more than $5,000, the organization must make a good-faith estimate, rounded to the nearest $10,000, of its lobbying expenses during the reporting period.

Organizations must also file a separate sheet on each general lobbying issue that was engaged, specific information about each bill or executive branch action, houses of Congress and federal agencies contacted, and the name and title of each employee who acted as a lobbyist. Online forms and instructions can be found at: *http://lobbyingdisclosure.house.gov*

Effective Strategies for Lobbying and Advocacy

- Get to Know Legislators—Give them the information they need to help the nonprofit organization meet its objectives.

- Identify Key Contacts—Survey the organization's network to discover who has a personal or professional relationship with key public policy decision-makers, and who contributes to political campaigns.

- Target Decision-Makers—Pay special attention to legislative leadership, the majority and minority chairpersons of relevant committees, and their staffs.

- Use Local Resources—Identify constituents connected to the organization, such as board members and organization members. Match them with their legislators, and assign them to meet with these particular legislators on issues of concern to the organization.

- Schedule Lobby Days—Many nonprofit organizations and other groups schedule a Capitol Lobby Day. Such events typically include a briefing on an important pending issue by the organization's executive director, a rally and/or press conference in the Capitol, scheduled office visits to local legislators and legislative leadership, and a closing session conducted by the organization's staff to exchange information gleaned from those visited.

- Schedule Press Conferences—Nongovernmental organizations can hold press conferences in the Capitol or on the steps of the Capitol.

- Circulate Petitions—While viewed as one of the least effective forms of lobbying, the presentation to a legislator or government official of a petition signed by thousands of persons is a worthy "photo opportunity" and may get some media coverage.

- Present Awards—Many nonprofit organizations present a "Legislator of the Year" or similar award to recognize key legislators for their interest in the issues of concern to that nonprofit. These awards further cement a positive relationship and ensure continued access to that legislator.

- Arrange Speaking Engagements—Most legislators are delighted to receive invitations to address groups of their constituents. Such gatherings provide opportunities to educate the legislator on issues of interest to the organization through questions and comments from the audience.

- Provide Contributions—Organizations exempt under Section 501(c)(3) may not establish political action committees. Other exempt organizations may do so and pay administrative and other indirect expenses of their affiliated Political Action Committees (PACs). However, money is still considered to be the mother's milk of politics. Those who make contributions find their access to public policy makers is vastly improved. As a general rule, the more an organization's activities are perceived to be in the public interest, the less need there is to rely on making political contributions to develop access and to deliver the organization's message. A 2006 publication of the Alliance for Justice, *The Connection: Strategies for Creating and Operating 501(c)(3)s, 501(c)(4)s, and PACs* is available for $35, including shipping and handling *(http://www.afj.org)*. It is an excellent guide for charities and social welfare organizations that want to influence the political process without violating federal laws and regulations.

- Request Public Hearings—Public hearings held by a legislative committee provide an opportunity for media coverage, a forum for an organization's point of view, and a way to galvanize support for an issue. Having an organization's clients fill a hearing room sends a clear message to the committee members and staff. While it is true that the suggestion by a committee chairperson to hold hearings on an issue may be a strategy to delay or kill a bill, public hearings can nevertheless be utilized by the organization to focus attention on an issue. A hearing can generate public and media support. It can provide a forum for improving the proposal, thereby minimizing opposition to the legislation.

501(h) Election

The U.S. Congress in 1976 enacted a law that expanded the rights of nonprofits to lobby. However, it was not until August 30, 1990, that the IRS and Treasury Department promulgated final regulations to implement this law. In the preceding 14 years, there had been a pitched battle between nonprofits and the Congress. Nonprofits fought diligently to preserve their rights to lobby under the Constitution and the 1976 law. Some in the executive branch also sought to deny those rights. The principal issue is the definition of the term "substantial," since the law prohibits 501(c)(3) nonprofits from carrying on "substantial" lobbying activities.

The regulations permit electing organizations to spend on lobbying, on a sliding scale, up to 20% of their first $500,000 in expenditures, and up to 5% of expenditures over $1.5 million—with a $1 million ceiling in each year. Organizations can spend no more than a quarter of their lobbying expenses on grass-roots lobbying (communications to the general public that attempt to influence legislation through changing public opinion).

These regulations exclude certain expenditures from lobbying, including—

1. Communications to members of an organization that brief them on provisions of legislation, but do not urge that they take action to change those provisions.

2. Communications to legislators on issues that directly affect the organization's own existence, such as changes to tax-exempt status law, or lobbying law.

Of major importance to nonprofits, the organization would no longer be subject to the "death penalty" (i.e., the total revoking of their tax-exempt status) for violations. There is a system of sanctions replacing that.

All 501(c)(3)s must report the amount they spend on lobbying on their Form 990 annual federal tax returns.

IRS Regulations on Lobbying

The August 1990 regulations of the Treasury Department with respect to lobbying are quite complicated. An excellent 57-page publication, *Being a Player: A Guide to the IRS Lobbying Regulations for Advocacy Charities,* is available from The Alliance for Justice, Eleven Dupont Circle, 2nd Floor, Washington, D.C. 20036 *(http://www.afj.org; 202-822-6070).* The guide explains in clear and precise terms what is permitted under these regulations, and includes many sample forms and worksheets. The cost is $15.

Citizens United v. FEC Case

In January 2010, the U.S. Supreme Court handed down a 5-4 decision in the case of *Citizens United v. Federal Elections Commission* that raised an issue about whether statutory limits on the exercise of free speech by charities is constitutional. The primary focus of the decision was to overturn two previous precedents *(Austin v. Michigan Chamber of Commerce,*1990, and *McConnell v. Federal Election Commissio*n, 2003), that had upheld statutory restrictions on campaign spending by corporations and unions. This case could, but not necessarily, have an effect on current statutory limitations on lobbying by tax-exempt organizations, including those that are exempt under section 501(c)(3).

Contacts With Legislators

1. When visiting a Legislator—

- Make an appointment, if at all possible.

- Arrive promptly, be warm and courteous, smile, and speak for five minutes or less on a single issue.

- Don't threaten or exaggerate your political influence. If you are really influential, the legislator will already know.

- Listen carefully to the legislator's response and take notes; be polite, but keep the legislator on the subject.

- Leave the legislator with something in writing on the issue, if possible.

- Request that the legislator do something to respond to the organization's position—vote in a specific way, take action on a problem, or send a letter to legislative leadership requesting action.

- Follow up the meeting with a thank-you note, taking advantage of this second opportunity to reinforce the organization's views and remind the legislator of the action requested.

- Do not feel slighted if referred to a staff member—legislators often have last-minute important meetings or unscheduled votes. Staff members are valued advisors who, in some cases, have as much or more influence than the legislator in the process and may have more time to help.

2. When writing to a Legislator—

- Restrict letters to one issue; be brief and concise.

- Clearly indicate the issue of concern, the organization's position on it, and the bill number, if known.

- Write the letter in a manner that will require a written response and include a return address.

- Use facts to support positions, and explain how the issue affects the organization, its members, and the community.

- Use professional letterhead, if appropriate. Type the letter, if possible, or write it neatly and legibly.

- Try not to indicate that the letter may be a form letter sent to scores of other legislators.

- Make the letter positive—don't threaten the loss of votes or campaign contributions.

- Follow up after the vote on the issue to indicate to the legislator that the organization is following his or her actions with interest and that it appreciated or was disappointed by that vote.

3. When telephoning a Legislator—

- Speak clearly and slowly.

- Make sure that callers identify themselves in a way that will permit the legislator to reach them or the organization by letter or telephone.

- Follow the guidelines listed above for writing and visiting that are equally appropriate for telephoning.

Tips:

- **Those who expect to spend a substantial amount of time in legislators' offices should register as lobbyists, even if they feel the law may not require them to do so. The judge of whether a person doing advocacy is in compliance with lobbying laws will not be that advocate.**

- **Comply with all state and federal reporting requirements.**

- **If the nonprofit corporation is a human service provider, invite local legislators to tour the facility and observe the services being provided.**

- **If the organization has members, invite local legislators to speak to the membership.**

- **Read the comprehensive, 158-page second edition of *The Nonprofit Lobbying Guide* that can be downloaded free at: *http://www.independentsector.org/***

lobby_guide. Other useful publications can be ordered or downloaded from the Alliance for Justice, *(http://www.afj.org)* including *E-Advocacy for Nonprofits* (2000, 82 pages, $25) and *Being a Player* (1995, 57 pages, $15).

- **Consider an e-mail advocacy campaign. Many organization members are more comfortable sending an e-mail to a legislator based on a sample provided on an organizational Web site than they would be writing a conventional letter.**

Chapter 18
Political Activity by Nonprofits

Synopsis: Charities are proscribed by law from engaging in electioneering. However, many political activities, such as candidate forums, questionnaires, awards, and compiling voting records, are not only permissible but are constructive activities for charities and other nonprofit organizations.

Introduction

Volunteer leaders and executives of nonprofit organizations are, generally, key opinion makers and play an important role, both in their organizations and in their personal lives, in shaping public policy. Many elected officials got their first taste of community service by serving as nonprofit board volunteers. Many elected officials continue to serve on nonprofit boards, and their expertise and political influence are often of great value.

Yet, there always has been a concern that nonprofits, particularly nonprofit charities, may be using taxpayer-financed subsidies to unduly influence the outcome of elections. This concern has been codified in federal and state law that, in general, prohibits 501(c)(3) organizations from helping candidates for public office and places severe restrictions on other tax-exempt organizations. Some state laws mimic federal law, prohibiting corporations and unincorporated associations, other than political action committees (PACs) and other organizations formed solely for political activity, from making contributions or expenditures in connection with the election of a candidate.

By federal law, a 501(c)(3) organization explicitly may "not participate in, or intervene in (including the publishing or distributing of statements), any political campaign on behalf of, or in opposition to, any candidate for public office." Moreover, any expenditures by a charity, for or against a candidate, can result in the loss of the organization's tax-exempt status, the assessment of a large excise tax, and potential fines against the charity's executives and volunteers. Charities may not endorse candidates or oppose candidates for public office. Generally, a person is considered to be a candidate for public office when he or she makes a public announcement to that effect, or files a statement with the elections commission of an intention to run.

Department of Treasury regulation §*1.501(c)(4)-I(a)(2)(ii)*, as amended in 1990, expressly forbids 501(c)(4) organizations from engaging in direct or indirect participation in political campaigns on "behalf of, or in opposition to, any candidate for public office" as part of its definition of "social welfare." However, a subsequent IRS Ruling (Rev. Rul. 81-95, 1981-1 C. B. 332) has interpreted that this regulation does not impose a total ban on political activity by 501(c)(4)s. The level of political activity that is permitted by 501(c)(4)s without jeopardizing their tax exemptions is still unclear. What is clear is that the political activity by the organization must not be a substantial part of its activities, and the activity must be consistent with the organization's social welfare mission, according to the May 1992 *Harvard Law Review* (p. 1675), which provides substantial guidance and applicable case law on this complicated legal issue. Other classes of exempt organizations, including those that are exempt under Section 501(c)(5), (c)(6), (c)(7), and (c)(8), also are permitted to engage in political activity, provided it is secondary to their primary purpose.

Among the types of expenditures that may be considered political activity are candidate travel expenses, fundraising expenses, polls, surveys, candidate position papers, advertising and publicity, and money paid to the candidate for speeches or other services. Expenses relating to nonpartisan voter registration drives are not considered political expenses.

Individuals who are associated with an exempt organization (or any other type of organization) may form an organization that is exempt under Section 527 of the Internal Revenue Code. Organizations exempt under this section are political action committees (PACs). These organizations have as their primary purpose engaging in political activity. They pay no federal tax on their operating income, but their investment income is subject to tax. Contributions made to them are not tax deductible. The excise tax that applies to political expenditures of social welfare organizations, exempt under Section 501(c)(4) of the Internal Revenue Code, does not apply to PACs.

These 527 organizations are coming under a lot of scrutiny. They are perceived as taking advantage of a loophole in the law that permits them to engage in "advocacy" activities that target the election or defeat of political candidates without any of the accountability and fundraising limits that apply to traditional political action committees. They are regulated by the IRS rather than the Federal Elections Commission (FEC). In August 2004, the IRS announced it would beef up its enforcement of public disclosure requirements that apply to these organizations, but the FEC had indicated that it would not take any action on enforcement until after the 2004 elections.

Examples, such as the Leadership Forum, America Coming Together, and Move On, raised tens of millions of dollars to influence the outcome of the 2004 Presidential election, all of it "soft money," without the traditional reporting requirements and contribution limits that applied to traditional political action committees under the McCain-Feingold campaign finance reform that went into effect in November 2002.

A 501(c)(3) organization cannot have its own PAC, but other exempt organizations are permitted to form one. Individuals associated with a 501(c)(3) may set up a "nonconnected political action committee," provided it receives no funds from the 501(c)(3), the individuals forming it do not imply any connection between the 501(c)(3) and the PAC, and the PAC is not controlled by the governing body of the 501(c)(3). For more details on this option, see FEC Advisory Opinion 1984-12.

Individual Political Activities

The Federal Election Campaign Act of 1971, as amended, prohibited all corporations, regardless of whether they are for-profit or nonprofit, from getting directly involved in federal political campaigns, with few exceptions. A 2002 law, known popularly as McCain-Feingold, prohibited the broadcast, cable or satellite transmission of "electioneering communications" paid for by corporations or labor unions from their general funds in the 30 days before a presidential primary and in the 60 days before the general elections. However, a January 2010 5-4 Supreme Court decision in the case of *Citizens United v. Federal Elections Commission* (No. 08-205) has determined that statutory restrictions on corporate and union funding of political campaigns are unconstitutional. In response, Senator Charles Schumer (D-NY) and Rep. Chris Van Hollen (D-MD) introduced the *Disclose Act* (S 3295/ HR 5175) to regulate campaign communications paid for by corporations, labor organizations, and nonprofits exempt from taxation under sections 501(c)(4), (c)(5) or (c)(6). The legislation was not approved before the Congress adjourned in 2010, but it did pass the House with a controversial amendment that was opposed by Independent Sector. This amendment would have exempted organizations that have been 501(c)(4)s in each of the previous ten calendar years that have at least 500,000 dues-paying members with at least one member in each state, and that receive no more than 15 percent of their total revenues from corporations or labor organizations.

Regardless of what the Congress decides to do about this issue, it is clear that volunteers and staff of charities have the same First Amendment rights as anyone else. There is no prohibition against such persons making political contributions, volunteering to work on a campaign, signing letters of support (provided any reference to their charitable organization affiliation clearly indicates that the reference is for identification purposes only), and issuing statements on a candidate's behalf. Moreover, the resources of the charity cannot be used for electioneering. Charitable organization leadership and staff should not write letters on a charity's stationery in support of a candidate. They should not turn the offices into a *de facto* campaign office for the candidate, using the telephone, copy machine, computer, and other resources, even during non-business hours.

Penalties

Beyond the sanctions of loss of tax exemption authorized by the 1954 Revenue Act, the Revenue Act of 1987 increased the sanctions available to the IRS in enforcing the prohibition against political activities. It also provided the IRS with the authority to seek an injunction to bring about an immediate cessation of violations that are deemed to be "flagrant." Most political campaign expenditures by 501(c)(3)s and 501(c)(4)s are now subject to a 10% excise tax applied to the organizations and a 2.5% excise tax (up to $5,000) applied to each of the managers of the organization who knew that a political expenditure was being made. This tax only applies if the expenditures were willful, flagrant, and not due to reasonable cause. If the illegal expenditure is not corrected, an additional 100% tax is imposed on the organization and 50% (up to an additional $10,000) on each manager who knew of the violation. Correcting the violation means that the managers tried to recover the contribution and took steps necessary to stop future violations.

While this area of law has a substantial gray area, there are several important general rules to be understood in guiding an organization's quasi-political activity. Each case decided by the IRS is fact-specific, and its rulings provide only general guidelines. The best advice for charitable organization leadership and staff is to provide a wide margin for error when contemplating involvement in political activities and not to engage in any activity that would even raise the specter of being improper, even if such an activity falls within the legal framework provided by current case law.

Quasi-Political Activities

Among the most common issues raised by charities are the following examples of borderline, quasi-political activities:

1. **Influencing Ballot Questions.** Federal law only prohibits organizations exempt under Section 501(c)(3) from engaging in political activity for or against a candidate for public office. Nothing in the law prevents efforts to influence ballot measures, such as constitutional changes, ballot initiatives, and referenda. These efforts, of course, must be insubstantial compared to the organization's activities in support of its primary purpose.

2. **Get Out the Vote Campaigns.** 501(c)(3) organizations may engage in nonpartisan get out the vote campaigns, but may not demonstrate any bias for or against any candidate or political party.

3. **Voting Records.** There is nothing illegal about a charity annually publishing a compilation of voting records of the Congress or the General Assembly. Some guidelines to follow are that the compilation should not be released only before an election and should list the voting records of all of the public officials or those in a relevant region (rather than in selecting only those who are up for re-election or who are targeted by the organization because they consistently vote for or against the organization's public policy positions). It should also involve a wide range of subjects, not imply organizational approval or disap-

proval of the public officials, and should not be disseminated beyond the membership or mailing list of the organization (i.e., the general public).

4. **Questionnaires.** It is not only permissible but advisable for charities to communicate with candidates, informing them of the organization's positions on issues and requesting their views. When candidates run for office, it is a vulnerable time for the shaping of their public policy positions. Many regret the positions they have taken during the election in response to a seemingly innocuous questionnaire. However, the use of these responses by an organization can be troublesome.

The IRS has ruled (Rev. Ruling 78-248) that it is permissible for charities to send a questionnaire to candidates and publish the answers in a voter's guide. However, the charities should make an effort not to demonstrate obvious bias in the questions, or to favor one candidate over another by making editorial comment. Organizations with a narrow range of interest, such as a pro-life or pro-choice group, are more in jeopardy by publishing the results of a questionnaire than groups with a broader range of interests, such as the League of Women Voters. If viewed by the IRS as a back door method to influence how your constituency votes, then questionnaires could place an organization's exemption in jeopardy.

5. **Public Forums.** Many 501(c)(3) organizations have a Candidates' Night to permit their volunteers and staffs to meet the candidates and question them about issues. This is not illegal, and it is expressly permitted by the IRS, provided it ensures "fair and impartial" treatment of the candidates (Rev. Rul. 86-95). However, such programs should be conducted with common sense. The moderator should be someone who can be impartial. All *bona fide* candidates should be invited, although it is not a prerequisite that they all accept the invitation for the event to be scheduled. Organizational leaders should refrain from making editorial comments about the positions of the candidates. Any account of the event in the organization's newsletter or other publication should be unbiased and should refrain from making editorial comment in favor of, or in opposition to, a candidate's views.

6. **Mailing lists.** The mailing list of a charity may be a valuable asset in the hands of a candidate. Many organizations get substantial revenue from selling or renting their mailing lists. There is no prohibition against selling a mailing list to a candidate for public office. However, giving a mailing list to a candidate is tantamount to making a political contribution. Also, all candidates must be given the same opportunity to purchase or rent the mailing list; no favoritism is permitted. As noted elsewhere in this publication, the sale or rental income from organizational mailing lists is potentially subject to federal unrelated business income tax, despite court rulings that decided they are not.

7. **Awards.** Many charities give "Legislator of the Year" or "Public Citizen of the Year" awards or similar citations to elected officials. However, making such an award just prior to an election in which the awardee is a candidate may be considered improper electioneering. From a practical viewpoint, even if this is done without any intention to help that candidate, a charitable organization's volunteers or contributors who may not like that particular candidate could view it as a disguised attempt at electioneering. It is a good policy to avoid providing awards to candidates during election periods.

Note: The above analysis is not intended to serve as legal advice about any particular set of facts, but only as a review of currently available reference materials on this issue. Consult a lawyer for a definitive answer to any particular legal situation.

Tips:

- If you as a nonprofit executive are a "political animal" who must get involved in partisan political activity, find another entity, such as a PAC or a political party committee, to channel those energies. Never use your organization's stationery for political purposes.

- Seek experienced and competent legal counsel before engaging in any political activity that falls into a gray area.

- Use permissible political activities to the advantage of the organization, such as candidate forums, candidate questionnaires, and awards to public officials.

- Pennsylvania has laws that apply to political action committees. You can find a information explaining reporting requirements on the Department of State's Campaign Finance Web pages at:

  http://www.dos.state.pa.us/portal/server.pt/community/campaign_finance/12731

- Review *The Rules of the Game: An Election Year Legal Guide for Nonprofit Organizations* published in 1996 and updated in 2010 by the Alliance for Justice *(http://www.afj.org)*. The cost is $30 per copy.

- Encourage members to make individual political contributions. It is good advice not to get involved in partisan politics, particularly if the organization has 501(c)(3) status. Those who do choose to participate in partisan politics should be scrupulous about separating personal political activities from those of the organization and not using organizational resources for partisan political activities.

- Keep informed about developments related to the Supreme Court's decision in the case of *Citizens United v. FEC* and how this decision will affect the legality of political activities of tax-exempt organizations.

Chapter 19
Communications and Public Relations

Synopsis: Organizations need to communicate their objectives, activities, and accomplishments effectively to attract funding, participation, and public support. Publications, media contacts, and workshops are among the methods used to do this.

Introduction

A well-planned public relations/communications strategy is important for two reasons. First, the organizational leadership has made a major investment in forming a nonprofit corporation, and a solid public relations effort will promote the organization's purposes. Second, few newly formed nonprofits begin with a silver spoon in their mouths. The first few years are often a fight for financial survival. Sound intraorganizational communications and building a solid public image through a public relations strategy are instrumental in building and maintaining a donor base and attracting grants and contracts.

But there is often a "Catch-22" at work here. New organizations must accomplish something useful quickly to obtain the credibility necessary to attract financial assistance. Yet, the organizations often need this financial assistance to accomplish something useful.

Public relations serves an important function. It puts the organization in a positive light and generates the essential public support needed to perpetuate it. An organization may be quietly successful in changing public opinion, advancing a legislative agenda, or providing vital services to worthy clients and its members. But if the right people—the board, funders, and potential funders and leadership—are unaware of the organization's successes, then its continued existence may be at risk.

There are thousands of creative ways to get the name of an organization in front of the public in a positive context.

Menu of Nonprofit Communication Tools

Among the conventional techniques nonprofits use are—

1. Organizational Brochure

Each nonprofit organization, from the largest to the smallest, should have a brochure. The brochure should clearly include the organization's name, address, telephone number, e-mail address, Web site and social networking addresses; its mission, its purposes and principal interests, its affiliations (if any); its federal tax-exempt status, and ways to make contributions; the names of its board members, advisory committee, and key staff people; and its major accomplishments. The organization's logo should appear on the brochure. If the organization is a membership organization, the brochure should provide information on dues and how to join.

The brochure should be distributed with all major fundraising solicitations. It should be a standard component of press packets, and should be distributed at speaking engagements made on behalf of the organization. All board members should have a supply of brochures to distribute to their friends and colleagues who may be interested in joining, contributing, volunteering, or assisting in other ways.

2. Print and Electronic Newsletter

No less than quarterly, the organization should publish a newsletter and distribute it free to all board members, all dues-paying members, significant opinion leaders on the issue(s) of interest to the organization, political leadership (such as members of the state legislature, local members of Congress, and local elected officials), the media, current and potential funders, and colleagues in the field.

Among the items the newsletter may contain are—

- recent board decisions;
- the organization's "wish list" of in-kind donations;
- legislative action in Washington, the state capital, and municipal government of interest to the membership and clients;
- planned giving information;
- schedules of upcoming meetings, workshops, conferences, and training sessions;
- messages from the executive director and/or board president;
- articles contributed by experts on the board or the membership about issues of interest to the readership;
- articles about organizational accomplishments, such as grants received, advocacy accomplished, coalitions joined, and letters of commendation received;
- profiles of people involved in the organization;
- general information about the status of issues of interest to the organization;
- new features of the organization's Web site;
- names of new donors;
- a list of all board members and staff;
- a form to join the organization, volunteer, or make a donation; and
- information on services and publications available from the organization.

The newsletter need not be fancy, but it should be as current as possible. It is advisable to select a creative and descriptive name for the publication and establish a master layout, so that subsequent issues will have the continuity of similar design.

The newsletter is often the only contact hundreds of influential people will have with an organization. As such, it is vitally important to present a professional, accurate, and eye-pleasing format. The newsletter should be carefully proofread and all typographical and grammatical errors eliminated. Make sure articles on one page continue correctly on subsequent pages.

Headlines should help busy readers find their way through the newsletter. Tricky headlines can be annoying. Double-check all headlines for appropriateness. Double check all names, telephone numbers, addresses, and Web site references.

3. News Releases

The media annually provide millions of dollars in free publicity to nonprofit organizations. The typical mode of communicating with the media is through the mailing, faxing, or e-mailing of a standard news release.

The news release is a pre-written "news" article that includes the name, organization, and work telephone number of the key organizational contact person at the top. If the release is really important, include the home telephone number, as well. The release should be dated, along with "For Immediate Release" or "Embargoed Until (insert date/time)" as appropriate.

Examples of topics for news releases are—

- the initial formation of the organization;

- an organization's official comment on a new law, legislative proposal, new regulation, or court decision affecting the organization's clients or members;

- an accomplishment of the organization;

- the release of a study or survey commissioned by the organization;

- the hiring or promotion of a staff member, or change of leadership within the organization; and

- awards given by or to the organization.

News releases are distributed to those who are most likely to print or broadcast them. A news release to a TV or radio station should be no more than six or seven sentences, and no more than two double-spaced pages for the print media. Most news releases will be edited before final publication or broadcast, although many neighborhood newspapers will print news releases word-for-word.

If the organization is based in Harrisburg, news releases can be distributed to most media outlets that cover the Capitol, including the AP wire service, by leaving 40 copies at the press center in the Capitol (Room E-524). The basic style of the body of a press release is—

- Precede the text with a catchy, descriptive headline.

- Put the most important sentence first.

- Place subsequent facts in descending order of importance.

- Include suitable quotes from organizational leadership when appropriate. The quotes should express a view/opinion, rather than providing a fact that could appear in the release narrative.

- Make sure the text answers the basic questions of "who," "what," "where," "when," "why," and "how."

4. Press Conferences

Organizations with a story of major interest to the public may want to consider holding a press conference. To do so, a media advisory is distributed in the same manner as a news release, telling the press where and when the press conference will be held, the subject, and speakers. It may be helpful to make follow-up calls to the news desks of local newspapers and broadcast stations.

At the press conference, written materials (a press packet consisting of a copy of a written statement, the organization's brochure, and materials relating to the topic of the press conference) should be distributed.

Another good idea is to arrange for a black-and-white photo to be taken of the organizational representative speaking at the press conference. The photograph may be accompanied by a picture caption and sent in a press packet to media outlets not covering the press conference. Take into account that 1-hour commercial photo developers may require several days to develop black-and-white film.

If the press conference is being held at the Capitol, special arrangements must be made in advance with the General Services Department's special events office (783-9100) for scheduling a site and providing a sound system. It is advisable to have the press conference at a site convenient to the press (i.e., the Capitol Rotunda or media center), but if the event is truly newsworthy, the press will attend.

Digital cameras have eliminated some of the frustration of having to wait for a picture to be developed commercially. The files of these pictures can be sent conveniently through the Internet as e-mail attachments to newspapers on deadline, or can be posted on the organization's Web site and social networking pages. The camera's resolution should be set high enough for good print quality.

A banner with the organization's logo, draped in front of the podium, creates a photograph that is useful for future annual reports, newsletters, and related publicity.

5. Public Service Announcements

Many TV and radio broadcasters regularly broadcast public service announcements (PSAs) for nonprofit organizations without cost. PSAs are an excellent and cost-effective way to get an organization's message, and its name, across to thousands of viewers and listeners.

The last line of such an announcement can be: "This message is brought to you by (the name of the organization) and this station as a public service." The rest of the announcement can be a 30-second sound bite of information of interest to people—how to obtain a free service, how to avoid health and safety risks, or even how to join or volunteer for the organization while accomplishing some vital objective in the public interest.

Before preparing a PSA, check with a potential broadcaster for the technical specifications for the form and format of the announcement. Some stations may be willing to produce your announcement without charge, as well as broadcast it.

6. Conferences and Workshops

Well-planned conferences and workshops can serve a useful public relations function. A one-day conference can bring together interested volunteer leadership and professionals in a shared field of interest, introduce them to the organization, increase networking among the participants, and advance the organization's interests. The charge for the workshop can be set to cover all anticipated costs, or even generate net revenue—provided it is planned well in advance and the plan is executed properly.

There are scores of major decisions to make in planning a conference, such as choosing speakers who will generate attendance and excitement, preparing and distributing the conference brochure, selecting the site for the conference, and arranging for exhibit space and advertising. There are hundreds of minor decisions that need to be made as well, such as choosing the type of name tag to use, deciding who staffs the registration table, and choosing the luncheon menu. There are many sources of advice on how to run a successful conference, many of which can be borrowed from the local library.

7. Intraorganizational Communication

Board and key contacts need to know what is happening beyond what they read in the organization's newsletter. Periodically, it is useful to send out "Action Alerts" or "Background Briefings" by mail or e-mail that describe the status of a problem and what they can do to participate in its resolution.

Some organizations have specially printed stationery for these messages. A sample letter may be included if the organization is encouraging its constituency to write advocacy letters. However, the organization should urge writers to use their own words rather than copy the sample exactly. The address or telephone number of the person they should contact should always be included.

8. Annual Report

Among the typical publications produced by nonprofit organizations is the annual report. Many nonprofits use this opportunity to supplement the financial information provided to stakeholders with a report on the operations of the nonprofit during the fiscal year.

The annual report can be professionally designed with a fancy layout, fonts, charts, graphics, and color pictures, which imply progress and success in meeting organizational goals and objectives. It can also be a word-processed report photocopied on plain paper. In either case, the annual report offers the opportunity to communicate what the organization has been doing on behalf of its board and membership, clients, funders, and the public, as well as its goals and plans.

9. Other Publications

Many nonprofits publish small booklets about various issues of concern, which are disseminated to their constituents and other interested parties. This is one more way to get the name of the organization in front of additional people, and it is another effective way to communicate the organization's views to those whose opinions count. Subjects of such publications include—

- the latest developments on issues of interest;
- how to contact government offices;
- how to lobby on behalf of the organization's issues; and
- information about the state legislature, and who serves on committees of interest to the organization.

These publications can also be considered the written equivalent of the public service announcement. Many institutions, such as hospitals, community centers, nursing homes, day care providers, and libraries, will distribute these public relations booklets without charge to the organization's target audience.

10. Membership/Board Surveys

Membership and board surveys can be, but may not always be, a useful tool to obtain information and feedback. The target of the survey may feel a sense of connection to the organization, and the survey will provide useful input from the membership.

Member surveys can be tailored to suit the needs of the organization. For example, many advocacy nonprofits periodically survey their boards and/or membership to determine who among the board and membership has influence or personal relationships with key public policy decision-makers. Surveys can be used to gauge the effectiveness of organizational programs and activities.

Free or low-cost software is available to administer online surveys. There are also free and low-cost commercial services that provide high-quality surveys, but may include advertising. Among the services to check out (features change quickly in the dot-com environment) are Survey Monkey. com *(http://www.surveymonkey.com)*, Free Online Surveys *(http://www.freeonlinesurveys.com)*, Vovici *(http://www.vovici.com)*, and BraveNet Web Services *(http://www.bravenet.net)*.

11. Speakers' Bureaus

Many groups, such as men's and women's clubs, fraternal organizations, educational organizations, membership organizations, and places of worship, have speakers at their regular meetings. Organizational leaders may wish to proactively seek invitations to discuss the activities of their organizations with these groups.

Such meetings may be the source of volunteers, donations, ideas, or simply good will and public support. Local newspapers (don't forget the "Shopper" newspapers) list many of these club meetings and their leaders. Addresses can be found in the telephone book or online, if they are not listed in the newspaper announcement. Members of the board can be deputized to speak on behalf of the organization. Many of them have associations with other organizations and clubs that would be delighted to host a speaker.

12. Newspaper Op-Ed Articles

Virtually all newspapers print feature-length opinion articles on their Opinion/Editorial (Op-Ed) pages. Many will include a picture and a line of biographical material about the author. The Op-Ed page is usually the page most widely read by a newspaper's readership, along with the Letters to the Editor page. It is an excellent forum to share an organization's ideas on an issue and bring attention to the organization.

There are many cases in which a thoughtful Op-Ed article resulted in legislation being enacted by Congress or the state legislature to address the issue raised by the Op-Ed piece.

13. Letters to the Editor

Letters to the Editor are an effective way to "talk back" to a newspaper when the organization believes an article or editorial unfairly and erroneously shapes an issue. They can also be an effective medium for reinforcing a position and permitting the writer to expand on that position from the perspective of the organization.

The general guidelines for writing letters to the editor vary from paper to paper, but they usually provide for writing on a single issue, being concise (no more than three paragraphs), using nonthreatening language, and providing information that might not be available to the readers from any other source.

14. Web Sites

Thousands of nonprofit organizations are establishing sites on the Internet (see Chapter 20). Web pages communicate information about donations; volunteer opportunities; products, services, and publications; and general facts about the organization. These Web sites can be prepared and maintained for very little cost and permit the general public to access information by computer from the privacy of their own homes and offices. Podcasts, blogs, wikis, message boards, and chatrooms are some of the techniques nonprofit organizations are using to build online communities to generate support.

15. Coalitions

There is strength in numbers. Two heads are better than one. Whatever the cliché, many organizations find a benefit to pooling their resources to accomplish an objective. One strategy is to form a coalition with other organizations to address an issue of vital importance (See chapter 23).

16. Social Networking Sites

Facebook, Twitter, LinkedIn, and Google+ are among the social networking sites that thousands of nonprofit organizations are using to advantage. These free platforms are raising money, finding volunteers, coordinating advocacy, providing forums for interaction and relationship building, and serving as a quick and inexpensive means to communicate with stakeholders. For more on this, see chapter 20.

Tips:

- **Use the power of the Internet to reach a global audience to foster relationships between your organization and potential future stakeholders. Review Chapters 20, 21, and 22 of this book for more ideas.**

- **Don't hold a press conference unless you feel that the information being shared is truly newsworthy. Be prepared for every reasonable question (and perhaps unreasonable ones, as well) from reporters that may not have any direct relationship to the subject matter discussed at the conference.**

Chapter 20
The Internet for Nonprofits

Synopsis: Nonprofits have an exciting, versatile resource in the Internet. Once connected, organizations can share information inexpensively and quickly, and they can use search engines and directories to find information. Nonprofits can set up their own Web sites, use social media, and generate donations and other revenue.

Introduction

The recent explosion of useful resources for nonprofits on the Internet is perhaps the most exciting positive development for this sector in years. Thousands of nonprofit institutions whose leadership had barely heard of the Internet 15 years ago are not only connected, but have their own Web sites and pages on Facebook, create podcasts and blogs, develop wikis, tweet the latest happenings on Twitter, and create online communities to build organizational support, utilizing advances in personal computing, such as tablets and smart phones.

Since the mid-1990s, when the Internet was first becoming popular, an entire generation of future (and current) employees, donors, volunteers, and clients has grown up with this technology being second nature.

Nonprofit executives have taken advantage of this revolution in communications by using the Internet to seek donations, Webcast events in real time, lobby members of Congress, advertise job openings, purchase office equipment and supplies, and hold online meetings and information sessions. They market their services, check references of prospective consultants, distribute board documents, reserve library books, generate grass-roots advocacy letters to government officials, research new laws and regulations, and download the latest Supreme Court decisions, all without leaving their offices.

Need a 990 tax return form? Download it from the IRS web site *(http://www.irs.gov)*. Need driving directions to your board meeting? Have a computer generate not only the directions but even a map, and e-mail them *(http://www.bing.com/maps/)* to your board members.

Prior to this communications revolution, if you wanted to distribute a document to a board, you had to photocopy the document, collate it, stuff it in envelopes, put correct postage and mailing labels on the envelopes, and mail it. The recipient would receive it two or three days later. Time could be saved by faxing the document, or broadcast-faxing it, to the list of recipients, but the cost of long-distance charges could be substantial. Via the Internet, the same operation results in almost immediate delivery of the documents to every person on the list with no mailing costs. The Internet has revolutionized the way all businesses operate, and the benefits to the for-profit world are just as applicable to the nonprofit sector.

Saving money, although of prime concern to nonprofits, is only one advantage of utilizing the Internet. Perhaps the most exciting aspect is that nonprofit executives can communicate inexpensively and efficiently with like-minded counterparts who may be in an office next door or on another continent. The culture of the Internet has made it easy for people who have something in common and information to share to find each other. It is also easy to begin a one-on-one or one-on-ten-thousand dialogue without having to laboriously screen out the other hundreds of millions of people who also are participating.

Many nonprofit executives report that attending a national conference results in serendipitous contacts with previously unknown colleagues who generate new ideas, new strategies for solving problems, interchanges that promote innovation, collaboration opportunities among people otherwise separated by geography, and useful social contacts. The Internet has become all this and more. The speed of communication among people has made a quantum leap as a result of the Internet. Nonprofits that don't take advantage of the opportunities afforded by this technology to save money, expand markets, and promote themselves may be left in the dust by competitors that do.

Practical Applications of the Internet

Among the most popular services and applications of the Internet are e-mail, text messaging, mailing lists, electronic newsletters, newsgroups, chat, blogs, social networking, podcasts, and wikis.

E-mail: Much of the information transmitted over the Internet is in the form of electronic mail. These are text communications that are sent from one person to another. E-mail is a "store and forward" system that permits someone to send a message to someone else for later retrieval. Each Internet user is given an Internet address that is used to send and receive these messages. E-mail messages also can have files attached to them. Using e-mail, one can avoid playing "telephone tag." But perhaps as much as 90% consists of "spam," unwanted junk e-mail.

The Web: Developing a functional, interactive Web site has become the most important priority for a new organization after filing one's incorporation papers. It is here that stakeholders visit and make first impressions of the organization. The Web site has not simply served as a repository for public files, but has become the most important tool organizations have to communicate with donors, volunteers, organizational leadership, and other stakeholders, using a variety of media, including video, photographs, text, and audio, all working together to encourage donations and other support that every nonprofit organization needs. The organization's Web site is the "online headquarters" of the organization that the public will choose to visit first (before any telephone calls or letters) to connect in some way.

Text Messaging: Text messaging is slowly overtaking e-mail as the method of choice in sending short communications to others via cell phones, with more than two billion individuals worldwide having text-message capacity. Research shows that the response to a text message is measured in minutes rather than in hours or days, as is the case with a typical e-mail message. For example, an organization might ask its supporters to enter a code into their cell phones with a text message, authorizing a small donation that appears on the donors' telephone bills. Utilizing this technique, the American Red Cross raised more than $30 million during a 10-day period for relief efforts in Haiti following the January 2010 earthquake. Spam messages comprise perhaps 10% of text messages, although this is likely to increase.

Electronic Newsletters: An electronic newsletter, sent by e-mail to those who have voluntarily requested to become subscribers, is becoming the model of choice for fundraising and friendraising. Unlike indiscriminately sent direct e-mail, this model of indirect fundraising appears to be both ethical and effective, and is considered a useful service by recipients. The electronic newsletter is a periodic e-mail that includes content that would be appropriate for an organization's print newsletter. The advantages are that compared to a print newsletter, there are no printing costs, no postage costs, no labels to be printed out and affixed, and there is minimal time-lag between the time the material is written and the time it goes to "press."

Newsgroups: A newsgroup is another form of Internet communication that provides for group discussion of a narrow topic. It is like a bulletin board in the supermarket, where you have to take action to see the messages posted there and read them. You have the opportunity to post a reply for others to see. Sending a message to a newsgroup results in each subscriber of the newsgroup having the capability of seeing the message without receiving it as an e-mail. Typically, someone makes a comment on a newsgroup, another person responds to the comment, and so on until there is a thread of related messages on a topic. Simultaneously, others online will start another thread of messages. All the messages are stored, often chronologically, and given a title, and viewers can pick and choose, using a newsgroup reader (specialized software to facilitate reviewing newsgroups) to decide which messages to look at. Although many newsgroups have been replaced by blogs and social networking pages, many still remain active.

Chat: Chat is the Internet equivalent of ham radio. Using chat software, you can have a "conversation" with someone by using the computer keyboard, all in real time. What you type and the response of the other participant(s) appears on your screen simultaneously. It is possible to have a nonprofit board meeting entirely by chat. Video conferencing, where all participants can see and hear each other, is quickly making the traditional chatroom described above obsolete. Most commercial providers provide for privacy among those who participate. More popular, however, are informal chats among those who just happen to frequent a chat room. More and more, these chat rooms are becoming specialized, so participants have something in common. Many Web sites, including those of nonprofit groups, use software, often provided free by commercial providers, that permits visitors to participate in chats. In return for the use of free chat rooms, the visitors often see advertising messages controlled by the software provider, not under the control of the organization that is sponsoring the individual chat room. For an example, see the chat site sponsored by the National Association of Social Workers and *The New Social Worker Magazine* at: *http://www.socialworkchat.org/*

Blogs: Short for "Web Log," a blog is a Web page that consists of a frequently updated journal or diary by an individual. The style of commentary is typically informal and personal, usually including links to additional online resources embedded within the content. Each entry is in reverse chronological order—the latest entry is placed on top. Each dated entry has its own Web address (called a "permalink"), making it easy for other blogs and search engines to link to any particular entry (rather than to the entire blog). Previous entries are archived on the blogger's site. There is a process that permits viewers to add their comments to each entry, which can be seen by all viewers. Many blogs have an RSS (for Really Simple Syndication) feed, a software application that lets viewers subscribe to blog updates by using an RSS reader, thus eliminating the requirement to visit each blog site individually to obtain access to updates of their favorites. In the nonprofit context, a blog might include the daily musings of an executive director of an advocacy organization, sharing her thoughts on a news development of the day, adding links to online articles that have come across her computer screen about that news, commenting on how her organization's stakeholders will be affected, and providing some insight into some of the internal debate within her organization about how to deal with it. For the nonprofit community, blogs provide another mechanism to improve interaction with an organization's stakeholders, enhance the bond with donors, and create a dialogue with outsiders while giving them an inside look at what the organization is trying to accomplish. The technical tools are easily accessible. Blogs serve many purposes for a nonprofit organization. If they are interesting or provocative, they draw readership—not only from the general public, but from the media and political leadership, as well. And these site visits often translate to new and more productive current donors, volunteers, advocates, and friends. Bloggers need to vigilantly monitor all comments, routinely deleting "comment spam" and inappropriate comments.

Social Networking Sites: Just a few years ago, social networking sites such as Facebook and MySpace were almost exclusively restricted to twenty- and thirty-somethings who used them to communicate about their college classes, their favorite songs, to share pictures, and to write about the highlights of their day. Today, with more than 500 million accounts on Facebook alone, almost everyone with access to a computer has one or more of these accounts, or has at least visited one or more sites. Nonprofit organizations have recognized that online social networking can be an effective technique to find volunteers, market their services, increase donations, and enhance already-created relationships they have with their stakeholders. Although initial results of using these sites to generate donations have been disappointing, so was online fundraising generally when organizations first began using it. Technology that promotes micro donations has improved substantially since then, as the Obama for President campaign proved in 2008. We are in the midst of a major change in culture, and sites such as YouTube, Twitter, LinkedIn and Facebook are changing the landscape. Nonprofit organizations are often slow to respond to such culture shifts, but those that proactively take advantage of new technology can benefit. The intent of these sites is to provide links that help connect individuals and groups to others that share some common interest or objective. And, by and large, they do this with unqualified success. According to a study by the University of Massachusetts Dartmouth's Center for Marketing Research, 96% of large charitable organizations are using some form of social media to communicate their messages (see: *http://www.umassd.edu/cmr/studiesandresearch/socialmediatopcharities/*).

Podcasts: Podcasting refers to the creation of audio files that can be uploaded to the Internet, using a process that allows subscribers to the broadcast to be informed when the audio program is available to be downloaded to the subscriber's audio player or computer. These files are typically in MP3 format and 5 to 60 minutes in duration, making them suitable for hearing on the subscriber's computer or personal audio player, such as an iPod or other MP3 player. The podcast craze is now sweeping the nation. It is adding another arrow in the quiver for nonprofit organizations that want to send a targeted audio or video message to stakeholders in a timely, convenient, and most importantly, cost-effective way. Podcasting permits the organization's staff to be the producer of a radio show (or TV show) rather than a third party, and gives them the ability to reach their target audience when they are most receptive to hearing what the organization wants to say about itself. What makes podcasting an incredibly powerful means of communication is that anyone in the world with an Internet connection can listen to podcasts at any time he or she chooses. This contrasts to cable TV and radio shows, which are on at a specific time and require action on the part of the viewer/listener to first know that there is a program of interest and then take steps to either listen to it in real time or record it. With podcasting, the subscriber is in complete control using the technology, deciding what content to subscribe to, and when to hear it. Podcasting affords the capability of listening to the program over and over again, having the ability to store it indefinitely, rewinding it, pausing it, deleting it, transferring the program to other media such as a CD-ROM, and distributing the files freely to others. Usually, there is no advertising to listen to, although there is no law against a charity making a subtle plea for donations to support its mission. To hear the program, all subscribers need is a media player, preferably portable, and an Internet connection. The broadcaster's costs for equipment are negligible, and the subscriber pays nothing for the service. Even if subscribers don't have an iPod or equivalent, the broadcaster's Web site can be designed to permit listeners to click on a button and listen while they sit in front of the computer screen, with the capacity to download the file for future use. For nonprofit organizations, podcasting is a natural fit, providing a forum to reach major givers with "insider" briefings about the organization, updates about programs funded by donations, details about a capital campaign, and opportunities to advocate on behalf of a public policy issue of importance to the organization. See page 195 for more details about podcasting.

Wikis: A wiki is a feature of a Web site that facilitates collaboration and participatory contribution among its users, who can add, remove, or edit content quickly and easily. Following Hurricane Katrina, a wiki was established permitting the public to create a master database of messages from those who were seeking information about missing friends and relatives, consolidating the message boards of dozens of those established by media outlets, disaster relief organizations, and others. Hundreds of volunteers, including this author, participated in the project and were delighted by the convenient opportunity to respond to the tragedy in a more tangible way than by simply donating money. Wikis can be public or password-protected, and software supporting this feature can be accessed for free or at minimal cost. For more details, read the *Exploring the World of Wikis* article at: The Tech Soup Learning Center *(http://www.techsoup.com/learningcenter)*.

Electronic Newsletters—How to Begin

Direct and indirect fundraising solicitations can be included in the newsletter, along with advocacy alerts, information about organization successes, upcoming fundraising events, calls for volunteers, notices concerning fee-based services, details about new laws and regulations that affect the organization's constituency, information about new Web sites of interest to stakeholders, jobs that may be available within your organization or similar ones, new features of the organization's Web site, and so on. Some organizations solicit advertising for their electronic newsletters, or embed simple links or a clickable link logo of a business partner who has agreed to pay a sponsor fee.

Unlike telephone and direct mail, an e-mail newsletter comes with little or no price tag other than staff time. It provides a valuable service to your donors and friends, and many look forward to receiving these regular communications in their in-box. I can't think of any downside to it. Typically, your organization's Web site will have a simple form that permits viewers to enter their e-mail address to subscribe to the newsletter. It is technically possible to maintain your electronic newsletter using your e-mail software. But doing so is cumbersome at best, and it uses up the available bandwidth your Internet Service Provider (ISP) permits. Many ISPs impose limits on the number of e-mails that can be sent with the identical message.

Consider third parties to administer electronic mail lists

Fortunately, free and low cost software packages (such as Dada Mail) are available on the Web that permit administration of electronic mailing lists. Many Web site hosts will permit you to send out thousands of e-mails to those who have opted in to receive them. If your host limits your use of e-mail, there are for-profit providers that will send your newsletter out for you using their own servers. In the event that you do not wish to tie up your own Web server, these third party services may be a good investment.

Here is some advice for planning your electronic newsletter:

- Provide the newsletter only to those who opt in by taking a positive step to subscribe, such as clicking on a button on your Web site. Sending out these e-mails to those who have not opted in is considered spam. At best, it is annoying. At worst, it could result in your ISP taking away your service, as well as infuriating your donors and other stakeholders.

- Advertise the availability of the newsletter on all organization materials.

- Make sure the electronic newsletter provides value to the readership, so subscribers won't automatically delete it or unsubscribe.

- Provide information in each newsletter on how to unsubscribe, preferably with a link to do so, and honor each unsubscribe request.

- Don't sell, rent, or give away your list of e-mail addresses.

- Although it is acceptable to include advertising in your newsletter, use it sparingly. If you are using a third-party mailing list service, be willing to pay a few dollars more to purchase the "premium" version rather than using the free version that includes advertising solicited by the application service provider. Some of the ads accepted by the application service provider may be considered inappropriate by your readership and reflect poorly on your organization.

- Provide an opportunity for subscribers to donate to your organization if they choose to, such as by providing a link to your Web site's donation form, publicizing a specific "wish list" of items that could be donated or financed, and including information about planned giving opportunities.

Some issues to consider when choosing whether to administer your mailing list on your ISP's or Web host's server or through an application service provider are:

- *The amount of bandwidth required.* If your newsletter is simple text and is sent out to only a hundred subscribers, your requirements will be less than if your newsletter contains high-resolution pictures in an HTML format and is sent to thousands.

- *Constraints of your application service provider.* You may be unable to send out your newsletter using your current Web host because of technical limitations.

- *How your subscribers will subscribe and unsubscribe.* This can be opt-in, opt-out, or even better, double opt-in, which means that subscribers who have hit the subscribe button receive an e-mail asking them to confirm that they want to subscribe before their e-mail address is entered into the subscriber database.

- *How bounced messages will be handled.* This includes addresses from those whose e-mail inbox is full or who no longer have an active e-mail address.

- *How you will deal with advertising.* Advertising, if you will permit it, can be solicited by your own organization, or inserted by an application service provider in exchange for the use of free newsletter administration software.

- *Who on the staff will be responsible for newsletter content and mailing list management.* There is work involved in creating the newsletter, soliciting advertisements and sponsorships, and dealing with bounced addresses.

HTML-Formatted E-Mail and Newsletters

Most people despise spam e-mails. But we sometimes are impressed by the design of some of these, utilizing slick fonts, graphics, backgrounds, pictures, and catchy special effects. Although there are advantages in keeping an electronic newsletter simple by keeping it text-only, an eye-catching electronic newsletter can have the same appeal as a well-designed print newsletter. Sending your newsletter in HTML format also provides you with the option of personalizing the messages.

Standard e-mail programs such as Outlook and Eudora permit limited formatting, such as using different typefaces, font sizes, bold, italics, and indenting. More sophisticated software, such as Dreamweaver, permits you to insert backgrounds, tables, and graphics. Another option is to use software and services that are specifically designed for sending out bulk HTML-formatted e-mail, such as EMailNow *(http://www1.networkforgood.org/for-nonprofits/fundraising/email-now)*, VerticalResponse *(http://www.verticalresponse.com/)*, or ConstantContact *(http://www.*

constantcontact.com/index.jsp). If you still feel clueless, you can simply hire an application service provider with experience in setting up HTML e-mails—there are scores of them. For an excellent article about some of the issues and options you might have, see: *http://www.idealware.org/ articles/fgt_email_newsletter_tools.php*

There are some technical issues to resolve if you do decide to send out HTML-based newsletters and e-mail. First, what you send will look different depending on the browser being used to view it. Some recipients may not be able to see it at all, depending on their e-mail program. You need to pre-test it using all of the most popular viewers, such as Outlook, Eudora, Thunderbird, Gmail, Yahoo Mail, AOL, and Hotmail. For more practical advice, you can visit the Techsoup Web site *(http://www.techsoup.org)* for articles about electronic newsletters and e-mail.

Application Service Providers may offer the option to have an alternate text version of your newsletter for those subscribers who prefer or can only access text.

Podcasts—Introduction

Back in the 1980s and 1990s when I was the CEO of a statewide association, I would get occasional requests to appear on a "live on tape" radio or TV show to discuss public policy issues with which my organization was engaging in advocacy. I would dutifully spend precious time preparing to be interviewed, drive to the station, and wait what seemed like hours for the interview to start. Almost without fail, the shows would broadcast at a time when it was quite unlikely that anyone would ever listen to what I had to say. It was rare that I ever heard from anyone who had actually listened to the program I was on.

Podcasting changes all of this. It makes *you* the producer of a radio show (or TV show), and gives you the ability to reach your target audience when they are most perceptive to hearing what you want to say about your organization.

Examples of podcasting by nonprofit organizations

Reverend Nancy McDonald Ladd of the Bull Run Unitarian Universalists in Manassas, Virginia, offers her weekly sermons by podcast, attracting an audience of members who live too far away to conveniently attend services, and the congregants' children who are away at college. A growing segment of the audience appears to be those who attend the Sunday service and want to hear the sermon again when it becomes available by RSS (Really Simple Syndication, the protocol that supports subscriptions of podcast and blog broadcasts) feed on Tuesday. According to national church leaders, Bull Run is just one of 25 Unitarian churches around the nation that podcast all or some of their weekly services.

The Collective Heritage Institute, also known as "Bioneers," is a nonprofit organization that promotes practical environmental solutions and innovative social strategies for restoring the Earth and communities. If you point your Web browser to *http://www.bioneers.org/radio/2011-radio-series/beloved-community,* you can find a directory of Bioneer's podcasts of 27 shows the nonprofit organization produced for public radio. You can hear them with the click of a mouse—a lot simpler than waiting for a radio broadcast.

On December 1, 2005, the Campaign to Make Poverty History joined with Gcast.com to launch the first ONE podcast. The World AIDS Day ONEcast featured former President of South Africa Nelson Mandela, Bono (U2 lead singer and co-founder of DATA—Debt, AIDS, Trade for Africa), and Chris Martin of Coldplay, along with members of the faith community and other ONE supporters. That month, Bono's charity ONE: The Campaign To Make Poverty History launched a monthly podcast focusing on AIDS, hunger in Africa, and other social issues.

How to Create a Podcast

The basic equipment needed to create a podcast consists of a microphone that connects to your computer, headphones, a computer, and an Internet connection. You can find detailed instructions on how to set up a podcast at sites such as Webmonkey *http://www.webmonkey.com* (search on the term "podcast") and Podcast411 *(http://www.podcast411.com/howto_1.html)*. The basic steps required are:

1. *Create your content.* This is accomplished by speaking into a microphone connected to your computer, or other devices that can create audio files. The content can be whatever you might include if the organization were producing its own radio show: highlights of the organization's accomplishments, pending public policy issues and advocacy efforts that listeners can participate in, details about a new general fundraising or capital campaign, new programs and services offered by the organization, or new features of the organization's Web site. Editing software can easily blend in music (make sure you have permission to use it) to open and close the program. Record directly into the computer using programs such as Audacity for Windows/Mac or GarageBand for Mac. Although it is not required, a good quality microphone and a room in which the sound isn't bouncing off the walls are of benefit.

2. *Save your content as MP3 files.* Use software such as RiverPast Audio Converter for Windows (http://www.riverpast.com) or Audio Hijack for MAC *(http://www.rogueamoeba. com/audiohijack/download.php).*

3. *Edit your files.* Among popular editing software titles for this purpose are *Audacity (http:// www.topdrawerdownloads.com/showdownload.php?company=Audacity&title=Audacity);* GarageBand *(http://www.apple.com/ilife/garageband/),* and Adobe Audition *(http:// download.cnet.com/Adobe-Audition/3000-2170_4-10324430.html).*

4. *Publish your podcast.* You have a choice of publishing it on your Web site or a site that serves as a catalog of podcasts (or both). Among the popular ones are:

   OurMedia.org *(http://www.ourmedia.org)*
   ITunes Music Store *(http://itunes.apple.com/us/genre/podcasts/id26)*
   Podcast Alley *(http://www.podcastalley.com/)*
   Podcast Bunker *(http://www.podcastbunker.com/)*
   iPodder *(http://www.ipodder.org/)*
   Digital Podcast *(http://www.digitalpodcast.com/)*

5. *Syndicate your podcast.* This entails sending it to subscribers. For details, see: *http:// www.wonderhowto.com/topic/syndicate/*

For a great tutorial on podcasting, see: *http://www.nten.org/uploads/podcasting_workshop.pdf*

Why podcasting is the future

I remember a few decades ago when personal stereos such as the Walkman became popular. Today, if you see someone walking down the street without talking into a cell phone, he or she is likely to have an earpiece connected to one of the 300 million iPods sold by Apple between November 2001 and April 2011. And this doesn't count the millions of iPod clones and smartphones with the capability of downloading and storing MP3 files. In a massive shift in popular culture, demand responsiveness is how people want their information, and podcasting fits this perfectly.

For charities, podcasting is a natural fit, providing a forum to reach major givers with "insider" briefings about the organization, updates about programs funded by donations, details about a capital campaign, and opportunities to advocate on behalf of a public policy issue of importance to the organization.

Online Communities

An online community is any Web site that attracts people who have something in common and allows them to contribute to content or discussions at the site. The types of services that are typically available are real time chat, forums or message boards, member directories, instant messaging, job/career information, shopping, and news and information. What members of the site have in common can be anything: their age, their social status, their profession, their religion, their politics, some health concern, or interest in a particular public policy issue.

What distinguishes online communities from other Web sites is that much of the content is contributed by visitors. This content may be moderated by the Web site administrator, although in many cases, it is not.

Challenges of Online Communities

1. Creating and maintaining an online community requires substantial time and effort.

2. Some visitors post inappropriate content, such as putting slanderous or libelous messages on the message board, posting commercial messages, violating confidentiality, or infringing on a copyright.

3. Some words used in real-time posting may be offensive, requiring the use of filtering software. It is difficult to choose which words to censor.

4. Online communities need an effective Code of Conduct.

Even when an online community is free, most require members to register and to select a user name and password. Doing so ensures that the organization has at least minimal control and can deny access to those who consistently violate the site's Code of Conduct. There are also marketing reasons to have a password-protected site, such as having access to information about those who visit.

Mobile Applications (Apps)

It took perhaps a decade for many nonprofit organizations to make a transition to conducting many of their interactions with stakeholders through the Internet via e-mail, electronic mailing lists, blogs, podcasts, and social networking pages rather than through printed matter such as letters, telephone calls, and face-to-face meetings. After a rocky start, our culture has embraced this transition with open arms—for good or for bad—and Internet access has become a part of our daily routine. Many of us are now connected to the Internet 24/7, perhaps turning off the alarm on our computers and phones that signal that we have received a new e-mail or text message only when we go to sleep.

This communications revolution is accelerating, and it has taken on a new direction since publication of the previous edition of this book. Everything that can be accomplished using one's personal computer can now be done using one's wireless phone. So-called "smart" phones such as the iPhone, Android, and Blackberry, and tablet computers such as the Apple iPad, Motorola Xoom, and Samsung Galaxy Tab, are replacing the PC and laptop as the gadget of choice to interface with the Internet. Today, one can have the Internet and all it offers literally in the palm of one's hand. Or the Palm of one's hand, if you choose that particular smart phone model. Savvy nonprofits are taking advantage of this new technology.

Nonprofits such as the Capital Area Food Bank of Texas, One Day's Wages, and the Salvation Army *(see: http://aynne.posterous.com/5-non-profit-iphone-apps-you-should-know-abou-1)* are using so-called "branded apps," customized smart phone applications, to raise money, organize supporters, and automatically post (and have their supporters view) messages to several social networking sites. When I visited the Detroit Zoo in 2010, I saw notices that I could download an app that would track my location, provide me with commentary about what I was seeing at that location, access announcements about events and animal feedings, view photos, and find friends who were visiting the zoo. All for $1.99.

And many others are developing mobile friendly Web sites (example: the Susan G. Komen for the Cure at *http://m.komen.org/*) that facilitate accessing the typical information one would find on a conventional Web site with a size that fits the screen of a typical smart phone.

Simple iPhone apps can now be created for a few hundred dollars using free templates. Looking for where to start? See a tutorial at: *http://www.smashingmagazine.com/2009/08/11/how-to-create-your-first-iphone-application/*

As I write this, Apple, which makes available apps for its popular iPhone, continues its policy of refusing to permit charities to market any app through its iTunes site that would provide direct credit card or PayPal donations to a charity, rather than those that direct donors to the charity's Web site. But I expect this policy may change as Apple becomes more comfortable with what its customers are demanding and comes up with safeguards to address its concerns.

QR Codes. QR codes are two-dimensional bar codes designed to be scanned and read by a cell phone, which contain data to open up a Web site, dial a telephone number, or send a text message, among other applications. The latest cell phones already come with QR readers, and apps may be downloaded for free to facilitate QR scanning. About 4,000 characters of data may be stored in the latest and largest version of this bar code system. First created in 1994, it has taken a long time for these to be in common use, but the smart phone revolution is going to make these ubiquitous, with scores of useful applications for nonprofit organizations. I would expect that it will not be long before a donor can see a print ad in a magazine or a Google ad on a Web site and effortless make a donation simply by scanning in a QR code. Or an organization's brochure may have a short version of a list of services along with a QR code, and a viewer can access "the rest of the story" without having to type in an entire URL into a browser, simply by scanning the accompanying QR code. Or, advocates could quickly sign on to an online petition to save an important government program simply by scanning a QR code. Or, well... you get the idea.

One thing about this technology trend appears certain. When I start the process of updating this chapter for the next edition of this book, much of what I have written will appear to be antediluvian.

Domain Names

A domain name is the part of the e-mail address after the "@" sign or the part of a Web address after the "www." For example, my personal e-mail address is: gary.grobman@paonline.com. Pa Online is my Internet Service Provider (ISP), and "com" indicates that it is a commercial provider. *Paonline.com* is the domain name.

Choosing a Domain Name for Your Organization

If you are just starting to develop a Web site for your organization, you will need to choose and register a domain name. Most organizations prefer to use "my organization.org" where "my organization" is the name of the organization. Go to a registrar's site (such as *register.com* or *networksolutions.com*) and do a search for the domain name you want. Most will have a simple form where you can type the domain name and click "enter" to find out if the name is available for registration. If someone else has already registered the name, you will get an "unavailable" answer. Depending on the registrar, you may get a listing of suggested domain names, related to your first choice, that are available. If the name is not available, you can do a "whois" search (try: *http://www.networksolutions.com/whois/index.jsp*) to find out who currently has the name registered. This information may be of use to you now or in the future. If the name is available, you are ready to register. If your first choice of domain name is not available, keep searching until you find a suitable alternative that is. In the meantime, you can do a "whois" search to find out who the current registrant is for your desired name, and when the registration expires. If it is due to expire soon, you can keep checking back to see if the registrant renewed it, or if he or she let it expire. Be aware that there is typically a "grace period" after expiration during which a domain name is still not available for registration. During that time (possibly two to three months), the former registrant can still renew it. Once the registrar releases it and makes it available for registration, anyone (including you) can register it.

Registering Your Domain Name

If you have found a domain name that you like and it is available, you are ready to register it. Simply go to a registrar's registration form and fill in the requested information. This will include the domain name, your name, the organization's name, address, phone number, e-mail address, and other pertinent information. If you already have a Web host, you will be asked for the host's DNS information. Otherwise, most registrars will "park" your domain name with a "Coming Soon" page until you have a host and are ready to publish your site. The registration process also requires that you pay for the domain registration, usually via secure online credit card payment. Have your credit card information ready. Once you have completed and submitted the online registration for your domain name, it may take a short time for the name to show up in the "root" registry, making your Web site accessible to all Web users around the world.

Domain Extensions

You have registered yourorganization.org. Should you register domains with other extensions, as well, such as yourorganization.com and yourorganization.info? One advantage of doing so is that anyone looking on the Web for "yourorganization" will be more likely to find you. Another is that it prevents someone else from setting up a Web site using your organization's name.

Developing Your Own Web Site

There are thousands of commercial services offering to design and administer Web sites for a fee. With a minimum of technical background, you can do it yourself. Free software is available that works with popular word processing programs to convert documents into HTML language. Open source content management systems, such as Joomla, are available free of charge and allow you to use templates to make your site look professional.

Among the types of information that can be found on typical Web sites of nonprofits are:

> educational pages, newsletter, annual report, press releases, brochure, how to contribute or volunteer, financial data, action alerts, job openings, information about board and staff members, publications, upcoming conferences and seminars, product catalogs and order forms, a way to e-mail the organization, and links to other organizations and government-based sites related to the mission and purpose of the organization.

Simply having a Web site is clearly not enough to bring your organization fame, friends, and fortune. The "build it and they will come" philosophy may work well for Hollywood baseball movies, but you need to take proactive steps to build a base of loyal visitors and keep them returning.

Encouraging First-Time Visitors

Building a Web site that encourages first-time visitors has become an art form. Page design, load time, color schemes, pictures, animations, graphics, and how content is linked from one page to another based on your visitors' needs have become important issues for Web page designers.

Unique content is the key

Of primary importance to nonprofit organization Web sites, of course, is the content itself. You can safely assume that a visitor is not likely to be visiting your site to be entertained, as there are thousands of commercial sites that do that quite well. In most cases, visitors will be pointing their browsers to your organization's site because they have an interest in the organization's cause and the information is not available anywhere else, or because they were directed there by some other source.

Take advantage of that knowledge, and put content on your site that will meet the specific information needs of your visitors. If you can do this in a pleasing format, fine, but don't sacrifice the unique content only you can provide—backed by the credibility of your organization's reputation—in exchange for "bells and whistles." A simply designed site with good content can be quite effective.

I offer additional advice for driving new traffic to your site:

Put a "Share" button on your home page. Part of what has become known as a "viral marketing" strategy, this allows visitors to send your pages to themselves and their social networks. such as Facebook or Twitter, an e-mail to someone he or she knows. Because the receiver of this message gets it from a friend and is likely to be interested in your site, that person is likely to visit it, and, perhaps, tell more friends. It is an electronic way to tell about your site using "word of mouth," or "word of mouse." You can find the code to incorporate this feature on your site at, among other places, *http://send-a-link.com, http://www.addthis.com* and *http://www.sharethis.com.*

Use metatags in your Web pages. Registering with search engines and directories doesn't guarantee that the person looking for information will find your organization in the search results instead of hundreds of others with similar information. Type the words "animal shelter" in the Google search engine, and it responds with two million "hits." Viewers are not likely to browse through more than a few of these pages. You want to take steps to help the search engine give you high placement compared to competing Web pages. One way to do this is using metatags—key words and descriptions that appear in your Web page source code and are used by search engines to rank the likelihood that your particular page will be useful to the searcher. Each search engine uses a different process to calculate the placement of search results. There are sites that are helpful in explaining all of the technical details about submitting to search engines and directories, and inserting the right metatags. Among the most popular free ones are Stepforth *(http://www.stepforth.com/archives/2003-news/ten-minute-optimization.html)* and Digital Web Magazine *(http://www.digital-web.com/articles/designing_for_search_engines_and_stars/).*

Maximize links to your Web site from other organizations. Develop a link strategy to get the message out about your site. One popular strategy is to identify Web sites that appeal to the same audiences as yours. You can do this by using search engines to search key words. Then e-mail the Webmaster for these organizations and offer to exchange links. You can have a separate "links" page on your site, with one-sentence descriptions. In this way, visitors to those sites who may not know about yours have the opportunity to visit with a simple click of the mouse.

Another form of exchanging links is participating in a Web ring. These are cooperative linkages of Web sites that have a common theme or topic. Each ring is administered by an individual Web site owner who screens requests to join the ring. For example, there are at least 23 Web rings on the topic of breast cancer. If your organization has a mission related to this topic and receives permission to join one of these rings, you will receive the appropriate code to place on your Web site. A visitor to your site and others that are members of the ring sees graphics and buttons that permit him or her to visit each site that is a member of the ring by clicking on them. This drives targeted traffic to your site from those who are visiting the sites of other members of the ring. For more information, check out *http://dir.webring.com/rw* and *http://www.ringsurf.com.*

Promote your Web site address on all organization materials. A final suggestion is to add your organization's Web site address to all of your organization's promotional items, brochures, newsletters, and conference/workshop materials. Put your site's address on your e-mail signature, your business cards, letterhead, and all of your advertisements—both print and online. It doesn't cost any more to do so, and this free advertising gets the word out.

Use social media to promote your organization and its work. Develop a Facebook page, a Linked-In group, and a Twitter presence. Your stakeholders are accessing these sites daily in what is becoming an activity of daily living. For an excellent primer on how to use the Internet to advantage for your organization, read *Connect Causes: Online Marketing Strategies for Nonprofit Organizations* by Walter Wymer and Stacey Landreth Grau (2011, Lyceum Books).

Encouraging Repeat Web Site Visits

Changing the content often is the most important step toward keeping loyal visitors returning. This requires a commitment that consists of two parts. First, content relating to your organization's activities, upcoming events, public policy and advocacy briefings, staff responsibilities, newsletter postings, and other information should be updated at least every week—more frequently if you are able to do this. Second, you need a strategy to let everyone know when there is updated information on your site.

Many Web-savvy organizations routinely keep focused on what needs to be updated on their sites by publishing weekly newsletters that are distributed by e-mail to stakeholders who request them (see page 193. You can archive back issues on your site and use the content of each newsletter as your reminder to systematically keep your Web site content current.

Letting Visitors Know About Your Site

Now that you've updated your site, you need to let visitors know about it. Your electronic newsletter can be the vehicle for informing your stakeholders and other site visitors of updates and new material added to your site. You can design your site with a "What's New" link that will make it easy for visitors to see what has been added recently. This can also be accomplished by putting a "NEW!" or "UPDATED!" icon beside a link to a page that was recently added or updated. It is also useful to add a line at the bottom of your home page divulging the date when the page was last updated. Doing this may even provide an incentive for you to update your site more often, so as to avoid the embarrassment of having too many days pass before any material is changed on your site. You can send an e-mail or press release to the publishers of electronic and print newsletters and electronic mailing lists informing them about the availability of new files and features on your Web site. And don't forget to let your Facebook, LinkedIn, and Twitter networks know about Web site updates. Take advantage of all of the free promotional resources you can!

Adding Features to Attract Visitors

Experienced Webmasters know that simply adding new content and telling people about it is not always enough to encourage repeat visitors. They use a variety of techniques. For example, offer something free, such as an electronic newsletter, contests (with prizes), surveys, or a downloadable screensaver with your organization's logo and URL. If your organization sells goods and services or charges for events, provide a printable coupon on your site that will give visitors a discount.

Add useful services such as a job bank, blogs, chat room, message board, or a library of informative issue papers that will encourage visitors to return again and again. Chat rooms and message boards are among the best techniques for building an online community—the ultimate goal you should have for promoting repeat visits. It is from building such an online community that an organization can substantially increase its pool of volunteers (virtual and otherwise), donors, advocates, and loyal supporters.

Use your Web site to conduct an auction of donated goods and services (see Chapter 22). This not only increases Web site traffic, but can generate supplemental revenue, as well.

Ask visitors to bookmark the site, using a custom-designed bookmark icon. Bookmarking provides a convenient way for a Web browser to "remember" your site's Web address. It may not be obvious, but having your Web site in a person's "favorites list" is one of the best strategies to generate repeat visits.

How do you add these tools to your site without busting your budget? See an online article on bookmarks by Dr. Ralph Wilson, which can be found at: *http://wilsonweb.com/wmta/bookmark. htm*. Visit sites such as BraveNet *(http://www.bravenet.com/)* and Presenter Media *(http://www. presentermedia.com/)*. Keep in mind that some free services may require advertising messages from the sponsor, and you may not wish to have these appear on your site. Some may offer these services/tools without advertising, for a fee.

Your Web site should not be a stagnant pond. Rather, it needs to be a vibrant river—flourishing, animated, dynamic, and zippy—making a measurable, positive contribution to your organization's communications and public relations efforts. An investment in some time and effort in building traffic to your Web site will help you in reaching your organization's goals.

Online Resources to Explore

Thousands of charities and other nonprofits have their own Web sites. There are scores of interesting and handy gateways to them and other sites that have substantial resources of interest to nonprofit organizations. Perhaps the best thing about accessing these Web sites is that they are free-of-charge to visit (other than the fee to your service provider for Internet access). Among them are:

1. Idealist
http://www.idealist.org/info/Nonprofits

This site is home to the popular Nonprofit FAQ, a searchable library of frequently asked questions (and answers) on nonprofit management, fundraising, technology, legal requirements, and almost every other practical facet of running a nonprofit organization. Bulletins are posted on the site with articles and late-breaking news of interest to the sector, and you can sign up to be notified by e-mail about newly available issues. For more on this site, see page 135.

2. The Foundation Center
http://foundationcenter.org/

The Foundation Center is an independent nonprofit information clearinghouse established in 1956. The Center operates five libraries and provides materials to hundreds of public libraries. The mission of the organization is to foster public understanding of the foundation field by collecting, organizing, analyzing, and disseminating information on foundations, corporate giving, and related subjects. The site has a searchable archives, an excellent reference on how to prepare grant applications (*A Proposal Writing Short Course,* accessible from the *Learning Lab* menu on the home page) and standardized grant application forms. There is access to an online librarian who will answer your questions about where to find resources and basic information of interest to nonprofits. Just fill out the online form with your question.

3. GuideStar
http://www2.guidestar.org

GuideStar is administered by Williamsburg, VA-based Philanthropic Research, Inc., a 501(c)(3), and publishes comprehensive reports about individual American charities. Its purpose is "to bring the actors in the philanthropic and nonprofit communities closer together through the use of information and communication technologies. GuideStar collects and analyzes operating and financial data from the IRS Form 990 and from voluntary submissions from the charities themselves." The database consists of more than 850,000 reports on individual charities, and the site is colorful, accessible, and well-designed. The database can be searched at no charge by any number of parameters, such as name, location, or type of charity. This is simply the best site on the Internet for finding financial information about charities. Charities can provide their reports and update them online at no charge. The site also includes links of interest to charities and essays about philanthropy in its *Nonprofit Resources* and *Donor Resources* sections.

4. Nonprofit Managers' Library
http://managementhelp.org/

While much of this site is targeted to the needs of Minnesota nonprofits (such as local grant information), it is an excellent resource for all. The site boasts updated files on ethics, fundraising, communications skills, marketing, organizational change, risk management, strategic planning, and much more, sorted by more than 70 categories and indexed with 675 topics. There are numerous useful links to outside organizations that make this site an excellent resource for those interested in grants, foundations, government information, and general information useful to nonprofits. The site also hosts a free Nonprofit Organization and Management Development Program (a.k.a., *Free Nonprofit Micro-eMBA*).

5. Philanthropy Journal Online
http://www.pnnonline.org

This online newspaper, based in North Carolina, is a service of Philanthropy News Network, a 501(c)(3). It posts breaking news stories of interest to the nonprofit community. The home page menu sorts these news stories (and feature stories, as well) by categories such as technology, volunteers, fundraising, and corporate giving. You can subscribe to the biweekly e-mail version for free.

6. The Chronicle of Philanthropy
http://philanthropy.com/section/Home/172

The site provides highlights from this print publication, which is the trade journal for America's charitable community. The tabloid-format biweekly is the number one source for charity leaders, fundraisers, and grant makers, and the Web site provides more than just a taste of what its subscribers receive in snail mail every two weeks. The site is updated every other week at 9 a.m. on the Monday before the issue date, and job announcements are updated on the Monday following that. You can sign up for a free weekly e-mail update of news and new features of the site, plus breaking news when it occurs. The principal categories of this site are gifts and grants, fundraising, managing nonprofit groups, and technology. Each of these headings is further divided by a news summary, workshops and seminars, and deadlines. Also on the site are front-page news stories, a news summary, conferences, Internet resources, products and services, and jobs. Most of the articles consist of one-sentence summaries but are still useful, particularly if you don't have the $72 in your budget to subscribe to the publication for a year. The "Jobs" link transports you to a searchable database of hundreds of positions available. In some respects, this searchability makes the Internet version of the *Chronicle* more useful than the conventional version. There is also a directory of "Products and Services." If you are a subscriber, you will have access to a handy, searchable database of archived issues.

7. The Nonprofit Times
http://www.thenonprofittimes.com/

This is the online version of the monthly tabloid newspaper. It has full-text articles from the latest issue, as well as classified advertisements. The Resource Directory, accessible from the home page, links to a database of vendors, consultants, and other professionals who serve the nonprofit community.

8. Independent Sector
http://www.independentsector.org

Independent Sector is the leading advocacy coalition in Washington that serves the nonprofit sector. This site is the first place to go for definitive statistics of interest about the nonprofit sector (click on *Nonprofit Information Center*). It also has files on ethics, advocacy, accountability, and leadership issues. There is current information about new laws and regulations affecting charities, as well as public policy advocacy updates.

9. HandsNet
http://www.handsnet.org

Founded in 1987, HandsNet links more than 5,000 public interest and human services organizations using the Internet to promote collaboration, advocacy, and information-sharing by the sector. The public pages are updated daily, and the members-only pages are considered to be the most valuable around for nonprofits that engage in advocacy. The site's Action Alerts provide numerous government links, state-of-the-art information on current issues (most of which is provided by member organizations whose niche includes that particular public policy issue), capsule summaries, sources to find more information about the issue, sample advocacy letters, and information about new legislation. While a generous sample of content is provided free, organizations are encouraged to join a fee-based *Web Clipper* service, which provides full access. A trial membership is free.

10. FirstGov.gov
http://www.firstgov.gov/Business/Business_Gateway.shtml

This site's strength lies in its convenient and user-friendly links to federal departments and agencies—executive, legislative, and judicial—and an easy-to-use guide to access publications of importance to nonprofits, such as the *Federal Register,* the *Catalog of Federal Domestic Assistance,* and access to the General Services Administration. It has a grid of federal agencies that permits easy access to each agency's home page, and a page on grants. Its search page can find information from more than a million government Web pages.

11. Volunteer Match/Impact Online
http://www.volunteermatch.org

This site provides a posting area for nonprofits to advertise volunteer opportunities that can be performed online, and it has excellent resources relating to "virtual volunteering." From the home page, click on "Virtual" for cutting-edge information about harnessing the power of those who are homebound, those who are unable to commit to a specific time and place to volunteer, or those who are simply too busy—but who have valuable skills they are willing to share. The "Volunteer Match" may help you find suitable volunteers for your organization who can transcend the limitations of geographical inaccessibility, as well as general volunteering resources.

12. Tech Soup
http://www.techsoup.org

TechSoup *(http://www.techsoup.org),* originally conceived by CompuMentor, a San Francisco-based nonprofit, has developed a reputation as being *the* place for nonprofits to visit for answers to questions about hardware and software, building Web sites, and taking advantage of all that technology can offer to help nonprofits achieve their vital missions. The content is all free and worthy of repeat visits. A service of TechSoup, DiscounTech is a partnership of America Online, Novell, Microsoft, CNET, and several national and community foundations and other computer-related for-profits. For more than a decade, CompuMentor has distributed donated Microsoft and other name-brand products. The strings attached to receiving donated software through this program are minimal: Eligible organizations are nonprofits and schools with valid 501(c)(3) status. Microsoft does not permit K-12 schools, political organizations, or religious organizations to participate in this program, or nonprofits from Washington State. Additional restrictions apply to those purchasing server products. Lotus products may not be purchased by organizations that advocate, support, or practice discrimination based on race, religion, age, national origin, sex, sexual orientation, or physical handicap. Overall, this is one of the best sites on the Internet for information about nonprofit technology issues, including hardware, software, connecting to the Internet, and finding discounts on products and services offered to nonprofit organizations.

13. Network For Good
http://www1.networkforgood.org

Network for Good is a charity portal founded in November 2001 by AOL-Time Warner, Cisco Systems, and Yahoo!. Charities large and small can find extensive resources here to assist in their online fundraising efforts. Even more valuable is the service it provides to charities that register, enabling them to place a "donate here" link on their own Web pages to permit donors to make secure, online contributions without the charity needing its own merchant account. By 2007, Network for Good delivered more than $100 million to more than 20,000 charities. I applaud the sponsors for their vision in helping small charities build an infrastructure to accept real-time credit card donations and help even the smallest charity benefit from this service.

14. Grants.Gov
http://www.grants.gov

While the searchable Catalog of Federal Domestic Assistance *(http://www.cfda.gov)* has been available free online in a searchable format since the mid-1990s, this site, launched in October 2003, takes the online search for federal government funding to a higher level. The objective of this site is to level the playing field so that all eligible organizations, regardless of their size or grantsmanship sophistication, can have a fair opportunity to receive federal grants. The site directs grant seekers to funding programs offered by 26 grant-making federal agencies that aggregately award more than $360 billion annually to state and local governments, academia, nonprofits, and other organizations. It not only makes it easier for organizations to find grants of interest; it streamlines the paperwork needed to apply for them and permits the entire process to be conducted online. All application forms, financial report data in support of organizational audit and performance measurement activities, grant management procedures, and information about grant programs have been standardized across these participating agencies. The site hosts everything an organization needs to find, apply, and manage a federal grant. Even grant notifications are made electronically. Site visitors download forms, work on them offline, and then submit completed applications electronically, saving hours of time and money. The site is divided into sections that help you engage in a six-step process, consisting of finding grant opportunities of interest, downloading the grant application package, registering with a Central Contract Registry, registering with a credentials provider, registering with grants.gov to submit grant applications, and logging on. There is a toll-free number to use to request assistance. This site is the first place to go if you have any interest in federal grant funds.

15. Nonprofit Good Practice Guide
http://www.npgoodpractice.org/

This site is a project of The Dorothy A. Johnson Center for Philanthropy & Nonprofit Leadership at Grand Valley State University. The searchable site is organized by ten topic areas, including "Fundraising and Financial Sustainability" and "Technology." You can find links to more than 3,000 articles, online courses (many of which are free), research papers, booklets, and case studies, all organized by topic. Although the strength of this site is in its organization of links to online resources found on other Web sites, it does have substantial useful content of its own. The Guide has a unique way of integrating both types of resources in a pleasing format that is both fun to browse and almost guaranteed to uncover some useful nugget that is worthwhile to print and save. Clicking on each topic area takes you to a page that opens with a list of "preferred practices" and "pitfalls"—in short, a list of "do's" and "don'ts." Although many of these initial offerings have been seeded by the center's seasoned executive director, Joel Orosz, Ph.D., there is a link that permits visitors to add to the lists and to submit information about new resources. Thus, the site is organic and is likely to become one of the leading sources nonprofit staff and board members can turn to for advice, once folks know it is available and it reaches the critical mass necessary to sustain itself as an online community. Another useful feature is a glossary, accessible from the home page menu. It defines more than 2,500 terms of interest to nonprofit organizations, some with hyperlinks that point your browser to supplemental information. All in all, this is one of the best new resources on the Internet for nonprofit organizations.

16. The Pennsylvania State Government Home Page
http://www.pa.gov/portal/server.pt/community/pa_gov/2966

This is the gateway for state government information—here you can find links to departments and agencies; executive orders, press releases, state budget proposals, financial reports, and speeches of the governor; local weather, terrorist threat information, tourist information, including calendars of events and maps; state lottery results; and links to federal, state, and local government offices. Department of Revenue forms, information about charitable organization disclosure, and a history of Pennsylvania are just a click away. The site is searchable and available in both colorful HTML and text formats.

17. Electronic Billroom
http://www.legis.state.pa.us/cfdocs/legis/home/session.cfm

This site became operational at the end of 1998. You can search the database by subject and obtain the full text of bills introduced during the Pennsylvania General Assembly from 1993 to the present. The bills are available in PDF format as well, so you can print them out just as they look from the Capitol document room. To find out what is happening in the PA House or Senate, visit *http://www.legis.state.pa.us* to access the home page.

18. Pennsylvania Department of State Corporation Bureau
http://www.dos.state.pa.us/portal/server.pt/community/corporation_bureau/12457

Here you can find definitive general information about record searches, name availability, name reservations, how to obtain copies of documents and get them in a hurry if you need them, filing and registration guidelines, fee schedules, and, perhaps most important, getting copies of forms you need online. There is a useful FAQ (Example: Q: Can corporate seals and corporate kits be obtained from the Corporation Bureau? A: No. They may be obtained from a local stationery store or any office supply store). There is also a link here to the Bureau of Charitable Organizations (see #19 below).

19. Department of State's Bureau of Charitable Organizations
http://www.dos.state.pa.us/portal/server.pt/community/charities/12444

This site has information about whether you need to register with the Bureau, and what forms you need to file, whether you work for a charity, represent an "institution of purely public charity" that must register as a result of Act 55, a fundraising counsel, or a fundraising solicitor. There are files of facts and statistics about charities in Pennsylvania, a complaints hotline, consumer information about charitable giving, a searchable database of charities registered with the Bureau, information about charities against whom the Attorney General's Office has issued cease and desist orders, and the full text of the charitable solicitation registration law, Act 202. Here you can download the Bureau's Annual Report and all forms and instruction booklets. You can follow links from the homepage to register your charity electronically.

20. Pennsylvania Association of Nonprofit Organizations
http://www.pano.org

This is a valuable site for accessing current information about public policy and advocacy of general interest to Pennsylvania nonprofits (click on "public policy"). The site has a directory of consultants where you can find fundraising and legal help. Click on "Forming a Nonprofit" for an FAQ focusing on practical advice. There is also a nonprofit organization jobs page, an online bookstore offering leading publications of interest to nonprofit organizations (including this book), information about training programs, and a 16-point set of tips on forming a nonprofit organization (click on "Forming a Non-Profit" from the homepage menu).

Tips:

- **Subscribe to a general nonprofit electronic mailing list to keep current with what your colleagues in the field are thinking and discussing.**

- **Use popular search engines and search on your own organization's name. Take steps to ensure that what you find is accurate and up to date.**

- **Protect your domain names by keeping your fees paid.**

- **For details about using the Internet to sell goods and services and to raise funds, see Chapters 21 and 22 respectively.**

Chapter 21
Nonprofit E-Commerce

Nonprofit organizations can effectively utilize the Internet to sell goods and services, and raise money. Those who take advantage of this must consider issues such as privacy, security, customer service, order fulfillment, and payment processing.

Introduction

The term *e-commerce* refers to business that is conducted electronically. It includes the marketing of goods and services, using the Internet to join an organization or subscribe to a publication, and automated customer service.

Technically, using the telephone to place an order also qualifies as e-commerce. So would using your debit card to make a purchase at your local convenience store. This chapter uses a narrower definition to describe business conducted over the Internet. It focuses on how nonprofit organizations can use the Internet to increase membership, market products and services, and respond to customer inquiries and complaints.

Customer service? Marketing? Products? Why does any of this have anything to do with the nonprofit sector? Many of us lose sight of the fact that a nonprofit organization is a form of business. Nonprofits and for-profits have many things in common. Both need capital to launch their operations; both need cash flow to pay their bills in a timely manner; and both need revenues to pay for staff, supplies, utilities, rent, equipment, printing, and other goods and services. Charities typically receive revenues beyond what is gratuitously donated by the public, the business community, or foundations. For example, they sell services. It is typical that a third or more of the revenue from a social service agency comes from user fees. Although many agencies charge on a sliding scale based on income, it is not unusual for them to charge a market rate to those who can afford to pay and use the surplus so generated to cross-subsidize those who cannot afford to pay the full costs of services.

The for-profit world has embraced e-commerce, recognizing that it is the future of how business-to-business (B2B) and business-to-consumer (B2C) purchasing will be conducted by millions, if not billions, of participants. The Internet is becoming a convenient way for consumers to make retail purchases. According to Forrester Research, e-commerce in the United States in 2009 accounted for sales of $155.2 billion, an 11% increase over the previous year, and continues its 10-20% annual growth rate despite a severe recession. One aspect of that organization's study that is perhaps of even more interest to nonprofit organizations is its finding that 42% of all retail purchases, $917 billion, were influenced by information consumers found on the Internet.

The business models and strategies used by for-profits can be adapted by nonprofits to generate revenue that will finance the expansion of nonprofit organizational programs and activities. At the very least, these techniques make it a bit easier to raise funds and thus reduce what must be one of the leading causes of stress and burnout among nonprofit executives and staff—the constant battle to raise dollars to balance organizational budgets.

For years, charities have generated income through a variety of programs and activities, such as selling newsletter subscriptions and other publications, collecting fees at conferences and workshops, operating thrift shops, conducting flea markets and running races, renting mailing lists, having auctions, scheduling fundraising dinners, and selling group outings to sporting events or theater performances.

The Web has made all of this easier, at least for many organizations, in two significant ways. First, it has provided organizations with a way to reach almost everyone, and to do this quickly and inexpensively. Using a combination of strategies, such as conventional mail, telephone, and media advertising, along with Web site and social networking site postings, mailing list postings, broadcast e-mail, and Web advertising, an organization can reach its target market and expand its reach. Second, using sophisticated technology, organizations can take advantage of homebound volunteers (at one end of the scale) and pricey, professional "back end" providers (at the other end of the scale) to do much of the work.

As a result of e-mail, the Web, electronic mailing lists, and real-time chat, the velocity of business transactions has made a quantum leap. The Internet has salient advantages over conventional sales marketing, such as—

- Overall marketing and order processing costs are lower using the Web.
- Organizations can reach a global, targeted market virtually instantaneously.
- A Web-based "store" is open 24 hours/day, seven days/week, and always has free parking.
- The playing field is leveled between small organizations and those with many more resources.
- Business transactions can be consummated electronically without the need for expensive labor or intermediaries, such as brokers.
- Internet search engines and directories bring potential customers to organizations without unreasonably expensive marketing efforts.
- Customer service can be almost completely automated.
- For-profit organizations with substantial expertise, labor, and sophisticated software will do the necessary "back office" work and make it appear to customers that the nonprofit organization is performing the work.

Setting Up an Online Store

If your organization sells products and services, you can enhance these sales by adding a secure online store to your organization's Web site. Before opening your store, think about costs, how you will handle online transactions, customer service issues, receipts and invoices, tax issues, and shipping.

Costs

What will an e-commerce-enabled Web site cost you? Surprisingly, less than you would think in terms of money (but likely more than you think in time). Here are some typical costs.

Web site hosting. Hosting services can be free for nonprofit organizations. A typical charge is $10/month. If you plan to take credit card information over the Internet, make sure that your Web host has the capability of supporting secure forms for this purpose. Secure online store hosting can be found for, perhaps, $30-$40 per month.

Software. Check out open-source software such as Joomla to manage your page content and add hosted shopping carts such as Big Commerce (*http://www.bigcommerce.com*)or Volusion *(http://www.volusion.com)*. Or hire someone to custom develop your site. Joomla is free while custom designers may charge you upwards of $100/hour.

Domain Name Registration. This costs up to $35 annually, although there are discounts for pre-payment, and some registrars such as Go Daddy *(http://www.GoDaddy.com)* and Register.com *(http://www.register.com)* will register a name for $10 or even less.

Content. Most nonprofit organizations create their own Web site content. It is not unusual to make a purchase or two of graphics or photographs suitable for the Web, but there are many sources that provide these items for free.

Site Maintenance. It takes time to update Web sites and respond to feedback from visitors. Some organizations are large enough to hire full-time Webmasters to design and maintain sites, and some have the executive director or a technically savvy volunteer do this.

Hardware. If you have a remote virtual Web site host, you don't need anything more than your standard office computer and monitor, which you can buy for perhaps $1,000 for an entire system, including CPU with modem, monitor, and color printer.

SSL Certificate. This ensures that the customers' credit cards and other personal information is secure (see page 216)

Marketing. This can be your largest cost. Advertising the site through print publications, post-cards, press releases, banner advertising on other sites, and similar strategies can bring more visitors, but can be expensive.

You can spend as little or as much as you want, but it is possible to obtain everything you need to set up an online store on your existing Web site for no cost. If you do not yet have a site (or even a computer), it is possible to buy everything you need for a one-time investment of $1,000, and a monthly payment of under $50.

Handling Online Financial Transactions

Qualifying for merchant status to accept popular credit cards such as Visa, MasterCard, American Express, and Discover is often routine. An organization typically approaches its bank to set up a merchant account. One can find hundreds, if not thousands, of financial institutions willing to establish merchant accounts on the Web. One way to find them is to search under the terms "credit cards" and "merchant accounts."

Startup fees, account maintenance fees, per transaction fees, and the bank's percentage of sales fee for processing each transaction varies by financial institution and may be negotiable.

Organizations will also need a system for transmitting the information about the transaction to the financial institution for processing—typically a terminal sold or leased by the financial institution—or computer software. The financial institution, within a few business days, credits the organization's account for the amount of the sale after deducting transaction charges. The card number, expiration date, and sales information is entered into the terminal or software (or transmitted through a real-time process, using an online ordering system), and the system verifies that the card is valid and the purchaser has not exceeded his or her credit limit. There is some paperwork involved, and occasionally a purchaser will challenge a charge, which can result in a loss of time and revenue, even if the charge is legitimate. On the other hand, entrepreneurial nonprofit organizations may lose out on revenue opportunities unless they satisfy the expectations of their customers by offering online credit card purchases.

An alternative to setting up a merchant account for credit card sales is to utilize the services of a third-party payment processor that will accept credit cards for you by using a secure, online platform. One such popular provider, PayPal *(https://www.paypal.com)*, not only provides this service but also gives access to tools that you can use to build your online store, such as shopping carts, invoices, and shipping/tracking management services. From the home page, click on "Merchant Tools" for details about these services. There are no setup fees to establish an account as a merchant. PayPal charges a fee of from 1.9% to 2.9% (depending on sales volume) plus 30 cents per transaction. There are additional fees for foreign currency transactions. More than 225 million individuals worldwide have PayPal accounts. The company was purchased by eBay in 2002 and is quickly becoming the standard for making and receiving online payments.

In June 2005, PayPal established Website Payments Pro to accept credit cards directly on your site without having a merchant account.

Customer Service

Depending on the products and services offered, many of the issues relating to customer service will be the same for a nonprofit as for a for-profit organization. Organizations will need to have policies for, and routines for, processing returns, exchanges, refunds, and shipping.

One obvious disadvantage of shopping over the Internet is that shoppers cannot touch and feel the product, or try it on or try it out. People are more willing to make purchases over the Internet when they feel that they can return the products if they are not completely satisfied. A refunds and returns policy should be posted on your site, and it should be a more liberal policy than one would expect to find at the local mall. This is good business practice; nonprofits certainly don't want to alienate a customer who is also a donor or potential donor. Among the issues that should be addressed are:

1. Will refunds be given in cash or credit for a future purchase?
2. How much time is permitted to elapse before returns will not be accepted?
3. Can returns be made unconditionally, or only for defective products?
4. Is there a restocking fee?
5. Must the product be returned in salable condition in the original packaging?
6. Will shipping and handling also be refunded, or only the product purchase price?
7. Will the organization pay for return shipping?
8. Will certain products not be returnable (such as publications, electronics, or jewelry)?

Receipts and Invoices

Products should be shipped with a receipt if pre-paid, or an invoice if payment is due. If they were not prepaid, the invoice should state the terms of payment, such as when the bill is due, and the percentage added to the bill per month for any outstanding balance. The receipt should include the name of the purchaser, the name of the organization, the description of the product(s), the price of each purchase, and the amount of tax and shipping. Generic accounting software programs such as Quickbooks, Quicken, MYOB Accounting, or Peachtree provide forms for standard invoices and receipts.

Collecting Taxes

Only the states of Alaska, Delaware, Montana, New Hampshire, and Oregon do not have a state sales and use tax. The sales tax applies to sales made within a state to a purchaser from that same state. The use tax applies to sales of products bought in one state and taken into another.

The use tax is intended to be paid by the purchaser and goes to the purchaser's state treasury, although this requirement is rarely, if ever, enforced. Generally, organizations are obligated to collect sales and use taxes on sales they make to customers within their own states.

There is a general moratorium on Internet sales taxes until November 1, 2014, courtesy of enactment of the *Internet Tax Freedom Act Amendments Act of 2007*, although legislation was introduced in July 2010, sponsored by Rep. Bill Delahunt (D-MA), to require consumers to pay state sales taxes on their Internet purchases. Sales taxes still must be collected for intrastate purchases in states with sales taxes, although enforcement of this requirement is spotty. Even if an organization is tax exempt, most states still require nonprofit organizations to collect sales taxes on sales they make to customers within the state.

Typically, states require organizations to obtain a sales tax license, and to transmit the collected taxes to the state using a provided form. It is advisable to check with a reputable local business organization, such as the Chamber of Commerce, to find out what the requirements are for collecting and transmitting state sales taxes in a particular state before engaging in the sale of goods and services there. For Pennsylvania requirements, see Chapter 26.

Shipping and Handling

Organizations need to decide how much they will charge for shipping and handling and display that information prominently on the site. Some shopping cart software provides for letting the customer decide how the product is to be shipped—automatically adjusting the amount for shipping and handling (such as by using a database provided by UPS or other shippers), based on how much the organization wants to add over the actual cost. They can charge a flat fee for shipping, charge by weight, charge by the number of products ordered, or provide for free shipping if the order exceeds a certain amount. Organizations should also consider policies with respect to out-of-country sales, which raise issues concerning payment, shipping, and customs duties.

Affiliate Marketing

New business models have emerged that permit nonprofit organizations to take advantage of technology and raise funds that would not have otherwise come their way. Even if your organization does not sell products or services of its own, you can generate revenue by marketing products and services of others through "affiliate" or "associate" programs.

The "affiliate" model was pioneered by Amazon.com. The Seattle-based company simply announced to the world that by placing specially coded links on your Web site, you can earn a commission on purchases of books, CDs, DVDs, videos, electronics, software, video games, toys, or home improvement items that are generated by those links.

Joining the Amazon Associates program involves visiting the Amazon.com site, clicking on the "Join Associates" link at the bottom of the home page, electronically submitting a form provided on the site (after reading and agreeing to the operating agreement), and using tools provided on the site to set up your links to Amazon.com and promote products. Each link has your Associate ID code embedded in it, so when someone buys something from Amazon.com through a link on your site, your organization gets a commission.

More than 2,000,000 Web sites have become Amazon.com associates. For nonprofits and for-profits alike, this simple, yet revolutionary, business model is generating valuable revenue without the need for any investment or exposure to risk.

Similarly, affiliate programs exist for many other online retailers and online services. Your organization can become an affiliate of eBay, Buy.com, allPosters.com, or CareerBuilder.com, for example. Typically, if a site offers an affiliate program, there will be a link for it somewhere near the bottom of the page, leading to an explanation of how to join and how the program works.

When considering whether to join an affiliate marketing program, think about how the site with which you will be affiliating fits with your organization's mission, as well as how you will incorporate the affiliate program into your own site. For example, if you are joining an affiliate program of an online bookstore (such as Amazon.com), will you place reviews and links to carefully selected books that are in line with your mission, or will you set up a complete store where your site's visitors can buy anything that is available in the affiliated store, encouraging your visitors to do all their shopping through your site, as a way of supporting your organization? Each of these approaches has its pros and cons.

Let's say your organization is an animal shelter. Using the first approach, you can create links to (and perhaps reviews of) books on animal care. This will keep the focus on your mission and promote products that your site's visitors are likely to be interested in. You can target these links to the visitor's interests, so a person who is reading an article about German shepherds will see a link on that page to a book on German shepherds. The conversion rate (from seeing the link to clicking on it to purchasing the item) on such links will be higher than that for random links that are unrelated to your site's content. You will need to monitor the links to make sure that they are up-to-date and the items are still available for purchase.

Using the second approach, you can build a store on your site using an automated data feed (if one is provided), and then "educate" your visitors to "support this site" by shopping there. If your visitors get in the habit of going through your site to make their purchases, you can do well with this method. They may buy animal care books, or they may buy office products, or both. Either way, you will earn the commission. However, keep in mind that you do not have complete control over the items that are shown through the data feed, and some items may not be consistent with the mission or character of your organization.

Charity Portals

Scores of for-profit and nonprofit dot-com companies are sprouting up, promising to take donations over the Internet by credit card, and funneling the donation—sometimes after deducting an administrative fee—to the charity. For charities that receive an unsolicited check in the mail from one of these portal companies, this is a windfall. For the donor, using a charity portal can be convenient and often provides anonymity, if requested.

The donor can use the site search engine to find a suitable charity, and there is often other content on the portal site to influence donation decisions. The administrative fee pays the bills and provides a profit to the service provider who runs the portal. Some make money by selling advertising on their sites. Others charge charities to be listed.

Some of these portals may not be legitimate. Many others are, but it is difficult to tell simply by visiting the Web site.

For many charities, being listed on these portals is a way to publicize the existence of the organization and the importance of its mission, even if donations received through participation are minimal. For others, being associated with a firm that takes a commission on donations is unacceptable. According to a report that appeared in *The Chronicle of Philanthropy*, the World Wildlife

Fund sent "cease and desist" letters threatening to take legal action if the sites did not remove its name from the list of organizations eligible to receive donations.

The Internal Revenue Service has raised questions about whether donations made through charity portals can be deductible for federal income tax purposes. Many are not likely to survive, since it takes a lot of marketing capital to draw people to the site to donate. In general, a site that requires charities to pay any kind of up-front fee is likely to be a scam.

How all of this will shake out is anybody's guess, but as more and more charities build their own Web sites that routinely accept donations by secure credit card forms, donations made through portals are likely to be a small slice of the online donation pie.

Perhaps the leading charity portal is Network For Good *(http://www1.networkforgood.org/)*, founded by America Online, AOL-Time Warner Foundation, Cisco Systems, the Cisco Foundation, and other cooperating charities. Its Web site boasts that it has raised over $500 million in donations so far to more than 60,000 charities, as of September 2011.

Online Shopping Malls

For-profit dot-coms have emerged that have established agreements with national retailers willing to offer discounts to online shoppers. These brokers will sign up charitable organizations for the purpose of driving traffic to the Web site of the retailers. Typically, the shoppers receive the same discount when they visit the retailer via the online shopping mall, and a percentage of the purchase is split between the charity and the broker. The charity encourages its stakeholders to shop at the online shopping mall by placing a link on its Web site. To find links to these sites, Google "charity shopping malls" or use the Yahoo Directory *(http://dir.yahoo.com)* and follow this path:

Directory > Business and Economy > Shopping and Services > Retailers > Virtual Malls > Charity and Fundraising Malls

Charity Auctions

The Internet provides many advantages if an organization has goods and services to auction off, particularly those obtained from celebrities. Many people will be interested in what an organization has to offer, even if they have never heard of the organization or don't care about its mission, if the goods and services are attractive.

An almost infinite number of items can be offered, and the auction can be conducted 24 hours each day year-round with the participation of people down the street or on the other side of the world. Innovative software makes the process relatively easy, and there are Web sites that help organizations seeking to harness this strategy. To find links to these sites, Google "charity auctions" or use the Yahoo Directory *(http://www.yahoo.com)* and follow this path:

Directory > Business and Economy > Shopping and Services > Auctions > Charity

One application service provider that is gaining a reputation as the leader in online charity auctions is Missionfish *(http://www.missionfish.org/about-us/us_about-us.html)*. Missionfish, formed in 2000, is a program of the Points of Light Foundation. Charities can register and run a charity auction using the tools on this site in the same way that members of the public do.

In November 2003, Missionfish launched eBay Giving Works, a program that permits hundreds of millions of eBay users to donate from 10-100% of their proceeds from eBay sales to a favorite 501(c)(3) organization. As of September 2011, this program had raised more than $228 million for U.S. charities. The charity must register to be eligible to receive these donations, but registration is free. According to the Web site, more than 20,000 nonprofits have registered.

Participating charities have online tools to review the types of goods being auctioned off. Why is this a useful feature? As one Missionfish press release points out, a charity that is dedicated to the protection of animals wouldn't want to be the beneficiary of an auction of fur coats! A charity benefits not only from the donation, but also from the exposure of having its name listed at the auction site. There are administrative fees involved for processing, but it is possible for a charity to encourage its stakeholders to participate in this form of auction, which requires no work for the charity other than cashing the donations.

Advertising

Another way you can generate revenue from your organization's Web site is to allow advertisements to be placed on it. The quickest and easiest way to earn money through advertising is to join Google AdSense or a similar program. Once you join, you will be able to log in to Google's AdSense site and generate HTML code to put on your site. Then ads will begin to appear on your site that correspond with key words in the content of your site. Google will send you a monthly check for a portion of the advertising revenue from these ads.

One downside to this is that you do not have complete control over the content of the ads that appear on your site. You can filter the ads to a certain extent, but it will take some staff or volunteer time to monitor the ads to make sure they are appropriate.

Instead of or in addition to this approach, your organization may decide to sell classified and/or banner advertising directly on your site. You will need to develop a policy stating what types of ads you will accept, your advertising rates, and so forth. And you will need to develop a "media kit" telling advertisers the benefits to them of advertising on your site, the amount of traffic the site experiences, the procedure for placing an ad, and how to make payment. If your site is a popular one that is getting a significant amount of traffic in your niche, this can be an excellent way to use your site to generate revenue.

Security and Privacy

Even putting e-commerce transactions aside, nonprofit organizations have many reasons to protect the security and privacy of the computer files they generate and the communications they send over the Internet. Human service organizations, for example, routinely use client files that, if disclosed in an unauthorized manner, could cause irreparable harm to their clients and result in lawsuits.

E-mail exchanges may involve sensitive personnel matters or contract negotiations with unions and other entities. Even if nothing sensitive is discussed in a file or e-mail message, an organization still does not want any prying person, within the organization or outside of it, to be able to browse through its business.

SSL and other Encryption Technology

Virtually every survey on Internet security has demonstrated the pervasive fear of providing credit card numbers over the Internet. The concern that unscrupulous merchants (or those who pretend to be merchants) will use the credit card information is mostly unfounded; even if this happened (and it does occasionally), there are limits on the amount of loss the consumer sustains (typically $50), and there is no exposure to loss if the problem is reported promptly.

The principal concern tends to be that hackers will somehow tap into the transaction and steal the credit card data. It is more probable that credit card data are stolen simply as a result of people, both merchants and consumers, being careless with the paper records of these transactions. Nonetheless, considerable effort has gone into making financial transactions over the Internet safe by encrypting (that is, disguising) the data so that only the intended sender and receiver can read it.

Although there are several protocols for encryption, the industry standard for e-commerce has become Secure Sockets Layer, or SSL. SSL was created by Netscape and is a feature of the company's Web browser software. The Netscape program uses what's known as a public and private key system and the use of a digital certificate.

Without having both the public and private keys, a message that is encrypted looks like gobbledygook. Each person has his or her own private key, which is kept very secret, and a public key, which is shared with others. The messages cannot be read without having both.

Certification/Authentication

Organizations that are serious about e-commerce should obtain an SSL certificate from a certifying authority to assure purchasers that they are who they say they are. A purchaser can see a lock icon or other indicator on his or her browser that authenticates encryption software if the organization has one of these certificates.

Many people will refuse to send their credit card information over the Internet unless the organization has a valid certificate. Server certificates are available commercially from many different companies, and the cost varies. Some free certificates are available, but there may be problems using free versions on some browsers and these are best used for testing purposes only.

The most widely-used certificate authority in the United States is VeriSign *(http://www.verisign. com)* along with its subsidiaries Thawte Consulting *(http://www.thawte.com)* and GeoTrust *(http://www.geotrust.com)*. Entrust *(http://www.entrust.com)*, GlobalSign *(http://www.globalsign.com)*, and Cacert.org *(http://www.cacert.org)* are among its competitors. One recurring problem is that the certificates may not work on all browsers, so make sure to inquire about this information.

Protection of Customer Data

Organizations can have all of the sophisticated encryption systems in place, but it won't do any good if employees keep the printouts on their desks or put them in an accessible file on their computers. Employees should take reasonable precautions to keep all customer data protected.

Firewalls

A firewall is a type of Internet security software that limits access to Web sites, allowing approved traffic in and out through a secure gateway. Firewalls can be downloaded for free (for example, find one at: *http://pfsense.com)* or obtained for thousands of dollars. See *http://www.interhack.net/pubs/fwfaq/* for a complete guide to firewalls.

Privacy Policies

Many commercial Web sites address privacy concerns by having a privacy policy posted online. The policy generally includes—

- what information will be collected on the site

- what information will be shared with others, and under what circumstances—for example, many organizations sell or rent their mailing lists.

- what information will not be shared with others—for example, obtaining a telephone number is helpful in the event of a problem with a customer's transaction. While many business organizations will request the telephone number for that purpose, they will keep the customer's telephone number confidential.

- what customers can do to keep their name and address confidential. This may entail simply clicking a box on an electronic form.

TRUSTe is an organization established to set up privacy standards and to provide sanctions against participants who violate the standards. Web sites that meet TRUSTe's strict privacy standards in the areas of notice, choice, access, and security and submit to TRUSTe's oversight program may display the organization's seal for a fee. This has become the Web privacy equivalent of the "Good Housekeeping Seal of Approval."

Cookies

One feature of the Internet that has contributed to fears about privacy violation is the cookie, a feature created by Netscape as part of its browser. Cookies are ASCII files (plain text) that can be created and accessed by a Web site visited by the browser. The file is stored in the browser directory, so using another browser results in the cookie not being readable by the originating Web site.

Cookies can be deleted, or the feature in the browser that creates them can be disabled. The benefit of the feature is that the cookie file lets the site being visited know something about the visitor and the visitor's interests by accessing it and permits the site to provide custom-designed information based on the cookie. Having a cookie can save a lot of time and keystrokes, because the site will "recognize" the visitor as a repeat visitor and "remember" what was done on previous visits. The downside is that the visitor may not wish to share this information.

Tips:

- **Look at the Web sites of similar organizations, and see how they handle issues such as returns, order fulfillment, privacy, and security.**

- **Make sure you are comfortable with the legal ramifications of e-commerce applications, such as privacy, security, copyright, and tax collection before launching an e-commerce initiative to generate revenue.**

Chapter 22
Fundraising on the Internet

by Gary Grobman and Gary Grant

Synopsis: The Internet assists, but does not replace, traditional fundraising efforts. While not without its problems, there are many creative ways to mount a successful online fundraising campaign. The Internet is a useful tool for development staff for use in prospect research, direct marketing, major gifts, corporate and foundation relations, and special events.

Introduction

On Tuesday evening, January 12, 2010, a magnitude 7.0 quake struck about 10 miles southwest of Haiti's capital, Port-au-Prince. Within minutes, Facebook and Twitter users viewed messages such as "Text 'HAITI' to 90999 to donate $10 to Red Cross relief efforts!" The American Red Cross raised $3.4 million just from text message donations in the first 36 hours following news of the disaster, an amount that increased to more than $31 million during the following four weeks. When another devastating natural disaster struck in Northern Japan on March 11, 2011, scores of charities competed to raise funds using the power of technology, harnessing social networking and other Web sites. The American Red Cross raised approximately $169.5 million during the first month of appeals, with text-message contributions accounting for more than $4 million of that total.

Of the $173 million raised by the International Red Cross within the first few weeks after the 2004 tsunami in the Indian Ocean, $73 million was donated via the organization's Web site, exceeding the total donated online after the September 11th terrorist attack. More than 45% of Catholic Relief Service's donations in response to the tragedy came online—almost $12 million. International relief organizations such as CARE, Save the Children, and Direct Relief International were all swamped with online donations. Doctors Without Borders/Médecins Sans Frontières (MSF), recipient of the 1999 Nobel Peace Prize, took what is believed to be an unprecedented step in January 2005 and raised almost $20 million for its tsunami relief efforts—and then decided that further fundraising would be counterproductive. According to a posting on the organization's Web site within about ten days after the disaster, the organization was inundated by donations, largely via its Web site's secure form. MSF noted that "at this time, MSF estimates that we have received sufficient funds for our currently foreseen emergency response in South Asia." MSF directed donors to donate either to the organization's general fund or to other international relief organizations.

In August 2005, hurricanes Katrina and Rita in the gulf coast of the U.S. resulted in 24-hour coverage by the news networks, followed by an almost constant appeal during commercial breaks to make cash contributions. More than a billion dollars appears to have been contributed online to the American Red Cross. In the first two weeks after Katrina, the Red Cross raised $439.5 million for relief efforts, and $227 million of that came in through the Internet—according to the September 15, 2005 article about it in the *Chronicle of Philanthropy*. Impressive!

The spike in online giving has continued unabated since we first starting writing about this topic in the late 1990s. According to South Carolina-based Blackbaud, a nonprofit technology consulting firm, cyber donations rose by 34.5 percent in 2010. Online donations accounted for 7.6 percent of all fundraising in 2010, which included data from nearly 2,000 nonprofits nationwide (*see http://www.nptrends.com/nonprofit-trends/2010-online-giving-trends.htm* for the full report dated February 15, 2011).

The *Chronicle of Philanthropy's* annual survey of online giving continues to show healthy growth, mirroring the results of the Blackbaud survey. Online giving expanding 34% in 2010 over the previous year for organizations in the Philanthropy 400—those charities that raise the largest amount of donations from private sources.

When we co-wrote the book *The Wilder Nonprofit Field Guide to Fundraising on the Internet* in 1999, our enthusiastic endorsement of using the Internet for fundraising was met with some healthy skepticism from the nonprofit community. There were lingering questions about security of data, privacy, and the cost—in both time and money—of buying and maintaining the hardware and software necessary to take advantage of this new medium for attracting donations. There were also cultural barriers to overcome—such as the level of comfort donors would have to share their credit card information online and the virulent reaction most of us have to unsolicited e-mail solicitations, often considered to be "spam." Adding to the confusion was a lack of clarity with respect to how state regulators viewed charitable contributions solicited via the Internet.

Additionally, there were trust factors with which to grapple, such as whether to authorize third-party, for-profit providers to manage technology issues for nonprofit organizations. Doing so would permit leadership and staff of nonprofit organizations to focus on their primary missions. But it would also entail trusting outside organizations, which may or may not share the nonprofit's values, with both charitable contributions and sensitive data. A damaging scandal in 2003 involving PipeVine, one such third party provider—ironically a nonprofit itself—profoundly affected how we view relationships between charities and outside vendors with respect to being the steward for charitable donations. PipeVine, a donation processing application service provider, was forced to shut down operations in 2003 after it failed to deliver an estimated $19.1 million in contributions it collected, most of which were on behalf of California's Bay Area United Way. It could be years before nonprofit organizations recover from the fallout of the PipeVine scandal and again become comfortable working with outside organizations in managing online fundraising efforts.

Now, as we survey the landscape and chronicle the successes and failures of online fundraising, we have to report that many of these same issues—security, privacy, cultural adjustment, trust, and government regulation—have yet to be completely resolved to our satisfaction.

We continue to urge caution regarding these issues, but our earlier strong endorsement of using the Internet for fundraising has proven warranted as it has clearly become a vital part of the operations of virtually every nonprofit organization. Today, the online donations generated by the Japan and Haiti earthquakes and the 2011 Mississippi River flooding and tornado outbreak have validated that the Internet is quickly becoming the method of choice for donors who want to respond immediately to do something tangible to help those in need, whether they live next door or on the other side of the globe.

"The Internet has gone from being one of several channels used by nonprofits for fundraising to being—in some cases—the primary vehicle being used to generate donations," says Dr. Harry Gruber, founder and CEO of Kintera. "Key reasons for this explosion in Internet fundraising are efficiency for the organization and convenience for supporters. Donors are realizing that it's much easier to make a difference immediately with an online gift than by mailing a check."

Internet fundraising has become much more than simply having a "donate here" button linked to a page that can process credit card transactions. Online donations to charities made through third-party online charity portals, such as Network for Good and JustGive.org, have skyrocketed; both recorded a doubling of the number of people making gifts in this manner between 2002 and

2003. Network for Good boasts on its Web site (as of April 2011) that it has raised more than $484 million for 60,000 charities since 2001.

The direct appeal by charities to give money is only one strategy available via the Internet. New models, assisted by sophisticated advances in technology, are providing innovative ways for charities to generate donor dollars.

According to The Hunger Site *(http://www.thehungersite.com/clickToGive/home.faces?siteId=1)*, visitor clicks on a button embedded on the site's Web page resulted in 671 million cups of food being donated for distribution to groups such as Mercy Corps and America's Second Harvest.

Much has changed in the ways charities use the Internet to raise funds in the 12 years since we first collaborated on a book about Internet fundraising. One conclusion we have drawn from watching this online communications revolution is that online fundraising is not likely to replace its conventional, off-line counterparts any time soon. We certainly do not recommend that organizations drop their direct mail programs, telephone solicitation, charitable auctions, and face-to-face appeals because of the availability of raising funds via the Internet. But we do see using the Internet for fundraising as another tool in the fundraiser's toolbox, with its distinctive advantages and disadvantages, and as an attractive strategy to pursue.

With the advance of technology and creative business models advanced by third-party providers, even the smallest nonprofit can build and display a Web-based fundraising "public face" that will generate both funds and public support. The "playing field" has been leveled on the Internet. Even the smallest nonprofit can create a sophisticated Web site with e-philanthropy and e-commerce functions that has the look and feel of the largest nonprofits with full-time Webmasters. The price of entry into building a highly attractive, professional Web site for the typical nonprofit is a few dollars a month for a host and some sweat equity. There are many Web hosting services that will even provide free Web space for nonprofits. Free and moderately priced content management software makes Web site design and content updating a breeze for the expert and novice alike.

If you are not taking advantage of the Internet to raise funds for your organization, you are missing out on an opportunity to take your organization to the next level. It is not as hard to raise funds on the Internet as you might think.

In putting together an online fundraising strategy, it is helpful to consider what makes online fundraising different from more conventional methods, such as direct mail, telephone solicitation, face-to-face meetings, and fundraising events. Doing so will permit you to take advantage of the strengths offered by online fundraising, and address how you will take into account its limitations.

Advantages of Internet Fundraising

Among the advantages are—

- *The Internet has a systemized culture that offers potential donors an invitation to find your organization.*

  Traditionally, nonprofit organizations reach out to potential donors by purchasing targeted mailing lists, advertising in print publications, and culling newspaper articles for information about those with substantial wealth for future follow-up communication. Through the use of links from other Web sites, search engines, social networking sites, online and print directories, and even word of mouth, potential donors will find your organization even if you have not found a way to contact them directly. Your organization can enhance this possibility by publicizing its Web site through news releases and other organizational communications and publications. See Chapter 20 for practical advice on attracting new visitors to your organization's Web site and keeping your visitors returning. The best such efforts lead donors to bookmark your site or link it to their personal home pages and blogs.

- *There is almost universal access to the Internet and increasing comfort with online transactions.*

Even those without their own computers have access to the Internet through their local schools and libraries, and free e-mail accounts are available to everyone with the motivation to sign up for one. People who only a few years ago didn't have an e-mail account eagerly participate in eBay auctions, purchase airline tickets and hotel rooms online, buy and sell securities, and examine PDF-format 990s online before they consider making a donation.

- *Potential donors can make "contact" with your organization 24 hours a day, seven days a week from anywhere in the world for virtually no incremental cost on their part.*

Donors can find your Web site's "donate here" button at any time of the day or night from any computer that has Internet access. Free or inexpensive software makes it practical for online forms to capture and process identifying information, payment information, and acknowledge a gift in the blink of an eye, providing the donor the instant gratification that is unavailable through many conventional fundraising methods. Compare making an online donation to the hassles of writing a check, filling out a paper form, finding a stamp and envelope, and taking the envelope to the post office. Or waiting for the organization's office to open in the morning to call in a pledge. By that time, your donor may have gone back to sleep and forgotten that he or she even wanted to make a donation.

- *In many cases, raising money online is cheaper and faster than traditional fundraising methods.*

Compare making a change in a direct mail fundraising brochure to making the same change to the online brochure. Solicitation materials can be modified electronically at any time at virtually no cost, with no extra charges for color. Full-color, glossy, print brochures are often thrown away without having been read and are costly to update. Online fundraising messages can incorporate animations, scrolling messages, and flashing screens that make Web pages more dynamic than their print counterparts. These flashy bells and whistles can be added at no additional cost. Almost instantaneously, and at virtually no cost, your computer can transmit thousands of electronic newsletters, each containing information of interest to your organization's supporters, as well as a subtle request for funds to finance a new service or program. There are no long distance charges, such as are incurred by a broadcast fax. Your telephones are not tied up if you use a Web-based service for this task. Responses (in the form of online donations) can literally come in within seconds, compared to the weeks required just to lay out and publish a print version of an organization's newsletter or fundraising brochure.

- *The Internet is less intrusive and less annoying than many conventional methods of fundraising.*

Direct mail and telephone solicitation appeals too often annoy and alienate. Both are getting less efficient: sending charitable bulk mail is getting more costly.

Telephone appeals are not as simple as in the past as a result of the popularity of "do-not-call" lists, caller ID, and other methods that potential donors use to screen calls from sources they do not know. To generate one donation from such a call, the organization must contact many individuals, most of whom will view your organization's contact as annoying.

Your fundraising message can be delivered by e-mail and read at a time that is convenient for the reader, who actually has signed up to receive it (along with other communications). While you won't want to send "spam" messages to ask for funds, there are several techniques you can use (see Chapters 20 and 21) that ethically and appropriately rely on e-mail to raise funds.

- *Internet fundraising can easily be integrated with other marketing and promotional materials and programs.*

Solicitations for donations can be coordinated with other features of an organization's Web site, such as being included in an electronic newsletter, posted on donor recognition Web pages, on links to an organization's sales of goods and services, and with testimonials about the organization that indirectly enhance opportunities for giving. Individuals will visit your Web site for many reasons other than to make a donation. A functional Web site can plant the seeds of future giving and make it convenient for those who make spur-of-the-moment gifts based on what they see on your site.

- *There are decreased transaction costs for Internet-based donation processing and donor outreach efforts.*

New business models make it easy to partner with third parties to streamline the on-line donation process and reach donors who otherwise might never have heard of the organization. Computers using sophisticated software automate many processes, such as accounting, database management, donor acknowledgment, and contact management, which previously relied on time-consuming work by staff. Many of these useful software packages can be purchased off the shelf, obviating the need to rely on third party providers.

- *There are increased opportunities to build positive relationships with the business community.*

Many for-profit businesses are willing to sponsor the Web sites of charities, usually with no more than a "thank-you" or a link (typically in the form of the sponsor's logo) from your site to the sponsor's own Web site. Internet models such as "click-to-give," online shopping malls, and charity portals are innovatively harnessing the power of the Internet to cement relationships between the business community and nonprofits that can carry over to relationships involving non-Internet collaborations.

Disadvantages of Internet Fundraising

Using the Internet for fundraising has its disadvantages, as well.

- *The online medium can be impersonal compared to face-to-face fundraising.*

  Online fundraising, with rare exceptions—such as when using real-time conferencing—is not face-to-face. The personal, human contact, with the ability to read, interpret, and respond to body language and other non-text cues, is an important component of fundraising, particularly when soliciting large gifts. There are limitations in relying on only what can be viewed on a computer screen to communicate.

- *Government regulation of online fundraising is unsettled.*

  There are unresolved legal and regulatory issues that have surfaced as a result of on-line fundraising. Among them are the degree to which the states regulate it, and what the roles are of third party for-profit dot-coms that agree to serve as intermediaries between donors and charities.

- *There are vulnerabilities as a result of having to rely on for-profit third parties.*

  Many charities are unwilling or unable to build the infrastructure to seek and process online donations. For-profit providers are available to offer these services (see Chapters 20 and 21). Many of them have no track record for reliability, ethical conduct, or financial stability. In addition, new business models have been created that involve partnerships and affiliation agreements with for-profits. The need for clear agreements between charities and these third parties raises issues of the transaction costs of creating contracts, motivation, opportunities for outright fraud, privacy with respect to sensitive donor and charity data, and the potential inability of a charity to control a third party's use of that charity's logo. Abuse by third party providers in the name of a charity can stain a reputation that took years to build. As we mentioned in our introduction, the PipeVine scandal of 2003 has placed a pall over relationships between charities and those who wish to help them raise funds. That said, there are scores of reputable for-profit application service providers (ASPs) that have exemplary relationships with their nonprofit clients.

Most charities are recognizing that, in almost every case, the advantages of using the Internet to supplement traditional fundraising far outweigh the disadvantages. Almost every major charity in the United States has reported raising significant revenues utilizing the Internet.

Most organizations do not dedicate staff solely to Internet fundraising. Instead, most development teams are integrating Internet approaches into their existing fundraising programs. So the question for these organizations is not necessarily, "How can I raise support online?" The more particular question may be, "How can the Internet enhance our annual appeals, our major gift program, our fundraising events, and our capital campaigns?"

Direct Marketing

Organizations of all types utilize basic direct marketing to reach the broadest possible public for support. Through mailing campaigns, these organizations strive to gain vital revenue to maintain their operations. The goals of a direct marketing effort are to build a mailing list as large as possible, as engaged as possible, and abundant with the names and addresses of those who support loyally, often in unrestricted dollars.

The challenges posed by direct marketing are ideally addressed by Web-based efforts. First, the Web provides a cost-effective way to help the public know about the organization. For large national organizations, a Web presence is absolutely vital and most likely to result in people seeking and finding their way to the organization. But even on the local level, a Web presence will lead to results.

The Community Food Bank (CFB) in Tucson, Arizona *(http://communityfoodbank.com)* set up its Web site hoping that the local community would learn about what it was trying to do and support its efforts. In only six months, the organization began seeing donations coming in every day through its Web site. A year later, donations of up to $1,000 were given regularly online.

Attract new donors

Direct marketing online may also attract a different kind of donor. The Community Food Bank was used to receiving support primarily from those over 50 giving through traditional direct marketing efforts. A survey of the organization's new online constituency demonstrated a dramatic increase in donors who were in their 30s and 40s. This younger contributor was being engaged for the first time thanks simply to an Internet marketing approach.

Build the giving "habit"

Web sites as a form of direct marketing are also credited for larger and repeated giving. Consider that most donors who respond to annual solicitations or direct marketing appeals give according to their income level. This contrasts with major donors, who give based on their assets. The size of an annual gift is based on disposable funds after meeting one's spending and saving needs at the time. When a gift is made only once each year, then the organization may only receive the contribution the person can afford in the particular month when the gift is made. Donors who give monthly will therefore tend to give larger gifts than those who give once in a year. Most donors do not save their disposable income each month to preserve their ability to give the largest contribution over the course of the year.

Promote monthly giving habits

For this reason, many organizations are seeing the value in promoting monthly giving habits. Donors who click to give often develop such habits. This is likely to be an especially effective mechanism for churches and temples to which contributions are often made in the form of monthly or weekly gifts. An online appeal may make it easier, especially for individuals who miss attending services in a given week. Any organization, however, that hopes to increase repeat giving will be served well by offering Web site giving options consistent with this approach.

Although monthly giving helps individuals maximize their philanthropy to organizations they care about, it is inconvenient to write a check that often. It requires time, stamps, and envelopes, and if any one of those is missing when the donor is ready to give, then the donor may not send the gift at all that month. Some organizations attempt to encourage frequent giving by mailing more often or soliciting pledges to be paid monthly and providing the materials to make the gift, but this is costly and may not appeal to all donors who are already inundated by mail.

Giving online addresses all of these concerns. It allows monthly giving habits to form without the inconveniences. Increasingly, people are getting used to paying their monthly bills online. Many donors are willing to support organizations in the same manner. Giving donors the option to automate giving or to give monthly shows that the organization is service oriented.

Cultivate a community of donors

Another aspect of Web-based direct marketing is the opportunity to cultivate a relationship with a large constituency. Direct marketers know that engagement is necessary to maintain their constituency's support over time. At a minimum, organizations need to communicate with donors and engage them in a participatory way. Personalization is important as organizations seek to build a real relationship with their donor public.

Conveying information can be a challenge if carried out primarily through direct marketing appeals. Letters and brochures convey only so much information. As a result, most are drafted to the needs of the largest segment of the donor public. A shotgun approach is necessary for effective fundraising. Thus, for example, if an environmental organization expects that the majority of its donors are more moved by hearing about its latest advocacy efforts than they are by learning about environmental impact research, then its appeals will likely focus on the former and neglect the latter. It's simply impractical to appeal to the smaller segments of the organization's constituency. A Web site, however, allows visitors to go to whatever topic interests (and moves) them, and these visitors can be invited to contribute while there.

Make giving easy

Several direct marketing fundraisers shared that online fundraising reduced barriers to giving. They advised us to **make sure the option to give is pervasive on your site.** The button to make a donation should exist on every page. Donors should not be required to leave what they are reading to navigate your site to find the place where a gift can be made. When possible, fundraisers can also relate the value of giving right at that point. How would $50 help advance the advocacy efforts of the organization? How would the same gift affect vital research supporting the cause?

Integrate and reinforce traditional direct appeals

Another helpful technique is to integrate mailings, phone appeals, and print ad forms of direct marketing with the organization's Web site. Repetition is often valuable in direct marketing. One message is easily missed. A letter can be tossed out because it is received at an inconvenient time. The Web site is a place where the same message can be viewed just because it's available when the donor wants to read it—even if that's at 3 a.m. Repetition helps to ensure that the message is seen.

Repetition may also strengthen the message. Seeing an image online that was previously seen in a magazine ad or reading a story that was heard in a phone call reinforces the message. The organization looks well organized and lively when something received in another medium is carried through online. This can demonstrate that the Web site is being maintained daily, consistently with other communications. Not everyone reads the "last updated" line to determine this.

One organization we spoke with tracks the relationship between its traditional media approaches and the Web site. A mailing, for example, will often refer the donor public to a particular place within the organization's Web site. The resulting traffic to that page can be tracked as another way to test the reaction to the mailing. From there, similar tracking can be done to determine if donors are then going to the donations page and making a gift. Over time, such research can be essential to perfecting a direct marketing approach to fundraising.

Engage donors in the organization

Communicating effectively with donors will help increase giving, but actively engaging donors can truly raise the bar on contributions. In an e-mail newsletter, the Brookfield Zoo offered recipients the chance to name the latest zoo baby. This kind of participation encourages individuals to click from the e-mail to the Web site and feel as if they are actively participating in the life of the organization.

The zoo's engagement, however, began earlier when individuals first opted to receive the e-mail newsletter (see Chapter 20). Giving people the chance to opt in is a major tool for direct marketing fundraisers. By opting in, the subscriber gives an organization permission to write (and to solicit). This is familiar to many membership organizations, universities, and clubs. Such organizations have long benefited from the bond their constituency has agreed to accept from the start. Other organizations have been disadvantaged by inherently temporary, arms-length, one-sided relationships. If donors send checks in response to a direct mail appeal, they are not necessarily going to view themselves as a part of that organization in the long term. But if they ask to receive communications online, they may do so—especially if the organization takes the opportunity to create a personalized and welcoming environment.

Establish a bond with discussion forums

Donor discussion forums are another form of engagement. They can help a constituency establish a bond with the organization and a relationship for appeals that feel more individualized.

Dads and Daughters *(http://www.thedadman.com/dadsanddaughters),* for example, is an organization that has grown around an opt-in discussion forum. DADS seeks to help fathers be successful parents for their daughters and engages them in addressing cultural and commercial messages that may negatively affect girls or damage their self-esteem. From the first page, visitors are encouraged to sign up for the electronic mailing list. The e-mail discussions are two-way. Participants can raise everyday parenting challenges and get input from other members. E-mail action alerts are sent to the list, as well as requests for support—from financial to in-kind needs. This works because each person has opted in and feels sufficiently engaged, so the requests for support are viewed as appropriate, even welcomed as convenient.

This approach is obviously more challenging for larger, well-established organizations, but any degree of engagement of one's donor public can enhance the level of giving, the frequency, and donor loyalty.

Even the simple act of registering at a site can create some level of engagement. Some organizations will encourage Web site visitors to register. Then when they return and "sign in," they get a degree of personalization from the site itself. Beginning with a "welcome back Mary" sign, the site can also be made to recognize various preferences or past activities. Online message boards, for example, may show what has been read and what has not.

Password protect the site

Having a password into a Web site encourages visitors to bookmark the site. By registering visitors, an organization can also request information. Visitors may voluntarily share a range of data on their interests, their contact information, including phone number, and even wealth information. Some organizations will retain credit card information with confidentiality. This can be done to make it even easier to give regularly. Donors don't even have to take their cards from their wallet or purse.

Prospect Research

Prospect research includes finding information not only on individuals, but also on corporate and private foundations and government agencies that will provide funds. It encompasses collecting and analyzing information to help fundraisers find out the ability and inclination of prospective donors to donate, and obtaining clues to the best strategy to assist donors in providing the largest gift that would feel comfortable to them. Good prospect research cannot guarantee successful "asks," but it can provide critical information about the background, needs, style, financial capacity, approachability, and interests of someone who can make or break your fundraising campaign. Before the Internet revolution, prospect researchers used newspapers and magazines, real estate records, data and mailing lists purchased from private companies or other charities, annual reports from businesses, industry association directories, and biographical directories (such as *Who's Who in America*) to cull for juicy leads. Today, there is a plethora of electronic sources, many free, dwarfing those available a decade ago.

Treat $50 donors today as if they will be $5 million donors tomorrow

One cannot ever know when any particular $50 donor today may become a potential $5 million donor tomorrow, and thus it is important to treat every donor and potential donor as if his or her donation is the most important the organization will ever receive. Yet the mathematics are that a single $5 million donation has as much purchasing power as 100,000 donations of $50 each, and with a lot less transaction cost. No wonder charities are willing to make substantial investments in prospect research.

Find prospects using free online databases

When Gary Grobman speaks at conferences making his PowerPoint presentations on the subject of online fundraising, one prospect research technique never fails to leave his audience ooohing and aaahing. He points his Web browser to *http://www.melissadata.com/lookups.* Then he clicks on "Campaign Contributors." Then he asks a fundraiser in the audience to provide him with a 5-digit ZIP Code of an upscale neighborhood in the area of his or her charity. When Gary submits that into the online form, it returns information about individuals who made contributions of at least $200 to a federal election campaign. Inevitably, the list is a "who's who" of philanthropists. It doesn't take much imagination to think about how such a database can be of use to fundraisers. Other sites that are favorites of professional prospect researchers include Edgar Online People *(http://www.edgar-online.com/)*, Hoover's Online *(http://www.hoovers.com/)*, Forbes.com *(http://www.forbes.com/)*, and David Lamb's Prospect Research Page *(http://www.lambresearch.com/)*. Some of these sites are free; others require a subscription.

Identify interests, motivations, backgrounds, and financial capacity

In 2003, Jerold Panas wrote a riveting two-part column in *Contributions* Magazine about his harrowing, semi-successful experience in making a $50 million "ask" on behalf of a university fundraising campaign. Obviously, the preparation required for such an endeavor is more than, let's say, seeking a $50 donation, because the stakes are so much higher. Veteran fundraiser and *Washington Post* columnist Bob Levey often tells the story of a neophyte fundraiser who approached the legendary philanthropist and *Washington Post* owner Katherine Graham seeking a major gift for a worthy cause, only to be immediately shown the door after calling her "Katie."

Major gift officers and other high-level fundraising and executive staff want to know their prospects. They want to understand their potential so they can make realistic assessments for future solicitations. They want to understand their personalities so they can approach them in the right way. They want to learn their motivations so they can focus on what appeals to each particular individual and avoid pitfalls that might turn them off to the organization. They want ideas for making initial introductions.

The Internet offers an efficient tool to access lots of publicly available information about individuals. Careful online research can answer many questions about potential donors.

Major Gifts

Major gift fundraisers work closely with a small set of an organization's top donors. Their donors contrast with annual supporters in making "stop and think" contributions ranging from once every few years to once in a lifetime. Major gifts tend to be given for special purposes—often restricted to projects with specific measurable outcomes. How do the Internet and the organization's Web site and electronic communications assist the major gifts team?

Don't use the Internet as a crutch

Fundraisers often view the Internet with great hope for finding the key information and insight they feel they need. The reality is that the Internet can be useful, but ought not be used as a crutch. For the most part, prospect research should be left to prospect researchers (if your organization has them), particularly for determining giving capacity. While many cannot help but "Google" a prospect before a visit or while planning an initial contact, fundraisers should be careful not to rely too heavily on cursory research or believe that they can truly understand the person from whatever they find. Major gift work still requires the traditional emphasis on face-to-face interactions for getting to know one's prospects and building a real relationship.

In addition to aiding in prospect research, the Internet can be a valuable aid in all aspects of major gift fundraising, including identifying new donors, cultivating relationships, solicitation, and stewardship.

Find hidden potential donors using the Internet

Identifying major gifts donors is one of a fundraiser's greatest challenges. Few donor prospects contact an organization requesting to have their relationships with the organization managed by a major gifts officer. Instead, they are often initially hidden. They may be hidden in the public at large, interested in the mission of your organization, but not yet connected. Or they may be hidden among the current annual donors. Some of the wealthiest individuals still give $25 or $50 gifts in response to direct mail appeals.

Sharing philanthropic news within your organization can also be an effective way to help encourage those who support far below their capacity to perhaps step forward and give more. Major gift stories provide a wonderful opportunity to communicate not only about the programs of the organization, but about the exciting support and endorsement a major gift demonstrates. To the extent possible, major gifts fundraisers want these stories to be shared broadly to set the highest possible bar on generous giving and to build a stronger culture of philanthropy throughout their donor constituency.

As you identify major donor prospects, the next step is to begin building a stronger affinity with the organization. This can mean several things, each of which may be enhanced through Internet tools.

Educate major donors about the organization

Potential major donors need to get to know the organization and its mission over time. There is an education process that must happen. While the most important efforts will be face-to-face, you can enhance these interactions and develop a closer connection through e-mail communications and referring donors to specific parts of your Web site. E-mail takes on a very different nature when the recipient knows the sender. If you are managing the fundraising for a political campaign, for example, and you tell a particular donor that the candidate will e-mail directly with some information, this is quite different from getting a general letter from the candidate to a larger number of people.

In short, e-mail can be a convenient form of communication but also extremely personal if it is combined with other one-on-one approaches. A fundraiser might send a note referencing a particular topic or article on your Web site for which they know the donor has interest. Fundraisers can facilitate communications with board members, leaders, and others as they help the donor understand how they operate and work to accomplish their goals. You might even have a program beneficiary write to a prospective donor to share information about the impact the organization has had.

If your organization has developed good case materials, you may want to adopt the common practice among successful fundraising programs of including case statements online in PDF format. You can see numerous samples of these simply by entering "case statement" into any popular search engine, or check the samples posted at:

http://staff.lib.msu.edu/harris23/grants/4fcelec.htm
and
http://www.capitalcampaigns.com/sampcasehosp1.html

In addition to educating donors about their organizations, fundraisers need to listen to major gift prospects and understand their needs, interests, and motivations. Again, the addition of Internet communication into the traditional mix can help escalate input both ways.

Keep track of the relationship between donors and the organization

Similarly, major gift donors and prospects often need to develop a relationship with leadership and trust in their ability to guide the organization successfully. Enhancing face-to-face relationships through online communications can increase the leadership's ability to engage with prospects. Your organization's leader can interact with higher quality communications as well as with a greater quantity of donors. Major gifts fundraisers should actively recommend, draft, and track e-mail conversations between leadership and top prospects.

Leadership should also remember to share valuable discussions with individuals who are supporting the organization. Remember to send a blind copy to relevant staff. Private conversations should be respected, but when appropriate, sharing information can avoid duplication of efforts or wasted time later.

Include contact information on the Web site

Although you may have given a donor prospect your card, it is common for anyone to misplace a number and seek you out through your Web site. Web sites that lack simple staff directories can create frustrations, and visitors may feel that you have failed to focus on helping them navigate your organization. With a staff directory, a donor will gain a more positive impression. Being able to "see" the staff they are trying to find will help make the communications seem more personal, warm, and friendly.

Ultimately, major gifts work leads to solicitations. Here your Web site can again support your efforts, beginning by detailing your organization's giving opportunities. Whether or not you have a case statement online, you should also detail major gift projects that can be funded. Because major donors tend to need specificity, it may be wise to give substantial details. Rather than just mentioning the organization's top giving levels, you can provide a description of how the organization can use gifts of $25,000 or $100,000 or $1 million. Your description can provide the impact, the visibility to the donor, and the reason why these opportunities are so high a priority.

Develop Web pages that encourage major gifts

While it may be unlikely that a donor will randomly visit your site and contact you interested in one of your top giving opportunities, the presence of these at the Web site can support gift discussions. Keeping these online reaffirms for donors that they authentically do represent the organization's top priorities. And you never know when your organization will receive a donation windfall as a result.

Planned Giving

In addition to presenting top gift opportunities online, you should also detail giving vehicles. Many organizations provide some information about planned giving options, estate gifts, and instructions for giving stock gifts or mutual funds. Such practical information can help donors as they consider making major contributions. Try to ensure that your site has all the details a donor would need and up-to-date contact information in case they have questions.

Here are some examples of planned giving pages:

> *American Red Cross* (http://www.redcrosslegacy.org)
> *Harvard Alumni (http://alumni.harvard.edu/give/college/gift-planning)*

In presenting both giving opportunities and giving vehicles, what can be particularly helpful are actual donor demonstrations. If donors are willing, you can share their stories as models for others. Major donors often are pleased to do this, because it ensures that their leadership gift is actually leading. Suppose you wish to show what a charitable gift annuity can do for a donor. While you probably don't want to share the exact financial details of any individual donor's gift annuity, you can still articulate and quote a donor to demonstrate why such gifts can be mutually advantageous.

The same can be done for giving options—adding a personal touch to your list of giving opportunities. In this way, you gain the endorsement of past donors to promote new major gift philanthropy. Donors might be asked to share what motivated them to make the gift. They can share their appreciation for the visibility or the chance a gift gave them to remember a loved one. They can articulate the impact they have seen their gift have and how that made them feel. All of this can make a significant difference to a new donor. It will also add value and interesting reading to the giving opportunities section, so you may have better reason to direct donors there.

Post donor recognition pages

Once you have secured a major gift, stewardship and recognition come into play. Here there are many options, and organizations may want to think through it carefully. There is no substantial research on the risks/benefits of recognizing gifts online. Some fundraisers are hesitant. Even if donors approve, they may worry about getting unwanted attention by being put online for their major gift. Organizations may worry that other organizations will fish for the recognition pages and immediately try to "steal away" their donors.

Others are more optimistic and see more value in the gains that publicizing a gift online can have. As we review these options, we leave it to the reader to weigh the pros and cons.

One method of recognizing gifts is to create an online donor board. Many organizations provide donor boards in their buildings, especially museums, universities, theaters, and other places that have high visitor traffic. Donors appreciate donor boards, because they provide visible recognition. Organizations enjoy the opportunity to encourage other gifts. Because Web sites often attract substantial visibility, an online board may be desirable. We may even see more of these in the future, in particular from organizations that do not have a suitable or sufficiently visible location for a traditional donor board.

Consider posting virtual donor plaques

If an organization is concerned that listing donor names on a donor board may lead to other competing organizations tapping into their donor constituency, it may consider using graphical donor "plaques" instead of a text list. A graphical plaque is even more attractive. It would mean that you put the donor's name on an image that appears like a real-life plaque. As an image, it cannot be found by regular search engine methods, provided that the donor's name is not used as the name of the image file.

A more detailed possibility for donor recognition is to build pages dedicated to donors. These can contain some combination of background on individuals and their families, and the programs they are funding. Such pages can be done in combination with a donor board, allowing individuals to click on the name for more information. Donor boards and donor pages offer the possibility for greater visibility and may make donors feel a greater sense of how they are creating a legacy for the organization.

A variation on this is the online press release. Oftentimes, donors hope for a press release in response to their gifts. Unfortunately, most newspapers and media outlets are not interested in pure philanthropic stories, short of the mega-gifts that happen from time to time. But a formal press release can be posted online and made visible to those visiting the Web site. While perhaps not as exciting as being in the *New York Times,* such visibility can at least be a practical compromise solution.

Again—be very careful to communicate with every donor as you do anything with his or her name online. Even seemingly harmless forms of recognition, such as attaching a name to a professorship or a program detailed online may upset a donor. Communicating in advance is necessary.

Special Events

A museum organizes an annual gala event. A health organization holds an annual bike-a-thon. A university seeks class gifts in preparation for its big reunion weekend. A political campaign organizes "meet up" events to raise money. A church group plans a concert to raise support.

Events, although all very different, are a mainstay in the fundraising menu of most every kind of nonprofit organization. But what does this have to do with the Internet? How can the Internet enhance such programs? How can it help them have a bigger impact? How can it help them grow over time? How can it help them attract larger numbers of people? How can it help increase their visibility?

Most special events fundraisers see their role as two-fold. First, they want to raise significant support for their organization while controlling costs. The second objective of special events is to create awareness and visibility for the organization. For this reason, gala events may be lavish affairs.

Increase visibility for your special event

Visibility as an objective serves multiple purposes. Walks, galas, and other high profile events, for example, have helped to educate and make the public more aware of devastating diseases, to move the government to support programs for the poor, and to build excitement about cultural events. Such events have direct mission benefits.

In addition, visibility can serve other fundraising goals. Fundraising events can help to identify new major gift donors or to recognize existing ones. They offer a special visible option for recognizing corporate philanthropy. They provide an opportunity to address a larger donor constituency and to build their knowledge of and commitment to the organization.

Attract corporate sponsorship with similar markets

Understanding the complex goals of a special event fundraiser, we can begin to look at how the Internet might be helpful. Let's focus first on corporate event sponsorship. Highly visible special events provide an opportunity to link corporations to philanthropy in a context that is often particularly valued by the company. If a company has a market that is similar to your organization's beneficiary public, then it may be particularly attracted to event sponsorship.

Events covered by the media often acknowledge such philanthropy in a way they never would otherwise. Outright major gifts almost never get major publicity, unless they are extremely large, i.e., in excess of $25 million. But the news will often show a corporate check presentation as small as $10,000, if it is done in the context of a public event of interest.

Develop a page for your special event

As fundraisers look for and approach potential event sponsors, the more visibility they can offer them, the more appealing their proposal will be. Using the organization's Web site to show how the sponsor's name will be featured is one valuable part of that package, particularly for organizations with heavy traffic. This can be done on a special page dedicated to the event, but linked from the organization's home page. Doing the same in mass e-mail communication to the organization's constituency about the event can be another aspect of this.

Is there value to a special page dedicated to an event like a gala? The short answer is "absolutely!" A page (or section) on a major event gives a fundraiser a chance to create an ongoing album for the event. It should contain photos of the most recent event, as well as substantive information about what the event is accomplishing. Over time, archived pages can be kept at the site, so visitors can look back to years past. A section of the Web site dedicated to a signature event can be a great point of pride for an organization and for its constituency as the program grows.

First time attendees will have a sense of the event if they visit the page. Individuals may encourage others to purchase seats or tables and may point friends to your site for this information. Previous attendees will enjoy seeing their own pictures there. Donors and sponsors may link to this part of your site.

Over the long run, an Internet presence for a major gala event can enhance the program. It can create loyalty in those who have attended in the past and help to broaden the appeal of the event significantly. The gala page can celebrate the visibility achieved each year—linking to news coverage it received.

Put the gala program booklet online

Ultimately, this will all serve to help raise the fundraising for a gala style event. Donors can give through the gala site. Individuals who cannot attend the event might especially enjoy being part of the fundraising action in this way. Some organizations may wish to put their program booklet online and raise the price for a page by adding an Internet version of the space in addition to the printed version. Auction items not purchased at the event can be auctioned off after the event, via the Web site.

In short, the Internet gala page can bring a major event to life *before* and help keep the excitement going *after* the actual event itself. As participants feel a part of the site through the images and perhaps the words they add there, they will feel more closely bonded to your organization. These feelings of connection to the event and the organization may help plant the seeds for budding major donor relationships.

Create a life-long bond

It is not enough for an organization to have donors merely invest in their mission itself. Investments are made at arms length and may be impersonal. Organizations want donors to develop an emotional and life-long bond—to become part of their family. Similarly, organizations should want their galas to be more than just wonderful parties that people attend because they are fun and for a good cause. It is better if they become family celebrations and gatherings that represent keystone moments on a shared journey to accomplish a vital public interest objective.

Universities and many private high schools and other educational programs know this, as they have long focused on the life-long bond alumni relationships can create. These are celebrated and funds are raised around special class years during reunions. Reunion weekends have organically spawned tremendous innovation and creativity through their Web presence.

The reunion site

All the elements described for galas are regular features of many reunion Web sites. These sites are graphic intense with pictures of alumni, faculty, and students. These pages are also highly interactive, encouraging visitors to be involved through the site for a year or even more before the actual event. They serve, in this way, to build excitement. Any high school reunion today is likely to have some activity develop through commercial sites such as Classmates.com, Facebook, or similar resources. By the time the event happens, classmates have already connected and begun talking and sharing with one another.

A typical university reunion site will provide the schedule of events (why should anyone depend on the printed version, which is so easily lost?). It will include a listing of the reunion committee members with e-mail addresses, so that everyone can provide input for the event early on. It will have a photo gallery, a full class list, and a variety of links to help graduates get caught up on information about the school today. It will have a section devoted to finding "lost" classmates who have moved away and for whom the event committee has no contact information.

Add a giving section

Of course, it will also have a giving section. These may describe special projects the class members have decided to join together to fund, or it could describe a variety of giving options. Reunion classes enjoy seeing how much they have raised, so a total to date is likely to be included. And just to further enhance the excitement of giving, there may be a friendly competition for the most dollars among different class years.

Many fundraisers feel that the purpose of special reunion fundraising efforts is to "bump up" giving over the alumni donor's lifetime. So while donors may give $25 each year their first few years out, perhaps by their 5th reunion, they will leap to $100 and may remain at about that level until their 10th or 25th, by which time they may leap to being $500 or $1,000 donors. In addition, reunions are events in which major gift giving becomes a special focus for fundraising. The reunion site is designed to help bolster these efforts. If their popularity is any sign, then they are succeeding. Just one of many enjoyable examples can be found in the online press release of a $5 million class gift from Denison University's 50th reunion *(http://www.denison.edu/offices/publicaffairs/pressreleases/reunion_2004.html)*.

Sometimes reunion sites are predominantly managed by volunteers. The organization might give over some control over the design so that volunteers rather than staff can develop the site. This can be a good idea for any school or organization that is concerned with the staff time it might take to manage a reunion site.

One of the conveniences of a reunion Web site is the ability for participants to register and pay for their participation in the event. Online registering, however, is turning out to be much more than just a convenience. It's turning out to be a boon for fundraising.

Special events that require registration

Today's walk-a-thon, bike-a-thon, and similar public fundraising events are benefiting hugely from organized online registration and fundraising. These kinds of fundraising events succeed when they are heavily attended. While a gala has limited seating and reunions are limited only to alumni graduates, walks can become enormous events in which hundreds or thousands participate. The sheer number of participants helps achieve the media coverage and visibility sought and the giving, because it's smaller on average, benefits by larger and larger attendance totals.

In years past, a family that was dealing with a devastating illness might join in a walk-a-thon to raise money for that cause. In the weeks before the event, they would take gifts and pledges through their personal solicitation of friends and family. They would call, write, or visit the individuals they were asking. It takes a significant commitment of time to do this.

Organize teams online

Today, most major walks organize their teams online. Commercial resources make this relatively simple to do. Typically, a person connected to the organization signs up online to be a team captain. The event's site will automatically allow a high degree of personalization. The volunteer can add personal pictures, personalize the message, and set his or her personal goals.

The sites then automate much of the fundraising (see *Personal Fundraising Pages* in this chapter). The volunteer just adds the names and addresses of those he or she knows (they can transcribe them all right from their e-mail address book) and decide if they want the pre-written solicitation or if they would like to make it their own. Their friends and family can click right from the e-mail message they get, give the gift by credit card (secured communications, of course), and then appear soon after on a scrolling banner of donors.

The volunteer's donors can return as needed to check on the progress toward the fundraising goal. They may even see the progress in a traditional fundraiser's "thermometer" and might decide to give a bit more to put the team over the top. The volunteer can get regular reports on progress. It's almost like giving them their own fundraising staff.

Generate financial support from nonparticipants

Many elements contribute to making this approach successful. It saves volunteers a lot of time, effort, and money, so they can be more active solicitors. Volunteer fundraisers can reach out to friends and family globally, yet personally. Because it is easier, it engages fundraising from those who may not be quite as focused or dedicated to the organization at this point. In the past, walk teams were comprised mostly of the diehard loyal donors and volunteers. Online fundraising broadens the participation. Many participants may not even attend the walk at all—but are happy to have helped raise the level of philanthropic support for something they do indeed care about.

In addition, donors report that fundraising in this way is simply fun. For many, asking for annual support from friends and family is an excuse to contact them. They may personalize their message for each one to catch up. How many of us need that excuse to contact Uncle Jack or our best friend from high school? The beneficiaries of this are the nonprofit organizations who are gaining greater support and more awareness and visibility for themselves and their missions.

Use automation and volunteers

In essence, this online fundraising technique is creating a mini-gala model, letting volunteers take over everything—providing a place for the event, food, invitations, and so on. All that the organization needs to do is to receive the check and use it wisely. Of course, to be very successful, the organization needs to support these efforts, providing the volunteers with good materials, both videos and printed, to make the event worthwhile for the participants. The most successful house party efforts may involve a phone-in period during which the candidate addresses multiple events simultaneously.

Innovative new and cutting-edge efforts such as these are in their early stages, but there are good signs that they represent how the Internet is creating a more diverse set of fundraising practices under the broad net of special events. They appeal particularly to a younger new generation of fundraising volunteer—individuals comfortable with utilizing technology to build grassroots efforts.

Many of these first generation efforts still have a rough feel to them. In the future, we will see them become more elegant and much more common, perhaps in other fundraising venues. How long will it be before we see a neighborhood food pantry or a church group using the Internet to support its fundraising in some of these ways and with some of these tools?

Make online fundraising event administration routine

We will also continue to see the Internet change special event fundraising in more dramatic ways. Organizations are already exploring the idea of using the Internet to actually be "at" a live event. Through video broadcasts over the Internet, it is now possible for individuals to attend seminars and hear speeches online. The Internet has become a common venue for certain fundraising events.

To sum up, the Internet's benefit for special events includes a number of very basic ideas, such as using a Web site to publicize and draw in more participants and even gifts before and after the event. It includes some important broader concepts, as well, such as employing the Internet to help build a different kind of connection to the organization, one that is more participatory and intimate while also more convenient.

Capital Campaigns

The capital campaign has become a way of life for many organizations, especially universities, public radio and television stations, and religious institutions. Not long ago, capital campaigns were held only occasionally and usually for a special need. Today, the planning for the next often begins as soon as the previous one ends. Capital campaigns build public excitement around fundraising. They serve to identify a set of needs and priorities, and in so doing make an organization's strategic plans a little more accessible to the organization's donor constituency. Capital campaigns also help make larger solicitations easier, creating urgency and the motivation of achieving a goal.

As capital campaigns have become more popular, they have given birth to the campaign Web site. As suggested above, the primary goals of a campaign Web site are to present the fundraising priorities and to generate excitement around giving.

Typical campaign sites include many or all of the following features:

- *A goal stated on the first page.* This can take the form of a graph or "thermometer" showing progress toward the goal. It will also include stories of key leadership gifts in the campaign.

- *Messages from the campaign chair or others about the effort.* Often these are presented in video or audio clips, as well as text, especially if high profile individuals or celebrities are helping to lead the campaign.

- *A case statement in PDF format.* The traditional case statement provides donors with a well-designed printed piece that explains the needs and attempts to motivate philanthropy toward them.

- *Detailed information about the institution.* Even institutions with complete Web sites will often reorganize and re-present their factual data, organizational structure, and history. Many campaign Web sites have a completely separate look from the main Web site of the organization. The purposes of doing this are to deliberately contrast with what the donors are used to on the site and thus grab their attention, or to create a more polished and prestigious look to appeal to high-scale donors. An organization with an extremely well branded look may simply want to draw greater attention by adopting a new campaign logo with different color schemes and page designs. The University of Chicago did this with its campaign Web site at *http://alumniandfriends.uchicago.edu/site/c.mjJXJ7MLIsE/ b.4464735/k.B7E4/Give.htm.* Here even the URL is unique. You can see the logo and color scheme versus the university's home page at: *http://www.uchicago.edu.* If the capital campaign is sufficiently large, then sub-branding or branding differently may be a good strategy. It may not be worth doing for smaller campaigns.

- *A list of needs and complete detail on them, as well as recognition levels.* These may be replicated in the case statement, but don't count on everyone printing out that document.

- *Pictures.* Appropriate pictures here are of people, program beneficiaries, and model construction planned. Some will include video feeds, allowing visitors to monitor 24 hours/day building projects under construction.

- *Current news.* News stories may help ensure that the site looks lively and up-to-date. The campaign Web site can be viewed as a secondary portal into the organization.

Market to donors rather than to the public

In essence, capital campaign Web sites recast the organization's online presence and market the organization very specifically to donors rather than the public at large. While the main gateway to the organization typically is focused on its mission, with philanthropy carefully and appropriately woven in, the campaign Web site can be unabashed in its drive for dollars. In a role reversal, fundraising becomes the highest priority on these pages, and the mission is woven in to show how essential fundraising is to meeting the organization's objectives.

Capital campaigns also often take place at large complex institutions and can serve an ancillary role of unifying multiple fundraising efforts. In a university, they bring together all of the college, graduate, and professional schools toward a common goal. They may connect geographically separate campuses, or organizations with separate chapters. The new Web portal can be a place to reflect that unity and to demonstrate the interconnectedness of an organization with multiple parts.

Online Fundraising Strategies

E-mail

E-mail is still considered the "killer application" of the Internet, and with good reason. For charities that abuse it, it may well, indeed, earn its name. A charity that purchases a disk with 20 million e-mail names on it and then indiscriminately e-mails a fundraising solicitation to the list is *likely* to make a name for itself. That name will be spelled "M-U-D." There is a consensus that using such a strategy is about as injudicious as one can get in using e-mail for fundraising. Our culture accepts the "cost" of wading through junk snail mail, most of it from tax-exempt organizations seeking contributions. Perhaps there is a feeling that the sender at least made some effort to weed out duplicates and, at least, is trying to target the mailing because even the charitable bulk mail postage rate is getting fairly steep these days. Printing fundraising letters, return envelopes, and the "free gift inside" of personalized mailing labels, calendars, or greeting cards must cost something, let alone the cost of designing and sending out the mailing.

Avoiding spamming

We do not (and should not!) as yet feel the same way about unsolicited e-mail. Pornographers, scam artists, crooks "phishing" for personal financial information, and purveyors of illegal drugs send a high percentage of the "spam" mail we all receive. Sending "spam" mail may associate an organization with these types of unsavory operations. No organization should want that.

The culture of participation in the Internet community is still evolving. What is not totally clear is what types of e-mail solicitation are acceptable, and what types are the most effective. Communicating organizational needs by e-mail to stakeholders who already have some relationship with the organization, such as donors, board members, and those served by the organization, is usually appropriate. Sending out online newsletters to an organization's stakeholders who have opted in to receive them is even better.

Using e-mail to interact with stakeholders

One legitimate use of direct e-mail is to simply interact with your stakeholders and provide them with information and services that bring them closer to your organization. E-mail is a cost-effective means for increasing direct communication between your organization's actual and potential donors. Because of the convenience of the "reply" button available within all e-mail programs, it also provides a convenient way for getting feedback. Sharing timely and informative news about what your organization is doing, and plans to do in the future, can keep your organization on the minds of your donors and maintain your visibility. Among information that can be shared with broadcast e-mails are the following:

- new features added to the organization's Web site
- requests for volunteers to help the organization with a program or service
- calls to action, such as to send letters or e-mails to public officials concerning an important, emerging public policy issue
- directions on how to participate in an online or offline survey
- information about an upcoming fundraiser
- details about an upcoming meeting or program (with driving directions).

Of course, even those who have expressed interest in your organization in the past may no longer maintain that enthusiasm. We recommend that you place instructions at the bottom of any mass-distributed e-mail on how to be deleted from the list for future e-mails.

Collecting e-mail addresses

Almost universally, online fundraising advocates agree that seeking a donor's e-mail address is a positive strategy, even if there are no current plans to communicate with those donors online. Plans can change. E-mail remains the fastest and cheapest way an organization can communicate, even if it may not be the most appropriate way in every circumstance. But simply having the capacity to contact every stakeholder quickly by e-mail is considered to be a top objective by those of us who give advice about online fundraising.

There are obvious strategies that will increase the percentage of donors who will give your organization their e-mail addresses. Organizations should routinely include "e-mail address" as a field in their donation forms and other forms (such as those used to request additional information from the organization). The online newsletter subscription is also a good method used to harvest e-mail addresses from donors and supporters. Some organizations require Web visitors to register with their e-mail addresses and other identifying information if they want to have access to some features of the site, such as the online community.

Turn your web site into a catcher's mitt

The organization's Web site offers lots of opportunities to obtain e-mail addresses, such as through electronic newsletter subscriptions, online surveys, information requests, e-mail feedback to the organization, and similar online transactions in which the e-mail address is routinely needed to respond. As Mathew Emery, of the application service provider Kintera, explained at a 2004 workshop on e-philanthropy sponsored by the Pennsylvania Association of Nonprofit Organizations, "The Web site has been (typically) treated like it's a brochure, but it's really a catcher's mitt. You want something on every single page where you can find something about the visitor." According to Emery, even if a donor doesn't make an online donation, online communications have a positive effect on direct mail. His organization found that there was a 10% increase in donations made as a result of a direct mail fundraising piece when an e-mail was sent to donors prior to sending out the direct mail.

"E-Mail to a Friend" strategies

Another fundraising strategy that appears to be effective is the online version of getting organization supporters to write personal letters to those they know, including friends and neighbors, appealing for donations. In the offline version, a charity might make a call to a past donor. Rather than requesting a direct donation, the charity requests that the donor send a note to ten or twenty neighbors requesting a donation. If the donor agrees, the charity provides the names of those it desires to solicit, perhaps a sample letter, and if appropriate, other support.

In the online version of this technique, donors are asked to e-mail their friends and relatives with a donor appeal. The solicitations are not considered spam, because they are coming from personal friends and relatives. Recipients of the solicitations see the communication coming from someone they know, rather than an organization, and are more likely to open the e-mail and respond.

There is increasing evidence that this type of e-mail solicitation is effective. One application service provider, Kintera, (acquired by Blackbaud in 2008), developed software to facilitate such online volunteer fundraising, called "Friends Asking Friends®." Hundreds of millions of dollars have been raised using this technique. It is particularly effective for specific fundraising events, in which an organization's supporters e-mail their online contacts about an upcoming charity auction, race/walk, or benefit concert. The Kintera software package has integrated links providing information and the ability to donate or register for the event, and tracks donations and responses (see *Personal Fundraising Pages* in this chapter).

In addition to the obvious "donate here" link on your organization's Web site, there are new business models that facilitate online fundraising. Among them are creating partnerships with businesses who will provide the charity with funds in exchange for marketing opportunities, holding online charitable auctions, soliciting tribute gifts, creating online shopping malls, and engaging in search engine marketing—which involves placing advertisements on search engine Web sites that will appear on the search engine query results of those searching on a term related to the organization's mission. For each of these, there are for-profit application service providers (ASPs) to whom organizations can outsource all of the work. Many charities that engage in these strategies do this work in-house.

"Donate Here" Buttons

One obvious way charities have raised funds is by placing a "donate here" link on their Web site's pages. Clicking on the button links the donor to a secure page (i.e., where the information sent by the donor is encrypted). The page will have an online form that permits the donor to make a contribution and pay by credit card or through PayPal. It will typically also have information about other methods for making donations, such as a form that can be mailed or faxed to the organization, a telephone number to call during business hours to make donations, and information about planned giving. It may also have an offer for a modest "thank you" gift for donors, such as a mug with the organization's logo, a calendar, or a t-shirt.

The page should provide the donor information you need to process the donation, such as payment information, address, telephone number, and e-mail address. The page should also include information such as the organization's address and telephone number, which the donor needs to mail in a check or call in a donation. Even for those donors who do not choose to take advantage of making an online donation, it is useful to request those donors' e-mail addresses on the donation form.

Even for those organizations without merchant accounts to process credit cards or an application service provider who will (see Chapters 20 and 21), a clearly visible "donate here" button can link to a page that can be printed out and mailed with a check.

Cause-Related Marketing (CRM)

In her 1999 book, *Cause Related Marketing—Who Cares Wins*, Sue Adkins defined cause-related marketing as "commercial activity by which a business with a product, service or image to market builds a relationship with a cause or a number of causes for mutual benefit." While the term is relatively new, cause-related marketing efforts are often traced back to the 1960s, when the Insurance Company of America offered to make a donation to CARE for every insurance policy it sold. It reached prominence, however, by virtue of a well-publicized effort of American Express begun in 1983, when it pledged to donate a penny to the Statue of Liberty restoration fund for each time its card was used to make a purchase. According to press reports, this strategy was successful in increasing card use by 28% in a single year while raising substantial funds for the Statue of Liberty restoration project.

Since then, scores of mainstream charities have partnered with for-profits to exploit their brand names and raise funds. CRM is not without controversy. A joke continues to circulate about this exploitation: Some see it as "tainted" money, while others see it as " 't ain't enough." Regardless, CRM collaborations are raising millions of dollars for charities, including the American Lung Association, the American Cancer Society, and our personal favorite—the recipients of the $.10 General Mills donates to our kids' schools when we buy their cereal with the "Box Tops for Education" coupons on the top.

Involve celebrities in cause marketing efforts

In some cases, cause-related marketing can involve three partners—the organization, the corporation, and a celebrity spokesperson. The fundraiser is looking for a good synergy that may influence everyone. A celebrity may want to help a good cause, but may also appreciate positive publicity and a boost to his or her public image. The corporation is seeking increased revenues, brand loyalty, and a positive corporate image. The charity is looking for revenues and increased awareness among the general public.

Relationships built around cause related marketing can be long-term. A good Internet strategy can help cement and maintain the relationship over time. Via e-mail, Web pages, and electronic newsletters, charities can communicate with their stakeholders about these cause-related marketing opportunities.

Tribute Gifts

Tributes are memorial gifts given in the name of a loved one, usually shortly after they die. Tribute gifts encourage family and friends to join together, and sometimes hundreds participate. Most fundraising offices do not have staff dedicated solely to tributes. Instead, they are folded into the work of other fundraisers, either in major gifts, direct marketing, special events, or other specialist or generalist fundraisers.

We mention tributes here because they often provide a particular challenge. Managing tribute gifts can be highly labor intensive. Often, the size of the tribute is not proportional to the amount of work it requires. Gifts need to be meticulously tracked and recorded. Communications need to be sent to the donors and to the family, keeping them apprised of each contributor and the total.

Soliciting tribute gifts requires sensitivity

While tributes are always highly valued and appreciated, fundraisers can see them as difficult to manage and distracting to the more proactive fundraising they are charged with doing. Smoothly managing tribute funds often goes unpraised, while the slightest error draws unwelcome attention and consequences. What manager wants to hear a complaint from a family at this deeply emotional time of their lives?

Furthermore, fundraisers have long sensed the potential to increase fundraising around tributes, but struggle with how to sensitively make an approach. Many of the largest gifts honor a lost loved one, but tribute gifts happen when a family isn't focused on philanthropy. The timing for discussing what the family could do is the worst possible, usually taking place around the funeral of a loved one. And often the connection, if there was any, was with the deceased, making it hard to re-engage with family members after enough time has passed. So, too often, the family and the organization part ways after a tribute fund is established, despite the possibility of greater support.

One new approach by Our Lasting Tribute *(http://ourlastingtribute.com)* seems interesting to us and may represent a creative way to use the Internet to increase giving through a culture shift in traditional philanthropy. Although this company utilizes written materials in its approach, as well as the Internet, we will focus on the role of the Internet here.

Imagine that a family wishing to establish a tribute did so through the creation of a mini-campaign online. Automated technology can allow a donor to set up a Web page connected to your organization's. At this Web site, the family can put pictures and details about their loved one and why they have designated your organization as their charity of choice. Others visiting could add their own thoughts, poems, prayers, and memories, and at the same time pledge their support to the fund.

Set up an online tribute page

An online tribute page can alleviate many of the managerial headaches of tribute funds while maximizing their potential and respecting the needs of the family at a difficult time. Visitors automatically know the exact fundraising total. Family members can be informed of gifts through e-mail, and while some paper acknowledgment and receipt is still needed, e-mail versions can help cut down significantly on problems, perceived or real, and in doing so, reduce the number of complaints. Because this Internet approach encourages families to come back to the question of philanthropy later, after the most difficult and immediate emotionally absorbing event, it can help resolve some of the timing and appropriateness issues associated with fundraising for tributes.

In short, the Internet may hold a key to helping to unlock the untapped potential in tribute funds. It can help to empower families to do more and to take greater satisfaction in the impact they are having in the name of a loved one. This may in turn lead to more substantial relationships with such families, and in some cases may even transform them into lifelong supporters or major donors.

Personal Fundraising Pages

Donors, be they casual or wealthy philanthropists, are more likely to give when asked by someone they know, or to whom they have some connection. Colleges and universities ask current students to volunteer to solicit alumni. Charities provide their supporters with donor materials, and ask that they mail solicitations to their neighbors with a personalized appeal. Organizations hold galas and other special events and encourage the well-heeled to invite their friends to attend, or to make a contribution if they cannot be there in person.

The technology revolution has added new wrinkles to many existing fundraising techniques, eliminating some labor-intensive aspects, and streamlining invitations, donor processing, acknowledgment and substantiation, and collections. Technology has also spurred the development of new, creative fundraising models. Among them are charity malls, online auctions, "click-to-give, " and electronic tribute gifts. Some of these models take advantage of using "personal" appeals of individuals to their friends, neighbors, and relatives, despite the fact that these appeals are highly automated and involve minimal labor on the part of either the charity or the solicitor.

One such model, the personal fundraising page, is rapidly catching on as an effective fundraising technique for charities on the cutting edge. It was successful recently in generating a donation from one of us, Gary Grobman, to a charity that he had not previously supported, the Leukemia and Lymphoma Society. Here's how it occurred.

ASPs can manage personal fundraising pages

In January 2005, Gary Grobman received an e-mail from a casual friend and neighbor, Shalom Staub of Harrisburg, PA. The message, not particularly long or detailed, said Shalom was participating in a 100-mile bike ride around Lake Tahoe in June to raise millions of dollars for this particular charity, and he was committed to raising $3,800 himself. He asked for Gary's participation by clicking on a link embedded in his e-mail. The link was to Shalom's personal fundraising page on Active.com. Gary complied, making a small donation online. Within minutes, he received two e-mails, one from the local chapter of the charity thanking him for his gift, and a receipt from the application service provider, Active.com. Apparently, scores of others responded to the appeal. In July, Gary received another "custom" e-mail from his cyclist friend saying that more than 1,900 bike riders raised $7 million, and that he more than met his fundraising goal. Attached to the e-mail were pictures of the event.

Active.com is a site managed by Active Giving Solutions, one of many application service providers who have developed software applications for personal fundraising pages. "We chose Active Giving Solutions for its customized technology and ability to integrate with our internal systems," said Richard J. Geswell, executive vice president, marketing and revenue generation for the Leukemia & Lymphoma Society, in a June 2005 press release. "We needed an easy tool to encourage and expand online fundraising by our participants. With Active's history of managing online transactions for participatory sports and its ties to the active lifestyle community, we're also looking forward to the additional exposure we gain through the partnership."

Perhaps the leader in the personal fundraising page model is Justgiving.com, with more than a million online donations received for its 1,200 nonprofit organization clients in the United States and Great Britain in its first five years of operations. A March 2005 survey of more than 1,000 Justgiving users validated the company's claim that making donations via this method is convenient, secure, and provides many other advantages over conventional methods of solicitation. One satisfied customer, Nathaniel Tilton, was diagnosed with Multiple Sclerosis in 2002. Rather than being impeded by his debilitating disease, he set a goal of running the Boston Marathon. Setting up his personal fundraising page on Justgiving.com, he raised more than $10,000 for his charity and finished the race in a respectable 4:43 on a hot day and challenging course (and likely passed Gary Grobman somewhere after Heartbreak Hill).

To Shalom Staub, this automated service relieved much of the anxiety and time involved in fund-raising.

"Some people who were distant to me, or who only knew of me through a friend or family member, donated quite generously," he told Gary in an e-mail. "Others who are closer friends of mine, failed to, which was frustrating. The point is, you just never know who might feel a personal connection to your cause and who might be willing to make a contribution—so don't be afraid to ask!"

The technology made his plea for support painless at every step. The cost to charities is reasonable, with typical transaction fees being 5% or less of donations made through the Justgiving platform. From the home page *(http://www.justgiving.com)*, you can find the personal fundraising pages of some of the top fundraisers who use the service, and the names and comments of their donors.

Also started in 1999, CharityFocus *(http://www.charityfocus.org/new/)* is a California-based 501(c)(3) that is run completely by volunteers. Its basic services, including setting up personal fundraising pages (see: *http://www.pledgepage.org)*, are free, although there may be charges for any third-party costs the organization incurs on your behalf.

Third party application service providers are becoming more sophisticated in meeting the customized needs of charities that want to encourage their donors to set up personal fundraising pages. Typically, these pages permit the participant to upload pictures, provide progress reports on the amount of donations received, and have colorful graphics that illustrate how close the participant is to meeting his or her fundraising goal. Anecdotal evidence is strong that charities, participants, and donors alike appreciate the convenience of this online giving option. And it is another effective strategy charities can use to add to their donor lists and publicize the important mission they have, even among those who may not be interested in making a donation.

Tips:

- **Purchase keywords from major search engines to attract donors to your Web site. Some organizations even purchase common misspellings of keywords!**

- **E-mail communications have a different tone than conventional letters. As one Direct Marketing manager shared, Web sites are all about the organization. The tone is focused on "we." Mail appeals, however, tend to start with "you," the donor. They bring the donor into the heart of the organization and reinforce the idea that the recipient is being asked to support "their" mission through "their" organization. Communications by e-mail, whether solicitations or not, should similarly focus on the donor.**

- **An element that may help in cultivating prospect relationships is to have a staff directory at your Web site, preferably including pictures. For one thing, just as major gift officers want to be able to read something about their donors and prospects, donors may want to investigate your leadership. Giving a bio online can help them do this.**

- **Make sure the option to give is pervasive in your site. The button to make a donation should exist on every page. Donors should not be required to leave what they are reading to navigate your site to find the place where a gift can be made.**

Chapter 23
Forming and Running a Coalition

Synopsis: Many nonprofit organizations form and participate in coalitions to accomplish objectives that would be difficult to achieve by themselves. There are significant advantages and considerations to forming a coalition, and the fact that they flourish is indicative of their value. This chapter discusses the pros and cons of creating and/or participating in coalitions.

Introduction

The tapestry of advocacy efforts at the international, national, state, and local levels is replete with collaborative initiatives that bring together diverse interests to accomplish a common goal. As a nonprofit organization seeks to accomplish its mission, its leadership often finds the value of creating formal and informal partnerships among like-minded organizations. As in any endeavor, there are traps and pitfalls in creating and running a coalition.

While it is often said that "two heads are better than one," it is equally rejoined that "too many cooks spoil the broth." Both of these clichés are often equally valid when applied to a coalition, and it is important for an organizational leader to be able to assess which one applies predominantly before embarking on coalition-forming.

The Coalition

A coalition is a group of diverse organizations that join together to accomplish a specific objective that is likely to be achieved more quickly and effectively than if the organizations acted independently. There are many types of coalitions, and the structure is often dictated by political as well as financial considerations. The prototypical coalition involving state government issues starts with a convener coalition partner who has identified an issue, usually of direct importance to the convener's organizational membership.

The convener then "rounds up the usual suspects" by soliciting membership in the coalition from constituencies that will participate in the coalition. He or she schedules periodic meetings of the coalition at which members share information about the issue and develop a strategy to accomplish a specific goal of the coalition that, as is often the case, is the passage of legislation to solve the problem. It is not unusual for the coalition to continue even after the legislation upon which it focused on is enacted into law.

Structures of Coalitions

- *Formal organization.* Some coalitions structure formally, creating a distinct nonprofit corporate structure, such as a 501(c)(3), which will permit the coalition to hire staff, seek tax-deductible contributions from the public, rent office space, and have a system of governance that parallels, in many respects, the constituent organizations that comprise the coalition. Obviously, one would not seek to create such a complex legal entity if the objective of the coalition was to be achieved in the short term. It is not atypical for a new 501(c)(3) coalition staff to spend much of its efforts raising funds to keep it in business rather than focusing on the actual mission of the coalition. Even if funding is stable, many formal coalitions spend an inordinate amount of time on intra-organizational issues, compared to achieving their stated purposes. An example of a formal coalition is Independent Sector *(http://www.independentsector.org).*

- *Semi-formal coalition.* These coalitions consist of organizations that have some financial resources themselves and are able to fund the activities of the coalition. While not incorporated as separate legal entities, these coalitions nevertheless may have office space and staff. The office space may be provided as an in-kind contribution from one of the coalition members, and the staff may or may not be employees of one of the member organizations. An example of such a coalition is the Public Education Coalition to Oppose Tuition Vouchers.

- *Informal coalition.* Most coalitions are informal, with a convener organizational leader, but with no dedicated organizational staff or budget, or separate bank account. The convener organization convenes the coalition, sends out meeting notices, holds the meeting in the convener's office, and staffs the coalition as a part of its routine organizational duties. Costs can be shared among coalition members, and the convener duty can be rotated among members. In general, member organizations are not bound by the positions taken by the coalition. An example of such a coalition in Pennsylvania is the Charities Build Communities Coalition, sponsored by the Pennsylvania Association of Nonprofit Organizations (originally named the Nonprofit Advocacy Network).

- *Group networks.* A group network is a type of informal coalition that has been formed to serve an information-sharing function with less emphasis on coordinated action. These networks have no staff, no budget, take no positions, and are useful in raising the consciousness of participants about a particular issue or set of issues. These networks also are valuable in bringing people together to "network," and to build trust among organizational leadership. While efforts to coordinate action on an issue are often the result of a network-based coalition, the network itself often does not take a formal role in the coordination; rather, the discussions among the participants during and after the meeting result in the synergistic effects of the network. Among examples of these coalitions in Pennsylvania have been coalitions formed to ban corporal punishment, increase welfare grants, support minimum wage increases, and expand the school breakfast program.

Advantages of Forming a Coalition

Coalitions focus attention among the media, opinion leaders, and those with advocacy resources on a specific issue. Any organization, no matter how large and powerful, has a limited ability to get its message across to the public, government officials, and the media. Building a coalition is an effective strategy to call attention to an issue, since messages not perceived to be important when heard from one organization may be considered important from another.

Coalitions bring together experts on a particular issue. A convener of a coalition often has a burning desire to solve a particular public-policy problem and has well-developed organizational skills, but may lack the technical expertise to develop the solution. Creating a coalition is a strategy to bring together experts in the field who collegially can participate in developing a solution.

Coalitions provide a forum to resolve turf issues and to limit destructive competition. Very few important public policy issues are so narrow that a single organization is the only one with a direct interest in their resolution. Virtually any public policy issue, particularly one that influences human services, affects a broad range of advocacy organizations, whether it impinges on children, schools, the environment, business, the disabled, or the aged. Trying to solve a problem without the "buying in" of key decision-makers is a recipe for disaster. Coalitions provide the framework for obtaining the cooperation of opinion makers who otherwise would be threatened by any effort to change public policy that violates their political turf.

Coalitions provide credibility to an issue and to the convener organization. One obvious application of this principle is the effort, often unsuccessful, of various extremist organizations not accepted in society, such as the KKK, to try to form or participate in coalitions that have a goal consistent with a community consensus. Another principle is that organizational messages viewed as self-interest are viewed negatively. When coalitions include organizations that are viewed to be acting in the public interest (such as those affiliated with the religious community or the League of Women Voters), it is more beneficial to have the organization's message delivered by a coalition.

Coalitions permit resources to be shared. Coalitions benefit by the resources of their membership, including money, volunteers, staff, office equipment, and meeting space. It is more cost-effective for an organization to form a coalition to permit resources to be shared, rather than having to pay the entire bill itself.

Coalitions provide a path to inform new constituencies about an emerging issue. For example, the religious-based advocacy community's constituency may not have access to detailed information about a specific state budget problem, other than seeing an occasional newspaper article. It is one thing for welfare recipients to write to their legislators requesting a grant increase, and another for middle-class taxpayers to write advocating for an increase based on economic justice, not self-interest. Coalitions provide a framework for expanding constituencies beyond those of the convener.

Coalitions result in positive public relations for a convener coalition-builder. New organizations build respect by forming and running a successful coalition. While the "credit" for a success achieved single-handedly can be savored, achieving that success is often much more difficult than with help from a coalition. By bringing other organizations together and working for a common goal, those organizations learn to work with the convener, to build trust, to get visibility for the new organization, and to make it more likely that the convening organization will be invited to participate in other coalitions.

Disadvantages of Coalitions

It is often difficult for members of a coalition to focus on an issue that is usually not the priority issue for any member of the coalition other than the convener.

Coalition members who are not the convener often have an agenda that differs from that of the convener. They may seek to exploit the coalition for their own goals in a manner that may be inconsistent with the purpose for which the coalition was formed.

Coalitions usually reach agreement on issues by consensus, which is sometimes difficult to achieve. When it is achieved, the result is often the lowest common denominator and dilutes the aggressiveness that might have been necessary to solve a problem.

Coalitions require considerably more time to make decisions than would be required by the convener acting alone. Many coalition members require major decisions to be discussed by their own boards. There is a lag time between when a decision is requested and when a decision can be made by a coalition, compared with an individual organization. Even scheduling a coalition meeting to discuss when a coalition consensus can be developed can be extremely difficult at times.

Many important coalition partners have organizational difficulties that make them accustomed to working independently rather than in coalition.

Coalitions can require substantial organizational work, such as preparing agendas, mailing materials, and coordinating meeting times.

To Form a Coalition or Not

There are many questions that should be answered, and an honest assessment made, in determining whether forming a coalition to solve a problem is constructive. Among them are:

- What is the outcome I wish to achieve with this coalition? Is it realistic to achieve it by myself? Are the chances for success improved with a coalition?

- Whose turf am I treading on by trying to solve this issue alone? Is there a more appropriate organization to form this coalition?

- Are there constituencies in my own organization that will react negatively if I form this coalition?

- How much will a coalition cost me in terms of money, time, and focus?

- Who should be invited to participate; who should not be invited?

- Will I have better access to outside experts if I form a coalition?

- Will my prospective coalition participants get along?

- How will the coalition dissolve after my goals are achieved?

- What kind of commitment do I need from participants, and is it realistic to expect to receive these commitments?

How to Form a Coalition

- Make sure that there are no major irreconcilable differences between coalition participants, either as a result of ideology or personal enmities.

- Identify all organizations that have a direct or indirect interest in the issue.

- Invite, if appropriate, organizations that would enhance the credibility of the coalition.

- Make sure that the effort is not perceived to be partisan.

- Invite outside experts to either serve on the coalition or speak to it.

- Consider business, labor, education, religious advocacy, good government citizen groups, health, local government, state government, federal government, beneficiaries of success of the coalition's objective, provider associations, lobbyists, experts on the issue, community leaders, foundation and other grantmaker representatives, charities, and religious leaders as coalition members.

Online Resources to Explore

Wisconsin Clearinghouse for Prevention Resources—Coalition Building
http://wch.uhs.wisc.edu/01-Prevention/01-Prev-Coalition.html

Community How To Guide on Coalition Building
http://wch.uhs.wisc.edu/docs/PDF-Pubs/CommunityHowToGuide.pdf

National Coalition Building Institute
http://ncbi.org/

University of Kansas Coalition Building Community Toolbox
http://ctb.ku.edu/en/tablecontents/sub_section_main_1057.aspx

Institute for Sustainable Communities
http://www.iscvt.org/

Tips:

- **Remember that if the objective of the coalition was the most central focus of all members of the coalition, they would have formed it first.**

- **Respect the fact that your coalition is perhaps one of many, and keep meetings short with the agenda focused. Encourage all in attendance to participate, but don't dominate the discussion yourself or let any other participant dominate. Reach consensus as quickly as possible, and then move on.**

- **Delegate the work of the coalition to participants (such as by forming committees when necessary to develop a consensus).**

- **Make the meeting pleasant by being hospitable (such as providing soft drinks or lunch).**

Chapter 24
Miscellaneous Administrative Issues

Synopsis: The offices of nonprofit corporations require computers, filing systems, and office equipment that are sensitive to organizational needs. The Postal Service offers discounted postage rates to organizations that prepare bulk mailings in a manner consistent with its format and regulations.

Office Equipment

Many small nonprofit corporations are headquartered in the residences of their incorporators. There are obvious limitations to that, particularly if the corporation needs to expand its "shoebox" existence. For those who rent or own office space, some basic equipment items to consider (and budget for) are—

- file cabinets (legal or letter size);
- postage meter, postage scales;
- copy machine;
- fax machine;
- telephone system, including cell phone;
- telephone answering machine or voice mail service;
- computer, printer, monitor, and peripherals, such as modem, scanner, mouse, flash drives
- electronic printing calculators; and
- office furniture (including desks, bookcases, supply shelves, cabinets, chairs, lamps, end tables, coat racks, umbrella stand).

Staffing Patterns

Thousands of registered nonprofits operate effectively with no paid staff, while others, such as colleges and hospitals, may have staff in the thousands. Salaries are, by far, the largest budget expenditure for organizations with paid staff. A typical "one man band" staff configuration has an executive director or director who performs all of the operations of the organization. There may be the need for some part-time assistance to do bookkeeping or help with a special project on occasion, but it is not impossible for one versatile person to run a highly successful organization. More typical is a two-person office—an executive/administrator and an administrative assistant/ secretary/clerk who performs the routine office management functions.

Nonprofits that can afford additional staff may have an assistant director, who may be responsible for publications, membership, or development (a euphemism for fundraising). Other typical generic staff positions of nonprofits are government relations representative, program director, publications specialist/newsletter editor, administrative assistant, public relations/community relations specialist, librarian, office manager, Webmaster, and data processor. Many nonprofits provide specific services that require staff with some particular educational credentials or training. Hospitals will hire doctors, nurses, social workers, and lab technicians. Colleges will hire professors and deans. The organization's mission may determine the types of specialists hired (see Chapter 12).

Many nonprofits choose to start small—hiring one staff member—and then expand with experience and fundraising, so there is a reasonable expectation that the budget can be supported in the long run. If a nonprofit is too ambitious at first, the staff may end up spending most of its time raising funds to support salaries, rather than accomplishing the mission of the organization.

Stationery/Logo

Every nonprofit corporation needs to have letterhead stationery to provide a professional first impression. This stationery need not be fancy or expensive, although it is generally a good practice to print stationery on bond paper with some cotton content, which is heavier than the 20-lb. stock used in the copy machine. Most corporate stationery has a graphic (also known as a "logo") that is uniquely descriptive of the corporation. This graphic can also be used on the masthead of a corporate newsletter; on the Web site; on mailing labels, brochures, and press packets, and other promotional literature. Paying an artist to draw a distinctive and creative logo is usually a good investment, although it is often possible to make one by using some of the popular "clip art" or graphics software programs. If you don't have a scanner, a computer store may be willing to scan logo art work, so it can be printed out in various sizes or "imported" into computer-generated publications as needed.

The letterhead should also include the organization's name, address, e-mail address, and Web site address. Most organizations also list their board members, officers, and key staff members, as well.

Filing Systems

The filing systems of nonprofit corporations usually evolve over several years and are as individual as each organization. Several factors should be considered in setting up a filing system.

Keep files of the corporation's internal operations separate from other files. For example, keep the files relating to tax-exempt status, corporation budget, office leases, insurance, taxes, Articles of Incorporation, membership, mailing lists, lobbying, and charitable registration in a different place from files about general political and public policy issues. A corporation should have correspondence files—one for "outgoing" and another for "incoming." One nonprofit always makes three copies of all outgoing correspondence—one for the "outgoing" file, one for the "incoming file" stapled to the incoming letter that generated the outgoing letter, and one for the subject file that relates to the issue of the letter. "External" files can be subject matter relating to the mission of the corporation. However, "internal" files will be similar from nonprofit to nonprofit. Among typical internal files are:

> allocations, annual report, Articles of Incorporation, bank statements, board meeting agendas, board minutes, board meeting packets, bookkeeping, brochure, budget, bylaws, computer, dues structure, expenses, financial reports, grass-roots alerts, insurance, mailing lists, newsletters, office equipment, office leases, payroll, personnel, photographs, planning, postal service, press mailing list, press clippings, press releases, printing, grants, publications, speeches and testimony, special projects, tax-exempt status, taxes, and Web site. Some of these files will have sub-categories (e.g., newsletter—previous, newsletter—current), and others will be categorized by year.

Computer

Perhaps there remain a handful of nonprofit executives who are quite satisfied replying to correspondence the old-fashioned way by either writing replies using pen and paper, or banging out an answer on the same trusty Remington typewriter they used when they were in college back in the 1970s. Many of them are satisfied with what they have—and don't begin to question this primordial existence until they are faced with having to type out 3,000 "personal" letters asking for funds to save their jobs or tire of personally addressing 6,000 newsletters each month. The computer is, with good reason, a fixture in the modern nonprofit office.

The good news is that in the hands of a knowledgeable operator, a computer can do a variety of tasks and save thousands of expensive staff hours. The bad news is that it can be expensive and complicated to learn, may be vulnerable to computer viruses and other cyberterrorism, and can "crash" at the most inopportune times.

Hardware/Software

This handbook provides only the most cursory review of basic computer buying decisions. It is geared to the small nonprofit interested in the advantages and disadvantages of purchasing a personal computer and the basic options.

Among many issues to consider when purchasing a computer system are:

- Who will be using the system, and will they be sufficiently trained?

- Is software available that is compatible with your hardware, and will this software be capable of providing the output you need?

- Are you paying for features or capacity you are unlikely to ever need?

- Is there sufficient follow-up support to answer questions, troubleshoot problems, and provide maintenance?

Basic Hardware Decision: Apple or IBM-Compatible

In the old days, these two types of computers were as incompatible as Beta format and VHS for VCRs. What were once uncrossable boundaries between these two hardware systems are now being crossed and integrated. Basically, the Apple-based Macintosh ("Mac") computers are considered to be more "user-friendly." On the other hand, IBM and IBM "clones" are generally less expensive and have more programs that are compatible, but require more knowledge on the part of the user. IBM and its imitators have developed software that imitates the user-friendliness of the Mac. Increasingly, the Mac-based hardware is permitting the use of files created using IBM-compatible software. Each system has those who swear by it and swear at it. The state-of-the-art is advancing so swiftly that this decision may become moot in the near future.

Typical Software for Nonprofits

There are thousands of programs available that are being used by various nonprofits. In general, several families of programs exist that are useful in a typical computer-based nonprofit office. Among them are:

- *Word Processing*—Microsoft Word, Corel WordPerfect, and OpenOffice.org Writer are among the most popular word processing programs. An advantage of word processing programs is that an entire document does not have to be retyped to make corrections or multiple copies. This is a major productivity enhancement if an organization desires to send a "personal" letter to 50,000 potential contributors.

- *Spreadsheet*—Lotus 1-2-3, Microsoft Excel, and OpenOffice.org Calc are among the most popular spreadsheet programs. In simple terms, the objective of a spreadsheet is to perform operations and calculations on numbers and automatically adjust a total when one number in a sum is changed. Spreadsheets are indispensable for bookkeeping, budgeting, and similar documents. Many spreadsheets contain graphics capability that permits numerical data to be displayed in pleasing and informative formats.

- *Database*—Lotus Approach, Corel Paradox, and Microsoft Access are among the most popular database programs. The objective of a database is to sort data into various fields, which can then be used to generate mailing lists, store information that can be sorted, and perform other similar tasks.

- *Desktop Publishing (DTP)*—Adobe InDesign, Microsoft Publisher, and Quark Xpress are among the most popular DTP or page layout programs. These programs "import" graphics and output from word processing programs and can manipulate the result on the screen in an eye-catching format. Text can be printed out in a variety of type faces and sizes, giving documents the appearance of having been professionally designed and typeset.

- *Presentation Software*—Microsoft PowerPoint, Lotus Freelance Graphics, Adobe Persuasion, and Harvard Graphics are among the most popular presentation software programs. These are used with LED screens to project speaker presentations of short bites of text and graphics for large audiences, and can be coordinated with music and video files.

There are software "suite" packages that provide the above types of programs all-in-one and are designed to work with each other. Some of the most popular are Microsoft Office, Corel Word Perfect Suite, IBM's Lotus SmartSuite, and OpenOffice.org (formerly known as "Star Office"). Before purchasing any software (which can be obtained for free or cost thousands of dollars), it is best to seek advice of those who are knowledgeable about the advantages and disadvantages of each program.

Nonprofits affiliated with a state or national association should check with the staff of that organization to ascertain what software packages are used. Often, these organizations share data among their affiliates in only one format. While software is available to make conversions between formats and hardware configurations, substantial time, energy, and money can be saved by having compatible computer systems.

Open Source Software

Open source software is quickly becoming the choice of thousands of charities for applications including operating systems (Linux), productivity office suite packages (OpenOffice), browsers (Mozilla Firefox), e-mail (Mozilla Thunderbird), databases (MySQL), and Web site design (Joomla). The term refers to software whose source code is public. Often, the software is licensed to users using a standardized form that sets rules for changing it and using it—but for the most part, there is no charge for using open source software. The open source software model is intended to encourage collaboration for the purpose of making a software product better for every user, rather than making money for the developer. Among the advantages are that you don't have to pay for periodic updates, you can put the software on as many computers as you like, and there is a community of software developers who collaborate to improve the product and eliminate bugs. However, keep in mind that there may not be stable technical support, quality control may be "iffy," and the software may not run on all operating systems. Generally, open source software tends to be high quality, and worthy for charities to consider.

Credit Card Sales

Nonprofit organizations are businesses and have many aspects in common with for-profit businesses. They sell products and services, such as memberships, publications, counseling, and tickets to events. They also solicit donations from the public, and it is not unusual for many contributors to be comfortable making these donations by credit card, either through secure forms on the Internet or, more conventionally, through the mail. Inexorably, we are becoming a cashless society, and the public increasingly relies on credit cards for financial transactions. Nonprofit organizations should consider whether having "merchant status" is advantageous. For more information about how to obtain this status, see Chapter 21.

Postal Service Issues

Nonprofit corporations typically generate a large volume of mail in the course of sending out annual reports, newsletters, program brochures, fundraising solicitations, surveys, grass-roots action alerts, and meeting notices. As a result of U.S. Postal Service advances in technology, mass mailings have become more complicated. Because of recent reforms that substantially change the way both organizations that qualify for nonprofit mailing status and others must prepare bulk mail, the USPS has expanded its outreach by providing educational programs.

The Postal Service offers free training on how to process bulk mailings. Call your U.S. Postal Service's regional bulk mail center to get information on the next scheduled workshop.

General Postage Rates

The U.S. Postal Service publishes the *Postal Bulletin*, which details the latest rates, fees, and changes in regulations. Subscriptions to this bi-weekly publication are available for $163/year. You can download back issues for free at: *http://about.usps.com/postal-bulletin/welcome.htm*

A more comprehensive publication, *Domestic Mail Manual*, is published twice annually, and is available electronically at *http://pe.usps.com/text/dmm300/dmm300_landing.htm*. Copies of the latest edition (2011) are also available from main post offices or from the Government Printing Office.

Postage Meters

Postage meters permit organizations to affix exact postage to letters and packages without the inconvenience of purchasing stamps of varying denominations. The postage is printed by the meter, and the organization pays in advance for the postage used. Most new postage meter systems permit postage accounts in the machine to be replenished by telephone/modem. Postage machines are not sold but, in accordance with federal law, are rented by commercial companies. A license is required from the Postal Service, but the paperwork is handled by the vendor. Pitney-Bowes is the firm that developed the system and is the leader in the field. Competing companies can be found in the Yellow Pages under "Mailing Machines and Equipment." The cost of renting a machine is about $20 per month and up, including a postage scale, depending on the system's sophistication.

Stamps.com and other competitors allow for a similar service that is Internet-based. Postage is provided by establishing an online account and printing out postage from your computer.

Bulk Mail Permit Procedures

The USPS has a terrific online tutorial for those who wish to set up a bulk mail operation. From the USPS home page *(http://www.usps.com)*, click on *Grow Your Business*. Then click on *Business Mail 101*.

Organizations that desire to participate in the bulk mailing program must first obtain an imprint authorization from the Postal Service using Form 3615. As of January 2011, the one-time-only imprint fee of $190 is good for both first and standard class (formerly known as "third class") mailing. Mailing permits must be renewed annually, and there is a $190 fee for first class and $190 for standard class. Organizations seeking nonprofit mailing status should file Form 3624. Forms are available online at: *http://www.usps.com/forms.* The Postal Service automatically forwards the correct form when it is time to renew the permits.

Having such an imprint entitles the organization to pay the postage in advance without having to affix postage to each individual piece of mail. The permit also provides a discount, provided there are at least 200 pieces or 50 pounds in the bulk mailing and the mailing is sorted and processed in accordance with post office regulations. Each piece must be correctly ZIP Coded or it will not be accepted.

Once in receipt of the imprint permit, the organization can affix the imprint to mail pieces using a rubber stamp, or they can print it directly on the piece.

The bulk mail discount can be large. The rate for a first-class letter rose to 44 cents per ounce (17 cents for each additional ounce) on May 11, 2009. That 17 cent charge increased to 20 cents in April 2011. A comparable piece of mail sent standard-class bulk rate can be sent for less than half of that amount, depending on how it was prepared. There are also substantial discounts to encourage barcoding of bulk mailings.

501(c)(3)s (or organizations that have the characteristics of such organizations) may qualify for the U.S. Postal Service's Special Bulk Rate. Organizations that may apply for this discount rate are agricultural, educational, fraternal, labor, philanthropic, religious, scientific, and veterans' nonprofit organizations. Organizations that are not eligible are auto clubs, business leagues, chambers of commerce, citizens and civic improvement organizations, mutual insurance associations, most political organizations, services clubs (such as Lions clubs and Rotary clubs), social and hobby groups, and trade associations. To apply, you need to file a PS 3624 form, which is available from any post office. The application will require you to submit your Articles of Incorporation, proof that your organization fits one of the eligible categories, a list of activities, a financial statement, and documents that show how your organization operates, such as brochures, newsletters, and board minutes. The Post Office reviewers pay close attention to any advertising you may have in your newsletter. For more details on this benefit to nonprofits, consult *Quick Service Guide 670* published by the U.S. Postal Service.

As of April 2011, the basic nonprofit rate for letters under 3.3 ounces was 19.1 cents (26.5 cents for other than nonprofit rate). This basic rate can be reduced further, depending on the nature of the presort and the destination. Use the online calculator at: *http://dbcalc.usps.gov* to calculate your bulk rate postage. For all rates, publications, and rate calculators, visit: *http://pe.usps.gov*

Automation

Bulk mail postage rates are substantially lower for mail that can be handled by automated equipment. Computer software is available at reasonable cost that will automatically place a U.S. Postal

Service-compatible barcode on each label generated by your computer. Even if you do not have barcoding capability, providing enough space for the Postal Service's equipment to optically read the address on each label and place its own barcode, while not reducing your postage rate, will qualify you for time-saving reductions in bulk mail preparation. Consult the U.S.P.S. for more information about this "upgradeable mail."

The entire system for presorting to comply with Postal Service regulations is too complicated to be described briefly. It has changed substantially since the last edition of this book. A thumbnail sketch of this system is provided below.

Size of Standard-Class Letter Mail

The dimensions of letter-size bulk mail are limited to the following:

> **length:** 5 inches - 11 1/2 inches
> **width:** 3 1/2 inches - 6 1/8 inches
> **thickness:** .009 inches - .25 inches (enough to send a 20-page newsletter of 20-lb. paper, folded once)
> **aspect ratio (length divided by height):** must be 1.3 inches - 2.5 inches

Standard Mail Sorting

To obtain bulk mail discount postage rates, mail must not only meet certain criteria to be considered "machinable" such as those relating to length, width, thickness, and aspect ratio, but must be delivered to the Post Office's business mail entry unit in trays sorted by ZIP Code. Note that trays are provided free by the USPS Business Mail Entry Unit. The following is a short version of how the mail should be placed in these trays:

> **Step 1:** Make up a tray or trays of mail going to your Post Office's origin ZIP Codes. Each bulk mail processing center has a list of such ZIP Codes, and these Sectional Center Facility (SCF) letters qualify for a reduced rate. They should be in ZIP Code order.

> **Step 2.** Make up a tray or trays of letters going to the same Automated Area Distribution Center (AADC). These should be in ZIP Code order. You can obtain a list of which ZIP Codes comprise each AADC from your Post Office (ask for Labeling List L801, AADCs—Letter-Size Mailings).

> **Step 3.** Make up a tray or trays of the remaining letters.

Tray Requirements

Trays should be at least 85% full. If not, skip the step that created that tray. The USPS wants you to provide them with full trays. "Full" is defined as at least 85% full, so choose either a one-foot tray or two-foot tray to comply with this requirement.

Trays must be enclosed by a tray sleeve and bound with polyethylene strapping. Strapping material can be purchased from a commercial office supply house. The trays must be labeled appropriately to reach the correct destination. The Postal Service can provide correct tray labeling information.

The applicable postage must be deposited in the organization's postage account if the current balance is not enough to cover the postage for the mailing. A mailing statement provided by the

Postal Service that identifies the organization, its bulk mail account, and the number of pieces being mailed for each standard-class category, must accompany each mailing.

The bulk mail operation is performed successfully by hundreds of for-profits and nonprofits alike every day. It can save thousands of dollars in postage compared with mailing every piece first class. It also saves the bother of affixing individual postage stamps. While it may appear intimidating at first, it becomes routine with practice.

In general, the Postal Service attempts to deliver standard class mail within ten days of receipt. Often, this mail is delivered just as expeditiously as first-class mail, although a four- or five-day time period for processing is not unusual. As a general rule, nonprofits should think twice before mailing anything standard class that absolutely *must* be received within 12 days after the organization delivers the mailing to the Business Mail Entry Unit.

Only certain U.S. Postal Service branches are equipped to process bulk mail. There are commercial services that specialize in processing bulk mailings. Some volunteer organizations will offer to help nonprofit organizations do bulk mail, as well.

Tips:

- **When creating a mailing list, it is useful to have the list in ZIP Code order or to be capable of sorting it in ZIP Code order. Otherwise, letters must be sorted by hand to take advantage of the bulk mail discounts.**

- **Most of the popular word processing programs will perform a ZIP Code sort operation and create mailing labels, and all of the database programs do. Many are capable of automatically inserting a barcode, which further reduces postage rates if printed in accordance with U.S. Postal Service regulations.**

- **Contact the U.S. Postal Service for help with bulk mail preparation or rates. A useful telephone number is: 1-800-238-3150—National Customer Support Center (USPS Web site: *http://www.usps.com*)**

Chapter 25
Nonprofits and Small Business Competition

Synopsis: Some small business advocates have charged that nonprofits have unfair advantages when they compete in the sale of goods and services. Legislation and regulations to remove these advantages are a clear threat to the ability of the nonprofit sector to function effectively.

Introduction

An issue has emerged on the agenda of small business advocates that could jeopardize the ability of many nonprofits to perform their vital missions. Tracing its beginning to the early 1980s, the issue of alleged unfair competition between nonprofits and small business earned its first stamp of legitimacy when the U.S. Small Business Administration issued a report in late 1983 entitled *Unfair Competition by Nonprofit Organizations with Small Business: An Issue for the 1980's.*

Small businesses had, until then, complained with muted voices that nonprofit corporations possessed advantages in the marketplace that hindered the ability of small businesses to compete. Among these advantages were said to be—

- tax exemptions—the most tangible benefit of nonprofits;
- reduced postage rates;
- tax deductions for those who contribute goods and services to nonprofit organizations
- Use of venture capital—the ability to use contributions and non-taxable surpluses for expansion, state-of-the-art equipment, and seed money for new activities that may compete with private enterprise;
- "captured referrals"—"sweetheart deal" arrangements between affiliated nonprofits that eliminate competition from non-affiliated businesses;
- use of plant, staff, supplies, and equipment donated or funded by grants to spur unrelated business enterprises that may compete with small business; and
- the "halo effect"—referring to the willingness of the public to do business with a nonprofit because of the perception that the organization is serving the public good rather than being operated for a private profit motive.

During the 1970s, nonprofit corporations were becoming increasingly sophisticated in their efforts to generate revenue. These efforts accelerated during the 1980s, when many social service nonprofits were hit by the loss of government funding during the retrenchment of domestic spending under the Reagan Administration. Nonprofit hospitals were a particular target of small business owners, who resented the establishment of laundry and pharmaceutical services that competed with them. Small business advocates continue to complain that state government has no effective mechanism to track funds that may be channeled between a nonprofit organization and its for-profit affiliates.

Also targeted nationally were YMCAs and their Jewish counterpart JCCs. Some of the YMCAs and JCCs began marketing their lucrative health club services to an "upscale" market segment to generate revenues to cross-subsidize services provided to their needier clients. Such facilities were caught in a "Catch 22." If they charged less than the market rates, they were accused of undercutting small business by taking advantage of their tax exemptions and other advantages. If they charged the same or more than the private health clubs, they were accused of operating just as any other business and thus, not deserving of any tax exemption. Private health clubs across the nation, through the guidance of their associations, participated in legal actions against several

YMCAs and instigated reviews by local taxing authorities designed to challenge the historical tax-exempt status of these facilities. An effort by nine private health clubs in the Pittsburgh area to challenge the tax exemption of the Golden Triangle YMCA in Pittsburgh was partially successful.

Colleges and universities garnered the wrath of small business owners who objected to college bookstores selling television sets and refrigerators, marketing surplus computer time, operating testing services, establishing travel agencies, or otherwise entering markets in direct competition with small business.

These small business owners found a voice in the Small Business Administration. On July 27, 1983, the Small Business Administration's Office of Advocacy held a one-day symposium on this issue, and followed up the conference with a November report entitled *Unfair Competition by Nonprofit Organizations With Small Business: An Issue for the 1980's.* This report charged that "traditional 'donative' nonprofits, such as the Red Cross and the Salvation Army, which rely primarily on gifts and contributions for their operating revenue, are being replaced by 'commercial nonprofits'... which derive all or nearly all of their income from the sales of goods or services they produce." The report charged some of the nonprofit sector with creating an oversupply of goods, and charging significantly less than the prevailing market rates as a result of exemptions from laws and regulations. The report concluded—

It is the responsibility of the Congress and the Executive Branch to make a systematic inquiry into whether these exemptions are still justified in light of the emergence of the commercial nonprofit sector.

Among other recommendations, the report called for:

- levying a higher tax on, or outright prohibiting, unrelated business activities by nonprofits,

- defining "substantially related" more clearly and narrowly for purposes of what constitutes an unrelated business,

- establishing a threshold above which a nonprofit engaging in unrelated business activities would lose its tax exemption, and

- eliminating the "convenience" exception for the payment of unrelated business income taxes.

Soon after the report was released, approximately 20 national business associations, many of which participated in drafting the 1983 SBA report, formed the "Coalition for Fair Business Competition" to lobby on behalf of business interests on this issue.

The issue of nonprofit competition with small business was among the most compelling of the issues reported by small business owners at the 1986 White House Conference on Small Business. Conference delegates designated it the number three issue on a list of 40 major concerns culled from a list of 2,232 proposed by small business owners nationwide. Legislation was introduced in several states in response to this conference.

Pennsylvania Background

On December 11, 1985, the Pennsylvania House of Representatives, by a vote of 195-0, passed a resolution to establish a seven-member bipartisan Select Committee to Study Nonprofits. The stated purpose of the Select Committee was to "study tax-exempt nonprofit organizations engaged in the sale of goods and services within the Commonwealth, especially with regard to the impact on small business."

The Select Committee held 16 days of hearings between March and August 1986. On November 25, 1986, the Select Committee issued its final report, which included nine recommendations. The report concluded that it was impossible to judge whether there was unfair competition by nonprofits because of the paucity of information on nonprofits in Pennsylvania. The report stated that Pennsylvania law is filled with "many loopholes and exemptions with regard to reporting requirements."

Among the report's nine recommendations were the following—

- establish an entity within the Pennsylvania Department of Revenue to determine which nonprofits are engaging in activities beyond the realm of the purpose for which they were incorporated;
- require all Pennsylvania nonprofits to file their IRS tax exemption code number and most recent federal income tax returns with the Commonwealth;
- require all nonprofits to disclose their "affiliations" with other corporations;
- restrict nonprofit entities from performing commercial business ventures in a nonprofit environment that takes advantage of tax exemptions;
- require that surpluses of nonprofits be used to fund their tax-exempt purposes; and
- prohibit the commingling of nonprofit resources with those of any for-profit within the same organizational structure.

Many in the Pennsylvania nonprofit community expected that the attention on this issue had concluded with the publication and distribution of the final report. It was, in fact, only a prelude. A follow-up resolution proposed a nine-member bipartisan Select Committee to study the possibility of direct and unfair competition resulting from nonprofits charging fees for their services. It raised the issue of potential adverse impacts of such competition, including forcing small businesses out of business and eroding the tax base. H. Res. 4 was adopted on February 5, 1987, by a vote of 189-5, and another series of hearings was launched.

Institutions of Purely Public Charity Act—Section 8

The Institutions of Purely Public Charity Act, Act 55 of 1997, was enacted on November 26, 1997, and is the culmination of the decade-long struggle between Pennsylvania small businesses and nonprofit organizations. With some irony, this law was supported by the National Federation of Independent Businesses (NFIB), and the legislation, the top priority of Pennsylvania charities for nearly a decade, was unlikely to pass without this support from such an unlikely source. Section 8 of this bill includes modest restrictions on nonprofit operations that were negotiated between charities and the small business community leadership. The principal restriction is that "(A)n institution of purely public charity may not fund, capitalize, guarantee the indebtedness of, lease obligations of or subsidize a commercial business that is unrelated to the institution's charitable purpose as stated in the institution's charter or governing legal documents."

This restriction does not apply to existing business arrangements. There are three major exceptions. The first is if the business "is intended only for the use of its employees, staff, alumni, faculty, members, students, clients, volunteers, patients or residents." The second exception is if "the commercial business results in sales to the general public that are incidental or periodic rather than permanent and ongoing." The third exception is if the institution "is formally requested to do so by the Commonwealth or a political subdivision." The law also includes an exception applicable to the use of facilities to host groups for educational purposes. The Department of State is authorized to administer an arbitration system to adjudicate small business complaints. Those unsuccessful may appeal the arbitrator's decision to a court of common pleas.

Federal Unrelated Business Income Tax (UBIT)

Federal law stipulates that nonprofit corporations pay federal taxes on unrelated business income. Corporations with at least $1,000 of such income are required to file a 990-T annually. Income is defined as "unrelated" if it is derived from a trade or business, is regularly carried on, and is substantially unrelated to the exempt purpose of the corporation. Income clearly exempt from UBIT includes that generated from activities performed by volunteers, from selling merchandise received as gifts or contributions, and dividends, interest, royalties, and capital gains. Also exempt is income from business operations conducted for the "convenience" of an organization's members, students, patients, and staff, such as a hospital cafeteria or college bookstore.

In 2010, the Internal Revenue Service reported that $2.3 billion in UBIT was collected from 23,796 nonprofit organizations for the 2007 tax year.

Both the Congress and the Internal Revenue Service have been skeptical about whether charities should have a broad exemption from paying taxes on business income. The House Ways and Means Committee's Oversight Committee held a series of hearings in June 1987 on the issue of changing federal policy on unrelated business income taxes. The subcommittee followed up on its hearings by issuing a press release on March 31, 1988, describing policy options on changes to UBIT, many of which caused concern in the nonprofit sector. The options included suggestions to narrow the "substantially related" test for exempting organizations from UBIT, repeal the "convenience" exception (which, for example, permits college bookstores and cafeterias to be tax exempt), apply UBIT to fitness/health clubs unless the program is "available to a reasonable cross section of the general public such as by scholarship or by fees based on community affordability," and apply UBIT to advertising income and allow deductions from UBIT only on direct advertising costs (a major concern to exempt nonprofits whose publications accept commercial advertising to defray expenses of the parent organization).

In March 1990, a revised report leaked from the subcommittee entitled *Summary of Main Issues in Possible Modification of Oversight Committee UBIT Options.* The draft proposal eliminated many of the controversial proposals that caused so much concern to nonprofits. While the "substantially related" test was retained in the proposal, the "convenience" exception was repealed. Most indirect and overhead expenses relating to advertising income would be deductible, but such expenses could not reduce net income by more than 80%. The subcommittee membership was unable to reach a consensus on UBIT proposals.

The Internal Revenue Service has aggressively audited some charities focusing on UBIT issues, and has taken charities to court to promote its policy of restricting UBIT exemptions. During the 1990s, the Internal Revenue Service expanded its attention to enforcement of UBIT and developed policies with respect to some of the borderline areas that were problematic to charities. Some cases involving the interpretation of what constitutes unrelated income were litigated. Several decisions on generic UBIT issues have been decided in favor of charities. Three examples have been cases involving mailing list rental income, affinity credit card income, and income from bingo games.

A case decided in August 1996 in U.S. District Court involving the American Academy of Family Physicians determined that the organization's income from a group insurance plan offered to its members underwritten by a private insurance carrier was not subject to UBIT. Again, the facts of this case may not be typical of conventional agreements between an insurance carrier and an exempt organization, but the opinion of the court on the issue was a favorable development.

Differences Between Nonprofits and For-Profits

There are clear and fundamental differences between the operations and motivations of nonprofits and for-profits. The buildings of some types of nonprofit charities and their for-profit counterparts may, in some cases, be similar. For-profit and nonprofit hospitals, nursing homes, day care centers, and recreational/youth service facilities may have the same equipment and physical plants, and they may provide some of the same services. Yet, these similarities often are exaggerated in an effort by some overzealous small business advocates to discredit the tax exemptions of those they perceive as competitors. The YMCAs in a growing number of communities particularly have endured vicious attacks from some private health club owners. In specific cases around the nation, these attacks have been given a credibility unsupported by the facts and have resulted in the loss of tax-exempt status.

Among the differences between nonprofit charitable organizations and for-profits are the following:

- A nonprofit charity is driven by its service mission philosophy rather than by the profit motive.

- A nonprofit charity serves those who cannot afford to pay full costs.

- Any excess revenue over expenditures is funneled back into the institution to further its exempt purpose.

- The charitable institution likely will remain in the community even if it suffers financial losses.

- The nonprofit charity is more accountable to its board for public service.

- The nonprofit charity often will proactively look for ways to respond to community needs without regard to any profit motive.

- A nonprofit charity may not compensate its employees higher than "reasonable" rates, as is evident from the successful prosecution of several television religious broadcasters who were paid exorbitant salaries and benefits.

- A nonprofit charity's board of directors is typically comprised of unpaid community leaders motivated by public service and serving the unmet needs of the community rather than making a profit.

- A nonprofit charity, because of its legal mission to serve rather than to make profits, often attracts thousands of hours of volunteer time and philanthropic contributions that further its purposes.

Tips:

- **Don't publicly advertise products and services in a manner that underscores price competition with the for-profit sector.**

- Refrain from entering markets that are not substantially related to the mission of your organization, and be prepared to pay unrelated business income taxes (UBIT) on income derived from activities not "directly" related.

- Review all activities that could be construed as commercial, and identify all those that require the filing of a 990-T and payment of UBIT.

- In exploring options for generating new revenue, be sensitive to meeting needs that are unmet by the for-profit sector, rather than relying on undercutting the price of goods and services already being offered in the marketplace.

- Support efforts to improve disclosure and accountability of the voluntary sector. Cooperate with expanded enforcement of laws governing this sector, so that the few nonprofits that are abusing the law do not stain the reputation of the entire sector.

- Periodically review the organization's bylaws and tax-exempt status purposes, and update these documents to reflect changing conditions.

Chapter 26
State and Local Tax Exemptions

Synopsis: Many nonprofit charities have been subject to challenges to their state and local tax exemptions in recent years. Legislation was signed into law in 1997 to constrain the misinterpretations by taxing bodies of a Pennsylvania Supreme Court case that provided a judicial definition of institutions eligible for tax-exempt status.

Sales and Use Tax Exemption

Pennsylvania has a 6% sales and use tax on most goods and many services. There is an additional 2% sales tax collected in Philadelphia as a result of a 1991 state law, and a 1% additional sales tax in Allegheny County as a result of a 1994 state law. Many charitable nonprofit organizations are legally exempt from paying this tax on purchases for their use. Organizations that believe they qualify for state sales tax exempt status need to submit qualifying information when they file the PA-100 form with the Department of Revenue, and must file an REV-72 form. This tax exemption is for purchases by the organization and does not extend to items sold by such organizations during fundraising efforts, unless the sale qualifies as an "isolated transaction." Answers to the questions on the form with respect to tax-exempt status should be sensitive to the issues discussed later in this chapter.

Sales and Use Tax Charitable Exemption Application Form

Organizations seeking exemption from paying Pennsylvania sales tax must submit an REV-72 to the Department of Revenue. The form, which consists of six pages of instructions and six pages that need to be filled out, was last revised in November 2006, and it reflects both statutory changes compelled by the enactment of the *Institutions of Purely Public Charity Act* and negotiations with the charitable community to streamline the form and reduce burdensome requirements.

The form is divided into two major sections titled *Registration* and *Financial Data*. Registration information is subdivided into subsections labeled *Institutional Information, Form of Organization, Organization Information, Affiliate Information, Officer Information,* and *Salary Information.* The Financial Information section is subdivided into subsections labeled *Basic Questions, Recipient Information, Goods or Services Provided,* and *Fundraising Activities.* Institutional Information and Form of Organization are straightforward requests for general information about the institution. Organization Information requests "a detailed description of the past, present, and planned future activities of the institution for a period of three years" including "a description of how beneficiaries are selected." Affiliate information requires disclosure of the date of affiliation, percent of ownership, and other general information. Officer Information requires disclosure of annual compensation, if any, for each officer, and other benefits and amounts of each. Salary information must be provided that discloses whether compensation is based in any way on the performance of the institution. The position, salary, and other compensation of the four highest paid individuals must be disclosed.

The financial data disclosure is quite extensive. Many of the questions track the various options for meeting the five-part HUP test found in Act 55 (see page 266). Even if an institution clearly demonstrates that it meets one of these options for "donating a substantial portion of its services," the disclosure form requests detailed information about how the organization meets virtually all of the options. For example, applicants must disclose the percentage of individuals receiving goods or services from the institution who receive a reduction of fees of at least 10% of the cost of goods or services provided to them.

In addition to filling out the form, applicants must also provide a copy of their governing legal document (Articles of Incorporation for corporations, bylaws for unincorporated organizations), most current financial statement (new organizations may submit a proposed budget), their most recent 990 annual federal tax return if they file one, and a copy of their IRS determination letter if they have one.

The Pennsylvania Constitution

Federal tax exemption status of an institution has no bearing on state exemption status policy. Article VIII, section 2(a) of the Pennsylvania Constitution provides the legal basis for the granting of tax exemptions in Pennsylvania. This section of the Pennsylvania Constitution provides that the General Assembly "may by law exempt from taxation" a narrow list of five types of institutions. Charitable institutions are among those potentially exempt, provided they are considered to be "institutions of purely public charity." See Appendix F for the full text of this section of the Constitution.

There is no definition of the term "institutions of purely public charity" in the Pennsylvania Constitution or in statute. Until enactment of the *Institutions of Purely Public Charity Act* (see page 273), the only guidance on this definition had been provided by the courts.

Pennsylvania Tax Exemption Law

The General Assembly has used the authority of the above section of the Constitution to provide tax exemptions to certain classes of institutions. The act of May 22, 1933 (P.L. 853, No. 155), known as the General County Assessment Law, as amended, provides that "...hospitals, academies, associations of learning, benevolence, or charity...founded, endowed, and maintained by public or private charity" are exempt from "all county, city, borough, town, township, road, poor and school tax." See Appendix G for the text of this act, which applies to counties of the first through third class [72 P.S. §5020-204(a)(3)]. A parallel law authorizes tax exemptions for such institutions in fourth through eighth class counties [72 P.S. §5453.202(a)(3)]. The act of March 4, 1971 (P.L. 6, No. 2, 72 P.S. §7204) provides an exemption from the state sales and use tax on "(T)he sale at retail to or use by (i) any charitable organization, volunteer firemen's organization or nonprofit educational institution..." See Appendix G for an excerpt from the text of these exemptions. State law (72 P.S. §7236) requires the organization seeking a tax exemption to affirmatively prove that it is entitled to an exemption.

Hospital Utilization Project v. Commonwealth of Pennsylvania (HUP v. PA)

Although the term "purely public charity" had not been defined with exactness under Pennsylvania statutes until 1997, case law has provided criteria establishing the parameters of a "purely public charity." In 1985, the Pennsylvania Supreme Court, after reviewing prior law stated:

> (It) may be safely said that whatever is gratuitously done or given in relief of the public burdens or for the advancement of the public good is a public charity. In every such case as the public is the beneficiary, the charity is a public charity. As no private or pecuniary return is reserved to the giver or any particular person, but all the benefit

resulting from the gift or act goes to the public, it is a 'purely public charity,' the word 'purely' being equivalent to the word 'wholly'...

The court elaborated further that receiving revenues from recipients sufficient to keep the institution in operation, so long as this revenue does not go beyond self-support, does not affect its status as a purely public charity. This principle is consistent with current Pennsylvania statute as well.

In its summary, the court concluded that "an entity qualifies as a purely public charity if it possesses the following characteristics:

- *advances a charitable purpose,*
- *donates or renders gratuitously a substantial portion of its services,*
- *benefits a substantial and indefinite class of persons who are legitimate subjects of charity,*
- *relieves government of some of its burden, and*
- *operates entirely free from private profit motive.'*

The HUP case should have had little or no bearing on the granting or denial of tax exemptions by the Department of Revenue or local governments. There was no new legal doctrine made by the case, and the decision was entirely appropriate given the facts of the case. Yet it is evident from reading the above five criteria outside the context of the cases in which these were developed that they are basic and general. The terms are unclear if viewed in a vacuum. What does the term "legitimate subjects of charity" mean? Does it mean only the poor? What about the term "substantial portion of its services"? Does this mean 75% or 5%? Does the provision of money rather than "services" preclude an organization from meeting these criteria?

The HUP case does provide appropriate guidance on the intent and meaning of the court's definition of "institution of purely public charity." For example, the only mention of the term "legitimate subjects of charity" in the HUP case is a quotation from its previous decision in the *YMCA of Germantown v. Philadelphia* (1936) case. In seeking to define a "purely public charity," the Court wrote:

Under this definition the characteristics of an organized charity are: First whatever it does for others is done free of charge, or at least so nearly free of charge as to make the charges nominal or negligible; second, that those to whom it renders help or services are those who are unable to provide themselves with what the institution provides for them, that is, they are legitimate subjects of charity.

Thus the term "legitimate subjects of charity" is broad enough to include those who use libraries and museums and attend symphony concerts.

The initial "judge" in a tax exemption case is usually the very unit of government that has the most to gain financially by the most narrow interpretation of tax-exempt status criteria. As has been demonstrated in several cases detailed below, these five criteria have been interpreted more narrowly than intended by the HUP decision, and in some cases, intentionally misinterpreted in order to maximize revenues for governmental units. Legislation was enacted by the General Assembly in 1997 to standardize and codify the meaning of the HUP criteria.

Department of Revenue Sales and Use Tax Regulations

The Pennsylvania Department of Revenue sales and use tax regulations affecting charities were published in April 1995 as a corrective reprint to the regulations published in the *Pennsylvania*

Bulletin on December 24, 1994. These regulations have been administratively replaced with informal rules that implement Act 55, the *Institutions of Purely Public Charity Act.*

Pennsylvania Tax Exemption Cases of Interest

Case 1: St. Margaret Seneca Place

A Commonwealth Court opinion of February 20, 1992, sent shock waves throughout the Pennsylvania charitable community. A three-judge panel overturned a lower court decision that had determined that a 156-bed Allegheny County nursing home had activities consistent with all five HUP criteria and the three statutory criteria as well, and thus was entitled to a refund of its property taxes for 1989. Using the logic of the Commonwealth Court opinion, virtually no modern charity would be eligible for tax exempt status in Pennsylvania. The court determined that, contrary to the findings of the lower court, St. Margaret's did not meet a single one of the five HUP criteria. To do so, the court had to stretch the intent of the HUP criteria to a point of absurdity and, according to many experts, did so. For example, the facility's Medical Assistance caseload was 48.5% of admissions, and the home lost hundreds of thousands of dollars by providing charity care to subsidize the difference between costs and Medical Assistance reimbursement. The court determined that accepting MA patients was analogous to an airline charging lower costs to different classes of persons in order to fill its seats—and thus this was a general business practice and not charity. The facility lost on two of the five HUP criteria because its executive testified that the facility would rather have a paying patient than someone who could not afford to pay because—

> *Given our current census and the number of Medicaid patients that we have now and the amount of charitable care that we are already providing, we would have to take the person who could afford to pay us something. We don't have unlimited resources in terms of funds to continue to take care of our deficits.*

To rule that St. Margaret's was not eligible for tax-exempt status, Commonwealth Court had to find that the facility failed on only one of the five HUP criteria or three statutory criteria. In ruling that the lower court was wrong on its interpretation of the HUP test on every single criterion as well as the three-part statutory test, the Court had to blatantly ignore substantial factual data that supported the facility's position. Some analysts suggested that the intent of the opinion was not to dispassionately weigh the merits of the case but to provide a political message to all Pennsylvania charities.

St. Margaret's appealed the case to the entire Commonwealth Court. In its appeal, the facility pointed out many obvious errors and omissions made by the Court that even the most zealous anti-charity judge disregarding political considerations would not have ignored. In addition, the facility noted that one member of the three-judge panel, Dan Pellegrini, "formerly served as Solicitor of the City of Pittsburgh, and in that capacity was very active in attempts to remove exemptions of many previously exempt institutions." Lawyers for St. Margaret's suggested that Judge Pellegrini's participation in this case would provide for "potential bias or appearance of impropriety." The appeal was denied. In May 1992, the facility appealed to the Pennsylvania Supreme Court.

For some in the nonprofit community, the Commonwealth Court decision in the St. Margaret's case was, in one respect, a positive development. Because the rulings in the case were so clearly absurd, the opinion became a useful tool in educating members of the General Assembly and the public about why a statutory solution was necessary.

The Nonprofit Advocacy Network organized an effort by more than a score of state-wide nonprofit charitable associations to file an amicus brief in this case. NPAN officials argued that there has never been such an obvious miscarriage of justice as occurred in this case, and this represented the best opportunity for the Pennsylvania Supreme Court to once and for all end the misinterpretation of its own ruling in the HUP case. Several other amicus briefs were filed by individual associations.

On April 20, 1994, the Pennsylvania Supreme Court ruled 5-1 in favor of St. Margaret Seneca Place. The court repudiated virtually every finding of Commonwealth Court, noting that the nursing home did, indeed, meet all of the five HUP criteria. Of importance to many charities is the finding that obtaining revenue from government sources to finance charity care was not a disqualification for charitable tax-exempt status. Also, the court ruled that a charity need not provide services that are "wholly gratuitous," a standard advanced by the lower court that, in effect, would have disqualified almost every modern charity from exemption. However, the opinion did not clarify the terms of the five HUP criteria beyond that which was necessary as a result of the actual facts in the particular case before the court, and thus did not obviate the need for statutory clarification provided by legislation such as Act 55.

Case 2: PA Institute of Certified Public Accountants (PICPA)

In October 1993, the Pennsylvania Supreme Court denied a sales tax exemption to the PICPA's educational foundation. The court ruled that the organization failed to meet several of the HUP criteria, including that it did not benefit the general public. About 38% of those attending PICPA seminars were not members of the organization. The court did not agree with the organization that government would have had to provide the educational services provided by PICPA if the organization did not provide them. Prior to the decision in the St. Margaret Seneca Place case, the PICPA case caused substantial concern in the charitable community because of the extremely narrow interpretation of the court on the issue of public benefit and relief of government burden. Even when an educational program is available to all who are interested, the court failed to recognize that "an indefinite class of persons" is being served. As one legal analyst pointed out, "by extending the court's logic, one wonders whether a medical school, law school, art school, or any other focused form of education qualifies as benefiting 'an indefinite number of people.' "

Case 3: Golden Triangle YMCA

In 1986, the Golden Triangle YMCA in downtown Pittsburgh relocated. The City of Pittsburgh challenged the tax-exempt status of this facility, whose clientele consisted of many "upscale" health club members paying substantial annual fees. The Allegheny County Board of Property and Assessment, Appeals and Review ruled that the facility should be taxed on a seventh of its assessed value because one floor of the seven-story building was a state-of-the-art health and fitness club that, the board determined, was not being used for charitable purposes. Both the YMCA and local taxing bodies appealed the decision. The city and county argued that the entire facility should be taxable, and the YMCA contended that the 140-year YMCA exemption from taxation was still valid. On November 22, 1988, Allegheny County Court of Common Pleas Judge Ralph Smith, Jr., ruled that the Golden Triangle YMCA failed to meet any of the five HUP criteria, all of which must be met in order for a facility to be an "institution of purely public charity" and eligible for tax-exempt status under the terms of the Pennsylvania Constitution.

The YMCA appealed the case to Commonwealth Court. In an opinion handed down September 29, 1989, the three-judge panel vacated and remanded the decision of the Allegheny County Court of Common Pleas. Commonwealth Court ordered that the lower court perform a use-by-use analysis of each floor of the facility and determine the extent the building was being used for charitable purposes. An appeal filed by the City and County of the Commonwealth Court decision, which was clearly a victory for the YMCA, was denied by the Pennsylvania Supreme Court.

On May 18, 1990, the court approved a settlement among the parties for the YMCA to make payments in lieu of taxes. The settlement stipulated that a percentage of the building shall be considered taxable, ranging from 15% for 1986 and 1987 up to 40% of the building's assessed value for the tax years of 1991-1995. The agreement provided that—

(i) the City, the County, the School District and the Board recognize the charitable nature of the YMCA in providing services to the citizens of the City of Pittsburgh and the County of Allegheny and the children attending the schools of the School District, (ii) the YMCA denies and continues to deny that it is liable for any real estate taxes as well as other taxes, recognizes the City's, the County's and the School District's fiscal needs and (iii) the parties hereto desire to avoid further expense, inconvenience and distraction of litigation.

Case 4: St. Luke's Hospital

Lehigh County Common Pleas Court Judge Robert K. Young handed down a decision April 19, 1990, in the St. Luke's property tax case validating that hospital's tax-exempt status. The decision affirmed the tax-exemption even though hospital income regularly exceeded expenses and most of its patient care was reimbursed. Judge Young ruled that St. Luke's met all five parts of the HUP test, and he established a formula for what constitutes "substantial" in the HUP test criterion "donate or render gratuitously a substantial portion of its services." The standard used by the judge was to require that the amount of uncompensated care be at least 75% of the amount of hospital "profit" (or 51% during a major construction program). The judge's definition of "uncompensated care" included bad debts, Medicare and Medicaid payment shortfalls, community education programs, and other costs advocated for inclusion in that term by the hospital industry. Despite the victory for St. Luke's, hospital officials for the 116-year-old facility filed an appeal, arguing that there may be some future circumstances where the facility might not be eligible for a tax-exemption under the court's formula, yet may still meet the criteria for exemption provided for by statute and the PA Constitution.

The local governments involved refused to accept the judge's ruling and petitioned the assessment board to again revoke the hospital's tax exemption. The board did so. In order to avoid more costly litigation after expending almost $300,000 in legal fees, St. Luke's surrendered to what some hospital officials characterized as "extortion." To avoid further challenges to its tax exemption, the hospital agreed to provide free drug testing of county inmates, build a fire station for the borough, do cholesterol screening and offer prenatal counseling to pregnant teens for the school district, and develop an Alzheimer's disease education program.

Case 5: Hamot Hospital

An Erie County Court of Common Pleas judge ruled on May 18, 1990, that the Hamot Medical Center was not eligible for tax-exempt status. Judge George Levin ruled that Hamot failed to meet four of the five HUP criteria, pointing out that the facility funneled more than $25 million in profits to its for-profit facilities for investment in a marina, real estate, and other for-profit ventures unrelated to medical care. Judge Levin also criticized the facility for having a profit-sharing plan for its employees, and for claiming that revenue it was unable to collect in court suits from those unable to pay their hospital bills constituted charity care.

Judge Levin's opinion included a finding that government receipts under a designed reimbursement system (e.g. Medicare and Medicaid) did not constitute maintenance by public charity. While Hamot officials appealed to the Pennsylvania Supreme Court for relief, they concurrently initiated negotiations with municipal government officials to provide for an out-of-court settlement. Hamot officials in 1992 agreed to make $4 million in annual in-lieu-of-tax payments. In addition, Hamot initiated a corporate restructuring geared to improving its chances of becoming an institution of purely public charity eligible for future tax-exempt status.

Case 6: Butler County Children's Center

A Butler County Common Pleas Court judge ruled on August 23, 1990, that the Butler County Children's Center was not eligible for its tax-exemption. The judge acknowledged that of the 142 children in the Center's Head Start program, 129 paid no fee and the rest were assessed on a sliding scale fee fixed by the state. The program was funded by Title XX, the United Way, and from fees. The judge ruled that this center did not "donate or render gratuitously a substantial portion of its services" because only 13 of the 142 students in the Head Start program were free non-paying, non-subsidized students. The Head Start funding was "taxpayers' money expended by a private agency, not public charity in the pure definition of public charity." The logic of this decision escaped virtually all human service agency advocates who would assert that the model of the Butler County center is exactly the kind of institution deserving of tax-exempt status.

Case 7: Jewish Federation of Reading

The Pennsylvania Department of Revenue on March 3, 1989, denied an application from the Jewish Federation of Reading for a sales tax exemption. The Federation appealed the decision to the Department's Board of Appeals, which reaffirmed the previous decision of denial on October 31, 1989. A seven-page decision of the board of Appeals detailed the reasons for denial. One significant finding of the board was that the Jewish Federation failed to "advance a charitable purpose" because the beneficiaries of its charity were other agencies and organizations rather than the public. Such a ruling was a direct contradiction of a 1973 Commonwealth Court case in which the United Way of Philadelphia was deemed to be an "institution of purely public charity." In addition, the board ruled that the Jewish Federation failed to "donate or render gratuitously a substantial portion of its services" because it provided funding rather than services. This ruling also was considered to be a threat to the tax-exempt status of all "umbrella" fundraising organizations, such as United Ways and foundations/community chests. The Board of Finance and Revenue unanimously approved the Federation's appeal and the tax exemption was restored.

Case 8: Washington and Jefferson College

The Pennsylvania Supreme Court on November 20,1997 handed down a 5-1 decision upholding a September 1995 opinion by Commonwealth Court that Washington and Jefferson College was entitled to tax-exempt status as an institution of purely public charity.

Case 9: Community Accountants

The Pennsylvania Supreme Court on March 29, 1996, issued a terse, one-page ruling in the Community Accountants sales tax case. The court upheld the decision of Commonwealth Court denying exempt status to the Philadelphia-based charity. The March 1995 decision of Commonwealth Court was problematic, because the standards used by the court to meet the HUP tests of "relieve government of some of its burden" and "an indefinite class of persons who are legitimate subjects of charity" were so narrow that few, if any charities could meet them. However, there are other decisions by the Supreme Court that provide enough guidance to prevent the Community Accountants standards from serving as a precedent for denying every charity's exemption. Also, the Community Accountants' function and mission is so different from that of most charities that many advocates for charities did not see this decision as necessarily having any major impact on how human service charities would be viewed by the courts with respect to meeting the five HUP criteria.

Case 10: Longwood Gardens

In the Longwood Gardens case *(Unionville-Chadds Ford School District v. Chester County Board of Assessment and Longwood Gardens, Inc.)* decided July 20, 1998 by a 6-1 vote, the Pennsylvania Supreme Court issued a strong opinion favorable to charities, but did not use Act 55, the *Institutions of Purely Public Charity Act,* as its template to judge whether the institution met each of the five HUP criteria.

Commonwealth Court had previously rejected the school district's claim that the term "legitimate subjects of charity" means only the poor, incapacitated, distressed or needy. Citing the 1878 case known as "Donohugh's Appeal" in which Philadelphia's public library was found to be tax-exempt, the Court embraced the interpretation that the term "legitimate subjects of charity" was intended to have a broader meaning that, in some cases, encompasses the entire public.

Also rejected was the argument made by the school district that the requirement that charities "relieve some of the burden of government" means that government would otherwise be required to provide what the charity is providing. Such an interpretation would, if left unchallenged, result in virtually all charities being unable to meet this prong of the HUP test, because there are few activities that government is legally required to perform. Instead, the court agreed with the conclusion of Common Pleas Court Judge Robert J. Shenkin that it was only necessary to show that the state and local government engaged in activities that were consonant with the mission of Longwood Gardens, and that there would be substantial costs to the public if Longwood Gardens' property had to be maintained by government rather than subsidized by a foundation.

The court rejected arguments that the fees charged to the public for admission, and for services provided by the facility's garden shop and restaurant, somehow tainted the institution's charitable status.

"Regardless of whether it shows a profit, the garden shop primarily advances and supports the institution's educational purposes through its sale of books and films on horticulture-related topics," the court stated in its opinion filed by President Judge James Gardner Colins. This perspective will be useful to many institutions that undergo challenges. Because few cases on charitable tax exemption advance to the Pennsylvania Supreme Court, a softening of the position on this issue by Commonwealth Court is a welcome development to charities.

The court agreed with the trial court's interpretation that since the admission fees covered less than 30 percent of operating expenses, the institution donated or rendered gratuitously a substantial portion of its services.

Case 11. Community Options

Commonwealth Court November 21, 2000, ruled 2-1 that Community Options, Inc. was liable for property taxes in 1995 and 1996, as well as all subsequent years. The New Jersey-based nonprofit operates group homes for those with mental retardation in eight states, including Pennsylvania. The decision reversed a ruling by Common Pleas Court that had granted exemption for all years after 1996. The Allegheny County Board of Property Assessment, Appeals and Review had revoked the organization's exemption starting with the 1995 tax year, which was partially restored by the Allegheny Court of Common Pleas. At issue was whether the organization relieved government of some of its burden. The trial court had ruled that the fact that almost all of the services provided by the organization were financed by county agencies was evidence that a government burden was not being relieved. However, Common Pleas Court ruled that Act 55, enacted in 1997, clarified the meaning of the term, and that the organization did, indeed, meet the safe harbors provided for by the statute, and thus was eligible for exemption beginning with the 1997 tax year. Commonwealth Court found that there was no testimony by the organization that it received significant non-governmental revenues to finance the care provided to these group home residents in Pennsylvania. It cited an earlier case involving the Community Service Foundation in which it ruled that this organization's programs were not substantially funded by private contributions, and thus a government burden was not being relieved. "Tax exempt status is properly reserved for organizations which abate government costs, not for those who perform government responsibilities as independent contractors," Commonwealth Court said in its opinion, written by Judge James R. Kelley and also signed by Judge Jim Flaherty.

Senior Judge Emil Narrick filed a dissenting opinion, expressing the view that the organization met the standard for relieving government of a burden in Act 55, and thus should be eligible for property tax-exemptions beginning in 1998. "The government was relieved of some of its burden," Judge Narrick wrote. "In 1997, with the enactment of the *Institutions of Purely Public Charity Act* (Act 55), Act of November 26, 1997, P.L. 508, as amended, 10 P.S. §§371-385, the General assembly in order to eliminate the vagueness of the term, further defined "institutions of purely public charity" and exempted from taxation certain institutions that did not meet the HUP standards." Community Options appealed the case to the Pennsylvania Supreme Court, which agreed on September 19, 2001, to hear it. On December 31, 2002, the Supreme Court reversed the Commonwealth Court decision, restoring the tax-exemption of Community Options for 1998 and future years.

Case 12: Alliance Home of Carlisle, PA

The Pennsylvania Supreme Court in April 2007 reversed a decision by Commonwealth Court that had denied a tax exemption to Chapel Point, an independent apartment that was a part of a Continuing Care Retirement Community (CCRC). The lower court had ruled that the apartment complex was not tax exempt because it did not offer admission to anyone who could not pay a steep entrance fee and be likely to afford monthly rent payments. The Supreme Court acknowledged that residents in these apartments received lots of services, and were entitled to be cared for in the Home's subsidized skilled nursing home or assisted living facility should they need that level of care. Perhaps more importantly, the Court recognized that while any statutory interpretation of the Constitution was not binding on the Court, Act 55 (see below) provided guidance as to what the General Assembly intended with respect to its legal authority to grant tax exemptions, and is not necessarily unconstitutional.

Institutions of Purely Public Charity Act (Act 55)

After nearly a decade of bitter wrangling among the Administration, the General Assembly, local government groups, representatives of the small business community, and the voluntary sector, Pennsylvania's charities won a major legislative battle with enactment of Act 55, the *Institutions of Purely Public Charity Act*. As previously mentioned, the Pennsylvania Constitution permits the General Assembly to grant tax-exempt status to "institutions of purely public charity," but does not define this term. Through more than a century of case law, the courts have defined this term. Act 55 codifies into law the five criteria of the *Hospital Utilization Project v. Commonwealth of Pennsylvania* case decided by the Pennsylvania Supreme Court in 1985 that determine whether a charity is an "institution of purely public charity" and eligible for property and sales tax exemptions. For each of these five broad criteria, this law provides measurable ways for charities to meet them.

Before Act 55, even a charity that met all five criteria could lose its exemption if a court determined that it did not meet a three-part statutory test found in the general assessment law of being "founded, endowed and maintained by public or private charity." Act 55 says that if a charity meets the five criteria relating to the constitutional definition, then it is considered to meet the three statutory criteria.

While all five criteria must be met to be considered an "institution of purely public charity," Act 55 provides options for how charities meet each of the standards. In general, all but sham charities should easily meet four of the five tests. First, to "advance a charitable purpose," a charity may accomplish "a purpose that is recognized as important and beneficial to the public and that advances social, moral or physical objectives." That is only one of the options for a charity to meet this criterion and is a catch-all for virtually every single one.

Second, the standard for "operating entirely free from private profit motive," with one exception, is a restatement of existing Pennsylvania law that applies to all nonprofits. Act 55 adds that "compensation, including benefits, of any director, officer or employee, (may) not (be) based primarily upon the financial performance of the institution." This does not prohibit financial performance from being a factor, however, and should not be a problem for conventional charities. Act 55 adds a new requirement that organizations include in their Articles of Incorporation a provision that upon sale or dissolution, it is prohibited for any surplus funds to be used for private inurement of any person (see Chapter 1).

Third, the criterion that the institution "must benefit a substantial and indefinite class of persons who are legitimate subjects of charity" is defined in the bill in a manner that will not be a barrier for legitimate charities. "Legitimate subjects of charity" is defined as "those individuals who are unable to provide themselves with what the institution provides for them." This is a direct quote from the HUP case. Opponents of the legislation have long argued that legitimate subjects of charity means only the poor and the sick. Act 55 explicitly rejects that interpretation. The new law clarifies that organizations other than charities, such as advocacy organizations, labor unions, fraternal organizations, and business organizations, may not qualify for exempt status.

Fourth, the standard to "relieve government of some of its burden" also explicitly rejects narrow interpretations of this criterion, and substitutes a broad standard that should not be problematic for legitimate charities. Some interpretations of this criterion have been so narrow that few, if any, charities could meet this test had the narrow interpretation prevailed.

Despite the broad, encompassing nature of these four criteria, it is still almost impossible for organizations that are not legitimate charities to pass all of these four tests, even if many non-charities are able to pass one or two. And what sets apart whether a charity is an "institution of purely public charity" or not is the definition of the fifth criterion, "donate or render gratuitously a substantial portion of its services."

Generally, this criterion is highly favorable to the charitable community. This law provides seven ways to meet this standard. The most likely way is for a charity to demonstrate that it "provides uncompensated goods or services that, in the aggregate, are equal to at least 5% of the institution's costs of providing goods or services." "Uncompensated goods or services" is defined broadly. For institutions with open admission policies (such as hospitals), the criterion can be met by providing uncompensated goods and services of at least 75% of the institution's net operating income, but not less than 3% of the institution's total operating expenses. Institutions that provide at least 5% of their goods or services wholly gratuitously can meet the standard, even if they cross-subsidize their operations by charging the other 95% more than the value of the goods and services provided wholly gratuitously.

Charities may include the reasonable value of volunteer assistance in their calculations of the donation of goods and services. Charities may average their data for the five most recently completed fiscal years. Theoretically, a charity could qualify under this definition by providing as little as 1% of its goods and services as charity.

Almost every legitimate charity should be able to meet the five-part standard of Act 55. What is not clear is whether the courts will agree that every definition of the five-part test is consistent with HUP. Unlike virtually every previous version of this legislation, the bill as enacted into law requires some charity to be done by the institution. Is the amount required enough? We won't know until the standard is tested in the courts, and a lot will depend upon which institution is the test case. The first exemption case to reach the Pennsylvania Supreme Court after enactment of this law, a challenge to the tax exemption of Longwood Gardens, resulted in a clear and convincing victory for charities. However, there was nary a reference to the provisions of Act 55 in the court opinion. Perhaps the Court will rely on the provisions of Act 55 in some future case. Or it may simply ignore Act 55 because it is a statute that should not have any effect on how the Court interprets the Constitution.

There are other provisions of interest in this law. For example, there is a section providing incentives for creating foundations to accept voluntary contributions from charities that will be funneled to local governments. Without this provision, local powerful local government interests would have maintained their opposition to the legislation, and may have successfully kept the bill bottled up in the Senate.

The burden of proof in local property tax cases is changed, providing a further barrier for local governments to challenge charities. There is a provision forbidding charities from starting unrelated businesses that compete with existing small businesses, although a loophole permits this "unfair competition" provided the charity gets a formal request from a political subdivision or the Commonwealth to do so. Existing businesses of charities that are considered "unfair competition" by the standards of the bill are not affected by this law.

Institutions that do not register under the *Solicitation of Funds for Charitable Purposes Act* must begin to make filings with the Bureau of Charitable Organizations, including sending copies of their 990 annual tax returns. Charities must now disclose information about relationships to other organizations, and pay a $15 filing fee. These disclosure provisions evolved from an effort launched more than 15 years ago by the late Rep. Italo Cappabianca (D-Erie).

Local Government Action

Local governments across Pennsylvania have been reeling in recent years from a crossfire of negative trends that have severely restricted their ability to provide municipal services. Among these trends have been—

- economic instability, exacerbated by the September 11, 2001 terrorist attacks, and subsequent federal and state budget cutbacks;
- cuts in federal government grants, other than for health care;
- increases in state and federal mandates to provide services without additional funding;
- an increase in the demand for services and a decrease in tax base— exacerbated by the implementation of state and federal welfare reform laws;
- the flight of the middle class to the suburbs;
- the burgeoning increase in tax-exempt property;
- the unwillingness of property owners to absorb additional tax increases; and
- the explosion of drug abuse, crime, AIDS, homelessness, and other social ills.

Several Pennsylvania cities were emboldened by the experiences of Pittsburgh municipal officials who were able to increase revenues by requesting that charities make "voluntary" contributions in exchange for not requiring them to expend hundreds of thousands of dollars in resources and staff time to fight exemption challenges. Among them have been—

Erie: In December 1992, the assessment board in Erie sent notices to the owners of more than 300 tax-exempt properties informing them that the properties would lose their exemptions beginning in January and they should begin to pay property taxes. The board pledged to hold hearings sometime in 1993 to determine if the properties were truly tax-exempt. Those that were determined by the board to be tax-exempt would be provided refunds. In early 1993, representatives of affected charities began negotiating with the City Solicitor and School District Solicitor to reach out-of-court settlements. In the majority of cases, tax exemptions were restored. Many other institutions, however, agreed to make payments-in-lieu-of-taxes, including all four Erie-area hospitals. Some charities retained their exemptions as the result of a March 29, 1994 ruling by Common Pleas Court Judge George Levin.

Harrisburg: Early in 1993, Dauphin County officials sent tax bills to the four general hospitals in the county, and followed this up with tax notices to nursing homes the following year. Most of the nursing home bills were withdrawn following the decision of the Pennsylvania Supreme Court in the St. Margaret Seneca Place case. The hospital cases were appealed to Common Pleas Court. In May and June 1996, Dauphin County Court of Common Pleas ruled that two of the hospitals failed to meet all of the HUP criteria, and thus were ineligible for exempt status. Commonwealth Court ruled in favor of two hospitals and against two others. The hospitals that lost appealed the decision, but a settlement was reached in which the hospital system that owns the two hospitals agreed to make payments-in-lieu-of-taxes to the school district, city, and county for five years.

Philadelphia: On June 30, 1994, the City of Philadelphia began the process of sending letters to many of its charitable institutions requesting voluntary payments-in-lieu-of-taxes and/or services-in-lieu-of-taxes of 40% of what they would owe in taxes without their exemptions, and announced that the city would challenge the exemptions of those that did not respond favorably. The rate was discounted to 33% for agreements made by December 1, 1994, and services could be provided for a third of the amount owed. Virtually every hospital agreed to participate, as well as several institutions of higher learning. The City sent scores of letters out to smaller human services agencies acknowledging that the City would not be requesting payments.

Why User Charges Are Not the Answer

As I write this, many Pennsylvania cities are distressed as a result of a recession that began in 2008 and has not abated well into 2011, with no end in sight. Municipal leaders in these cities are once again considering how to "encourage" nonprofits to participate in revenue-raising.

No reasonable ways exist to measure the public services that are directly utilized by charitable nonprofits.

Property taxes, by themselves or disguised as "user charges," neglect the factors by which these institutions have earned their tax exemptions in the first place. In accordance with state law, these institutions have been founded, maintained, and endowed by public and private charity. They are, for the most part, created to provide benefits to the community. The tax exemption provided to these organizations is a benefit that is returned to the communities many times over. The amount of financial support accruing to municipalities by taxing charities is generally not believed to be substantial. At least one study done in Wisconsin showed that 67% of the state's tax-exempt property belonged to government, and that an additional 10% was owned by religious organizations. All of this property would continue to be exempt under legislative proposals to authorize municipalities to impose user charges on tax-exempt property. While the reduction in local property taxes that would result if such legislation were enacted would be negligible, the impact on the charities themselves would be real and would threaten their continued viability. By state law, all incremental revenue over expenses of these charities is returned to the operations of the organization. There is no profit that is distributed into private pockets. Thus, the payment of taxes would result in a limited set of options for charitable nonprofits, all of which are injurious.

The first option is that charities can decide that they are unable to continue operations, since the property tax payment required could be substantial in comparison to their total budgets. A second available option is to reduce services. A third option is to increase the cost of their services, but doing so often makes the service inaccessible to those who most need them.

In any one of these cases, the cost of reducing the activities of these charities is eventually borne by the community. That is why these organizations have been granted tax-exempt status in the first place—to assure that their total resources are dedicated to meeting community needs.

Even with tax-exempt status, times are tough for these institutions. Government support for many nonprofit charitable activities has substantially declined since 1981. Demographic trends—including the aging of our population, the increase in homelessness, drug abuse, single-parent families, domestic violence, children living in poverty, and the increasing economic necessity of two parents in the family working in order to make ends meet—have resulted in the demand for more free and subsidized services. Private enterprise has, in recent years, invaded the traditional turf of nonprofit human service agencies. In virtually every case, the for-profit business has marketed its services to garner the most lucrative market segment, siphoning away clients who generated incremental revenue that was used by the nonprofit charities to cross-subsidize services for the needy. By skimming off this market share, private enterprise has placed an additional burden on the charitable nonprofit sector.

Finally, economic instability in Pennsylvania has had an impact on not only an increase in service demand, but also a decrease in the revenue depended upon by charities, including fees for service and charitable contributions. As this book was going to press in October 2011, the national and state economy stubbornly remained in a deep recession, with unemployment hovering at the 9% level. The state capital of Harrisburg was poised to slip into receivership, unable to pay its bills.

Justification For the Charitable Tax Exemption

There has been much discussion above about the legal basis for tax-exempt status in Pennsylvania. The Constitution provides that the General Assembly may by law exempt from taxation certain classes of institutions. That the General Assembly has done so is not something that the charitable community should take for granted. At any time, the General Assembly can pass legislation either revoking or restricting the extent to which this exemption is granted for "institutions of purely public charity." Thus it is imperative that charities continue to reinforce the public policy reasons why this exemption deserves to be protected and continued.

Some of the reasons are:

1. Charitable nonprofits augment and, in some cases, replace the role of government in responding to and preventing society's problems. Tax-exempt status is an acknowledgment

that these organizations have been deputized to act in the public interest and to improve societal conditions, rather than to serve any private interest. As a result, such tax-exempt organizations have a special responsibility to ensure that their programs and activities are consistent with these principles and that the level of accountability is on par with the government's.

2. Nonprofit charities have many advantages in responding to societal problems that are not available to government. Among them are:

- Nonprofit charities can be galvanized to attack a problem much more quickly than can government. Those who disagree with this need only consider how long it took for government to respond to problems such as AIDS, homelessness, and drug abuse compared with individual nonprofit charities. Clearly, nonprofits can respond to problems before a political consensus is developed by either the public at large or a legislative body. Charitable nonprofits can, in many cases, direct resources toward solving the problem without the typical government bureaucracy and lag time between the identification of a problem and the approval of a statute, budget, regulation, request-for-proposal (RFP), and the actual expenditure of funds to solve the problem.

- Nonprofits can effectively and efficiently respond to and solve problems that are localized in nature. This is a politically difficult task to accomplish under our present governmental system. Our political system often requires that a problem be universal in nature before resources are allocated to it. Also, politics make it more likely that government will be unable to target resources to solve a problem because there is often a cost to obtaining the necessary votes to pass a law.

- Nonprofits attract volunteers. Volunteers, both on boards and doing the actual work of the agency, include many who would not be attracted to government service and the constraints of government-affiliated organizations.

- Nonprofits can provide services when government programs, because of a limit on tax revenues, cannot expand. Charitable nonprofits often fill the void between what government provides to those who are destitute and what the for-profit sector provides to those who can afford the market rate for services. These charities provide services to those caught in the middle, who are not "poor enough" for government entitlement programs, but yet would be denied services by the for-profit sector. By charging fees for services on a sliding scale, these nonprofits are able to serve many who would otherwise not be served. This permits government to concentrate on serving only the neediest, while private business serves those who can afford to pay market rates.

The entire public benefits from the improvement of society resulting from the activities of these organizations. The tax exemption provided to charities is a cost to the entire public, but is only a small fraction of the public benefit accruing from these activities. Beyond the monetary benefit of this exemption, which permits these charities to commit all of their resources to the mission of the organizations, there is a principle involved. The tax exemption is an acknowledgment that the public values this type of altruistic activity and has foregone the collecting of taxes. It makes a statement that these organizations play an important role in strengthening the safety net that the government alone cannot offer.

It is in the public interest to promote the health of these charitable organizations, because government could not perform their missions as creatively, efficiently, or as cost-effectively.

Tips:

- To protect tax-exempt status, serve clients who cannot afford to pay the full cost of services and make services accessible to some clients who cannot afford to pay at all.

- Periodically quantify the dollar amount of free and subsidized services provided to the organization's clients and to the public at large.

- If state and local tax-exempt status is desired, develop a careful and honest outline of how the organization complies with state and local criteria. If staff members feel that compliance with these criteria is problematic, then consider changing operations to reasonably meet them.

- View or download Pennsylvania Department of Revenue tax forms at:

    http://www.revenue.state.pa.us

Chapter 27
Mergers and Consolidations

Synopsis: Mergers involving nonprofit organizations are increasingly common and require planning. There are steps that should be taken when planning for a merger between nonprofit organizations to meet legal requirements and promote a successful transition.

It wasn't too long ago that many nonprofit boards considered liquidation to be a preferable alternative to mergers. Considering the loss of identity was just too painful, and the term "merger" conjured up a vision of a corporate shark gobbling up weaker entities. Since then, mergers and consolidations among nonprofit organizations have become increasingly common, spurred in part by cost-containment pressures that have been affecting the delivery of social services for several decades now, particularly in the healthcare industry. The lingering recession that began in 2008 and just never seems to go away has also motivated many nonprofits in Pennsylvania to merge.

Managed care, cuts in Medicare and Medicaid, DRG payments, and increased competition have been among the factors that have induced hundreds of nonprofit mergers among hospitals. There are increasing incentives for all nonprofit organizations to improve their efficiency and effectiveness. With the entry of for-profit organizations into providing services historically provided by nonprofits, competition for service dollars has increased. To create new sources of revenue, even staid nonprofits have become entrepreneurial and are offering services that may only be indirectly related to their core mission. Unwittingly, they may be siphoning off revenue from colleague agencies.

Factors That Trigger Merger Consideration

Among the events that trigger consideration of nonprofit mergers are:

- Organizations that deliver similar services recognize that economies of scale can be achieved.

- Organizations that are struggling financially seek a partner to stave off bankruptcy and liquidation.

- National organizations may place restrictions on local affiliates, such as having a minimum asset level, technology capability, and service menu, which cannot be met without combining with another local affiliate.

- Two nearby agencies find themselves engaging in destructive competition.

- Changes in leadership capability, both of staff and within the board, may trigger a strategic plan that recognizes an organization's inability to continue with the status quo.

- Scandal or other ethical challenges might surface in which merger or consolidation is seen as an alternative to liquidation.

- Changes in the outside regulatory environment or economic environment (e.g., managed care) may make it more attractive to increase economic power to maintain a viable market niche.

- A loss of membership may make it difficult or unfeasible to continue.

- The organization's mission has been accomplished successfully.

Generally, the reasons for suggesting a merger can be divided into three categories:

Economic reasons: A merger will help the organization become more efficient, take advantage of economies of scale, increase its access to members and/or clients, help it raise more donations and grants, and contain costs. The nonrenewal of a major grant that provided overhead expenses to the organization can threaten its continued existence. There is no longer the cash flow necessary to continue the operation.

Programmatic reasons: Organizations recognize that a strong synergy can be created by combining each organization's expertise to create new programs or offer a streamlined menu of existing services to a common population, permitting clients to avoid having to negotiate two or more organizational systems and venues to access services.

Strategic reasons: Strategic reasons include—

- An organization may be in a precarious state either economically or programmatically.
- Competition from for-profits or other nonprofits is becoming destructive, and funders are complaining.
- The board might be losing interest.
- A long-term CEO may be retiring, and there is no one to take his or her place with the vision necessary to lead the organization.
- The staff is demoralized because of an ineffective CEO who cannot be removed for political reasons.
- The public or funders have lost confidence in the organization as a result of ethical lapses or a reputation for poor quality.
- An organization in the outside environment is identified that, if a merger occurred, would create a strong collaboration.

How to Begin

At a 1997 workshop session on nonprofit mergers sponsored by the Pennsylvania Association of Nonprofit Organizations, William Morgan of Performance Industries and Paul Mattaini of Barley, Snyder, Senft & Cohen distributed a list of areas to consider when contemplating a merger.

Among the issues they raised were—

- the importance of infusing key leadership with the view that merging is a viable option;

- whether the CEO will find a way to sabotage the merger because of ego;

- whether the merger will fit into the organization's mission;

- finding the right candidate to merge with, and finding the right staff (such as an attorney, accountant, and consultant);

- bringing together the two organizational cultures; and

- handling the public relations and community relations aspects.

Steps to Merger

1. Each participating board should adopt a resolution in favor of the general principle of merging.

2. Each board should appoint a merger committee of board members and staff.

3. An outside, experienced merger consultant should be jointly hired to structure negotiations, with the cost shared by the participating organizations.

4. Meetings should be scheduled among the parties to discuss the goals of the merger, determine whether merging is feasible and makes sense for all parties, and negotiate, over time, the details, such as the change in the mission and values, new name, staffing, logo, merger budget, board selection, bylaws, personnel policies, location, and what happens to staff who are no longer needed.

Budgeting

Mergers cost money. There are likely to be legal fees, consultant fees, audit fees, personnel costs relating to layoffs, moving costs, costs relating to covering the liabilities of the non-surviving corporation (which may be substantial, and responsible for triggering the merger idea in the first place), and even providing new building signs, printing new stationery and business cards, and designing a new logo.

As David La Piana writes in *Nonprofit Mergers: The Board's Responsibility to Consider the Unthinkable*,

> *Although it is unlikely that the financial position of two merging organizations will immediately improve as a result of a merger, well-conceived and -implemented mergers can raise staff morale, better focus the organization's activities, and increase overall energy levels—that will help the new group tackle difficult problems. Thus, a successful merger can offer relief and renewed hope for nonprofit boards, staff, and donors, and, most importantly, benefit clients because of the greater energy, increased funding, and better management possible with a more stable organization. In contrast, poorly conceived mergers may simply bring together two weak organizations that compound each other's problems.*

Obstacles to Merger

Virtually every article about the difficulty of merging two or more organizations refers to the two scourges that often scuttle the best laid plans: "turf" and "ego." Many, if not most, mergers of nonprofit organizations involve a financially strong organization merging with an organization that is merging to stave off bankruptcy or liquidation. The surviving organization will have one chief executive, and it is often a traumatic and, at times, potentially humiliating experience for the chief executive of the non-surviving organization to hand over the reins of decision-making. It is not unusual for an otherwise "routine" merger to be derailed by petty squabbling over the name of the combined organization, the logo, or the office space that will be provided to the staff of the non-surviving organization.

Legal Requirements

The legal procedures for mergers and consolidations that involve nonprofit corporations can be found in state law. Obviously, experienced, professional legal advice is necessary to carry out a successful merger.

Tips:

- **Merging organizations is not a "do it yourself" task. Always consult qualified professionals.**

- **If you are unable to assure employees that their jobs will not be in jeopardy as a result of a merger, plan to offer outplacement services.**

- **Don't take advantage of a merger situation by humiliating a party to a merger by flexing your power. The Golden Rule makes perfect sense in this situation.**

Chapter 28
Quality Issues

Synopsis: Quality is as important to nonprofit organizations as it is to for-profit businesses, if not more so. Nonprofits need quality programs to compete for donations, clients, board members, workers, and political support.

Introduction

Those who govern and manage nonprofit organizations are increasingly finding them subject to many of the same economic pressures as their for-profit counterparts. Their operations often resemble their for-profit competitors in both organizational structure and corporate culture. They are increasingly led by those trained in business rather than social work, and their mentality and administrative style often reflect this. Stereotypically, they often make the "bottom line" paramount above the needs of clients.

One nonprofit CEO with whom I spoke recognized the inconsistency of trying to run a human service organization and retain his "humaneness," while at the same time being forced to make rational business decisions that could mean the firing of "nice" people who were hurting the performance of his organization. He commented to me that his management credo was to be "ruthlessly altruistic."

In many cases, the products and services once provided solely by nonprofit, charitable organizations are now being provided by for-profits. One can often find health clubs, hospitals, schools, nursing homes, and day care centers—both for-profit and nonprofit—competing for clients on an equal basis within communities. When there is this direct competition, particularly in the delivery of human and educational services, cost is just one factor in a customer's decision. Quality of service is often even more important, and nonprofits that offer high-quality products and services obviously have a competitive edge. Those that can't offer quality may find themselves out of business.

Many thousands of other nonprofit organizations don't have direct economic competition from others providing the same service. There is only one United Way affiliate in each community, one Arts Council, one Arthritis Foundation, and one Special Olympics affiliate. Except under unusual circumstances, it is unlikely that another organization will sprout up to directly challenge one of these. It would be easy to jump to the conclusion that having a monopoly of this nature would mean that quality and performance are not as important as they are to those with direct, head-to-head competition for providing a particular product or service. That conclusion would be flawed.

Why Quality is Important to Nonprofit Organizations

Quality is important to all nonprofit organizations. None is immune from the consequences of neglecting it. Charities rely on loyal customer support. Even if a nonprofit is not involved in direct economic competition, there is substantial competition for things that indirectly affect the viability of organizations. Among them are—

- **Competition for government and foundation grants.** Most charitable nonprofits depend on grants to supplement any client fees they receive. Foundations are acutely aware of organizations that have poor reputations with respect to skimping on service quality. No one wants to be associated with such an organization. It is no wonder that first-class organizations often have little trouble attracting funding, because everyone wants to be associated with them.

- **Competition for private donations**. Would you make a donation to a charity that had a reputation of treating its clients like animals? Unless that organization is the Society for Prevention of Cruelty to Animals (SPCA), you are more likely to look elsewhere for a charity worthy of your donation.

- **Competition for board members.** Why would anyone want to serve on the board of a second-class nonprofit and risk being condemned or otherwise embarrassed by the media, the political hierarchy, and clients? There are only so many skilled, committed civic leaders in each community who are willing to donate their time and expertise to serve on nonprofit boards, and it is clearly not attractive to serve on the board of a charity with a reputation for poor quality.

- **Competition for volunteers.** What can be said for board members goes double for service delivery and other volunteers. No one wants to be associated with an organization with a reputation for poor quality. Many volunteers see their volunteer work as a springboard for a career, and volunteering for a pariah in the community does not serve their interests.

- **Competition for media.** The media play an important role in helping a nonprofit charity promote its fundraising, encourage clients to utilize its services, and improve employee morale. Poor quality can result in the media ignoring an organization or, worse, highlighting its shortcomings for the entire world to see.

- **Competition for legislative and other political support.** Nonprofit charities have benefited from the support of political leaders—directly through the provision of government grants, and indirectly through the provision of favors such as cutting government red tape and legislation to help solve problems of the organization and those of its clients. Political leaders are certainly not going to be responsive to an organization if they receive letters of complaint about the organization's poor quality.

- **Competition for qualified employees.** Particularly during times of low unemployment, quality nonprofits have less employee turnover and find it easier to attract employees to fill vacancies and for expansion.

The consequences of poor quality, or the reputation (public perception) of poor quality, can result in the board of directors throwing up its hands and deciding to liquidate the organization. Or, in extreme cases, a state government agency may step in and liquidate the organization. Imagine the aftermath of a child care agency that failed to perform a quality background check on an employee who was later found to be a child abuser. A hospital that failed to adequately verify whether a staff member it had hired was adequately board-certified could be exposed to a major stain on its reputation, in addition to potential legal liability.

As pointed out by Dr. John McNutt of the University of Delaware, most, if not all, states look at the community benefit provided by a nonprofit organization in considering whether it is eligible for nonprofit status in the first place. Quality and community benefit are inextricably linked.

In 1998, a scandal affected international organizations that raise funds for child welfare. Who knows how many millions of dollars will not be contributed to these organizations because some official did not feel it was important to inform donor sponsors that their sponsored child had died several years earlier?

The Cost of Poor Quality

The cost to organizations with poor quality standards can be substantial. Just read the newspapers and you can find many examples. Owners of assisted living homes have failed to see the value of installing sprinkler systems and, as a result, have seen the loss of life and of their properties. Doctors have mistakenly removed the wrong kidney from a patient. Hospital maternity ward staff members have given newborns to the wrong parents. The ramifications far exceed the financial loss and loss of prestige to the organization—human suffering for the clients and potentially huge, successful lawsuits against the nonprofit organization as a result of a preventable lapse in quality-related policies.

An Associated Press article on the January 8, 2002 front page of my home town newspaper reported that the American Red Cross disposed of 49,000 pints of blood collected after the September 11th disaster because of a lack of storage space. Many will think twice before responding to an urgent call from that organization for blood donations, despite the obvious need to continually replenish the nation's blood reserves.

Quality in the Nonprofit Organizational Context

For the typical nonprofit that doesn't deliver client services, quality should mean much more than the ability to answer the telephone on the first ring. It means having a newsletter without typographical errors. It means having an attractive, periodically updated Web site. It means spelling the names of donors correctly in substantiation letters. It means delivering on promises made to legislators for follow-up materials. It means having conferences at which participants feel they get their money's worth. It means ensuring that each board member has the necessary and appropriate information to make governing decisions. It means that volunteers know in advance what is expected of them.

For those who deliver direct human services, it means, among other things—

- treating each client with the dignity he or she deserves;
- respecting confidentiality;
- respecting client privacy;
- providing on-time services;
- providing timely resolution to legitimate complaints;
- providing services in a safe and secure setting;
- providing services in a facility that is accessible, clean, and functional;
- delivering services provided by competent, trained personnel;
- ensuring that services meet high standards and respond to the clients' needs;
- obtaining informed consent from clients before services are provided;
- seeking constant feedback from clients to improve the delivery of services; and
- using advances in technology to improve communication between the organization and its clients.

Tips:

- **Consider providing all organization staff with training that focuses on improving quality.**

- **Make it organizational policy to promote "continuous quality improvement" of every program, activity, and work process.**

- **Continually seek feedback from organization funders, clients, and staff to identify problems before they evolve into serious quality deficits.**

Chapter 29
Change Management

Synopsis: Change management strategies, such as Total Quality Management, Business Process Reengineering, Benchmarking, Outcome-Based Management, and Large Group Intervention, are potential ways to improve nonprofit organizational quality and performance.

In the context of this chapter, "change management" does not refer to a prescription for getting rid of the people who run the organization. Rather, it is a menu of management strategies to change the philosophy of management to accomplish an objective or set of objectives such as, for example, improving efficiency and competitiveness, motivating employees and increasing their job satisfaction, or reducing absenteeism. In this sense, "change" is used as a noun rather than a verb.

There is general agreement among scholars, practitioners, and management experts that organizations must adapt to changing conditions if they are to survive. Technology advances, markets change, the requirements and expectations of customers evolve, the needs of workers are altered as a result of demographics, economic conditions, and changes in culture, among other things.

Businesses, both for-profit and nonprofit, go out of existence every day. This is attributable to many causes. There may be an organizational scandal that causes the public to lose confidence or the government to take action. There may be quality lapses. The services provided by an organization may no longer be needed, or a competitor skims off a lucrative market share. The organization's operations may be too economically inefficient to support it. Government funding priorities or regulatory requirements may shift, leaving an organization in the lurch. The list of possible causes is endless.

For years, the for-profit business community has utilized formal change management strategies to improve operations and keep organizations competitive and vibrant, improve efficiency, generate loyalty, and maintain or expand support from customers. It has only been recently that the nonprofit community, with health care institutions leading the way, started implementing some of these strategies. The material appearing here is based on my book, *Improving Quality and Performance in Your Non-Profit Organization*, which was published in January 1999.

Among the most popular change management strategies being considered by nonprofit organizations are Total Quality Management (TQM), Business Process Reengineering (BPR), Benchmarking, Outcome-Based Management (OBM), and Large Group Intervention (LGI).

Total Quality Management (TQM)

TQM is an innovative, humanistic, general approach to management that seeks to improve quality, reduce costs, and increase customer satisfaction by restructuring traditional management practices. It requires a continuous and systematic approach to gathering, evaluating, and acting on data about what is occurring in an organization. The TQM management philosophy includes the following:

- It asserts that the primary objective of an organization is to meet the needs of its "customers" by providing quality goods and services, and to continually improve them. In the nonprofit organization context, customers include not only the direct recipients of services, such as clients, but the organization's board, elected and appointed government officials, the media, and the general public.

- It instills in all organization members an *esprit de corps* that ensures them that *having quality* as the number one goal is an important tenet. *Every* organizational member is responsible for quality, even if it is related to an issue beyond the scope of his or her job. Eliminating the "It's not my job" mentality becomes an achievable organizational objective.

- It continuously searches for ways to improve every activity, program, and process. It does so by constantly seeking feedback from the organization's customers and promoting suggestions from all sources, both external and internal, on how to improve.

- It rewards quality, not only internally, but from its suppliers. It recognizes that poor quality from its collaborators, be they suppliers or other organizations, affects its own quality.

- It recognizes that staff must receive continuous training to improve their work performance.

- It encourages all components of the organization to work as a team to solve problems and meet customer needs rather than compete against each other.

- It empowers workers at every level. It permits them to be actively engaged in decisions that affect the organization and to constantly look for ways to improve it.

- It permits employees the opportunity to have pride in what they produce for the organization and to see the fruits of their labor measured in the quality of the service they provide, rather than just receiving a paycheck.

- It promotes a planning process geared toward continuously improving quality in *everything* the organization does.

TQM principles are finding their way into nonprofit settings other than healthcare, such as community centers, arts organizations, and human services agencies. Focusing on the needs of the "customer" rather than on the "bottom line" is a value with which the nonprofit sector should feel comfortable compared with its for-profit counterparts. When a nonprofit organization's leadership becomes excited about TQM, this excitement can become contagious, provided that the behaviors of the leaders are consistent with their words. When it "happens," those in a TQM environment notice the difference, whether they work there or benefit from the organization's services. Workers feel empowered. Clients notice a positive difference in staff attitudes. Everyone associated with the organization feels good about it.

Business Process Reengineering (BPR)

If your heart stops beating and you keel over breathlessly, a professionally trained medical professional can often revive you by administering CPR. But if it's your *organization's* heart that fails, BPR, administered by professionally trained consultants or by those within an organization, is increasingly becoming the TLA ("three-letter acronym") of choice for cutting-edge managers. BPR is a successor to TQM as the latest management bromide for reviving comatose organizations.

Business Process Reengineering is defined by Michael Hammer, BPR's leading guru, as "the fundamental rethinking and radical redesign of business processes to achieve dramatic improvements in critical measures of performance (cost, quality, capital, service and speed)."

Fanatical interest in Total Quality Management peaked in the 1980s, but its once-pervasive influence seems to have waned in recent years. One of the reasons often given for TQM's apparent decline in the United States is that the philosophy of slow, incremental, and continuous improvement is generally inconsistent with American culture. Perhaps this is so; American organizational leaders are perceived as more impatient to see the tangible results of their business management interventions compared with their Asian, African, and European counterparts. They want to see quantum leaps of measurable improvement rather than the tortoise-paced improvement promised by TQM advocates. The tenure of many organizational leaders is short; several CEOs may come and go before TQM is fully implemented and shows results.

A major strategy involved with BPR efforts is to look at a business process involving many tasks that have been performed by several specialists. Then, the specialists are replaced with generalists (or the specialists are retrained to become generalists) who can handle all the tasks of the process and have access to all of the information they need to do it.

BPR requires a new way of thinking. Unlike TQM, which requires the involvement of everyone in the organization, BPR is necessarily implemented from the top. It is the zero-based budgeting of business processes, contending that, at least theoretically, the past should have no bearing on what is planned for the future. It makes the assumption that organizations have evolved incrementally, reflecting a history of culture, tradition, technology, and customer needs that may not be particularly relevant today. BPR suggests that managers step out of the constraints of their current physical plant, work processes, organizational charts, and procedures and rules, and look at how the work would be performed if they were starting from scratch.

BPR requires an organizational leader to step back and answer the question: If I were building this organization today from scratch, knew what I know now, had the technology and human resources that I have now, and knew the customer needs that I know now, would I still be doing things the same way? More often than not, the answer is a resounding "No!" In the nonprofit environment, this might mean redesigning data collection and reporting, client intake, billing, purchasing, and every other process.

In many cases, new and more efficient technology is available. For example, a human service agency may receive a telephone call from a client requesting even a minimal change in service as a result of some change in circumstances. The person answering the telephone may have to put the person on hold and call the client's caseworker, who has the client's case file. The caseworker may have to put the person on hold and check with the supervisor for a decision on whether to waive a rule, and the supervisor may have to meet with the caseworker to make the decision.

After a BPR implementation, the person answering the telephone for the agency may be able to pull up the case file on a computer screen and be preauthorized to approve a change in services within a constraint programmed into the computer by the organization. Or the person answering the telephone may be able to give the caller technical advice on how to solve a problem by searching a "frequently asked questions" file on a computer screen, instead of transferring the call to a technical specialist.

Another way of looking at this is that everyone in the organization is conventionally functioning solely as his or her part of a process rather than on the overall objective of the organization. The receptionist answers the telephone. The case manager holds the file for a particular set of clients.

The supervisor makes decisions authorizing variances from agency rules. BPR permits a work process to change so that the true objective of the process—responding to the client's needs—does not require the intervention of several people in the organization. The revolutionary advances in information technology permit this.

With the use of networked computers and an educated labor force, it is possible for a single person to process and troubleshoot an entire order that previously may have required being passed serially from person to person in the organization, taking many days to complete. And the more hands involved, the higher the probability of an error.

Among the major principles of BPR are—

- Use modern technology to redesign work processes rather than work tasks, concentrating on permitting a single person to achieve a desired outcome/objective.

- Let the worker who uses the output of a process also perform the process. For example, instead of having a purchasing department make purchases of pencils and paper clips for the accounting department and other departments, the accounting department orders its own pencils and paper clips and other "inexpensive and nonstrategic" purchases.

- Let those in the organization who collect information be the ones who process it. For example, when the public relations department wants to send out its newsletter to a mailing list, it should be able to generate the mailing labels itself rather than having to make a request to a data processing department.

- Treat decentralized organizational resources as centralized, utilizing information technology to bring them together. A college with several satellite campuses, for example, could link its bursars so that a student making a payment at either the main office or a satellite campus would have the payment show up in the records of the registrars of all of the campuses.

- Electronically link disparate parts of an organization to promote coordination.

- Let those who perform the work make the decisions, thereby flattening the pyramidal management layers and eliminating the bureaucracy and delay that slow down a decision-making process.

- Use relational databases and other technology to collect and store information only once, eliminating both redundancy and error.

Generally, BPR often enables a single person to perform all of the steps in a process by using information technology. One byproduct of BPR is that the need for many employees may be eliminated. This saves a lot of money for organizations. One downside is that BPR may have the effect of terrorizing a work force.

Benchmarking

Benchmarking refers to the process by which organizations study how similar organizations perform their business processes and learn how to adapt those that are most efficient, innovative, and successful. Obviously, no two organizations are alike, and there is no guarantee that copying something from another organization will automatically work well in your own. But certainly there is value in exploring how other organizations perform some of the tasks your organization does, and discussing what efficiencies they may have found that would improve your business operations. For-profit organizations have been doing this in a formalized way for many years. Nonprofit organizations are just recently recognizing the value of benchmarking.

There are two types of benchmarking that nonprofit organizations might wish to consider. The first, internal benchmarking, looks at your organization and projects future goals, including a process by which employees are encouraged to meet performance targets. External benchmarking, on the other hand, tries to determine the "best practices" of similar organizations. Rather than reinventing the wheel, external benchmarking permits you to allocate minimal resources to finding how others have solved a problem, or have exponentially increased productivity with respect to some process, rather than having to discover that on your own.

Many nonprofit organizations are not only willing to share this information, but are quite proud to do so. The fact that competition among nonprofit organizations is almost always either friendly or nonexistent promotes benchmarking in a manner that avoids some of the troublesome potential conflicts and ethical dilemmas in the for-profit context.

Jason Saul, writing in a chapter on benchmarking in *Improving Quality and Performance in Your Non-Profit Organization*, says that nonprofits should typically consider benchmarking in three general categories: A **process** (such as screening job applicants or organizing inventory in a food bank), a **policy** (such as a salary structure or incentive plan), or a **program** (such as welfare-to-work or educational incentives).

Three approaches taken to benchmarking include:

1. *technical approach*—using computer models, statistics, spreadsheets, and other quantitative methods;

2. *committee approach*—bringing in a team of experts from outside your organization to gather data and make judgments about which changes would be beneficial to the organization; and

3. *survey approach*—combining the above two models by creating a team of individuals from within the organization to identify which processes should be benchmarked, define the measures and organizational performance, obtain "best practices" information, and implement these practices.

Saul, who is the co-founder of The Center for What Works, a Chicago-based clearinghouse for those studying solutions to social problems, recommends a seven-step process for benchmarking. It includes self-assessment, measuring performance, assembling the team, data collection, evaluating practices, translating best practices, and continuously repeating the process.

Outcome-Based Management (OBM)

To improve quality in a larger organization, simply adopting a progressive management philosophy such as TQM or BPR is not going to suffice in today's modern competitive business climate. As an organization grows, there are more pressures for accountability, not only internally from a board of directors, but externally from elected officials, government funders, foundation funders, individual donors and volunteers, and the public. Leaders of large organizations generally do not have the ability to visualize every aspect of their organization's operations and assess what is going on just by looking out their office windows, or by engaging in informal conversations with their staff and clients. The proverbial "one-minute manager" is an ideal construct that is not particularly well suited to crystallizing the information a CEO needs to make judgments on how to allocate precious resources.

To accomplish the important task of determining what is really going on within a large organization, most organizations have a Management Information System (MIS), which permits the aggregation of data in a form that can be analyzed by a manager, enabling him or her to see trouble spots and make adjustments in operations and to generate reports required by the government, funders, auditors, and the board of directors.

For many larger nonprofits, particularly those that depend on government and foundation grants rather than private donations, the objective of "meeting clients' needs" has become a more formalized process. Times have changed within just the last decade or so. Traditionally, measures of organizational performance for human service organizations were based on a model more appropriate for industrial processes, where raw materials were turned into finished products. In the language of industrial systems analysis, inputs (the raw material) were processed into outputs (the finished product).

In adopting an analogous frame of reference to industry, the conventional thinking was that human service agencies took in unserved clients (input), provided services (process), and changed them into served clients (output). In this way of thinking, organizations improved their output by increasing the number of clients served.

An exciting new way of looking at the output of an organization is called outcome-based management (OBM) or "results-oriented accountability" (ROA). Most recently, results-oriented management and accountability (ROMA) has become the buzzword describing this general tool. OBM focuses on program outcomes rather than simply quantifying services delivered. Program outcomes can be defined as "benefits or changes for participants during or after their involvement with a program" (from *Measuring Program Outcomes: A Practical Approach, United Way of America*).

For example, an organization with a mission of reducing drug abuse may have a stellar record of attracting clients through a flashy outreach program. It may be exemplary in convincing doctors in the community to donate thousands of hours of free services to the program, thereby reducing unit costs per client. It may have few complaints from the clients, who feel the staff are competent and treat them with dignity. An analysis of conventional data might indicate that there is little room for improvement. But, perhaps, data are not collected on whether those treated for drug abuse by the organization are successfully able to become independent, avoid future interactions with the criminal justice system, and abstain from drug use for an extended period of time—all measurable outcomes for a successful substance abuse program. If most of these clients are back on the street abusing drugs, is that organization providing successful treatment, even if drug abuse services are being provided? Are funders and taxpayers getting a fair return on their investment?

In the outcome-based management model, the number of clients served is an input. The outcome is considered to be a measurement of the change in the condition of the clients after receiving the services. For example, if thousands of clients are served, but the condition of the clients has not improved, then the outcome is zero, even if the services were provided 100% on time, every client received a satisfactory number of hours of services, and there were no client complaints. It is no longer indicative of the effectiveness and value of an organization to only collect data on how many clients sought services, how many of these were accepted into the client stream rather than being referred or turned down, how many hours of service were provided, and how much each service cost and was reimbursed. Outcome data, together with the above process data, are needed to measure the effectiveness and value of an organization.

In addition to a significant change in attitude about the accountability of the private nonprofit sector, the passage in 1993 of the *Government Performance and Results Act,* PL 103-62, changed the way federal agencies plan, budget, evaluate, and account for federal spending. The intent of the act is to improve public confidence in federal agency performance by holding agencies accountable for program results and improving congressional decision-making. The act seeks to accomplish this by clarifying and stating program performance goals, measures, and costs "up front." These changes were implemented beginning in September 1997.

For some organizations, the shift to outcome-based management will have modest cost implications. It may mean more data being collected from clients during intake. It may mean follow-up surveys to see what happens to clients after they have availed themselves of the organization's services. When this information is available, it is of extraordinary value to those who design, administer, and deliver those services.

What makes outcome-based management an easy sell to the human services sector is that it is common sense. What is the point of investing thousands, if not millions, of dollars of an organization's resources if the end result is not accomplishing what is intended by the investment—improving the lives of the organization's clients?

Our human service organizations have been established to make people's lives better. When our organizations change their focus to concentrate on doing what it takes to make people's lives better, as opposed to simply providing human services, it is much more likely that this worthy goal can be accomplished successfully. Such a philosophy is compatible with the values of most in the sector, who often make financial sacrifices to make a difference in the lives of those who need human services.

In cases in which the data show that an organization is successfully providing services, but those services are not having the intended effect on the clients, the organization's leadership should be the first to recognize that it is wasteful to continue business as usual. Outcome-based management is a powerful tool that allows organizations to allocate their precious resources to do the most good. If successfully implemented, it also can provide the ammunition to fight the increasing public cynicism about what is often perceived to be a poor return on investment of tax dollars, and provide a competitive edge to organizations that adopt it.

Large Group Intervention (LGI)

Large Group Intervention (LGI) is the generic name given to a family of formal change management strategies that involve placing large parts of an organization, or even the entire organization, in simultaneous contact with one another to plan how the organization is going to change. Proponents and users of LGIs believe these methods are particularly well suited to organizations seeking to establish a shared vision of their future and to build a road to get there. Some LGI models are designed specifically for organizations seeking to change the way their work is done (e.g., through reengineering or business process redesign).

Although many different LGI models have been developed and are in current use, they generally have common origins and are rooted in similar principles. Among these principles are getting the "whole system" into interactive discussion, using a carefully designed mixture of communication elements and processes designed to make effective use of participants' emotions as well as thoughts, and facilitating effective dialogue while validating differing perspectives.

Large Group Interventions are usually staged in a setting away from the workplace, where participants can focus on the objective at hand without the distractions of the normal work environment. Artificial boundaries within organizations, such as functional departments, are routinely and intentionally fractured to facilitate communication and participation. These boundaries often get in the way of addressing important needs of organizations.

Strategies such as TQM and BPR, as well as strategic planning itself, demand that each member of the organization think about the needs of the entire organization rather than his or her piece of it. "Democratic" participatory efforts by organizations may facilitate their members to see beyond the borders of their individual organizational niche and develop the spirit required to make TQM not simply a "program" but a working philosophy.

The general philosophy inherent in planning change is recognizing that there is resistance to change within organizations. Change is more likely to be successfully implemented when people affected can participate in the process, influence the process, and prepare for its consequences.

Much more than a device for overcoming psychological resistance, LGI is an effective approach to substantially improve the planned change and achieve more desirable results for the organization. One dimension of additional benefits is more effective communication about the planned changes. Plans become far less distorted when everyone affected is hearing the same message at the same time, rather than having it communicated through the grapevine, through regular hierarchical channels, or not at all.

Another advantage of LGI is that those affected by the changes can provide invaluable input. It is rare that a few layers of management (or a subset of the full breadth of functions) within an organization can have an adequately detailed grasp of the whole. In most change management strategies, those at the bottom of the hierarchy, who are usually the most aware of the "nuts and bolts" of current reality, are often frozen out of the planning process. Most LGI models bring in a broad base of stakeholders to brainstorm together and to weed out problems and unintended consequences that often are otherwise built into initial designs for change, because they are invisible to the unrepresentative group of staff traditionally involved in planning.

A third advantage of LGI is that it builds a diverse and broad base of support for planned changes. Useful in all cases, this advantage becomes particularly powerful when circumstances alter, planned changes need to be modified, and time is of the essence. Circumstances that otherwise could be expected to derail well-laid plans can be addressed by a robust and already engaged subset of the organization. Plans are far more open to effective alteration midstream when developed via an LGI approach.

LGIs tend to bring together people from various hierarchical levels within the organization, who otherwise may have minimal direct interaction. Many organizational development experts believe that bringing large groups of organizational members together pays an additional dividend of creating positive social linkages among organizational members that would otherwise not have been created. Large Group Interventions create a new and different organizational bonding, which increases networks of informal communication within an organization and makes for more robust capabilities.

All of this can occur in a three-day period, significantly curtailing the process time of conventional change management planning.

Permitting workers affected by planning to participate in the planning process is one strategy to erode resistance to organizational change, in addition to generating fresh ideas from people who have expertise as a result of doing their jobs every day. They may have shied away from making valid, responsible suggestions, not only because "no one ever asked us," but because they may feel that their views are not important, or that management does not have an interest in listening to them.

Among the most popular models for LGIs are the Search Conference, Future Search Conference, and Real-Time Strategic Change. For additional details about these interventions, consult the book *Improving Quality and Performance in Your Non-Profit Organization.*

Tips:

- **Don't fall into the "goal displacement" trap by concentrating more on the paperwork involved in making a TQM program run than on the actual change in culture and staff attitudes that make TQM an attractive change management strategy.**

- **Consider the steps that might be necessary to undo a change management strategy in the event that it simply doesn't work for one reason or another.**

- **Avoid the undesirable outcome of making your organization more streamlined, efficient, and effective, but with employees who can't stand to be there anymore.**

- **Incorporate useful concepts in this chapter, such as benchmarking and outcome-based management, into your strategic planning process in the event your organization engages in such planning.**

Chapter 30
Organization and Program Evaluation

Synopsis: A formal program evaluation process is often a requirement of funders, but is otherwise an important exercise to determine whether nonprofit organizations and programs are effective. There are two major types of evaluations—formative and summative. Evaluations may be performed by in-house staff or outside consultants, and each has its advantages and disadvantages. Regardless of who performs an evaluation, organizations should engage in a thorough planning process.

Introduction

In the opening to his seminal book *Utilization Focused Evaluation*, the required textbook in the graduate school course on program evaluation that I took at Penn State, Michael Quinn Patton relates the following parable:

> *In the beginning, God created the heaven and the earth.*
> *And God saw everything that He made. "Behold," God said, "it is very good." And the evening and the morning were the sixth day.*
> *And on the seventh day God rested from all His work. His archangel came then unto Him asking, "God, how do you know that what you have created is 'very good'? What are your criteria? On what data do you base your judgment? Just exactly what results were you expecting to attain? And aren't you a little close to the situation to make a fair and unbiased evaluation?"*
> *God thought about these questions all that day and His rest was greatly disturbed. On the eighth day God said, "Lucifer, go to hell."*
> *Thus was evaluation born in a blaze of glory...*

I love this story for many reasons, but I think it crystallizes in my mind some of the dilemmas of program evaluation in a humorous way. To those who run programs, an evaluation is often perceived as a way outsiders find fault with how they operate their programs and make decisions. To the evaluators, they often find that staff are not forthcoming because of a fear that blame for any shortcomings will fall on them. Yet, it clearly makes no sense for those who run and fund programs not to step back occasionally and determine whether what they are doing is really working as they expect, and how their programs could be improved.

Evaluation is a general term that describes determining whether an existing organization or a particular program of an organization is fulfilling its purposes, goals, and objectives, and if it is achieving results from its efforts and allocation of resources. The term is also used in the context of determining how well an organization's employees are functioning.

Organizations are increasingly being asked to engage in formal evaluation exercises by stakeholders, including the organization's own board, government grantors, private foundations, and donors. Many subsectors within the nonprofit sector, such as hospitals, universities, and nursing homes, are required to have periodic formal evaluations by the private agencies that have been formed to provide accreditation. Virtually every government or foundation grant includes a requirement for an evaluation of the program being funded at the end of the grant period. And, as described in Chapter 29, the scope of evaluations has ratcheted upward with a movement to focus on program outcomes, evaluating not simply whether an organization is doing the work that it says it is doing—such as providing so many hours of counseling—but determining whether those who are receiving the organization's services are actually having their lives and the community in which they live changed for the better as a result of having received those services. According to the Government Accountability Office, the *Government Performance and Results Act of 1993* was enacted "to shift the focus of government decisionmaking and accountability away from a preoccupation with the activities that are undertaken—such as grants dispensed or inspections made—to a focus on the results of those activities, such as real gains in employability, safety, responsiveness, or program quality." The United Way of America displayed leadership in adopting an outcome-based approach and advocating for its implementation by nonprofit organizations funded by its affiliate umbrella fundraising charities.

Program evaluation has in recent years become a routine requirement, as nonprofit organizations are increasingly being asked to be accountable for the dollars being spent to further their missions. And this is a good thing, generally. It certainly doesn't make much sense to spend government tax dollars and funds gratuitously donated by foundations, corporations, and the public on programs that are not accomplishing much. Even the fact that there will be an evaluation of a program can serve as motivation to continue to improve its operation, so as to avoid the consequences of a poor evaluation. Evaluations often uncover flaws in program management that might not otherwise be discovered, thus improving the delivery of services to those who need them and making programs both more efficient and effective. For the leadership of nonprofit organizations, this is valuable information.

One downside is that those involved in programs being evaluated often view evaluations as something that is being done *to* them rather than *with* them, and there can be a real fear that a poor evaluation, regardless of whether this is performed by an outside consultant or in-house staff, could result in a program being terminated, putting their jobs at risk. Evaluations cost money and other scarce resources, and they often require staff to put aside their work of providing services to participate in the data collection process.

The intent of formal program evaluations is to provide objective assessments of what is going on in an organization and/or its programs. Ideally, the evaluation should be carried out by someone experienced in the tools and techniques of program evaluation, and who has no bias with respect to judging the program and its staff. This is easier said than done. It is quite clear that it is much more subjective and a clear conflict of interest for the staff of an organization's programs to be the ones who evaluate their own organization or program. Yet, evaluations performed by outside consultants can be expensive, and such consultants often do not have the background and know the staff well enough to reach conclusions about what might improve a program.

Regardless of who carries out the evaluation, the more "objective" the evaluator can be, the more likely the evaluation will address program shortcomings in a fair way. Evaluations should be focused on making programs better in the future rather than pointing the finger of blame, and crafted in language that provides a clear roadmap for implementing constructive changes.

What is Program Evaluation?

Program evaluation is a form of research. It involves data collection and analysis of that data. Program evaluation is a process that involves the systematic collection of information about an organization to determine how well the organization or its individual programs are working, and what might be done to improve performance. Information that is collected might include the program's activities; program outputs; program outcomes; program work processes and policies; data about program quality; how stakeholders, including clients, perceive the program; and judgments about ways the organization's program could improve to reach its stated goals.

There are two general forms of a program evaluation. A *summative evaluation* is one that focuses primarily on the effectiveness of a particular program. Typically, a summative evaluation is conducted after a program is completed, and its purpose is to determine whether the program is effective enough to continue. This is the type of evaluation most requested by funders, who need to determine whether to continue funding the program for future years. A *formative evaluation* is one that is used to determine how a program might be improved. Formative evaluations look at a program's strengths and weaknesses, problems that exist with implementation and how they might be addressed, changes in the program that are being suggested by stakeholders, unintended consequences of program implementation, and new ideas that might be tested to improve performance. Stakeholders are staff and board of the organization, its funders, those who directly benefit from its services (*clients, patients,* and *consumers* are among the terms used by organizations to describe recipients of their services, and each one has a connotation that can be viewed as positive or negative, depending on the organization's culture), community leaders, government leaders, and the public at large.

The distinction between the two is that *summative* implies a final judgment about the program; *formative* does not. As related in Patton's book, Bob Stake, an evaluation theorist at the University of Illinois, came up with an apt metaphor to describe the difference:

> When the cook tastes the soup, that is formative; when the guests taste the soup, that's summative! (Patton, 1997, p. 69).

Why Program Evaluation is Performed

The most common reason why program evaluation is performed is somewhat obvious—it is required by an organization's stakeholder with power to require it (such as an accreditation body), or a grantor (such as the government or a foundation). Yet there are clear benefits for an organization's board or CEO to insist that a program or the entire organization be periodically evaluated.

Benefits include—

- Evaluations uncover flaws in a program, which can lead to corrective action, improving service delivery, outcomes of clients, and more efficient use of scarce organizational resources.

- They can help determine whether a program is really doing what it was designed to do.

- They validate that a "good" program is really a "good" program by having this determined by an objective third party, rather than the organization itself.

- They help program staff step back and reflect on what they can do to improve efficiency and effectiveness of a program. Staff can brainstorm and communicate ideas to someone trained in looking for patterns, and who may have experience in working with other organizations that have responded to the same type of problems. Program staff may otherwise be too engrossed in providing the services and have little time to consider how the delivery of these services could be improved, or communicate about program policies that they feel are barriers to overcoming problems.

Who Performs a Program Evaluation

There are generally three options in deciding who will perform a program evaluation: using an outside consultant, using staff from the organization itself, or using a combination of the two.

For example, an outside consultant may design and direct the evaluation with organization staff performing a major role in collecting and analyzing the data. Outside evaluators are often found in research think tanks and educational institutions. There are also many private consultants who offer this service.

Each option has its own advantages and disadvantages:

Outside Consultants:

Advantages

- Outside consultants typically have special training in how to perform formal program evaluations.
- They can be more objective than an in-house staff evaluator, as they have no direct stake in the findings of the evaluation.
- They have experience working with other organizations and can provide a perspective that in-house evaluators do not have.
- They can do much of the work of an evaluation, freeing the organization's staff from tasks that would otherwise disrupt their routines.

Disadvantages

- Outside consultants are expensive compared to in-house evaluators.
- They are likely to not have too much background about the organization.
- They are likely to not have as much background about the program's recipients.
- They may be unable to get close enough to the program to understand what is really going on.
- They may be willing to provide an organization with a more "positive" evaluation than warranted by the facts, knowing that this may enhance their potential for obtaining future evaluation contracts from the organization.

In-House Staff

Advantages

- In-house staff are likely to be less expensive than outside consultants.
- They are more likely to understand the program's objectives.
- They are more likely to understand the programs themselves, their target populations, and their other stakeholders.
- They are more likely to understand and be sensitive to the internal politics of the organization and already know the staff, organization structure, and culture.

Disadvantages

- In-house staff are more likely to be perceived as being less objective than an outside consultant.
- They are less likely to know how other, similar organizations are dealing with work processes.
- They may be too busy doing their other tasks for the organization to do a good job evaluating.

Combination of the Two Models

Some organizations use an evaluation method that combines these two models. An outside consultant can direct the evaluation, develop the methodology, and analyze the data, while staff can do the leg work and collect the appropriate data. Or a staff member can direct the evaluation and a consultant can make sure the data collection and analysis are both appropriate and valid. This assures that there is some outside technical expertise that can be accessed, but that staff feel more buy-in to the results if they have a major role in participating in the evaluation.

Obviously, whatever model is chosen must be consistent with the practices and standards of the stakeholder requiring the evaluation.

Planning for Program Evaluation

The planning for program evaluation begins at the point at which a program is conceived, often at a point before funding is obtained to implement it. First, each program needs to be associated with a concrete, measurable set of goals and objectives. What must be measured are aspects of the program that relate to how well the organization is providing its services. This is typically done by compiling a set of outputs and outcomes that are hoped to be achieved before a program is started. A list of these benchmarks is typically provided to a funding organization in advance of funding as part of the grant application. Although it seems to be common sense, organizations don't always design their management information systems to capture this data, even though doing so saves a lot of time and effort when it is time to perform an evaluation.

For example, let's consider a program to assist homeless people in a community in not engaging in using illegal substances and alcohol. In applying for grant funds for such a program, an organization would likely provide data on how many people in the community are homeless and how many of them use illegal drugs and/or alcohol. The organization would carefully document the lack of other programs that sufficiently provide these services, to demonstrate that this new program would not be duplicative and would fill a need. The organization that received a grant to provide such a program would have intake of homeless clients with a drug or alcohol problem, provide treatment, and then attempt to keep track of these clients over time and measure whether they still use illegal drugs and alcohol after completing the program. Of course, this is not so simple; homeless people tend to be transient. It may not be possible to know whether someone is using drugs and alcohol (although it may be possible to know that clients are being admitted to other programs in the area for treatment, or are entering the criminal justice system for drug- and alcohol-related crimes—data that could serve as a surrogate for other data that would be much harder to collect). But the point is that data should be routinely collected that will help evaluators determine whether a program is being effective, and it makes sense to have a system in place that has this data collected *before* it is required for an evaluation rather than after.

An excellent model for planning an evaluation can be found at: *http://managementhelp.org/evaluation/program-evaluation-guide.htm#anchor4294569952*

Another useful document is provided by the Office of Planning, Research & Evaluation of the Department of Health and Human Services' Administration for Children and Families (OPRE). In Chapter 6 of this free, online, evaluation guide, the Office recommends that organizations consider scores of issues when designing their program evaluation. Among them are recommendations to—

1. *Designate the evaluation framework.* This includes the program objectives; evaluation questions; evaluation time frame; and a discussion of the context for the evaluation, par-

ticularly the aspects of the organization, program staff, and participants that may affect the evaluation.

2. *Consider procedures and methods.* These include those that will be used to obtain the evaluation data and answer the evaluation questions. Organizations need to decide where the data will come from (e.g., client records, staff interviews, observations by evaluators of clients receiving services, data already collected by the MIS system), whether the data will consist of samples or comprise the entire population being studied, what types of survey instruments will be used (such as e-mail questionnaires, telephone interview questions, focus groups), how to keep the information collected confidential and secure while respecting the privacy of respondents, how to design consent forms permitting the release of data from individuals, who will administer the instruments or otherwise collect the data, and the methods that will be used to analyze the data.

3. *Select your evaluation design.* The design should allow you to assess whether participation in the program is *really* responsible for making a difference seen in the recipients or is perhaps caused by some other factor(s). This gets to the issue of causality. For example, let's assume that you run a drug treatment center that provides services to individuals. Your data show that those who received services used illegal drugs less after one year in the program. One interpretation is that the program was effective in reducing drug use. But there are other possible explanations: Perhaps the price of drugs increased beyond the ability of these individuals to afford them. Or, perhaps new laws and increased drug law enforcement put drug pushers in jail, so that users no longer had easy access to drugs. Or perhaps these individuals simply "grew up" and no longer felt the need to use illegal drugs.

Evaluators often use scientific procedures to eliminate threats to validity, as they are called, that call the explanation of results of a study into question.

For example, there are a lot of threats to validity when evaluators rely on a simple pre-test/post-test design of an evaluation. That is, the evaluator measures some variable that is considered important (e.g., drug use) before services are delivered, and measures the same variable in the individuals after the services are delivered.

Many threats to validity are eliminated by using a control group. The evaluator may randomly assign two groups of individuals, one group receiving the treatment and the other not receiving any treatment, and then do pre-test/post test to determine if there are any differences between the two groups. There are problems with this procedure, as well, as it may be unethical for an organization to deny services to those who need them simply because of an evaluation experimental design. But putting ethical considerations aside, using a control group with random assignment is much preferable to a simple pre-test/post-test research design in determining whether the program itself is the cause of improvement in program recipients. Many nonprofit organizations can ethically use control groups in their evaluations, because the demand is so great for their services that there is often a large waiting list of unserved clients.

But the bottom line remains. As the OPRE document summarizes, evaluations are designed to answer basic questions such as:

- Did program participants demonstrate changes in knowledge, attitudes, behaviors, or awareness?
- Were the changes the result of the program's interventions?

Those who are trained in administering evaluations have a lot of research and statistical tools, including effective experimental designs, at their disposal to get valid answers to these questions.

4. *Manage and monitor the evaluation.* This involves how staff will be trained and monitored with respect to working on the evaluation, making sure the survey instruments are culturally appropriate and clear, making sure staff are informed about what is going on and their responsibilities to cooperate with the evaluation, and validating that the evaluation will answer the right questions.

The full text of the OPRE document can be accessed at:

http://www.acf.hhs.gov/programs/opre/other_resrch/pm_guide_eval/reports/pmguide/ chapter_1_pmguide.html

Conclusion

Many nonprofit executives have a fear of program evaluation, but in most cases, this fear is unfounded. For those who are committed in the sector to serving the needs of the most vulnerable in our society, program evaluation is one of the most useful tools available to improve the management of nonprofit organizations. A nonprofit organization's board and staff leadership have a stake in identifying what is working and not working in their programs. They have an obligation to document to funders and the public that their dollars are being used wisely, and that the organization is accountable for the trust placed in it to provide services that are appropriate and high quality. In many cases, an evaluation provides the evidence that the organization is meeting its obligations and worthy of being funded. As more and more evaluations of organizations occur, the knowledge base of what works and what doesn't is expanding, and society is the main beneficiary of this effort.

Tips:

- **Design organization programs before implementation begins so that evaluations can be performed easily if and when they are required.**

- **If you are performing the evaluation in-house, determine what the interests are of stakeholders, such as funders.**

- **Take advantage of the data collected and analysis of that program to improve your organization's performance, rather than simply considering it to be an exercise.**

Appendix A
Sample Articles of Incorporation Legal Notice

NOTICE IS HEREBY GIVEN that Articles of Incorporation were filed and approved by the Department of State and the Commonwealth of Pennsylvania, on (insert date), for the purpose of incorporating (insert name of corporation), under the provisions of the Pennsylvania Nonprofit Corporation law of 1988, as amended.

The corporation is incorporated under the Nonprofit Corporation Law of the Commonwealth of Pennsylvania, and the corporation does not contemplate pecuniary gain or profit, incidental or otherwise. The nature of the activities to be conducted and the purposes to be promoted or carried out by the corporation, shall be exclusively within the purview of Section 501(c)(insert) of the Internal Revenue Code of 1986, or the corresponding provisions of any subsequent tax laws of the United States. Without limiting the generality of the foregoing, the purposes of the corporation shall be: (insert).

(insert Name of Corporation Secretary or Law Firm)

Appendix B
Sample Bylaws

Bylaws of the _____

Note: Bylaws are an important legal document, and should be examined, if not drafted, by an experienced attorney. The intent of this sample is to provide a list of traditional provisions of bylaws of nonprofit organizations. I recommend that bylaws be custom-designed to serve the needs of the organization.

INTRODUCTION and PURPOSE

1. These bylaws constitute the code of rules adopted by the _____, a nonprofit organization, for the regulation and management of its affairs. The purposes of the corporation are to _____ and, further, to engage in any other lawful business purpose to be conducted on a not-for-profit basis. In carrying out such purposes, the corporation shall not exercise any powers not permitted to be exercised by an organization exempt under Section 501(c)(3) of the United Stated Internal Revenue Code of 1954.

MEMBERSHIP

2. The Corporation shall have no "members."

DIRECTORS

3. Definition of Board of Directors: The Board of Directors is that group of persons vested with the management of the business and affairs of this Corporation subject to the law, the Articles of Incorporation, and these bylaws.

4. Qualifications: Directorships shall not be denied to any person on the basis of race, creed, sex, religion, sexual orientation, or national origin.

5. Number of Directors: The Board of Directors shall consist of _____ or more natural persons. The number of directors shall be determined from time to time by Resolution of the Board of Directors.

6. Terms and Election of Directors: The Directors shall serve a maximum of _____ terms beginning at the January board meeting, and ending at the January board meeting approximately one year thereafter, until they resign or are removed in accordance with the provisions of these bylaws.

7. Procedure at Board Meetings: The rules contained in the Handbook on Parliamentary Procedure ("Robert's Rules of Order") shall govern the meetings of the board of directors.

8. Resignations: Any Director can resign at any time by delivering a written resignation to the President of the board or to the Secretary of the Corporation. Resignations of directors shall become effective immediately or on the date specified therein and vacancies will be deemed to exist as of such effective date.

9. Removal: Any director may be removed at any time (with or without cause) by a vote of 4/5ths of the total number of incumbent directors (not counting vacancies or the director subject to the removal action) at a meeting of the board of directors properly called in accordance with the terms of these bylaws. Directors may be removed by a majority vote of the board of directors at a properly called meeting with a quorum attendance when he or she misses three consecutive regular meetings.

10. Vacancies: Vacancies can be created by resignations, removals, or an increase in the size of the board of directors. Vacancies on the Board of Directors can only be filled by a majority vote of the remaining Directors, though less than a quorum.

11. Place of Director's Meetings: Meetings of the board of directors, regular or special, will be held at the primary place of business for this Corporation or at any other place within or without the _____ metropolitan area as provided or such place or places as the board of directors may designate by resolution duly adopted.

12. Meetings: Board meetings shall be held at least four times each year. Special meetings of the Board of Directors may be called by:

    A.   at least two-thirds of the Board of Directors
    B.   the President
    C.   the Secretary upon the written request of at least two-thirds of directors.

13. Notice of Board Meetings: Notice of all board meetings shall be given to each board member no less than five (5) days prior to the meeting.

14. Waiver of Notice: Attendance by a Director at any meeting of the Board of Directors will constitute a waiver of notice of such meeting except where such Director attends the meeting for the express purpose of objecting, at the beginning of the meeting, to the transaction of business because the meeting is not lawfully called or convened.

15. Quorum: A third of the incumbent directors (not counting vacancies) shall constitute a Quorum for the conduct of business. At Board meetings where a quorum is present, a majority vote of the Directors attending shall constitute an act of the Board unless a greater number is required by the Articles of Incorporation or any provision of these bylaws. Attendance by conference call whereby all members physically present at a board meeting can hear any participant not physically present and vice-versa shall constitute being present for purposes of determining whether a quorum is present.

16. Self Dealing: No director shall use confidential information gained by reason of being a member of the board of directors for personal gain to the detriment of the corporation.

OFFICERS

17. Roster of Officers: The Corporation shall have a President, Vice President, Secretary, and Treasurer.

18. Selection and Removal of Officers: All officers shall serve _____ year terms. Officers shall be elected by the Board of Directors at the board's first meeting of the calendar year or as soon as practical thereafter. Officers shall remain in office until their successor has been selected. The Board of Directors may elect a single person to any two or more offices simultaneously, except that the offices of President, Vice President, Treasurer, and Secretary must be held by separate individuals.

19. President: The President will perform all duties incident to such office and such other duties as may be provided in these bylaws or as may be prescribed from time to time by the Board of Directors. The President shall preside at all board meetings and shall exercise parliamentary control in accordance with Roberts Rules of Order.

20. Vice-President: The Vice-President shall perform the duties of the President in the absence or unavailability of the President, or when the office of President is vacant.

21. Secretary: The Secretary will keep minutes of all meetings of the Board of Directors, will be the custodian of the corporate records, will give all notices as are required by law or these bylaws, and generally, will perform all duties incident to the office of Secretary and such other duties as may be required by law, by the Articles of Incorporation, or by these bylaws.

22. Treasurer: The Treasurer will have charge and custody of all funds of this Corporation, will oversee and supervise the financial business of the corporation, will render reports and accountings to the Directors as required by the Board of Directors, and will perform in general all duties incident to the office of Treasurer and such other duties as may be required by law, by the Articles of Incorporation, or by these bylaws or which may be assigned from time to time by the Board of Directors.

23. Removal of Officers: Any officer elected or appointed to office may be removed by the Board of Directors whenever in their judgment the best interests of this Corporation will be served. Such removal, however, will be without prejudice to any contract rights of the Officer so removed.

INFORMAL ACTION

24. Waiver of Notice: Whenever any notice whatever is required to be given under the provisions of the law, the Articles of Incorporation, or these bylaws, a waiver of such notice in writing signed

by the person or persons entitled to notice, whether before or after the time stated in such waiver, will be deemed equivalent to the giving of such notice. Such waiver must, in the case of a special meeting of members, specify the general nature of the business to be transacted.

25. Action by Consent: Any action required by law or under the Articles of Incorporation or by these bylaws, or any action which otherwise may be taken at a meeting of either the members or board of directors may be taken without a meeting if a consent in writing, setting forth the action so taken, is signed by all of the persons entitled to vote with respect to the subject matter of such consent, or all directors in office, and filed with the secretary of the Corporation.

COMMITTEES

26. Appointment of Committees: The Board of Directors may from time to time designate and appoint one or more standing committees as it sees fit. Such committees shall have and exercise such prescribed authority as is designated by the Board of Directors.

27. Executive Committee: The officers of the Corporation designated in these bylaws shall constitute the executive committee. The board of directors may, if it so chooses, appoint other persons to serve on the Executive Committee. The President shall act as chairperson of the executive committee. The Executive Committee shall have such authority as may be given to it from time to time by Resolution of the Board of Directors.

OPERATIONS

28. Fiscal Year: The fiscal year for this Corporation will be the calendar year, unless the Board otherwise so designates by majority vote.

29. Inspection of Books and Records: All books and records of this Corporation may be inspected by any Director for any purpose at any reasonable time on written demand.

30. Loans to Management: This Corporation will make no loans to any of its Directors or Officers.

31. Execution of Documents: Except as otherwise provided by law, checks, drafts, and orders for the payment of money of this Corporation shall be signed by at least two persons who have previously been designated by a Resolution of the board of directors, unless the Board by majority vote approves authorizing one person for this purpose in cases of payments for amounts of less than $500 in the aggregate for any single purpose. Contracts, promissory notes, leases, or other instruments executed in the name of and on behalf of the Corporation shall be signed by one or more persons who have been authorized and directed to do so by the board of directors. No contract shall be valid unless it is authorized or ratified by a properly adopted Resolution of the board of directors.

32. Conflict of Interest and Whistleblower Policies. This Corporation shall have a conflict of interest policy consistent with the Sample Conflict of Interest policy of the Internal Revenue Service and a whisleblower policy.

33. Dissolution. Upon the dissolution of the corporation, assets shall be distributed for one or more exempt purposes within the meaning of section 501(c)(3) of the Internal Revenue Code, or the corresponding section of any future federal tax code, or shall be distributed to the federal government, or to a state or local government, for a public purpose. Any such assets not so disposed of shall be disposed of by a Court of Competent Jurisdiction of the county in which the principal office of the corporation is then located, exclusively for such purposes or to such organization or organizations, as said Court shall determine, which are organized and operated exclusively for such purposes.

AMENDMENTS

34. Amendments. The Board of Directors may alter, amend, suspend or repeal these Bylaws at any regular or special meeting called for that purpose, except as restricted by state or federal law.

PUBLIC STATEMENTS

35. Authority to make Statements. No person, except for the President or staff authorized by the Board to do so are authorized to make any public statements, whether written or oral, purporting to represent the official policy, position, or opinion of this Corporation, without first having obtained the approval of the Board of Directors.

36. Limitation on Statements. Any person who is authorized to make any public statement, whether written or oral, purporting to represent the official policy, position, recommendation or opinion of the Corporation, shall first make it clear that he or she is representing the Corporation. Thereafter, throughout the entire presentation, he or she shall confine his/her presentation only to those matters which have been properly approved by the Corporation. He or she shall not at the same time present any statement purporting to represent any other firm, group, or organization or purporting to represent his or her own personal views.

37. Indemnification: _____ (optional provisions relating to state or federal law that apply to the indemnification of officers/directors and limitations on liability that apply to the organization's volunteers).

CERTIFICATION

I hereby certify that these bylaws were adopted by the Board of Directors of the_____at their meeting held on _____.

_____
Secretary

Appendix C
Addresses of IRS Field Offices in Pennsylvania

Altoona
Paine Webber Building
1601 Eleventh Ave.
Altoona, PA 16601
(814) 944-3532

Bethlehem
3 W. Broad St.
Bethlehem, PA 18018
(610) 865-8208

Butler
Holly Pointe Center
Room 201
220 S. Main St.
Butler PA 16001
(724) 282-4531

Cranberry
230 Executive Drive
Cranberry TWP, PA 16066
(724) 772-5111

Erie
1314 Griswold Plaza
Erie, PA 16501
(814) 456-8967

Harrisburg
Federal Building
228 Walnut St.
Harrisburg, PA 17108
(717) 777-9650

Horsham
200 Lakeside Drive
Horsham, PA 19044
(215) 887-6134

Johnstown
Penn Traffic Building
319 Washington St.
Johnstown, PA 15901
(814) 533-4221

King of Prussia
601 South Henderson Rd.
King of Prussia, PA 19406
(610) 992-5130

Lancaster
1720 Hempstead Rd.
Lancaster, PA 17601
(717) 291-1994

Media
Rosetree Corp. Center
Building 1
1400 N. Providence Rd.
Media, PA 19063
(610) 891-6002

Monroeville
4314 Old William Penn Highway
Monroeville, PA 15146
(412) 856-1913

Philadelphia
600 Arch St.
Room 1232
Philadelphia, PA 19106
(215) 861-1225

Pittsburgh
William S. Moorhead Federal Building
Suite 1113
1000 Liberty Avenue
Pittsburgh, PA 15222
(412) 395-5667

Reading
201 Penn St.
Reading, PA 19601
(610) 320-5154

Scranton
Suite 600
409 Lackawanna Ave.
Scranton, PA 18503
(570) 961-2493

State College
2038 Sandy Drive
State College, PA 16803
(814) 234-8735

Washington
Jefferson Court Plaza
Upper Level
162 W. Chestnut St.
Washington, PA 15301
(724) 229-5985

Wilkes Barre
Stegmaier Building
7 North Wilkes-Barre Blvd.
Wilkes-Barre, PA 18702
(570) 821-4076

Williamsport
330 Pine St.
Williamsport, PA 17701
(570) 326-1632

York
2801 Eastern Boulevard
York, PA 17402
(717) 757-4977

Appendix D
Addresses of Legal Journals (for Advertising Articles of Incorporation Filings)

Adams County
Adams County Legal Journal
111-117 Baltimore St.
Gettysburg, PA 17325
(717) 337-9812 Extension 336

Allegheny County
Pittsburgh Legal Journal
400 Koppers Bldg.
7th Ave. Pittsburgh, PA 15219
(412) 261-6255

Armstrong County
Armstrong County Legal Journal
Armstrong County Courthouse
Kittanning, PA 16201
(724) 543-2500

Beaver County
Beaver County Legal Journal
788 Turnpike Street
Beaver, PA 15009
(724) 728-7622

Bedford County
Bedford County Legal Journal
P.O. Box 440
Bedford, PA 15522
(814) 623-8611

Berks County
Berks County Law Journal
544-546 Court St.
P.O. Box 1058
Reading, PA 19063
(610) 375-4593

Blair County
Blair County Legal Bulletin
115 Logan Blvd.
Altoona, PA 16602
(814) 943-1496

Bradford County
Bradford County Law Journal
206 S. Keystone Ave.
Sayre, PA 18840
(570) 888-2244

Bucks County
Bucks County Law Reporter
135 E. State St.
P.O. Box 300
Doylestown, PA 18901
(215)348-9413
1-800-479-8585 X106

Butler County
Butler County Legal Journal
222 S. Main St.
Butler, PA 16001
(724) 285-1717

Cambria County
Cambria County Legal Journal
P.O. Box 157
Johnstown, PA
15907-0157
(814) 255-3221

Cameron County
none

Carbon County
Carbon County Law Journal
P.O. Box 6
Jim Thorpe, PA 18229
(610) 379-3795

Centre County
Centre County Legal Journal
Box 57

Bellefonte, PA 16823
(814) 355-5474

Chester County
Chester County Law Reporter
15 W. Gay St.
PO Box 3191
West Chester, PA 19380
(610) 692-1889

Clarion County
none

Clearfield County
P.O. Box 521
Clearfield, PA 16830
(814) 765-6555

Clinton County
none

Columbia County
none

Crawford County
Crawford County Legal Journal
403 Chestnut St.
Meadville, PA 16335-2902
(814) 333-2398

Cumberland County
Cumberland Law Journal
32 South Bedford Street
Carlisle PA 17013
(717) 249-3166

Dauphin County
Dauphin County Reporter
213 N. Front St.
Harrisburg, PA 17101
(717) 232-7536

Delaware County
Delaware County Legal Journal
Bar Association Bldg.
Front & Lemon Sts.
P.O. Box 466 Media, PA 19063
(610) 566-6625 Ext. 23

Elk County
none

Erie County
Erie County Legal Journal
302 W. 9th St.
Erie, PA 16502-1427
(814) 459-3111

Fayette County
Fayette Legal Journal
84 E. Main St.
Uniontown, PA 15401
(724) 437-7994

Forest County
none

Franklin County
Franklin County Legal Journal
100 Lincoln Way East, Suite E,
Chambersburg, PA 17201-2291
(717) 267-2032

Fulton County
none

Greene County
Greene Reports
Courthouse
Waynesburg, PA 15370
(724) 852-5237

Huntingdon County
none

Indiana County
Indiana Law Journal
307 Savings & Trust Co. Bldg.
Indiana, PA 15701
(724) 465-5651

Jefferson County
Jefferson County Legal Journal
316 Main St.
Brookville, PA 15825
(814) 849-1237

Juniata County
none

Lackawanna County
Lackawanna Jurist
338 N Washington Ave.,
Floor 3
Scranton, PA 18503-9161
(570) 969-9161

Lancaster County
Lancaster Law Review
28 E. Orange St.
Lancaster, PA 17602
(717) 393-0737

Lawrence County
Lawrence Law Journal
c/o Lawrence Co. Government Center
New Castle, PA 16101
(724) 656-9774

Lebanon County
Lebanon County Legal Journal
Room 305
Law Library Municipal Bldg.
Lebanon, PA 17042
(717) 274-2801 X 2280

Lehigh County
Lehigh Law Journal
1114 Walnut St.
Allentown, PA 18102
(610) 433-6204

Luzerne County
Luzerne Legal Register
Room 23
Courthouse
Wilkes-Barre, PA 18711
(570) 822-6712

Lycoming County
Lycoming Law Assn.
321 Pine St., Ste 217
Williamsport, PA 17701
(717) 323-8287

McKean County
none

Mercer County
Mercer County Law Journal
P.O. Box 1302
Hermitage, PA 16148
(724) 342-3111

Mifflin County
none

Monroe County
Monroe Legal Reporter
P.O. Box 786
Stroudsburg, PA 18360
(570) 424-7288

Montgomery County
Montgomery County Law Reporter
100 W. Airy St.
P.O. Box 268
Norristown, PA 19404
(610) 279-9660

Montour County
none

Northampton County
Northampton County Reporter
155 S. Ninth St.
Easton, PA 18042
(610) 258-6333

Northumberland County
Northumberland Legal Journal
P.O. Box 126
Sunbury, PA 17801
(570) 286-7777

Perry County
none

Philadelphia County
The Legal Intelligencer
1617 JFK Blvd., Sts.
1750
Philadelphia, PA 19103
(215) 557-2300

Pike County
none

Potter County
none

Schuylkill County
Schuylkill Legal Record
Law Library
Schuylkill County Courthouse
401 N. Second Street
Pottsville, PA 17901
(570) 628-1235

Snyder County
none

Somerset County
Somerset Legal Journal
P.O. Box 501
Somerset, PA 15001
(814) 445-4021

Sullivan County
none

Susquehanna County
none

Tioga County
none

Union County
none

Venango County
none

Warren County
none

Washington County
Washington Co. Reports
523 Washington Trust Bldg.
Washington, PA 15301
(724) 225-6710

Wayne County
none

Westmoreland County
Westmoreland Law Journal
129 N. Pennsylvania Ave.
Greensburg, PA 15601
(724) 834-7260

York County
York Legal Record
137 E. Market St.
York, PA 17401
(717) 854-8755

Appendix E
Foundation Center Regional Foundation Reference Collections

Aliquippa
Beaver County Library System
109 Pleasant Dr., Ste. 101
Aliquippa, PA 15001
(724) 728-3737

Allentown
Allentown Public Library
1210 Hamilton St.
Allentown, PA 18102
(610) 820-2400

Bethlehem
Northampton Community College
Paul and Harriett Mack Library
3835 Green Pond Rd.
Bethlehem, PA 18020
(610) 861-5360

Blue Bell
Montgomery Co. Comm. College
The Brendlinger Library
340 DeKalb Pike
Blue Bell, PA 19422
(215) 641-6596

Bristol
Margaret R. Grundy Mem. Library
680 Radcliffe St.
Bristol, PA 19007
(215) 788-7891

East Stroudsburg
East Stroudsburg University
Kemp Library
200 Prospect Ave.
East Stroudsburg, PA 18301
(570) 422-3594

Erie
Erie County Public Library
160 E. Front St.
Erie, PA 16507
(814) 451-6927

Franklin
Franklin Public Library
421 12th St.
Franklin, PA 16323
(814) 432-5062

Harrisburg
Dauphin Co. Library System
East Shore Area Library
4501 Ethel St.
Harrisburg, PA 17109
(717) 652-9380

Hazleton
Hazleton Area Public Library
55 N. Church St.
Hazleton, PA 18201
(570) 454-2961

Lancaster
Lancaster Public Library
125 N. Duke St.
Lancaster, PA 17602
(717) 394-2651

Free Library of Philadelphia
Regional Foundation Center
1901 Vine St., 2nd Fl.
Philadelphia, PA 19103
(215) 686-5423

Philadelphia
The Johnson-UGO Fd. Library
United Methodist Neighborhood
Services
804 North Broad St.
Philadelphia, PA 19130
(215) 236-1003

Phoenixville
Phoenixville Public Library
183 2nd Ave.
Phoenixville, PA 19460
(610) 933-3013

Pittsburgh
Carnegie Library of Pittsburgh
4400 Forbes Ave.
Pittsburgh, PA 15213
(412) 622-3158

Pittston
Nonprofit and Community Assistance Center
1151 Oak St.
Pittston, PA 18640
(570) 655-5581

Reading
Reading Public Library
100 S. 5th St.
Reading, PA 19602
(610) 655-6355

Scranton
Albright Memorial Library
500 Vine St.
Scranton, PA 18509
(570) 348-3000

Sharon
Community Library of the
Shenango Valley
11 N. Sharpsville Ave.
Sharon, PA 16146
(724) 981-4360

Washington
Citizens Library
55 S. College St.
Washington, PA 15301
(724) 222-2400

Williamsport
James V. Brown Library
19 E.4th St.
Williamsport, PA 17701
(570) 326-0536

York
Martin Library
159 E. Market St.
York, PA 17401
(717) 846-5300

Appendix F
Constitution of Pennsylvania, Article VIII, Section 1 and 2, Taxation and Finance--Uniformity of Taxation

Section 1.
All taxes shall be uniform, upon the same class of subjects, within the territorial limits of the authority levying the tax, and shall be levied and collected under general laws.

Exemptions and Special Provisions
Section 2. (a) The General Assembly may by law exempt from taxation:

(i) Actual places of regularly states religious worship:

(ii) Actual places of burial, when used or held by a person or organization deriving no private or corporate profit therefrom and no substantial part of whose activity consists of selling personal property in connection therewith;

(iii) That portion of public property which is actually and regularly used for public purposes;

(iv) That portion of the property owned and occupied by any branch, post or camp of honorably discharged servicemen or servicewomen which is actually and regularly used for benevolent, charitable or patriotic purposes; and

(v) Institutions of purely public charity, but in the case of any real property tax exemptions only that portion of real property of such institution which is actually and regularly used for the purposes of the institution.

(b) The General Assembly may, by law:

(i) Establish standards and qualifications for private forest reserves, agriculture reserves, and land actively devoted to agriculture use, and make special provision for the taxation thereof;

(ii) Establish as a class or classes of subjects of taxation the property or privileges of persons who, because of age, disability, infirmity or poverty are determined to be in need of tax exemption or of special tax provisions, and for any such class or classes and standards and qualifications,and except as herein provided may impose taxes, grant exemptions, or make special tax provisions in accordance therewith. No exemption or special provision shall be made under this clause with respect to taxes upon the sale or use of personal property, and no exemption from any tax upon real property shall be granted by the General Assembly under this clause unless the General Assembly shall provide for the reimbursement of local taxing authorities by or through the Commonwealth for revenue losses occasioned by such exemption;

(iii) Establish standards and qualifications by which local taxing authorities may make uniform special tax provisions applicable to a taxpayer for a limited period of time to encourage improvement of deteriorating property or areas by an individual, association or corporation, or to encourage industrial development by a non- profit corporation; and

(iv) Make special tax provisions on any increase in value of real estate resulting from residential construction. Such special tax provisions shall be applicable for a period not to exceed two years.

(v) Establish standards and qualifications by which local taxing authorities in counties of the first and second class make uniform special real property tax provisions applicable to taxpayers who are long-time owner-occupants as shall be defined by the General Assembly of residences in areas where real property values have risen markedly as a consequence of the refurbishing or renovating of other deteriorating residences or the construction of new residences.

Appendix G
Excerpt from Act 2, Session of 1971,
PART III. EXCLUSIONS FROM TAX

§ 7204. Exclusions from tax

The tax imposed by section 202 shall not be imposed upon...

(1) The sale at retail or use of tangible personal property (other than motor vehicles, trailers, semi-trailers, motor boats, aircraft or other similar tangible personal property required under either Federal law or laws of this Commonwealth to be registered or licensed) or services sold by or purchased from a person not a vendor in an isolated transaction or sold by or purchased from a person who is a vendor but is not a vendor with respect to the tangible personal property or services sold or purchased in such transaction: Provided, That inventory and stock in trade so sold or purchased, shall not be excluded from the tax by the provisions of this subsection.

*****

(10) The sale at retail to or use by (i) any charitable organization, volunteer firemen's organization or nonprofit educational institution, or (ii) a religious organization for religious purposes of tangible personal property or services other than pursuant to a construction contract: Provided, however, That the exclusion of this clause shall not apply with respect to any tangible personal property or services used in any unrelated trade or business carried on by such organization or institution or with respect to any materials, supplies and equipment used and transferred to such organization or institution in the construction, reconstruction, remodeling, renovation, repairs and maintenance of any real estate structure, other than building machinery and equipment, except materials and supplies when purchased by such organizations or institutions for routine maintenance and repairs.

Excerpt from The Fourth to Eighth Class County Assessment Law:
(Title 53--Municipalities Generally)

§ 8812. Exemptions from taxation.

(a) General rule.--The following property shall be exempt from all county, borough, town, township, road, poor, county institution district and school real estate taxes:

(1) All churches, meetinghouses or other actual places of regularly stated religious worship, with the ground annexed necessary for their occupancy and use.

(2) All actual places of burial, including burial grounds and all mausoleums, vaults, crypts or structures, intended to hold or contain the bodies of the dead if used or held by a person or organization deriving no private or corporate profit from the enterprise and no substantial part of whose activity consists of selling personal property in connection therewith.

(3) All hospitals, universities, colleges, seminaries, academies, associations and institutions of learning, benevolence or charity, including fire and rescue stations, with the grounds annexed and necessary for their occupancy and use, founded, endowed and maintained by public or private charity as long as all of the following apply:

(i) The entire revenue derived by the entity is applied to support the entity and to increase the efficiency and facilities of the entity, the repair and the necessary increase of grounds and buildings of the entity and for no other purpose.

(ii) The property of purely public charities is necessary to and actually used for the principal purposes of the institution and not used in such a manner as to compete with commercial enterprise.

Act 55 (Excerpt)

Note: *The following is the section of Act 55, the* Institutions of Purely Public Charity Act, *which provides a measurable standard for meeting the "donate or render gratuitously a substantial portion of its services" test of Hospital Utilization Project v. Commonwealth of Pennsylvania.*

(d) COMMUNITY SERVICE.--

(1) The institution must donate or render gratuitously a substantial portion of its services. This criterion is satisfied if the institution benefits the community by actually providing any one of the following:

(i) Goods or services to all who seek them without regard to their ability to pay for what they receive if all of the following apply:

(A) The institution has a written policy to this effect.

(B) The institution has published this policy in a reasonable manner.

(C) The institution provides uncompensated goods or services at least equal to 75% of the institution's net operating income but not less than 3% of the institution's total operating expenses.

(ii) Goods or services for fees that are based upon the recipient's ability to pay for them if all of the following apply:

(A) The institution can demonstrate that it has implemented a written policy and a written schedule of fees based on individual or family income. An institution will meet the requirement of this clause if the institution consistently applies a formula to all individuals requesting consideration of reduced fees which is in part based on individual or family income.

(B) At least 20% of the individuals receiving goods or services from the institution pay no fee or a fee which is lower than the cost of the goods or services provided by the institution.

(C) At least 10% of the individuals receiving goods or services from the institution receive a reduction in fees of at least 10% of the cost of the goods or services provided to them.

(D) No individuals [individual in enrolled bill] receiving goods or services from the institution pay [pays in enrolled bill] a fee which is equal to or greater than the cost of the goods or services provided to them, or the goods or services provided to the individuals described in clause (B) are comparable in quality and quantity to the goods or services provided to those individuals who pay a fee which is equal to or greater than the cost of the goods or services provided to them.

(iii) Wholly gratuitous goods or services to at least 5% of those receiving similar goods or services from the institution.

(iv) Financial assistance or uncompensated goods or services to at least 20% of those receiving similar goods or services from the institution if at least 10% of the individuals receiving goods or services from the institution either paid no fees or fees which were 90% or less of the cost of the goods or services provided to them, after consideration of any financial assistance provided to them by the institution.

(v) Uncompensated goods or services which in the aggregate are equal to at least 5% of the institution's costs of providing goods or services.

(vi) Goods or services at no fee or reduced fees to government agencies or goods or services to individuals eligible for government programs if any one of the following applies:

> (A) The institution receives 75% or more of its gross operating revenue from grants or fee-for-service payments by government agencies and if the aggregate amount of fee-for-service payments from government agencies does not exceed 95% of the institution's costs of providing goods or services to the individuals for whom the fee-for-services payments are made.

> (B) The institution provides goods or services to individuals with mental retardation, to individuals who need mental health services, to members of an individual's family or guardian in support of such goods or services or to individuals who are dependent, neglected or delinquent children, as long as the institution performs duties that would otherwise be the responsibility of government and the institution is restricted in its ability to retain revenue over expenses or voluntary contributions by any one of the following statutes or regulations or by contractual limitations with county children and youth offices in this Commonwealth:

(I) Sections 1905(d) and 1915(c) of the Social Security Act (49 Stat. 620, 42 U.S.C. §§ 1396d(d) and 1396n(c)).

(II) 42 CFR 440.150 (relating to intermediate care facility (ICF/MR) services).

(III) 42 CFR Pt. 483 Subpt. I (relating to conditions of participation for intermediate care facilities for the mentally retarded).

(IV) The act of October 20, 1966 (3rd Sp.Sess., P.L. 96, No. 6), [50 P.S. § 4101 et seq. (3rd Sp.Sess.)] known as the Mental Health and Mental Retardation Act of 1966.

(V) Articles II, VII, IX and X of the act of June 13, 1967 (P.L. 31, No. 21), [62 P.S. §§ 201 et seq., 701 et seq., 901 et seq., and 1001 et seq.] known as the Public Welfare Code.

(VI) 23 Pa.C.S. Ch. 63 (relating to child protective services).

(VII) 42 Pa.C.S. Ch. 63 (relating to juvenile matters).

(VIII) 55 Pa. Code Chs. 3170 (relating to allowable costs and procedures for county children and youth), 3680 (relating to administration and operation of a children and youth social service agency), 4300 (relating to county mental health and mental retardation fiscal manual), 6400 (relating to community homes for individuals with mental retardation), 6500 (relating to family living homes), 6210 (relating to participation requirements for the intermediate care facilities for the mentally retarded program), 6211 (relating to allowable cost reimbursement for non-State operated intermediate care facilities for the mentally retarded) and 6600 (relating to intermediate care facilities for the mentally retarded).

(vii) Fundraising on behalf of or grants to an institution of purely public charity, an entity similarly recognized by another state or foreign jurisdiction, a qualifying religious organization or a government agency and actual contribution of a substantial portion of the funds raised or contributions received to an institution of purely public charity, an entity similarly recognized by another state or foreign jurisdiction, a qualifying religious organization or a government agency.

(2) The institution may elect to average the applicable data for its five most recently completed fiscal years for the purposes of calculating any formula or meeting any quantitative standard in paragraph (1).

(3) For the purposes of calculating the number of individuals for use in the percentage calculations in this subsection, educational institutions may use full-time equivalent students as defined by the Department of Education.

(4) For purposes of this subsection, the term "uncompensated goods or services" shall be limited to any of the following:

(i) The full cost of all goods or services provided by the institution for which the institution has not received monetary compensation or the difference between the full cost and any lesser fee received for the goods or services, including the cost of the goods or services provided to individuals unable to pay.

(ii) The difference between the full cost of education and research programs provided by or participated in by the institution and the payment made to the institution to support the education and research programs.

(iii) The difference between the full cost of providing the goods or services and the payment made to the institution under any government program, including individuals covered by Medicare or Medicaid.

(iv) The difference between the full cost of the community services which the institution provides or participates in and the payment made to the institution to support such community services.

(v) The reasonable value of any moneys, property, goods or services donated by a primary donor to an institution of purely public charity or to a government agency or the reasonable value of the net donation made by a secondary donor to a primary donor. As used in this subparagraph, the following words and phrases shall have the following meanings:

"NET DONATION." In the case of a donation of money, property or identical goods and services made by a secondary donor, the difference between the value of the donation made by the secondary donor and the value of the donation made by the primary donor, provided such value is positive.

"PRIMARY DONOR." An institution which makes a donation of any money, property, goods or services to an institution of purely public charity.

"SECONDARY DONOR." An institution which receives a donation of any money, property, goods or services from a primary donor and then makes a donation back to that primary donor within three years of having received such donation.

(vi) The reasonable value of volunteer assistance donated by individuals who are involved or assist in the provision of goods or services by the institution. The reasonable value of volunteer assistance, computed on an hourly basis, shall not exceed the Statewide average weekly wage as defined in section 105.1 of the act of June 2, 1915 (P.L. 736, No. 338), [77 P.S. § 25.1.] known as the Workers' Compensation Act, divided by 40.

(vii) The cost of goods or services provided by an institution licensed by the Department of Health or the Department of Public Welfare to individuals who are unable to pay provided that reasonable and customary collection efforts have been made by the institution.

(viii) The value of any voluntary agreement as set forth in section 7(c).

Appendix H
New Year's Resolutions for Nonprofit Executives

by Gary M. Grobman
(reprinted with permission from *Pennsylvania Nonprofit Report*)

It's December, and another year has slipped by. Replacing calendars on the wall is often an excuse for introspection. I've made some New Year's resolutions of my own, and it's not too late for you to do so if you haven't. Let me make a few suggestions.

1. Become an exemplary, ethical individual, every minute, every day. Don't use organizational resources for personal use and don't tolerate others in your organization who do. Consider whether you are creating conflicts of interest with your decisions. Don't cheat on your expense account. Register your organization with the state agency that regulates charitable organizations if you are required to do so. Consider registering with that agency and disclosing information even if you are not required to do so because your fundraising is under the threshold requirements. Be honest with your board and staff (most boards are much more tolerant of mistakes made than they are of lying about it, anyway!). Your standard of ethics reflects not only upon you and your organization, but also upon our sector as a whole. The shock waves surrounding the New Era debacle and the United Way fiasco in the 1990s are still being felt. The public is becoming more cynical about how charities operate. Don't be someone who adds to this sense of cynicism. It's also easier to sleep at night when you know you didn't do something dishonest or questionable during the day.

2. Make sure you have a healthy, vibrant personal life. It is so easy running an organization to become consumed by the pressures, challenges, and demands that accompany leadership and neglect your health, family, hobbies, and vacation needs. If you are one of those who find it impossible to leave the office to take vacation, remember that even the President plays golf and takes vacations, and he's a really busy executive! If your organization is such that it can't survive with you away for a few days, then that is a sign that something is unhealthy with either you or the organization. Fix it. And then go take a hike (on the Appalachian Trail). If you are getting too many evening calls from your board chair or (God forbid!) unnecessary calls in the middle of the night, politely inform him or her that you are no longer willing to take these calls, and that there are 900 numbers available for late night companionship needs.

3. If your organization can afford it, consider making a voluntary contribution to a local government or a foundation established to support local governments. There is some legitimacy to the view of local governments that charities use their services and do not pay for it, and this places a strain on their ability to function. There is also legitimacy to our sector's view that as charities, we should be exempt from taxes or involuntary monetary payments. Yet many in our sector recognize that we have a partnership with local governments to make society better. One way to do so is to help our local governments, on a voluntary basis, when we can do so. If your organization cannot or will not provide money, then offer services.

4. Be sensitive to the legitimate concerns of small business. Small business people are not the enemies of charities. They serve on our boards. They provide us with valuable products and services. They purchase our products and services. How would you feel if you invested not only your entire life savings but your entire emotional capital in a business, and a local charity used its profits as ven-

ture capital to establish a commercial business (i.e., designed not to serve any charitable mission but to generate net revenue) to compete head-to-head with yours, and had the advantage of not paying taxes, paying cheaper postage rates, had volunteers, access to capital, and the public relations value that comes from being a "charity"? There is clearly a role for charities to generate revenue to fund services for the community. But there is a right way and a wrong way of doing this. The Jewish Community Center or YMCA that places advertisements in general circulation newspapers seeking corporate memberships touting that its fees are slightly lower than the private health club a mile away is probably not violating any laws. But they are violating the spirit of why the JCC health club and YMCA are eligible for tax-exempt status. The hospital that markets its laundry service to the general public may be paying unrelated business income taxes on its revenue, but this style of marketing creates tensions within the small business community, and for good reason. Should my public library be offering best-sellers and videos for fees that undercut existing small businesses? A gray area, and we could argue that one for a long time. But my point stands: Before establishing or expanding a commercial business under the aegis of charitable tax-exempt status, even if it is not violative of any unfair business competition provisions of your state law, think twice. There are ways to generate income by providing services and products that don't step on toes.

5. Join and support a state advocacy association. The non-profit charitable community faces problems and challenges that are too big for any individual to face alone. There are associations based in most state capitals and Washington whose job is to identify these problems and challenges, devise a strategy to meet them head on, and coordinate advocacy. Many of these organizations are starved for membership and resources because it is easy for a charity to avoid its responsibilities and let the burden fall on the "other guy." There is strength in numbers, and if you run an agency that thinks it can save a few dollars by not making an investment in its future, you're being short-sighted. And while you are at it, join a professional organization, as well.

6. Get some continuing education to improve your ability to manage your organization. Whether it is in the grants writing, computer, management, strategic planning, time management, or board/staff relations areas, virtually every nonprofit organization manager can benefit by some outside training. Taking a course also offers a break from the office routine and brings you in contact with peers from other disciplines. It's good for networking, good socially, good for your brain, and, best of all, many organizations will pay all of the costs!

7. Take advantage of the Internet, and set up social networking pages and use mobile apps that hawk your products and services. The communications revolution shouldn't leave you and your organization behind. Each day, thousands of "newbies" access these sites, which have become the access points of choice for information about volunteering, charitable giving, news and views, demographic data, and contacts within your field. A modest home page; active presence on Twitter, Facebook, and LinkedIn; blog; and online store can be established and maintained for surprisingly low cost and effort. And, believe it or not, it's lots of fun.

8. Invite your local legislators to visit your agency and/or meet with your board. Whether at the City Council/County Commissioner, state legislature, or Congressional level, the decisions made by our elected officials affect our organizations, our clients, our volunteers, our board members, and us. There are many benefits in establishing a relationship with these officials before you need something from them. This is especially important if your agency is the recipient of government funding, or hopes to be in the future.

Appendix I: Sample Financial Reports: Association for Research on Nonprofit Organizations and Voluntary Action (ARNOVA)

ASSOCIATION FOR RESEARCH ON NONPROFIT ORGANIZATIONS AND VOLUNTARY ACTION

STATEMENTS OF FINANCIAL POSITION
JUNE 30, 2010 AND 2009

ASSETS

	2010	2009
Cash and cash equivalents	$ 338,175	$ 88,359
Cash held by others	36,215	19,953
Investments	808,987	1,030,330
Grants receivable	23,000	75,000
Accounts receivable	52,511	40,460
Prepaid expenses	11,348	23,427
Inventory	5,798	6,009
Property and equipment, net	8,479	21,371
	$ 1,284,513	$ 1,304,909

LIABILITIES AND NET ASSETS

Liabilities		
Accounts payable	$ 8,398	$ 15,477
Accrued payroll and benefits	17,824	17,463
Deferred member dues	41,264	59,621
Total liabilities	67,486	92,561
Net assets		
Unrestricted		
Undesignated	619,706	540,329
Board designated	317,992	317,992
	937,698	858,321
Temporarily restricted	260,154	334,852
Permanently restricted	19,175	19,175
Total net assets	1,217,027	1,212,348
	$ 1,284,513	$ 1,304,909

See accompanying notes to financial statements.

2

ASSOCIATION FOR RESEARCH ON NONPROFIT ORGANIZATIONS AND VOLUNTARY ACTION

STATEMENT OF ACTIVITIES
YEAR ENDED JUNE 30, 2010
(With Comparative Total for the Year Ended June 30, 2009)

	2010				2009
	Unrestricted	Temporarily Restricted	Permanently Restricted	Total	Total
Support and revenue					
Grants	$ -0-	$ 194,500	$ -0-	$ 194,500	$ 150,000
Membership dues	95,357	-0-	-0-	95,357	106,443
Conference revenue and sponsorships	102,337	21,250	-0-	123,587	159,065
Publications	96,777	16,000	-0-	112,777	98,268
Contributions	10,936	61,017	-0-	71,953	69,963
Interest income on cash and cash equivalents	385	-0-	-0-	385	1,969
Other	1,127	-0-	-0-	1,127	5,101
Net assets released from restrictions	367,993	(367,993)	-0-	-0-	-0-
Total support and revenue	674,912	(75,226)	-0-	599,686	590,809
Expenses					
Program					
Conference	201,793	-0-	-0-	201,793	234,161
Publications	101,177	-0-	-0-	101,177	109,950
Membership services	101,150	-0-	-0-	101,150	86,749
Scholarships and awards	31,982	-0-	-0-	31,982	31,125
Other programs	42,801	-0-	-0-	42,801	36,520
Total program expenses	478,903	-0-	-0-	478,903	498,505
Management and general	136,412	-0-	-0-	136,412	162,443
Fundraising	8,424	-0-	-0-	8,424	7,431
Total expenses	623,739	-0-	-0-	623,739	668,379
Change in net assets from operations	51,173	(75,226)	-0-	(24,053)	(77,570)
Other income (loss)					
Investment return, net	29,013	528	-0-	29,541	28,816
Loss on disposition of property and equipment	(809)	-0-	-0-	(809)	-0-
Total other income	28,204	528	-0-	28,732	28,816
Change in net assets	79,377	(74,698)	-0-	4,679	(48,754)
Net assets, beginning of period	858,321	334,852	19,175	1,212,348	1,261,102
Net assets, end of period	$ 937,698	$ 260,154	$ 19,175	$ 1,217,027	$ 1,212,348

See accompanying notes to financial statements.

3

Appendix J
National Organizations and Publications of Interest

American Society of Association Executives and the Center for Association Leadership
1575 I Street, NW
Washington, D.C. 20005-1103
phone: (202) 371-8315
E-mail: asaeservice@asaecenter.org
Web Site: *http://www.asaenet.org*

Association for Research on Nonprofit Organizations and Voluntary Action
550 W.North Street, STE 301
Indianapolis, IN 46202
phone: (317) 684-2120
Fax: (317) 684-2128
Web Site: *http://www.arnova.org*

The Foundation Center
79 Fifth Avenue/16th Street
New York, NY 10003-3076
phone: (212) 620-4230; fax: (212) 807-3677
E-mail: feedback@foundationcenter.org
Web Site: *http://foundationcenter.org*

Independent Sector
1602 L Street
Suite 900
Washington, D.C. 20036
phone: (202) 467-6100; fax: (202) 467-6101
E-mail: info@independentsector.org
Web site: *http://www.independentsector.org*

Mandel Center for Nonprofit Organizations
Case Western Reserve University
10900 Euclid Avenue
Cleveland, OH 44106-7167
phone: (216) 368-2275; fax: (216) 368-8592
Web Site: *http://mandelcenter.case.edu/*

National Council of Nonprofits
1101 Vermont Avenue, NW; STE 1002
Washington, D.C. 20005
phone: (202) 962-0322; fax: (202) 962-0321
E-mail: ncna@ncna.org
Web Site: *http://www.councilofnonprofits.org*

BoardSource
750 9th Street, NW
Suite 650
Washington, D.C. 20001-4590
phone: (202) 349-2500; fax: (202) 349-2599
E-mail: ncnb@ncnb.org
Web Site: *http://www.boardsource.org*

Association of Fundraising Executives
4300 Wilson Boulevard
Suite 300
Arlington, VA 22203
phone: (703) 684-0410; fax: (703) 684-0540
E-mail: info@afpnet.org
Web Site: *http://www.afpnet.org*

National Publications of Interest

Nonprofit Issues (monthly)
PO Box 482
Dresher, PA 19025-0482
phone: (215) 542-7547; fax: (215) 542-7548
E-Mail: info@nonprofitissues.com
Web Site: *http://www.nonprofitissues.com*

Nonprofit Times (monthly)
Circulation Department
201 Littleton Road
Second Floor
Morris Plains, NJ 07050
phone: (973) 401-0202; fax: (973) 401-0404
E-mail: circmngr@nptimes.com
Web Site: *http://www.thenonprofittimes.com/*

Chronicle of Philanthropy (biweekly)
1255 23rd Street, NW
Washington, DC 20037
phone: (202) 466-1200; fax: (202) 446-2078
E-Mail: help@philanthropy.com
Web Site: http://philanthropy.com/section/Home/172

Nonprofit and Voluntary Sector Quarterly
340 West Michigan Street
Canal Level - Suite A
Indianapolis, IN 46202
Phone: (317) 684-2120 / Fax: (317) 684-2120
phone: (317) 278-8981; fax: (317) 684-8900
E-mail: nsvq@sp2.upenn.edu
Web Site: *http://www.sp2.upenn.edu/nvsq/*

Contributions Magazine
28A Park Street
Medfield, MA 02052
phone: (508) 359-0019; fax: (508) 359-2703
E-Mail: info@contributionsmagazine.com
Web Site: *http://www.contributionsmagazine.com*

Appendix K
About the Author

Gary M. Grobman (B.S. Drexel University; M.P.A. Harvard University, Kennedy School of Government; Ph.D., Penn State University) is special projects director for White Hat Communications, a Harrisburg-based publishing and nonprofit consulting organization formed in 1993. The title of Dr. Grobman's doctoral dissertation is *An Analysis of Codes of Ethics of Nonprofit, Tax-Exempt Membership Associations: Does Principal Constituency Make a Difference?* He is an adjunct faculty member of several colleges and universities.

He served as the executive director of the Pennsylvania Jewish Coalition from 1983-1996. Prior to that, he was a senior legislative assistant in Washington for two members of Congress, a news reporter, and a political humor columnist for *Roll Call.* He also served as a lobbyist for public transit agencies. In 1987, he founded the Non-Profit Advocacy Network (NPAN), which consisted of more than 50 statewide associations that represent Pennsylvania charities. He currently is the Harrisburg Contributing Editor for *Pennsylvania Nonprofit Report.*

He serves as Vice President of the Greater Harrisburg Concert Band and Treasurer of the Harrisburg Area Road Runners Club. He also served on the board of directors of the Citizen Service Project, and was the Treasurer of that statewide 501(c)(3), which was established to promote citizen service in Pennsylvania.

He is the founder of the Ph.D. Culture Project *(http://www.facebook.com/phdculture)* and the author of two related books—*Just Don't Do It!: A Fractured and Irreverent Look at the Ph.D. Culture* (Ph.D. Culture Project and Science and Humanities Press) and the *Ph.D. Culture Project Cartoon Book* (with Jerry King).

He is the author of *The Holocaust—A Guide for Pennsylvania Teachers, The Nonprofit Handbook, Fundraising Online: Using the Internet to Raise Serious Money for Your Nonprofit Organization* (co-authored with Gary Grant), *Improving Quality and Performance in Your Non-Profit Organization, The Nonprofit Management Casebook, The Nonprofit Organization's Guide to E-Commerce,* and other books published by White Hat Communications and Wilder Publications (now Fieldstone).

Appendix L
Pennsylvania Nonprofit Handbook—Ninth Edition
Reader Survey/Order Form

Return Survey To:
White Hat Communications
PO Box 5390
Harrisburg, PA 17110-0390

My name and address (please print legibly):

1. I would like to suggest the following corrections:

2. I would like to suggest the following topics for inclusion in a future edition:

3. I have the following comments, suggestions, or criticisms:

4. I would like to order _____ additional copies @$34.95 each plus $8 shipping and handling first book, $1 each additional book. Pennsylvania purchasers please add 6% sales tax or include a copy of exemption certificate from the Pennsylvania Department of Revenue. Note: Quantity discounts are available.

For Further Reading

General

Conners, Tracy D. *The Nonprofit Handbook: Management* (2nd Ed.). New York: Wiley & Sons. 2001.

Hopkins, Bruce R. *Starting and Managing a Nonprofit Organization: A Legal Guide* (5th Ed.). New York: Wiley & Sons. 2009.

Mancuso, Anthony. *How to Form a Nonprofit Organization* (9th Ed.). Berkeley, CA: Nolo Press. 2009.

Ott, J. Steven and Shafitz, Jay M. *The Facts on File Dictionary of Nonprofit Organization Management.* New York, NY: Facts on File Publications. 1986.

Pakroo, Peri. *Starting & Building a Nonprofit: A Practical Guide* (4th Ed.). Berkeley, CA: Nolo Press. 2011.

Sand, Michael. *How to Manage an Effective Nonprofit Organization.* Pompton Plains, NJ: Career Press. 2005.

Chapter 1/Chapter 2/Chapter 3

American Bar Association. *Guidebook for Directors of Nonprofit Corporations.* Author. 2003.

Hopkins, Bruce R. S*tarting and Managing a Nonprofit Organization: A Legal Guide* (5th Ed.). New York: Wiley & Sons. 2009.

Hutton, Stan. *Nonprofit Kit for Dummies.* Hoboken, NJ: For Dummies. 2010.

Kirschten, Barbara L. *Nonprofit Corporate Forms Handbook.* New York, NY: Clark Boardman Co. 2010.

Stephens, Joyce. *Bylaws: Writing, Amending, Revising.* Clearwater, FL: Frederick. 2000.

Chapter 4

Andringa, Robert C. and Egstrom, Ted W. *Nonprofit Board Answer Book.* Washington, DC: Board Source. 2002.

Carver, John. *Boards That Make a Difference. A New Design for Leadership in Nonprofit and Public Organizations.* San Francisco, CA: Jossey-Bass. 2006.

Conrad, William R. Jr. and Glenn, William E. *The Effective Voluntary Board of Directors: What it Does and How it Works.* Chicago, IL: Swallow Press. 2003.

Grace, Kay Sprinkel. *The Ultimate Board Member's Book.* Medfield, MA: Emerson and Church. 2008.

Hopkins, Bruce. *Nonprofit Governance: Law, Practices and Trends.* New York: Wiley. 2009.

O'Connell, Brian. *The Board Member's Book: Making a Difference in Voluntary Organizations.* New York: The Foundation Center. 2003.

Widmer, Candace and Houchin, Susan. *The Art of Trusteeship: The Nonprofit Board Member's Guide to Effective Governance.* San Francisco, CA: Jossey-Bass. 2000.

Chapter 5

About.com. (2003). *How to Draft a Mission Statement.* Retrieved October 13, 2011, from *http://management.about.com/cs/generalmanagement/ht/MissionStatemen.htm*

Angelica, Emil. *The Fieldstone Alliance Guide to Crafting Effective Mission and Vision Statements.* St. Paul, MN: Fieldstone Alliance. 2001.

Morrisey, George. *A Guide to Strategic Thinking: Building Your Planning Foundation.* San Francisco: Jossey-Bass.1996.

MPowerUniversity. *Vision Statements in Just a Few Steps—Or Your Money Back!* (Kindle Format). Katy, TX: MPowerUniversity. 2011.

O'Hallaron, Richard and O'Hallaron, David. *The Mission Primer: Four Steps to an Effective Mission Statement.* Richmond, VA: Mission, Inc. 2000.

Taylor, Ron. *The Mission Statement: A Framework for Developing an Effective Organizational Mission Statement in 100 Words or Less* (Kindle Format). Amazon Digital Services. 2011.

Chapter 6

Barry, Bryan W. *Strategic Planning Workbook for Nonprofit Organizations.* St. Paul, Minnesota: Amherst H. Wilder Foundation. 1997.

Bryson, John & Alston, Farum. *Creating Your Strategic Plan: A Workbook for Public and Non-profit Organizations.* San Francisco, CA: Jossey-Bass. 2011.

Burkhardt, Patrick J. & Reuss, Suzanne. *Successful Strategic Planning: A Guide for Nonprofit Agencies and Organizations.* Newbury Park CA: Sage Publications. 1993.

Mintzburg, Henry. *The Rise and Fall of Strategic Planning.* New York: MacMillan. 1994.

Steiner, G. A. *Strategic Planning: What Every Manager Must Know.* New York: Free Press. 1979.

Chapter 7

Anderson, Albert. *Ethics for Fundraisers.* Bloomington, IN: Indiana University Press. 1996.

Harmon, Curran, Spielberg & Eisenberg, LLP. *What the "Intermediate Sanctions" Law Means for Nonprofit Organizations.* Washington, DC: Alliance for Justice, 1996.

Independent Sector. *Ethics and the Nation's Voluntary and Philanthropic Community.* Washington, DC. 1991.

Josephson Institute of Ethics. *Making Ethical Decisions.* Marina del Rey, CA: Author. 2002

Pettey, Janice Gow. *Ethical Fundraising: A Guide for Nonprofit Boards and Fundraisers.* New York: Wiley. 2008.

Svara, James. *The Ethics Primer for Public Administrators in Government and Nonprofit Organizations.* Sudbury, MA: Jones & Bartlett Learning. 2006.

White, Doug. *The Nonprofit Challenge: Integrating Ethics into the Purpose and Promise of Our Nation's Charities.* New York: Palgrave Macmillan. 2010.

Chapter 8

Blazek, Jody. *IRS Form 1023 Tax Preparation Guide.* New York: Wiley. 2005.

Busby, Dan & VanDrunnen, John. *2011 Church and Nonprofit Tax and Financial Guide.* Grand Rapids, MI: Zondervan. 2011.

Godfrey, Howard. *Handbook on Tax-Exempt Organizations.* Englewood Cliffs, NJ: Prentice-Hall. 1983.

Hansmann, Henry. *The Rationale for Exempting Nonprofit Organizations From Corporate Income Taxation.* New Haven, CT: Institute for Social Policy Studies. 1981.

Harmon, Gail and Ferster, Andrea. Dealing With the IRS. *Nonprofit Times.* May 1988.

Hopkins, Bruce R. *The Law of Nonprofit Organizations* (10th Ed.). New York: John Wiley & Sons. 2011.

Kirschten, Barbara L. *Nonprofit Corporate Forms Handbook.* New York: Clark Boardman Co. 1993.

Mancuso, Anthony. How To Form Your Own Nonprofit Corporation (10th Ed.). Berkeley, CA: Nolo Press. 2011.

Trompeter, Jean E. *Formation and Qualification of a Charitable Organization.* Milwaukee Lawyer. Fall 1983.

Chapter 9

Brooklyn In-Touch Information Center. *How to Assess Board Liability.* Fact Sheet for Nonprofit Managers (#6). Brooklyn, NY: Brooklyn In-Touch Information Center. 1988.

Chapman, Terry S.; Lai, Mary L; and Steinbock, Elmer L. *Am I Covered For? A Comprehensive Guide to Insuring Your Non-Profit Organization* (3rd Ed.). San Jose, CA: Consortium for Human Resources. 1992.

Edie, John. *Directors and Officers Liability Insurance and Indemnification.* Washington, DC: Council on Foundations. 1991.

Herman, Melanie. *Ready in Defense: A Liability, Litigation and Legal Guide for Nonprofits.* Nonprofit Risk Management Center. 2003.

Jackson, Peggy; White, Leslie, & Herman, Melanie. *Mission Accomplished: A Practical Guide to Risk Management for Nonprofits.* Leesburg, VA: Nonprofit Risk Management Center. 1999.

Johnson, R. Bradley. *Risk Management Guide for Nonprofits.* Alexandria, VA: United Way of America. 1987.

Minnesota Office of Citizenship and Volunteer Services. *Planning It Safe: How to Control Liability & Risk in Volunteer Programs.* Minneapolis, MN: Author. 1998.

Peat, Marwick, Mitchell and Co. *Directors' and Officers' Liability: A Crisis in the Making.* New York, NY: Peat, Marwick, Mitchell and Co. 1987.

Chapter 10

American Institute of Certified Public Accountants. *Audits of Certain Nonprofit Organizations.* New York, NY: American Institute of Certified Public Accountants. 1981.

Coe, Charles. *Nonprofit Financial Management: A Practical Guide* (Wiley Nonprofit Authority). New York: Wiley. 2011.

Dropkin, Murray & Halpin, James. *Bookkeeping for Nonprofits: A Step-by-Step Guide to Nonprofit Accounting.* San Francisco, CA: Jossey-Bass. 2005.

Dropkin, Murray, Halpin, Jim, & La Touche, Bill. *The Budget-Building Book for Nonprofits: A Step-by-Step Guide for Managers and Boards* (2nd Ed.). San Francisco: Jossey-Bass. 2008.

Drucker, Peter F. *Managing the Nonprofit Organization.* New York: Harper Collins. 2006.

For Dummies. *Nonprofit Bookkeeping and Accounting for Dummies.* Hoboken, NJ: For Dummies. 2009.

Foster, Mary, Becker, Howard; & Terrano, Richard. Miller. *Not-for-Profit Reporting.* New York: Aspen Publishing. 2001.

McLaughlin, Thomas. *Streetsmart Financial Basics for Nonprofit Managers.* New York: Wiley. 2009.

Olenick, Arnold J. and Olenick, Philip R. *Making the Non-Profit Organization Work: A Financial, Legal and Tax Guide for Administrators.* Englewood Cliffs, NJ: Institute for Business Planning. 1983.

Shim, Jae, Siegel, Joel, & Simon, Abraham. *Handbook of Budgeting for Nonprofit Organizations.* Old Tappen, NJ: Prentice Hall. 1996.

Zietlow, John & Hankin, Jo Ann. *Financial Management for Nonprofit Organizations: Policies and Practices.* Wiley. 2007.

Chapter 11

Albert, Sheila. *Hiring the Chief Executive: A Practical Guide to the Search and Selection Process.* Washington, DC: National Center for Nonprofit Boards. 2000.

Barbeito, Carol. *Human Resource Policies and Procedures for Nonprofit Organizations.* New York: Wiley. 2006.

Becker, Sarah and Glenn, Donna. *Off Your Duffs and Up the Assets: Common Sense for Non-Profit Managers.* Rockville, NY: Farnsworth Publishing Co. 1984.

Bernstein, Leyna. *Creating Your Employee Handbook: A Do-It-Yourself Kit for Nonprofits.* San Francisco: Jossey-Bass Publishers. 1999.

DeLuca, Matthew. *Nonprofit Personnel Forms & Guidelines.* New York: Aspen. 1994.

Drucker, Peter F. *Managing the Nonprofit Organization.* New York: Harper Collins. 2006.

Hauge, Jennifer C. & Herman, Melanie. *Taking the High Road: A Guide to Effective and Legal Employment Practices for Nonprofits* (2nd Ed.). Washington, DC: Nonprofit Risk Management Center. 1999.

Muller, Max. *The Manager's Guide to HR: Hiring, Firing, Performance Evaluations, Documentation, Benefits, and Everything Else You Need to Know.* New York: Amacom. 2009.

Pynes, Joan. (2009). *Human Resources Management for Public and Nonprofit Organizations: A Strategic Approach.* Sacramento, CA: Jossey-Bass. 2009.

Smith, Shawn & Mazin, Rebecca. *HR Answer Book, An Indispensable Guide for Managers and Human Resources Professionals.* New York: Amacom. 2004.

Stratton, Jeff. *Nonprofit Personnel Policies.* Horsham, PA: LRP Publications. 2007.

Chapter 12

Bagley, Esq., Bruce. Necessary v. Nosey—Guidelines and Strategies for Hiring. *PA Society of Association Executives' Society News.* April 1996. pp. 20.

Brown, Jane Newell. *The Complete Guide to Recruitment: A Step-by-Step Approach to Selecting, Assessing and Hiring the Right People.* London, UK: Kogan Page. 2011.

Fader, Sonny. *365 Ideas for Recruiting, Retaining, Motivating and Rewarding Your Volunteers: A Complete Guide for Non-Profit Organizations.* Atlantic Publishing Co. 2010.

Half, Robert. *On Hiring.* New York, NY: Crown Publishers. 1985.

Muller, Max. *The Manager's Guide to HR: Hiring, Firing, Performance Evaluations, Documentation, Benefits, and Everything Else You Need to Know.* New York: Amacom. 2009.

Pennsylvania Human Relations Commission. *Pre-Employment Inquiries: What May I Ask? What Must I Answer?* Harrisburg, PA: Author.

Rogers, Henry C. *The One Hat Solution—Rogers' Strategy for Creative Middle Management.* New York, NY: St. Martin's Press. 1986.

Stettner, Morey. *The New Manager's Handbook.* New York: McGraw Hill. 2006.

Chapter 13

Conners, Tracy. *The Volunteer Management Handbook: Leadership Strategies for Success.* New York: Wiley. 2011.

Ellis, Susan. *The Volunteer Recruitment (and Membership Development) Book.* Philadelphia, PA: Energize. 2005.

_____ *From the Top Down: The Executive Role in Volunteer Program Success.* Philadelphia, PA: Energize. 1996.

Fader, Sonny. *365 Ideas for Recruiting, Retaining, Motivating and Rewarding Your Volunteers: A Complete Guide for Non-Profit Organizations.* Ocala, FL: Atlantic Publishing Co. 2010.

Friedman, Jill. *Boomer Volunteer Engagement.* Bloomington, IN: AuthorHouse. 2010.

Masaoka, Jan. *The Nonprofit's Guide to Human Resources: Managing Your Employees & Volunteers.* Nolo. 2011.

Chapter 14

Kramer, Donald. Pa. Passes Solicitation Act With New Rules, Penalties. *Nonprofit Issues* December, 1990.

Morgan, Lewis & Bockius. *The Solicitation of Funds for Charitable Purposes Act.* Philadelphia: Morgan, Lewis & Bockius, May 1991.

Wickham, Kenneth. Testimony Presented to House Finance Committee Regarding HB 2046 and HB 2047: November 1, 1989. Harrisburg, PA: United Way of Pennsylvania. 1989.

Chapter 15

Bray, Ilona. *Effective Fundraising for Nonprofits: Real-World Strategies That Work.* Berkeley, CA: Nolo. 2010.

Collins, Sarah. (Ed.). *The Foundation Center's User Friendly Guide—Grant Seeker's Guide to Resources.* New York: The Foundation Center. 1994.

Dove, Ken. *Conducting a Successful Fundraising Program: A Comprehensive Guide and Resource.* San Francisco: Jossey-Bass. 2001.

Helwing, Richard & Figure, Eileen. *199 Fun and Effective Fundraising Events for Nonprofit Organizations.* Ocala, FL: Atlantic Publishing Company. 2010

Kelly, Kathleen. *Effective Fund-Raising Management.* Mahwah, NJ: Lawrence Erlbaum Associates. 1998.

Mutz, John & Murray, Katherine. *Fundraising for Dummies* (3rd Ed.). Hoboken, NJ: For Dummies. 2010.

Saul, Jason. *The End of Fundraising: Raise More Money by Selling Your Impact.* San Francisco, CA: Jossey-Bass. 2011.

Weinstein, Stanley. *The Complete Guide to Fundraising Management* (The AFP/Wiley Fund Development Series). Wiley. 2009.

Chapter 16

Browning, Beverly. *Grant Writing For Dummies* (4th Ed.). Hoboken, NJ: For Dummies. 2011.

Blum, Laurie. *The Complete Guide to Getting a Grant.* New York: Poseidon Press. 1993.

Chelekis, George C. *The Action Guide to Government Grants, Loans and Giveaways.* New York: Perigee Books. 1993.

Collins, Sarah. Foundation Fundamentals: *Fundraising Guides* (8th Ed.). New York: The Foundation Center. 2008.

Collins, Sarah & Dion, Charlotte. *The Foundation Center's User-Friendly Guide: A Grantseeker's Guide to Resources* (4th Ed.). New York: The Foundation Center. 1996.

Geever, Jane C. *The Foundation Center's Guide to Proposal Writing* (5th Ed.). New York: The Foundation Center. 2007.

Karsh, Ellen. *The Only Grant-Writing Book You'll Ever Need: Top Grant Writers and Grant Givers Share Their Secrets* (3rd Ed.). Basic Books. 2009.

Payne, Mary Ann. *Grant Writing DeMYSTiFied.* New York: McGraw-Hill. 2011.

Quick, James M. & New, Cheryl C. *Grant Seeker's Budget Toolkit.* New York: Wiley and Sons. 2001.

Thompson, Waddy. *The Complete Idiot's Guide to Grant Writing* (3rd Ed.). Alpha. 2011.

Chapter 17/Chapter 18

Avner, Marcia. *The Lobbying and Advocacy Handbook for Nonprofit Organizations.* St. Paul, MN: Wilder Foundation. 2002.

Berry, Jeffrey. *A Voice for Nonprofits.* Washington, DC: Brookings Institution Press. 2005.

Caplan, Marc and Nader, Ralph. *Ralph Nader Presents a Citizen's Guide to Lobbying.* New York: Dembner Books. 1983.

Fitch, Bradford. *Citizen's Handbook to Influencing Elected Officials: Citizen Advocacy in State Legislatures and Congress: A Guide for Citizen Lobbyists and Grassroots Advocates.* Alexandria, VA: TheCapitol.Net, Inc. 2010.

Jansson, Bruce. *Becoming an Effective Policy Advocate.* Florence, KY: Brooks Cole. 2010.

Litwack, Maury. *Capitol Plan—A Comprehensive Washington Advocacy Strategy* (Kindle Edition). Capitol Plan Publishing. 2010.

Prakash, Aseem & Gugerty, Mary Kay. *Advocacy Organizations and Collective Action.* Cambridge University Press. 2011.

Richan, Willard. *Lobbying for Social Change* (3rd Ed.). New York: Routledge. 2007.

Smucker, Bob. *Nonprofit Lobbying Guide* (2nd Ed.). Washington, DC: Independent Sector. 1999.

Chapter 19

Beckwith, Sandra. *Publicity for Nonprofits: Generating Media Exposure That Leads to Awareness, Growth, and Contributions.* Kaplan Publishing. 2006.

Bonk, Kathy, Tynes, Emily, Griggs, Henry, & Sparks, Phil. *Strategic Communications for Nonprofits: A Step-by-Step Guide to Working with the Media.* San Francisco, CA: Jossey-Bass. 2008.

Fitch, Bradford. *Media Relations Handbook: For Agencies, Associations, Nonprofits and Congress—The Big Blue Book.* TheCapitol.Net, Inc. 2010.

Winston, William & Kinzey, Ruth Ellen. *Using Public Relations Strategies to Promote Your Nonprofit Organization.* Binghamton, NY: Routledge. 2000.

Chapter 20

Fouts, Janet. (2010). *# SOCIALMEDIA NONPROFIT tweet Book01: 140 Bite-Sized Ideas for Nonprofit Social Media Engagement.* Cupertino, CA: Happy About. 2010.

Hart, Ted. (2010). *Internet Management for Nonprofits: Strategies, Tools and Trade Secrets.* New York: Wiley. 2010.

Hart, Ted, Greenfield, James, & Haji, Sheeraz. *People to People Fundraising: Social Networking and Web 2.0 for Charities.* New York: Wiley. 2008.

Kanter, Beth, Fine, Allison, & Zuckerberg, Randi. *The Networked Nonprofit: Connecting with Social Media to Drive Change.* San Francisco, CA: Jossey-Bass. 2010.

Madia, Sherrie Ann. *The Social Media Survival Guide for Nonprofits and Charitable Organizations.* Basecamp Communications. 2011.

McPherson, Richard. *Digital Giving: How Technology is Changing Charity.* iUniverse. 2007.

Neff, David. *The Future of Nonprofits: Innovate and Thrive in the Digital Age.* New York: Wiley. 2011.

Warwick, Mal. *Fundraising on the Internet: The ePhilanthropyFoundation.org's Guide to Success Online* (2nd Ed.). San Francisco, CA: Jossey-Bass. 2008.

Chapter 21/Chapter 22

Grobman, Gary. *The Nonprofit Organization's Guide to E-Commerce.* Harrisburg, PA: White Hat Communications. 2001.

Grobman, Gary and Grant, Gary. *Fundraising Online.* Harrisburg, PA: White Hat Communications. 2006.

Holden, Greg. *Starting an Online Business for Dummies* (6th Ed.). Foster City, CA: IDG Books Worldwide. 2010.

Sanders, Michael. *Joint Ventures Involving Tax-Exempt Organizations* (2nd Ed.). New York: Wiley and Sons. 2002.

Tureen, Edward. *The Nonprofit Internet Companion* (2nd Ed.). Washington, DC: SEK Publications. 2000.

Warwick, Mal. *Fundraising on the Internet: The ePhilanthropyFoundation.org's Guide to Success Online* (2nd Ed.). San Francisco, CA: Jossey-Bass. 2008.

Chapter 23

Brown, Cherie R. *The Art of Coalition Building—A Guide for Community Leaders.* New York: American Jewish Committee. 1984.

Clifton, Robert L. & Dahms, Alan. *Grassroots Organizations: A Resource Book for Directors, Staff, and Volunteers of Small, Community-Based, Nonprofit Agencies* (2nd Ed.). Long Grove, IL: Waveland Press. 1993.

Kahn, Si. *Organizing: A Guide for Grassroots Leaders.* Washington, DC: NASW Press. 1991.

Tydeman, Ann. *A Guide to Coalition Building.* Washington, DC: National Citizen's Coalition for Nursing Home Reform. 1979.

Van Dyke, Nella & McCammon, Holly (Eds.). *Strategic Alliances: Coalition Building and Social Movements (Social Movements, Protest and Contention).* Minneapolis, MN: University of Minnesota Press. 2010.

Wolff, Tom. *The Power of Collaborative Solutions: Six Principles and Effective Tools for Building Healthy Communities.* San Francisco, CA: Jossey-Bass. 2010.

Chapter 24

Dabel, Gregory J. Saving Money in Nonprofit Organizations: *More Than 100 Money-Saving Ideas, Tips, and Strategies for Reducing Expenses Without Cutting Your Budget.* San Francisco, CA: Jossey-Bass. 1998.

Mancuso, Anthony. *How To Form Your Own Nonprofit Corporation* (9th Ed.). Berkeley, CA: Nolo Press. 2009.

Chapter 25

Deja, Sandy. *Nonprofit Organizations, Business Ventures, and the IRS: Your Guide to the Unrelated Business Income Tax Law.* Whole Nonprofit Catalog 6. Spring 1988.

Dewan, Bradford N. *Operation of a Business by Non-Profit Tax-Exempt Organizations.* Economic Development and Law Center. March-April 1986.

Gallaway, Joseph M. *The Unrelated Business Income Tax.* New York: John Wiley. 1982.

Grobman, Gary. *The Issue of Competition Between Non-Profit and For-Profit Corporations* Harrisburg, PA: Pennsylvania Jewish Coalition. 1994.

Hopkins, Bruce. Hearings on Nonprofit 'Competition.' *Nonprofit World* 5 (Sept-Oct. 1987).

Kotler, Philip and Andreasen, Alan R. *Strategic Marketing for Nonprofit Organizations.* Englewood Cliffs, NJ: Prentiss-Hall, Inc. 1987.

Lehrfeld, William J. More Unrelated Business Tax Issues. *Philanthropy Monthly.* October 1984.

Skloot, Edward (Ed.). *The Nonprofit Entrepreneur.* New York: The Foundation Center. 1988.

United States Congress, Joint Committee on Taxation. *Tax Policy: Competition Between*

Taxable Businesses and Tax-Exempt Organizations. Gaithersburg, MD: U.S. General Accounting Office. 1987.

Wellford, Harrison and Gallagher, Janne. *The Myth of Unfair Competition by Nonprofit Organizations*. New York: Family Service Association of America. 1985.

Chapter 26

Bookman, Mark. *Protecting Your Organization's Tax-Exempt Status*. San Francisco: Jossey Bass. 1992.

Gillespie, Catherine H. Court Denies Tax Exemption for Nonprofit Nursing Home. *Nonprofit Issues*. Philadelphia, PA: Montgomery, McCracken, Walker and Rhoads. March 1992.

Grobman, Gary. *The Issue of Tax-Exempt Status for Pennsylvania Non-Profit Charities*. Harrisburg, PA: Pennsylvania Jewish Coalition. 1994.

Hopkins, Bruce. *The Law and Tax-Exempt Organizations* (6th Ed.) New York: John Wiley and Sons. 1992.

National Council of Nonprofit Associations. *State Tax Trends*. Volume 2, No. 4. Summer 1994.

Stepneski, Rob. Rising Tax Pressure Hits Nonprofits. *NonProfit Times*. April 1993.

Van Til, Jon. Tax Exemptions Reconsidered. *NonProfit Times*. June 1993.

Wellford, Harrison & Gallagher, Janne. *The Myth of Unfair Competition by Nonprofit Organizations*. New York: Family Service Association of America. 1985.

Chapter 27

Cavadel, Joel. *Nonprofit Mergers. Unpublished report on legal consideration relating to nonprofit mergers in Pennsylvania*. 1996.

Dickmeyer, Louise. *No Risk No Reward: Mergers of Membership Associations and Nonprofits*. Andover, MN: Expert Publishing, Inc. 2009.

La Piana, David. *Nonprofit Mergers Workbook Part I: The Leaders Guide to Considering, Negotiating, and Executing a Merger*. Nashville, TN: Fieldstone Alliance Books. 2008.

McCormick, Dan H. *Nonprofit Mergers: The Power of Successful Partnerships*. New York: Aspen Publishers. 2000.

McLaughlin, Thomas. *Nonprofit Mergers and Alliances*. Wiley. 2010.

Sanders, Michael. *Joint Ventures Involving Tax-Exempt Organizations:* 2011 Cumulative Supplement (3rd Ed.). New York: Wiley. 2011.

Chapter 28

AL-Tabbaa, Omar. *Boosting Organization Performance through Adopting Quality Models: The case of EFQM model applied within the nonprofit sector*. Lap Lambert Academic Publishing. 2011.

Crosby, Philip B. *Quality is Free*. New York: Mentor Books. 1992.

Garvin, David A. *Management Quality: The Strategic and Competitive Edge*. New York: Free Press. 1988.

Grobman, Gary. *Improving Quality and Performance in Your Non-Profit Organization*. Harrisburg, PA: White Hat Communications. 1999.

Chapter 29

Brothers, John, & Sherman, Ann. *Building Nonprofit Capacity: A Guide to Managing Change Through Organizational Lifecycles*. Jossey-Bass. 2011.

Bunker, Barbara Benedict and Alban, Billie T. *Large Group Interventions: Engaging the Whole System for Rapid Change*. San Francisco: Jossey-Bass. 1997.

_____ What Makes Large Group Interventions Effective? *Journal of Applied Behavioral Science* 28(4). 1992.

Carter, Reginald. *The Accountable Agency.* Thousand Oaks, CA: Sage Publications. 1983.

Creech, Bill. *The Five Pillars of TQM: How to Make Total Quality Management Work for You.* New York: Penguin Books. 1994.

Deming, W. Edward. *On Some Statistical Aids Toward Economic Production. Interfaces,* v5, n4. Aug. 1975. The Operations Research Society of America and the Institute of Management Sciences. 1975.

Friedman, Mark. *A Guide to Developing and Using Performance Measures in Results-Based Budgeting.* Washington, DC: The Finance Project. 1997.

Hammer, Michael. *Reengineering Work: Don't Automate: Obliterate.* Harvard Business Review, July-Aug. 1990, pp. 104-112. 1990.

Hammer, Michael. and Champy, James. *Reengineering the Corporation: A Manifesto for Business.* New York: HarperBusiness. 1993.

Hammer, Michael and Stanton, Steven A. *The Reengineering Revolution: A Handbook.* New York: HarperBusiness. 1994.

Light, Mark. *Results Now for Nonprofits: Strategic, Operating, and Governance Planning.* New York: Wiley. 2011.

Peters, Thomas J. and Waterman, Jr., Robert H. *In Search of Excellence: Lessons from America's Best-Run Companies.* New York: Harper and Row. 1982.

Richmond, Frederick and Hunnemann, Eleanor. *What Every Board Member Needs to Know About Outcomes.* Management and Technical Assistance Publication Series n2, Harrisburg, PA: Positive Outcomes. 1996.

Rouda, R. & Kusy, M., Jr. Organization Development—The Management of Change. *Tappi Journal* 78(8): 253, 1995.

Steckel, Richard and Lehman, Jennifer. *In Search of America's Best Non-Profits.* San Francisco: Jossey-Bass. 1997.

Watson, Gregory H. *The Benchmarking Workbook: Adapting Best Practices for Performance Improvement.* Portland, OR: Productivity Press. 1992.

Chapter 30

Carter, Reginald. *The Transparent Accountability Paradigm: An Outcome-Based Management Approach for Government and Nonprofit Organizations.* East Lansing, MI: Transparent and Accountability Manager Press. 2011.

Festen, Marcia & Philbin, Marianne. Level Best: *How Small and Grassroots Nonprofits Can Tackle Evaluation and Talk Results.* San Francisco, CA: Jossey Bass. 2006.

Gray, Sandra T. Evaluation with Power: *A New Approach to Organizational Effectiveness, Empowerment, and Excellence.* San Francisco, CA: Jossey-Bass. 1997.

Wholey, Joseph S., Hatry, Harry P., & Newcomer, Kathryn E. *Handbook of Practical Program Evaluation.* San Francisco, CA: Jossey-Bass. 2004.

KEY WORD INDEX

A

abuse, 65, 68, 88, 93, 96, 97, 98, 143, 224, 238, 275, 277, 278, 286, 294

accountability, 11, 23, 26, 44, 55, 63-64, 67, 70, 71, 72, 73, 76, 94, 96, 97, 101, 114, 147, 176, 263, 264, 278, 293, 294, 295, 300, 305, 310

accounting, 20, 23, 24, 26, 60, 69, 86, 93, 94, 95, 96, 98, 99, 100, 101, 102, 103, 104, 108, 109, 120, 121, 142, 204, 212, 223, 269, 271, 282, 292, 310

accrual basis of accounting, 99, 102, 108

advertising, 10, 31, 61, 87, 111, 122, 150, 151, 166, 175, 185, 186, 189, 191, 192, 193, 194, 201, 202, 204, 205, 210, 211, 214, 216, 221, 240, 256, 262, 263, 329

affiliates, 77, 137, 139, 170, 213, 214, 254, 259, 265, 281, 285, 300

affiliate marketing, 213, 214

AIDS, 13, 195, 196, 275, 278

Amazon.com, 213-214

American Cancer Society, 13, 241

Americans With Disabilities Act, 84, 114, 123

annual meeting, 35, 125

annual report, 16, 24, 32, 41, 70, 118, 137, 148, 151, 152, 154, 159, 184, 185, 200, 228, 252, 255

application service provider (ASP), 194, 195, 215, 220, 224, 239, 240, 241, 243, 244

applications, 17, 28, 31, 67, 77, 115, 118, 122, 135, 197, 198, 203, 265

for 501(c)(3) status, 76, 77-79, 81, 145

for funding and grants, 32, 41, 42, 46, 55, 148, 151, 153, 157, 158, 159, 160, 162, 163, 203, 206

for domain name (see domain names)

for incorporation 31, 32

ARNOVA, 18, 98, 331

articles of incorporation, 23, 24, 27, 28, 29, 30, 31, 32, 33, 35, 41, 75, 77, 78, 139, 145, 252, 256, 266, 274, 307, 308, 309, 310, 311

articles of dissolution, 30, 32, 33, 78, 93, 274, 312

auctions, 151, 202, 210, 215, 216, 221, 222, 234, 240, 243

charity (see charity auctions)

audit, 24, 41, 69, 93, 97, 101, 102, 103, 104, 139, 140, 142, 153, 162, 206, 262, 282, 294

authentication, 217

B

awards, 122, 134, 136, 154, 169, 175, 178, 179, 183

balance sheet, 96, 98, 99, 139

bank accounts, 16, 19, 20, 24, 28, 116, 246

benchmarking, 289, 292, 293, 297, 303

blogs, 187, 190, 191, 195, 197, 202, 222, 330

board development, 40, 42

board minutes, 23, 24, 31, 35, 40, 41, 43, 44, 56, 91, 103, 252, 256, 310

board of directors, 19, 21, 23, 25, 27, 28, 30, 32, 35, 37, 38, 39, 46, 49, 88, 102, 113, 126, 263, 286, 293, 294, 308, 309, 310, 311, 312

board surveys (see *surveys*)

bookkeeping, 20, 24, 97, 101, 102, 105, 251, 252, 254

BPR (see *business process reengineering*)

budget,

budget deficits,

organization, 60, 75, 106, 268

bulk mail, 16, 223, 238, 251, 255, 256-258

Bureau of Charitable Organizations, 19, 137, 140, 207, 275

business process reengineering (BPR), 289, 290-291, 295

bylaws, 16, 17, 19, 23, 27, 30, 33, 35-38, 39, 40, 41, 42, 43, 46, 47, 48, 78, 86, 87, 126, 139, 252, 264, 266, 283

C

campaigns, 64, 166, 173, 195-196, 224, 228

fundraising, 64, 65, 152, 145, 155, 219, 230, 232

political, 30, 169, 171, 172, 175, 176, 177, 179, 192, 230, 232

capital campaigns, 192, 196, 197, 224, 237-238

cash, 95, 96, 98, 99, 100, 101, 146, 212, 219

basis of accounting, 99, 102, 108

cash-flow, 95, 96, 100, 101, 209, 282

cause-related marketing, 241

chairperson (of the Board), 23, 35, 37, 39, 41, 43, 44, 46, 47, 48, 56, 57, 61, 68, 107, 113, 126, 131, 329

change management, 289-297

charity auctions, 215, 240

child labor law, 113, 115

Chronicle of Philanthropy, 122, 134, 153, 154, 204, 214, 219, 220, 333

churches and synagogues, 166, 195, 225, 232, 236, 325

Notes

Notes

Join the Pennsylvania Association of Nonprofit Organizations

PANO is a 501(c)(3) nonprofit organization dedicated to helping Pennsylvania nonprofits operate efficiently and effectively. PANO can show how to improve management practices, increase the public's understanding of nonprofits, and positively impact policies affecting nonprofits.

PANO offers—

- Advice on management, board, and funding issues
- Insurance and management plans that save you money
- Up-to-date education and information services
- Advocacy with the state government in Harrisburg
- Networking opportunities with nonprofit staff and board members
- Information on philanthropic opportunities
- Research and planning

PANO's members include executive directors, administrators, board members, and staff of hundreds of nonprofit organizations of all types and sizes.

Your membership in PANO will increase your knowledge of nonprofit management and improve the efficiency of your organization like no other single investment, thanks to the services and information offered. For more information contact PANO at:

PANO
777 East Park Drive, Suite 300
Harrisburg, PA 17111
(717) 236-8584
http://www.pano.org

The Pennsylvania Nonprofit Handbook, 9th Edition
by Gary M. Grobman

The Pennsylvania Nonprofit Handbook, 9th Edition is the most up-to-date and useful publication for those starting a nonprofit or for those already operating one. This 344-page, 30-chapter Handbook was originally published in 1992 with the help of more than two-dozen nonprofit executives and attorneys. Each easy-to-read chapter includes a synopsis, useful tips, and resources to obtain more information. This essential reference tool includes:

- Information about current laws, court decisions, and regulations that apply to nonprofits in Pennsylvania
- Practical advice on running a nonprofit, including chapters on grant-writing, communications, fundraising, quality management, insurance, lobbying, personnel, fiscal management, nonprofit ethics, and 21 other chapters
- Information on applying for federal and state tax-exempt status
- How to write effective grant applications
- How to hire and fire
- Internet resources for nonprofits
- How to develop a strategic plan
- How to plan for a program evaluation

We know you will find The *Pennsylvania Nonprofit Handbook* to be an essential resource for every library's reference collection.

ISBN13: 978-1929109-32-6
8½ x 11 softcover
344 pages including index
$34.95 U.S.

The Pennsylvania Nonprofit Handbook *is must reading. While it will have value as a reference tool to be consulted when needed, I highly recommend that you read the book cover-to-cover to familiarize yourself with the panoply of issues that face the modern nonprofit in the United States.*

Joe Geiger, Executive Director
Pennsylvania Association of
Nonprofit Organizations

Table of Contents

The Nonprofit Management Casebook

The Nonprofit Management Casebook
by Gary M. Grobman
ISBN: 978-1929109234
5½ x 8½ softcover
172 pages including index
$16.95 U.S.
2010

The Nonprofit Management Casebook: Scenes from the Frontlines is unlike any other management casebook available. The 16 cases that comprise this volume are written in a style that will keep you turning the pages for more! Each case is designed for maximum educational value, illustrating key management concepts, many of which are unique to the sector. Highlighted are issues relating to fundraising, ethics, governance, personnel management, board-staff relations, and financial management.

Each case is set in a different type of organization, among them a long-term care facility, a family service agency, a hospital, a think tank, an institution of higher learning, a foundation, and an advocacy organization, providing readers with a sense of the diversity of the sector. These vibrant cases sing with authenticity and plausibility, yet are crafted to be read simply for pleasure.

Each case is followed by discussion questions that are designed to engage students in spirited discussion. Academic reviewers have been unanimous in giving this new text a "thumbs up," and we know you will be delighted with these stories, either as a required assignment or simply for enjoyment.

I really look forward to using these cases in my classes! It's a wonderfully broad collection....

Peter Dobkin Hall, Ph.D., Hauser Center, Harvard University

An Introduction to the Nonprofit Sector

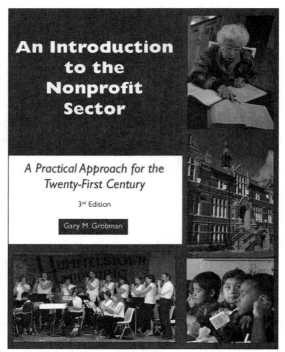

Introduction to the Nonprofit Sector 3rd Edition
by Gary M. Grobman
ISBN: 978-1929109-27-2
8½ x 11 softcover
401 pages including index

An Introduction to the Nonprofit Sector: A Practical Approach for the 21st Century is an introductory text on the nonprofit sector and nonprofit organizations. It provides an overview of the history, theory, and scope of the nonprofit sector. It discusses issues facing nonprofits, such as legal and regulatory issues, ethics, quality, fiscal, and liability issues. It also provides practical guidelines for writing mission and vision statements, strategic planning, hiring, firing, lobbying, communicating, using the Internet, and other functions of nonprofit organizations. Each chapter includes a synopsis at the beginning, as well as discussion questions, activities, and bibliographic references at the end. An index is included.

This book is an excellent resource for introducing students to the nonprofit sector and for providing nonprofit managers with the basic information they need to start or run a nonprofit organization. It is comprehensive in its scope, ranging from the history, theory and legal foundations of the sector, to the very practical issues of governing and managing a nonprofit organization. While well grounded in literature and current information sources, it is clearly written and easy to use as either a classroom text or a ready desk reference.

Dennis Young, Ph.D.
Director, Nonprofit Studies Program, Georgia State Univ.
Past President of the Association of Research on Nonprofit
Organizations and Voluntary Action (ARNOVA)

Related Titles Published by White Hat Communications

Introduction to the Nonprofit Sector, 3rd Ed. (2011)

The Nonprofit Handbook, 6th Ed. (2011)

The Nonprofit Management Casebook (2010)

Fundraising Online (2006)

Improving Quality and Performance in Your Non-Profit Organization, Kindle Ed. (1999)

PLEASE SHIP MY ORDER TO:

NAME _____

ADDRESS _____

ADDRESS _____

CITY/STATE/ZIP _____

TELEPHONE NUMBER _____

❑Enclosed is a check for $_____ made payable to "White Hat Communications."

❑Please bill to my:　　❑Mastercard　　　　❑Visa　　　　❑American Express　　　❑Discover

Card # _____

Expiration Date_____　　VISA/MC/Discover 3-digit # on back of card _____　　AMEX 4-digit # on front of card _____

Name as it appears on card _____

Signature _____

Billing address for credit card (if different from above) _____

Billing City/State/Zip _____

QUANTITY	TITLE	PRICE	AMOUNT DUE
_____	THE PENNSYLVANIA NONPROFIT HANDBOOK, 9th Edition	$34.95	_____
_____	INTRODUCTION TO THE NONPROFIT SECTOR, 3rd Edition	$39.95	_____
_____	THE NONPROFIT MANAGEMENT CASEBOOK	$16.95	_____
_____	THE NONPROFIT HANDBOOK, 6th Edition	$34.95	_____
_____	OTHER_____	$____	_____

SHIPPING	$	_____
SUBTOTAL	$	_____
PA SALES TAX (if applicable)	$	_____
TOTAL DUE	$	_____

Shipping charges: $8.00 first book/$1.50 each additional book in U.S. $12.00 per book to Canada. *Please contact us for rates on rush orders or other methods of shipping, as well as rates to addresses outside the U.S. and Canada.*

PA Sales tax: 6% tax for orders from Pennsylvania, unless accompanied by Pennsylvania Department of Revenue sales tax exemption certificate.

Visit our Web site to order online at:
http://shop.whitehatcommunications.com

Send order form and payment to:
WHITE HAT COMMUNICATIONS
P.O. Box 5390
Harrisburg, PA 17110-0390

Federal EIN: 25-1719745